AMERICAN INDIANS AND STATE LAW

AMERICAN INDIANS AND STATE LAW

Sovereignty, Race, and Citizenship, 1790–1880

DEBORAH A. ROSEN

University of Nebraska Press
Lincoln and London

Portions of chapters 1 and 2 originally appeared in "Colonization through Law: The Judicial Defense of State Indian Legislation, 1790–1880," in *American Journal of Legal History* 46, no. 1 (January 2004): 26–54.

Chapter 7, "The Politics of Indian Citizenship," was first published in a slightly different form as "Pueblo Indians and Citizenship in Territorial New Mexico" in *New Mexico Historical Review* 78 (Winter 2003): 1–28. © University of New Mexico Board of Regents. All rights reserved.

∞

Library of Congress Cataloging-in-Publication Data
Rosen, Deborah A., 1955–
American Indians and state law: sovereignty, race, and citizenship, 1790–1880 / Deborah A. Rosen.
p. cm.
Includes bibliographical references and index.
ISBN 978-0-8032-3968-5 (cloth : alk. paper)
1. Indians of North America—Legal status, laws, etc.—United States—States—History. 2. Indians of North America—Government relations—United States—States—History. 3. Citizenship—United States—States—History. 4. United States—Race relations—States—History. 5. State rights—United States—History. I. Title.
KF8205.Z95R67 2007
342.7308'72—dc22
2007021326

Set in Minion.
Designed by Ashley Johnston.

For Susan

Contents

TABLES

PREFACE

~

During the century following the end of the Revolutionary War, the states governed American Indians in a variety of ways, belying the common assumption that Indian policy and regulation in the United States was exclusively within the federal government's domain. With support from judges who accepted justifications based on state sovereignty, state legislatures extended their authority over Indians in two stages. During the early national period, states began regulating Indians, as well as whites' interactions with Indians. After the Civil War a number of states took the next step and bestowed citizenship rights on Indians. Some states simply imposed citizenship on all resident Indians; others offered political rights on a basis that was both selective and elective, that is, available only to certain Indians deemed suited to citizenship and granted only upon the request of the individual Indian. In parallel fashion—though necessarily relying on different constitutional arguments—western territories also took on local management of Indians and determined the extent to which Indians would be made part of the political community. These state and territorial actions constituted significant advances toward incorporating Indians into American society and imposing direct rule over them.[1]

Thus, local governments took the lead in addressing key questions arising from the presence of Indians in territory over which whites claimed domination: Should Indians be permitted to remain in white settlement areas, and if so, should their autonomy be respected? Should Indians be subjected to obligations and laws defined by the white community? Should they have the privileges of membership in that community? Once admitted as members of the community, how should they be classified in the existing racial hierarchy? The states' answers to these questions between 1790 and 1880 set important precedents for American Indian policy. How state and territorial officials approached these issues, and how they justified their resolution, is the focus of this book.

The one-sided manner in which the states posed these questions brushed aside the crucial underlying jurisdictional question and imagined the possibility of only one answer: The European discourse of conquest provided the foundation for whites' continuing presumption that they held legitimate authority over Indians and their land. The belief was so entrenched that white Americans rarely questioned it. Thus, when states sought access to Indian territory and resources or wanted to exert control over Indians, they represented the federal government as the main barrier, ignoring the possibility that tribal sovereignty might reasonably present any legal or moral obstacle. Repeatedly, state officials injected the language of states' rights into debates about the status of Indians within state boundaries. They placed questions of their authority over Indians within the framework of federalism. This approach not only provided them with considerable constitutional leverage in matters relating to Indians but also had the potential to reinforce state sovereignty arguments made in closely related contexts, such as defending against federal interference with slavery, asserting the right to grant or withhold state citizenship rights, and resisting federal civil rights legislation.

State officials assumed not only that American legislatures had inherent authority to enact laws governing Indians but also that American courts were the sole appropriate judicial forums for discussing matters involving whites and Indians, and that Indian voices and opinions were not necessary or relevant to consider as part of the decision-making process. A state's course of action was determined by its particular economic and political interests, and questions of how Indians should be treated were often shaped by whites' racial and cultural prejudices. State lawmakers and judges had little incentive to weigh Indian perspectives or inherent rights when they made their case for authority over Indians. But that did not mean they did not take into account the reality of the Indian presence and Indian resistance; they had to consider such factors in practice, even if they did not always speak openly about them. Because the subject of this book is state and territorial policies, laws, and judicial decisions pertaining to Indians, most of the primary sources were written and produced by white government officials. However, it is important not to treat government policy as a unilateral matter in which Indian voices played no part, nor as merely an abstract topic that excludes the relevance of Native American experiences. During the period under study, Indians spoke out vehemently on such issues as Indian status and land rights. Indians expressed themselves in courtroom proceedings, public speeches, and printed publications, as evidenced in the criminal cases at the heart of the book's discussion of the issue of tribal sovereignty and state jurisdiction in chapter 1. Indian perspectives were also voiced during legislative hearings, as shown in the later analysis of nineteenth-century debates over whether states should grant citizenship to Indians.

The two main themes of this book—the decentralized nature of much of American Indian policy, and the gradual local assertion of direct rule over Indians—necessitate a focus on state and territorial law. Because of that focus, federal legislation, treaties, and judicial opinions receive little attention here. Since federal government policy provided a broader context in which state officials acted, brief discussion of a few federal cases and statutes relating to the issue of state authority is unavoidable. An attempt has been made, however, to minimize discussion of U.S. government policies and decisions—even if they were important to the development of U.S.–Indian relations—in order to retain a primary focus on what was happening at the local level.

Despite the pervasiveness of state regulation of Indians, there are few publications focusing on state Indian policies, laws, and court cases in the period from 1790 to 1880 (or, for that matter, the period from 1880 to the present). In fact, in a recent review essay, Donald Fixico concluded that "[t]he question of state-tribal relations has been seriously understudied."[2] Likewise, few scholars have examined local regulation of Indians in U.S. territories during that era. Studies of white-Indian government relations have concentrated overwhelmingly on the Indians' relations with the federal government. It is understandable that scholarly studies have focused on federal law and policy, since relations with Indian tribes is officially a matter delegated to the federal government. As Vine Deloria and Clifford Lytle point out, "[t]here is no inherent power in any of the fifty states to deal with Indians at all."[3] Nevertheless, the states have extensively regulated Indians throughout American history.

Where the topic of state Indian law between 1790 and 1880 is mentioned in scholarly publications, it tends to be peripheral to the author's main focus. However, books and articles on some related subjects, either in the same time period or in a different one, can provide useful information and context. In particular, scholarship on the following topics can be relevant: nineteenth-century federal law, Indian dispossession, and the historical roots of present-day Indian land claims. Examples of prominent publications in each field are discussed in turn.

Some broad studies of nineteenth-century federal law pertaining to Indians indirectly touch on the role of the states. Although such scholarship rarely addresses issues of state law explicitly, historical themes and patterns identified by scholars of federal law are also evident in the history of state law. Moreover, some principles of U.S. law have implications for the authority of the states in Indian matters. Thus the scholarship on federal law is pertinent to this book on the states. For example, in a powerful book entitled *American Indian Sovereignty and the U.S. Supreme Court: The Masking of Justice,* David Wilkins explains how the Supreme Court's decisions pertaining to Indians have been "characterized by self-interest, political expediency, and cultural arrogance." Those are qualities that also typify state court opinions. Also evident in state government approaches to Indians is the European-derived colonizing legal discourse that historically has shaped and justified federal Indian law, as described by Robert Williams in *The American Indian in Western Legal Thought: The Discourses of Conquest.* This mythic intellectual framework, which subordinates and ignores contrary Indian visions of justice, has affected legislative and judicial decision making at both the state and the federal level. Other scholarly publications focus on the contractual nature of tribes' historical relationship with the United States, which logically should preclude unilateral state and federal regulation of Indians. For example, David Wilkins's discussion of the "reserved rights doctrine"—the principle that Native peoples reserve and retain all rights that they have not expressly relinquished—should apply equally to their interactions with individual states as it does to their interactions with the United States (see "From Time Immemorial: The Origin and Import of the Reserved Rights Doctrine"). Works that emphasize the treaty process as the only appropriate manner in which to work out the terms of the relationship between the United States and Indians, such as David Wilkins and Vine Deloria's *Tribes, Treaties, and Constitutional Tribulations,* have even stronger negative implications for state authority over Indians. Since only the federal government has constitutional power to make treaties, adherence to Wilkins and Deloria's principles would presumably go a long way toward protecting tribal sovereignty, lodging American negotiating authority exclusively with the federal government and preventing the states from meddling in Indian affairs.[4] Although state law is not the main focus of these important studies, the studies do make points that are relevant to analysis of the states' statutes and judicial decisions.

Two major studies that have federal law as their main focus do directly address important issues relating to state jurisdiction over Indians. First, in *American Indians, American Justice*, Vine Deloria and Clifford Lytle point out the federal government's acknowledged obligation to serve as a shield against states' attempts to apply their laws within Indian territory; they also discuss Indians' rights and benefits that states must offer equally to Indians as to others. When Indians have taken their disputes to court, the authors find, they tend to gain more supportive decisions from federal forums than in the states, though federal courts have not been entirely consistent or successful in protecting Indians from state intrusions. Deloria and Lytle conclude that cultural differences, racial prejudice, and economic competition have often resulted in tense Indian-state relationships over the course of American history. Second, David Wilkins and Tsianina Lomawaima's book *Uneven Ground: American Indian Sovereignty and Federal Law* devotes a chapter to analyzing the clauses in late-nineteenth-century western state constitutions, state enabling acts, and territorial acts that explicitly precluded state or territorial authority over Indians and Indian lands. Of the eleven state constitutional disclaimer clauses, only one (Kansas, 1861) was enacted during the period under study in this book, but Wilkins and Lomawaima's discussion of the broader historical and current problems in state-tribe relationships is highly pertinent. They conclude that state attempts to regulate Indians often violate disclaimer clauses, and there needs to be more vigorous enforcement of those state constitutional provisions. The authors also make the more general point that, absent Indian consent, states have no constitutional justification for imposing their jurisdiction on Indian tribes, and even in the absence of disclaimer clauses, such imposition conflicts with tribal sovereignty, treaty provisions, and federal authority under the Constitution.[5]

Scholarship examining Indian dispossession during the period under study also often contains material that is relevant to the study of state law, even though such studies sometimes concentrate more on federal policymaking than on the states and usually do not focus specifically on legal matters. Particularly fine examples of monographs in that category are David Wishart's *An Unspeakable Sadness: The Dispossession of the Nebraska Indians*, and Craig Miner and William Unrau's *The End of Indian Kansas: A Study in Cultural Revolution, 1854–1871*. These books describe the roles of federal Indian agents, missionaries, fur traders, railroad and timber company employees, land speculators, and Natives themselves in the dispossession of Indians during the nineteenth century; they also comment on the function of state and territorial officials in the process, though that is not their main focus. A book that concentrates more on the state government's policies relating to Indian removal, while also providing insights on the role of private interests, is Laurence Hauptman's outstanding study of Indian policy in New York, *Conspiracy of Interests: Iroquois Dispossession and the Rise of New York State*.[6]

Studies of Indian dispossession can be relevant even if they focus on a time period that precedes the focus of this book. An important example of pertinent colonial American history is Jean O'Brien's *Dispossession by Degrees: Indian Land and Identity in Natick, Massachusetts, 1650–1790*, which describes how Massachusetts dislodged Indians from their land in a way that set relevant precedents for the early national and antebellum eras. As O'Brien points out, "much of what occurred in relations between Indians and English colonizers prefigured later developments in U.S. Indian policy. . . . Reservations, removal, and allotment . . . , and at least the semblance of the notion of a trust relationship all can be found in one form or another in colonial Massachusetts."[7] Studies of tribes that have retained their territory, or at least a portion of it, during and after the colonial period are just as relevant. For example, James Merrell's *The Indians' New World: Catawbas and Their Neighbors from European Contact through the Era of Removal* examines how the Catawbas adapted to the presence of English colonists and survived on their South Carolina land into the nineteenth century.[8]

In addition, studies of present-day land claims incorporate some relevant history from the early national and antebellum periods. Studies of Massachusetts Indians' claims are particularly notable, such as Jack Campisi, *The Mashpee Indians: Tribe on Trial*; Paul Brodeur, *Restitution: The Land Claims of the Mashpee, Pasamaquoddy, and Penobscot Indians of New England*; Robert N. Clinton and Margaret Tobey Hotopp's article "Judicial Enforcement of the Federal Restraints on Alienation of Indian Land: The Origins of the Eastern Land Claims"; and essays about the Mashpees by James Clifford, Francis G. Hutchins, Jack Campisi, and Jo Carrillo in *Readings in American Indian Law: Recalling the Rhythm of Survival*. Similar publications examine ongoing New York Indians' land claims, such as *Iroquois Land Claims*, a collection of essays edited by Christopher Vecsey and William A. Starna that contains significant historical content pertaining to New York state policy during the early national period. Articles examining other present-day challenges to state law—most notably Robert B. Porter's "Legalizing, Decolonizing, and Modernizing New York State's Indian Law"—also provide highly relevant context.[9]

Although the publications in these three areas—federal policy, Indian dispossession, and land claims—provide some useful material, they do not focus on state and territorial Indian regulation, leaving much of the terrain unexplored. However, there are some notable exceptions, books and articles that are beginning to fill this critical gap in the literature on state and territorial law pertaining to Indians between 1790 and 1880. Tim Alan Garrison broke important ground by devoting a book to state court decisions relating to Indians, a subject that has received almost no scholarly attention. His 2002 monograph, *The Legal Ideology of Removal: The Southern Judiciary and the Sovereignty of Native American Nations*, is a superb in-depth analysis of three key southern court cases (accompanied also by discussion of the two famous federal cases) relating to Cherokee and Creek status under Georgia, Alabama, and Tennessee law in the 1830s. The book is a vital corrective to the dominant scholarly focus on U.S. Supreme Court cases. For the Cherokees in the 1830s, it was actually the state court decisions, rather than the Supreme Court's opinions, that were more influential and had greater impact in practice.[10]

Like *The Legal Ideology of Removal*, Brad Asher's *Beyond the Reservation: Indians, Settlers, and the Law in Washington Territory, 1853–1889* focuses on local courts' role in managing relations with Indians. However, while Garrison analyzes the resolution of legal issues in appellate courts, Asher concentrates on actual stories of individual Indians in trial courts. He makes an important contribution in explaining the ways in which Indians came to fall under the local jurisdiction of whites. Asher makes it clear that even though America's western territories were formally subject to rules and regulations of Congress, and even though most Indians there were formally confined to reservations and under federal administration, in practice the boundaries between Indians and whites were porous, there was considerable interaction between the two groups, and local bodies exercised significant regulatory and adjudicatory jurisdiction over Indians. His book substantiates the principle that territorial legislatures and territorial courts were both local institutions, and they exercised functions that paralleled those of their counterparts in the states.[11]

Several shorter scholarly works also address the issue of law in the states. The importance of looking at local actors when studying Indian law and policy is demonstrated in an article by Cynthia Cumfer. Writing about Indian policy in Tennessee, Cumfer analyzes the evolution of frontier settler and Cherokee perspectives on Indian-white relations and Native sovereignty during the early national period and examines how the intel-

lectual developments affected state policymaking. Focusing on a later period, Ann Marie Plane and Gregory Button also examine policymaking in a
single jurisdiction. On the weighty issue of Indians' citizenship status in
the states, their article on ethnicity issues underlying the Massachusetts
Indians Enfranchisement Act makes a rare contribution. Finally, although
the issue of Indians' position under state civil and criminal laws in early United States history has not yet received any comprehensive scholarly treatment, Sidney Harring has made a significant contribution in the
background chapter in his study of the 1883 case *Ex parte Crow Dog*. The
second chapter of that book begins with the 1830 Cherokee case *Georgia v.
Tassels* and then proceeds to survey the extent of state criminal jurisdiction
over Indians in the nineteenth century.[12]

These books on federal policy, Indian dispossession, land claims, removal cases in the southeast, and trials in Washington Territory, as well as the
articles relating to Indian policy, provide useful information and models
for the study of state and territorial law in early American history.

This book examines the law pertaining to the status and rights of Native
Americans in the states and territories from 1790 to 1880, analyzing policymaking and judicial decision making at the local level. The introduction
provides a foundation by describing Spanish and English approaches to
Indian policy during the colonial period and explaining how the United
States relied on similar theories after the American Revolution. Following
that introduction, the central portion of the book is organized around
three topics: part 1 focuses on "Sovereignty," part 2 on "Race," and part
3 on "Citizenship." In the first part, chapters 1 and 2 address how Indians
and whites in New York and Georgia viewed the issue of tribal sovereignty, describe the manner in which state legislatures regulated Indians, and
consider the way judges throughout the country relied heavily on state sovereignty arguments to justify such regulation. In part 2, chapters 3, 4, and 5
assess how the issue of race was handled in courtrooms, legislative cham-
bers, and constitutional conventions. The first two chapters in this part
of the book evaluate the ways in which state legislatures treated Indians
as a distinct racial group and explore racial issues arising in Louisiana
and other state courts, especially disputes over racial classification, suits
for freedom based on maternal Indian ancestry, and disagreements over
how the Civil Rights Act of 1866 and the Fourteenth Amendment affected laws that discriminated against Indians on the basis of race. Chapter
5 then analyzes shifts in the rhetoric of race, culture, and political status

during the debate over Indian political rights in Michigan and Minnesota constitutional conventions spanning from 1835 to 1867. The third part of the book studies the politics of Indian citizenship rights in one eastern and one western jurisdiction. Specifically, chapter 6 appraises the process by which Indians were declared citizens by the Massachusetts legislature, including the perspectives of whites and Indians in the commonwealth, while chapter 7 examines battles in the executive and judicial branch over Pueblo Indian citizenship in the Territory of New Mexico. Finally, the conclusion brings together the themes of the book and analyzes some of the larger patterns evidenced by the material discussed in chapters 1 through 7, focusing particularly on the important role of the states and territories in extending direct rule over Indians.

I am very grateful for the thoughtful and knowledgeable input of the anonymous readers for the University of Nebraska Press; they provided invaluable suggestions for improving my book manuscript. I also appreciate the contributions of the editors and staff at the University of Nebraska Press in bringing this book to publication. In addition, chapter 7 of the book, which was previously published in slightly different form as an article in the *New Mexico Historical Review*, benefited greatly from the judicious advice offered by the journal's editor, Durwood Ball.

I appreciate the archival assistance provided by Marie Windell and John Kelly of the Special Collections Department of the Earl K. Long Library at the University of New Orleans and by José L. Villegas Sr. of the New Mexico State Archives and Records Center. Lafayette College students Robert Alessi, Tiffany Blakey, Phillip Dudley, Andrea Kotrosits, and Michael Sparrow provided useful research assistance through their participation in the Excel Scholar program. I am also thankful for the superb service I received from the Interlibrary Loan Department of Skillman Library at Lafayette College.

AMERICAN INDIANS AND STATE LAW

INTRODUCTION

The Colonial Foundations of Indian Policy

The status of indigenous peoples in the Western intellectual scheme has been a continuing dilemma since the arrival of the first Europeans in the Americas. Once European explorers discovered the existence of the "New World," resolved that they had the right to travel to and through that world, and decided that it was not only within their rights but also in their power to determine the status of the peoples they encountered there, they debated whether Indians should be treated as separate nations, as citizens, or as wards. The intellectual consideration of this issue focused on a number of questions. Should Indian nations' autonomy be recognized—and, if so, should their dominion over all, or just part, of the Americas be acknowledged? If tribal sovereignty was not to be conceded, should Indians be included in the European-American community and regarded as equals under the law? Or should they be assigned a distinctive status as persons subject to paternalistic protections and ineligible to participate in the political or legal processes? Furthermore, if the plan was to include indigenous people under European jurisdiction, two additional correlative issues needed to be decided. Would Indians ideally live together with colonists, or would they reside in separate communities? And finally, from where in the colonial governing structure would Indian regulations emanate, the central metropolis or the colonial frontiers where settlers actually met Indians?

Europeans considered a number of options for dealing with the Indians: assimilation and incorporation of the Indians as equals, integration of Indians into colonial society but as a subordinate people, domination and regulation of Indians while keeping them separated from white communities, recognition of Indian tribes as independent and autonomous entities, or removal of Indians from white society completely through either extermination or expulsion. Europeans—and, later, European-Americans—would at various times experiment with all five of these approaches.

In practice, of course, the decision as to Native people's status in relation to the colonies was not up to the Europeans alone. The Indian nations remained committed to protecting their own sovereignty. Therefore, even though most Europeans could not voluntarily accept the idea of Indian autonomy because it conflicted with their justifications for exploring and appropriating territory in the Americas, in actuality, limited military capability in the colonies meant that they sometimes had no choice but to acquiesce in the independence of Indian nations. However, many Europeans viewed this situation as not only undesirable but also temporary. Keen to exclude the possibility of permanent autonomous Indian nations and reluctant to admit openly to a policy of removal, Europeans focused their theoretical analyses on the first three options listed above.

Although some early colonizers spoke of incorporating and assimilating Indians, in practice European laws typically treated indigenous people as incapable inferiors, neither entirely separate nor integrated as equals. Even though Europeans shared many common assumptions about Native people and about government, however, there were also notable differences in how the two main colonial powers in North America approached the issues of Indian status and colonial governance. Spain and England were both determined to regulate Indians, but they made different choices about how they wanted Indians to fit with colonial settlements and about how centralized their administration would be.

SPANISH COLONIAL NORTH AMERICA

In the sixteenth century, the Spanish claimed vast stretches of land in the Americas containing millions of Indians as well as huge quantities of silver. Scholars of Spanish colonial history have concluded that the material wealth of the conquered territory gave the king the incentive to centralize colonial authority in the metropolis more effectively than was evident in early English colonial history. The fact that the Spanish monarchy was comparatively absolutist and authoritarian in character further reinforced the tendency toward centralization of imperial administration. The crown tried to keep tight control over the two primary Spanish colonial officials, the viceroys of Peru (South America except for Portuguese Brazil) and New Spain (Mexico, the Caribbean, and Central America). Furthermore, the king did not allow the colonists to establish representative assemblies, nor were the appointed local government entities allowed to exercise independent authority. Instead, the king and his Council of the Indies had the last word in legislating and adjudicating colonial matters. Naturally, distance from the metropolitan core and its coercive powers left local settlers with some flexibility as to how legislation imposed from the center was carried out in the periphery on a day-to-day basis. Officially, however, the colonists were allowed little autonomy, and consequently formal laws pertaining to Indians in the Spanish empire issued primarily from Madrid.[1]

From very early in their interactions with the indigenous people of the New World, Spanish thinkers debated the question of what laws should apply to the Indians. A few of them argued that Indians should be allowed to continue as separate communities under their own institutions and laws, either because those intellectuals saw Indians as intelligent, competent, and capable of self-government or because they regarded the Indians as childlike and weak-willed and subject to abuse and corruption by more sophisticated and aggressive Europeans. The vast majority of European writers rejected the argument for Indian autonomy, however. For the Spanish, the presumed superiority of Christian European civilization was seen as justifying the conquest and subjugation of people they perceived as barbarous infidels, who would thereby be exposed and converted to Christianity and Christian civilization. The goal of saving savage souls provided the foundation for late fifteenth-century papal bulls authorizing Spain to assert guardianship over the peoples of the Americas and to claim paramount title to their lands. In theologically based Spanish colonial legal discourse, there was no room for independent Indian self-government.[2]

Having rejected the notion of Indian autonomy, and eager to exploit the labor of Native peoples, the Spanish needed to find a way to incorporate Indians into their society. Some of those who saw the Indians as people of equal intellectual capacity as Europeans argued that they should be assimilated into colonial Spanish society and that Spanish law should fully apply to them. It seemed to the Spanish, however, that Indian resistance to Spanish religion and culture provided evidence that they were not yet suited to become integrated into Spanish society as citizens. By the end of the sixteenth century—after decades of brutal exploitation and abuse of the Indians—the Spanish decided that, out of concern for social welfare and social justice, they should provide the Indians of New Spain with legal protection, effectively treating them as wards of the government.[3] The special protective laws of the late sixteenth and seventeenth centuries were codified and included in the *Recopilación de Leyes de los Reinos de las Indias*, a collection of Spanish statutes pertaining to the colonies that was published in Madrid in 1680. In North America, where the Spanish colonial empire extended into the present-day U.S. states of New Mexico, Arizona, Utah, Colorado, Nevada, California, Texas, Florida, Mississippi, and Alabama, these laws had little effect on the tens of thousands of Apache, Comanche, and Navajo Indians inhabiting the plains and mountains of the hinterland but clearly were intended to protect the sedentary Pueblo Indians, sixty thousand of whom lived in towns along the Rio Grande in 1600.

Most of the laws relating to Indians appeared in Book 6 of the *Recopilación*, where the first law, originally enacted in 1580, mandated generally that the Indians be "protected, favored, and sustained." Title 10 of book 6 included twenty-three laws explaining how the Indians were to be well treated and not "excessively" exploited, while title 6 contained fourteen laws describing a government official known as the *protector de indios*. Other Spanish laws protected the Pueblo Indians' communal land from encroachment. Each pueblo was entitled by custom to one league (about 2.6 miles) in each cardinal direction from the church—four square leagues, or 17,712 acres, dubbed the "pueblo league." Laws prohibited Indians from selling this communal land, thus protecting the physical integrity of the pueblos. Furthermore, the laws provided that non-Indians ("Spaniards, Negroes, Mulattoes, or Mestizos") were prohibited from living in Indian towns, that Spanish livestock was not to be kept on Indian farmlands, and that Spaniards were forbidden to establish farms so close to Indian towns and fields that their livestock might cause damage to Indians' property. Other protective laws in the *Recopilación* provided that because of their poverty Indians should be given "special consideration in the matter of prices for provisions and other goods," that the Indians' own laws were to be respected, that the Spanish governors were to recognize the beliefs of the Indians and to tolerate their religious customs as long as they did not conflict with Catholicism, and that local Spanish officials were not to take food or other property from the Indians nor force the Indians to work for them without wages.[4]

The very existence of these paternalistic laws suggests the underlying reality: the Spanish soldiers, settlers, and priests encroached on Indian land, attacked Indian religion, disregarded Indian laws and customs, forced Indians to pay tribute in the form of goods or labor (known as the *encomienda*), and subjected Indians to violent physical punishments if they showed signs of resistance. The Spanish did not simply go about their search for riches in the New World, leaving the Indians alone. Rather, since conversion of the Indians was central to their religious rationale for being in the Americas and since Indian labor was essential for making the colonies productive, it was inevitable that Spanish interactions with the Indians would be highly intrusive. Indeed, their stated purpose of Hispanicizing and Christianizing the Indians meant assimilating them into Spanish culture and, eventually, merging them into Spanish society. Such a goal could not be achieved without extending Spanish law to cover the Indians, exposing them to direct rule by the Spanish. Thus, in Mexico City, the General Indian Court claimed jurisdiction over lawsuits with Indian defendants, whether initiated by colonists or by Indians. In settlements remote from Mexico City, such as New Mexico—which is the subject of a case study in chapter 7—such matters were typically handled by the governor.[5]

Yet although Indians were subject to Spanish colonial jurisdiction, they were not generally regarded as citizens. In ordinary discourse, the term "citizens" referred only to settlers and did not include Indians, not even the settled Pueblo Indians.[6] It was possible for Pueblo Indians to give up their pueblo affiliation and become Spanish citizens, however. Evidence can be seen in late eighteenth- and early nineteenth-century documents relating to conflicts in the Pueblo of Santa Clara that led some members to leave the pueblo. In the midst of tensions in the pueblo in the mid- to late 1780s, a Spanish colonial document referred to one Juan Pubijua as a Santa Clara Indian who "was living away from the pueblo as a Spanish citizen." Then, in 1815, a dispute erupted between Indians of the Pueblo of Santa Clara and former members of the pueblo, called Canjuebes, who had abandoned their connection with the pueblo and become Spanish citizens but who still claimed lands within the pueblo grant. The local alcalde, Miguel Lopez, brought the matter to the acting governor. The alcalde sided with the Canjuebes, but the acting governor decided in favor of the pueblo, and the commandant general at Durango, Bernardo Bonavia, agreed with the acting governor. Bonavia explained that the Canjuebes could continue to hold the lands in dispute only if they returned to become part of the pueblo community. If they wanted to retain Spanish citizenship, they had to follow the laws applicable to other Spanish citizens and buy lands outside the pueblo.[7] Thus for most of the colonial period the Spanish attempted to keep the line between "Indian" and "citizen" clear but permeable. Pueblo Indians could sometimes become citizens, but only by giving up their place in their own community.

The status of the Pueblo Indians was beginning to change during this same time period. By the end of the eighteenth century, many Spaniards came to see the protective laws as overly paternalistic and inconsistent with liberal ideals coming out of Enlightenment thought, such as the principle of equality under the law. By the early nineteenth century, the Spanish began revising the protective laws. When Napoleon removed the Spanish king from the throne, the Spanish parliament met at Cádiz from 1810 to 1812 and drafted liberal laws and a new Constitution. In its proposed legislation, the Cortes of Cádiz declared the legal equality of all people of Mexico, including both Spaniards and Pueblo Indians. Indians were declared to be full Spanish citizens with equal legal rights and with no special protections. The proposed laws also provided that vacant public lands and unneeded communal lands, including unused communal Indian lands, could be converted to private ownership.[8]

Because the Constitution of 1812 and the liberal laws were not accepted by the Spanish crown until 1820, the year before Mexico declared independence from Spain, the changes did not have the opportunity to affect the colonies before independence.[9] But the liberal legislation enacted at the end of the Spanish period was incorporated into Mexican law from the beginning of the Republic. Consequently, the formal status of Pueblo Indians changed significantly in 1821. Agustín de Iturbide's Plan of Iguala, which was declared on February 4, 1821, and reached Santa Fe on September 11, 1821, proclaimed that all Mexicans "without any distinction between Europeans, Africans, nor Indians, are citizens." The Treaty of Cordova (August 24, 1821), the Declaration of Independence (September 28, 1821), decrees of the first Mexican Congress (February 24, 1822, and April 9, 1823), and the Constitution of 1824 also guaranteed the equality of all Mexicans.

The effect of these provisions was to eliminate the special protections accorded Pueblo Indians during the colonial period. They were no longer treated as wards of the state entitled to special legislation and their own official protector. They were now citizens. What did abolition of the colonial protective system mean for the Pueblo Indians? Historian Woodrow Borah concluded that "[t]he legal equality that came with independence and the new constitutions quickly turned out to carry with it very real loss." It resulted in the seizure of communal lands and resources and increased abuse of Indian labor. "An end to legal tutelage," Borah wrote, "meant exposure to far greater exploitation and simple ravage."[10] Historians G. Emlen Hall and David J. Weber have concluded, however, that although the Indians were indeed left more vulnerable, in fact they were able to preserve most of their communal land base during the period from 1821 to 1846. Furthermore, Hall and Weber have pointed out, the Pueblo Indians quickly adapted to their status as citizens and used the new language of citizenship rights to protect their traditional communities. For example, when they appealed to the governor not to allow their vacant lands to be sold off by the government, they made the argument based not on their special rights as Indians but, rather, based on the customary rights of Mexican citizens, including "the right of ownership and security that every citizen . . . enjoys in his possessions." They argued that the sanctity of property rights meant their well-established prior ownership rights to land could not be infringed. Members of the New Mexico *diputación*, or assembly, agreed with the argument, and as a result they decided they would not seize unused portions of pueblo lands and sell them off to non-Indians. The assembly did allow individual Indian land sales, so the Pueblo Indians of New Mexico lost some of their property during the Mexican period. But Mexican respect for the Indians' property rights prevented extensive seizure of pueblo lands. Thus, despite the liberal policies of the Mexican government and the citizenship status of Pueblo Indians in the Mexican Republic, most pueblo lands were still intact in 1848, when the Treaty of Guadalupe Hidalgo ceded northern Mexico to the United States.[11]

ENGLISH COLONIAL NORTH AMERICA

Although English colonists encountered fewer Native peoples in North America than the Spanish had, they, too, had to consider the issue of the appropriate status of Indians in the European-American political structure.[12] The English justification for settling in the Americas after the Reformation differed in some ways from that of the Spanish. Protestant England shifted the colonizing discourse to focus on the idea that New World land was a vast, underdeveloped wilderness occupied by infidels, and a Christian people who could make the land more productive had a superior claim to it. Although English enterprises focused more on taking control of land than of indigenous people, however, Indians did factor into English justifications. Under English domination, not only would under-utilized New World lands be made productive, as God intended, but the Indians would be introduced to the true gospel. The English envisioned utilizing trade with the Indians as a way of leading them to Christianity and civilized life. Under natural law and the law of nations that supplemented the legal framework for colonization by the seventeenth century, although Indians might physically possess land, ultimate sovereignty over it lay with the English.[13]

Although both the Spanish and the English sought to spread civilized European ways to the New World, historians have identified a distinction between the Spanish goal of incorporating indigenous people into the social order and an English tendency to expect Indians to remain outside the Anglo political, legal, and social community. The English were more interested in displacing Indians from land than in assimilating them into colonial society. The Spanish settled among the Indians, incorporated them as forced laborers, engaged in extensive efforts to convert Indians to Catholicism, and frequently intermarried with Indian women. In contrast, the English were more concerned with settling their own farming families in the New World and cultivating the land there, made a much less concerted effort to Christianize Indians, disapproved of cohabitation or intermarriage with Indians, and tended generally to exclude Indians from their communities. Reflecting their recognition of the separate status of tribes, the English often negotiated with tribal leaders to arrange for the transfer of Indian territory to the colonists. Once they had ceded land, the Indians were expected to move beyond the perimeter of English colonial settlement.[14] The line between Spanish and English policy should not be too sharply drawn, however, since the English colonists did integrate some Indians into their society to varying extents. Thus, although the English in America may have had some tendency to regard Indian tribes as independent entities apart from the Anglo-American political organization, they nevertheless believed it was necessary not only to regulate colonists' interactions with Indians but also to regulate the Natives' lives in many ways.

The non-absolutist nature and weak financial position of the English monarchy affected the political relationship between the metropolis and the colonies. Unlike Spain, England had an elected legislature that counterbalanced the crown's power, especially after the Glorious Revolution strengthened Parliament's position. It was therefore natural that the colonists might expect their own elected representatives to moderate royal power. Furthermore, the crown's lack of funds to subsidize colonization (and the absence of vast quantities of precious metals that could have provided a self-sustaining source of economic support for imperial governance) meant that English colonies were founded and maintained by private individuals or groups who had to make their settlements attractive to potential immigrants by offering a form of shared governance. As a consequence of these factors, although matters of transatlantic trade were directed from London, the individual colonies retained considerable autonomy over local issues. Each of the English colonies had its own elected assembly to enact legislation on a range of subjects, including Indians. Consequently, there was not one uniform English code of laws governing Indian policy. Instead, lawmaking on this topic was decentralized, with each colony developing its own set of rules regarding Indians within its borders.[15]

Massachusetts—which is the focus of a case study in chapter 6—provides an example of an English colony's regulation of Indians along the east coast of North America. New England was occupied by a number of Algonquian Indian tribes, including Wampanoags, Mahicans, Mohegans, Pequots, Narragansetts, Pocumtucks, Pawtuckets, Nipmucks, and Abenakis. Over the course of the colonial period, the governments established separate communities for most of the colonies' Indians. In Massachusetts, the communities included Mashpee, Gay Head, Chappequidick, Christiantown, Herring Pond, Fall River, Deep Bottom, and Dudley. In colonial (and later state) legislation, the various Indian groups came to be referred to by those community names.[16]

Indians in Massachusetts were regulated, controlled, and limited by laws that restricted their freedom of movement and choice of dwelling places; forbade them from powwowing or worshiping "false gods"; tightly regulated trade between English settlers and Indians; and prohibited settlers from selling liquor, guns, horses, or boats to Indians.[17] Because it was considered important to uphold the principle that only the government had the authority to "extinguish" Indian claims to land, other laws prohibited individual settlers from privately buying or leasing land from the Indians without the consent of the General Court.[18] An effort to protect Indians at the beginning of the eighteenth century meant that they effectively lost their right to make contracts when Massachusetts passed laws prohibiting colonists from suing Indians for debt, or limiting the amount they could sue for, and laws requiring colonists' contracts with Indians to be signed in front of two justices of the peace.[19] Other eighteenth-century statutes forbade Indians from binding themselves or their children out for labor as apprentices or servants without permission of two or more justices of the peace or other colonial agents, thus depriving them of their right to control their own labor.[20] Although Indian slavery was not extensive in Massachusetts, laws requiring that shipmasters importing Indian slaves had to pay a duty and present a certificate asserting the Indians' slave status, laws providing that Indian prisoners could be sold and transported out of the colony, and laws referring to any "Indian, negro or molatto servant or slave" indicate that some Indians were enslaved there.[21] Natives not only were deprived of rights enjoyed by other people living in Massachusetts but also were not consistently subject to the same legal system as the colonists. In the seventeenth and eighteenth centuries, the government appointed special justices to hear and determine disputes among Indians.[22]

Providing in 1652 that Christian Indians were authorized to establish their own "praying towns" under English jurisdiction, Massachusetts Bay officials signaled that although they wanted Indians to take on the Christian religion and English culture and to be subject to English law, they still preferred to keep the Indians separate. On the positive side, the 1652 law seemed to guarantee Indians self-government in those townships, just as the English enjoyed in their towns. Furthermore, Plymouth Colony's law of 1665 allowing Indians some self-government seemed to indicate some positive progress.[23] But by the end of the century legislation severely limited Natives' autonomy. In New Plymouth, as early as 1682, the legislature provided for the appointment of an overseer to supervise the Indians in each town.[24] The Indian towns were becoming increasingly similar to the reservations that would emerge much later in American history.[25] Then in 1747 the Massachusetts General Court took an important step toward making all Indians in the merged colony wards of the government by appointing guardians for Indian tribes, three for each Indian settlement in the province. Those guardians were empowered to take control of the Indians' lands, which meant that they had the power to allot "sufficient" land to each Indian, lease out the rest of the land, and bring lawsuits on behalf of the Indians for any trespasses committed on Indian land.[26] For a brief period right before the American Revolution, one Massachusetts tribe, the Mashpee, was allowed some degree of self-government. Most notably, according to the 1763 statute incorporating the town of Mashpee, only two of the five overseers had to be English, and all five were chosen by the Indians. As it turned out, however, even that limited degree of self-government was short-lived.[27] Thus, for a century and a half, the Indians of Massachusetts were not allowed to enjoy either equal rights or significant autonomy. Clearly they were bound to lose in such a political environment.

The laws of other English colonies echoed the Massachusetts statutes. In the South, however, Indian slavery was not merely indirectly referred to but, rather, was directly and frequently regulated. For example, in the preamble to a 1755 statute, the Georgia legislature noted the fact that "in his Majestys Plantations in America Slavery has been introduced and Allowed and the people commonly called Negroes, Indians, Mulatos, and Mestizos have been deemed Absolute Slaves." The statute proceeded to state that, along with "Negros," "Mulatos," and "Mestizos" who were not free at the time of the law, all Indians in the province (excepting "free Indians in Amity with this Government"), and all of their children, were "hereby declared to be and remain for ever here-after absolute Slaves." Similar language appeared in Georgia legislation of 1765 and 1770.[28] South Carolina had the largest population of Indian slaves and regulated them extensively, along with "negro" and "mulatto" slaves; like Georgia, South Carolina exempted "Indians in amity with this government" from the presumption of slave status.[29] Indian slavery appears to have been more marginal in the other colonies. Indian slaves were mentioned, though not as extensively regulated, in seventeenth- and eighteenth-century laws of North Carolina, Virginia, Maryland, New Jersey, Pennsylvania, New York, Connecticut, and Rhode Island.[30]

Other categories of laws pertaining to Indians were more similar in the three regions of the English colonies. New England, southern, and middle colonies all regulated the purchase of Indian land and regulated trade with Indians, demonstrating a particular concern about trade in liquor.[31] On some levels such regulation helped Indians retain their separateness from, and therefore their independence of, English settler society and culture. However, the English did not allow the Indians to remain truly independent. Laws reinforcing separation were of limited value to the Indians since the legislation also left little room for independence: the English denied the Natives not only equality but also autonomy.[32]

THE AMERICAN REVOLUTION AND
INDIAN POLICY IN THE NEW NATION

In the mid-eighteenth century, Britain attempted to exert more centralized control over Indian policy in its colonies. In 1755 the imperial government appointed two superintendents of Indian affairs to manage Britain's relationship with the Native peoples, and six years later Board of Trade approval came to be required for any purchase of land from Indians. In 1763, concerned about Indian rebellions that had erupted along the frontier during the early 1760s and convinced that colonists' encroachments into Indian territory provoked hostility from the tribes, King George III prohibited the colonists from extending their settlements west of the Appalachian mountain ridge into Indian territory. The British and the eastern tribes formalized the separation of colonists and Indians in treaties of the 1760s that established boundaries extending through both the southern and the northern colonies. The Americans were unwilling to accept such a limitation on their acquisition and use of land, however, and the Proclamation of 1763 proved impossible to enforce. Numerous squatters simply settled west of the mountains, and speculators began purchasing lands directly from Indian tribes.[33]

Britain also encountered resistance in response to its other efforts to tighten control over the colonists by enforcing the trade and navigation acts more vigorously and demanding that Americans contribute more taxes to support the troops defending the empire along its borders in North America. Americans insisted that the British government was violating their natural rights in a number of ways, including restricting their freedom to settle where they chose, taking away their property without their consent, and imposing a standing army on them. In 1776, the colonists declared their independence from Britain; seven years later the Treaty of Paris recognized the independent country, with a western border along the Mississippi River. Although pre-Revolutionary Americans had objected that the king's use of prerogative power to control western land was a violation of their natural rights, the new nation's Constitution, ratified in 1788, conveyed the same kind of power over western territory to the federal government. The new nation was no more willing than the king or the colonial governments had been to allow unregulated private purchases of Indian land—and no more willing to recognize the Indians' natural rights to ownership of the land they occupied. One frontier governor's late eighteenth-century letter illustrates how the colonial English justification for expanding into Indian lands continued to hold sway in the new Republic: "By the law of nations, it is agreed that no people shall be entitled to more land than they can cultivate," Tennessee governor John Sevier wrote. "Of course no people will sit and starve for want of land to work, when a neighbouring nation has much more than they can make use of."[34] In other words, Indians' underutilization of their territory justified American seizure of those lands.

During the Confederation Period, the United States initially claimed that it held title to Indian lands by the "right of conquest." When it soon became apparent that the country did not have the military or economic wherewithal to act unilaterally with regard to Native peoples, the government modified its stance by acknowledging that the Indians had a right to retain possession and ownership of their lands. So, rather than seizing land pursuant to a theoretical and mythical right of conquest, the United States returned to the previous practice of acquiring Indian lands through bilateral agreements with Indians.[35] Congress officially articulated the new position in the Northwest Ordinance of 1787. Thereafter, a U.S. policy of negotiating treaties with Indian tribes became well established. Yet later, when the tribes no longer posed a military threat and were no longer ceding territory quickly enough to satiate American land hunger, greater ambivalence about treaty relationships with Indian tribes emerged, and some Americans claimed that the past practice of negotiating with tribes was a mere fictional convenience rather than a legal mandate.[36] By the 1820s the official view had shifted back to asserting a right of conquest that gave the United States underlying title to Indian lands. The United States borrowed from (and somewhat modified) old European concepts to explain its right to exercise authority over Indians and their territory.

As leading legal scholar David Wilkins has explained, in 1823, when the U.S. Supreme Court at long last ruled on the validity of Revolutionary era private purchases of frontier land from Indians in *Johnson v. McIntosh*, it not only endorsed the notions of "discovery" and "conquest" as foundations of United States authority over Indians and their lands but also established several other major principles: "the inferior status of Indian property rights . . . , the allegedly inferior cultural standing of tribes, the impaired ability of tribes to sell their 'incomplete' title, and the 'so-called' diminished political status of tribes." Although the Court's reasoning in *Johnson* was based on a "distorted, historically inaccurate, and legally fictitious discussion of the doctrine of discovery," Wilkins writes, the notions established by the decision "have had lasting implications for indigenous–nonindigenous relations."[37]

The *Johnson* decision not only challenged Indian property rights but also addressed the question of how Indians fit into the American political community. Chief Justice John Marshall explained that ordinarily conquered people "are incorporated with the victorious nation, and become subjects or citizens of the government with which they are connected . . . and that the rights of the conquered to property should remain unimpaired." But, Marshall wrote, such a policy was not possible in North America because "the tribes of Indians inhabiting this country were fierce savages, whose occupation was war, and whose subsistence was drawn chiefly from the forest. To leave them in possession of their country, was to leave the country a wilderness." It was "impossible to mix" with the Indians in such a way as to form a common society, nor could they be allowed to retain exclusive control over their underdeveloped territory.[38] In this portion of the decision, the Chief Justice thus took a position on the question of what the goal of American Indian policy should be—an issue on which Americans held conflicting views.

American Enlightenment thinkers of the late eighteenth century believed that Indians were capable of learning to be just like Europeans and that the two groups could eventually amalgamate in one society. Accordingly, they advocated a policy of "civilizing" Indians—teaching them about Christianity, agricultural practices, private property ownership, proper gender roles—to prepare them to assimilate. Social reformers of the 1820s continued the project of acculturating Indians. The end goal was absorption of Indians into the American political and social community, where the most idealistic reformers envisioned they would be governed equally with other citizens. At least in its anticipated outcome—Indians living with and ruled by European-Americans—this approach mirrored the Spanish colonial model.

But many Americans did not believe that Indians were capable of changing their religious and cultural practices. Although many of these Americans, often out of a sense of religious duty, were willing to support the civilization program, their racist and ethnocentric presumptions led them to doubt the ultimate assimilability of Indians. That is, supporting acculturation did not necessarily mean advocating assimilation. Because these Americans saw Indians as both unworthy and dangerous neighbors, they advocated a policy of separation rather than amalgamation. In a sense, these were the heirs to the old English colonial model of separation between Europeans and Indians. Because whites sought ever increasing amounts of land in post-Revolutionary America, in practice "separation" usually meant removing Indians.

The two competing notions about Americans' relationship with Indians—assimilation versus separation—co-existed in the United States during the early national period. However, most white Americans and government officials initially leaned toward separation. Although federal government officials were fairly consistent in espousing and funding civilization programs, they also did everything they could to persuade Indians to move further west, thus making their lands available to whites. And once it became plausible to argue that the removal of Indians was necessary to protect them while they underwent the civilizing process, the federal government was able to rationalize what effectively amounted to forced expulsion, the most extreme form of separation.

Americans living on the frontiers distant from the center of the U.S. government were among the strongest advocates for separation, but they did not view all forms of separation as equally desirable. They tended to support—indeed, eagerly instigated—separation in the form of Indian removal out-of-state. They were less keen on separation within state boundaries. In their view, the presence of separate Indian communities within the state impeded white settlement, migration, use of natural resources, and implementation of transportation projects. In-state separation of Indians was also viewed unfavorably because the federal government was likely to assert authority over distinct Indian communities within states, depriving states of control over both the Indian lands and the Indians themselves. The dilemma of what to do about Indians living within state borders led local officials to shift their approach to Indian policy over the course of the period from 1790 to 1880. At first, during the early decades after the American Revolution, state governments tended to accept and even enforce the separation of whites and Indians while still asserting some degree of authority over Indians. However, over the course of the nineteenth century the states gradually moved toward asserting complete jurisdiction over Indians remaining within their boundaries wherever possible—not because they felt more comfortable with Indian neighbors but because the alternative was losing (or never obtaining) control over what was deemed to be state territory and all its inhabitants. Thus, as is shown in this book, at the state level the form of rule over Indians changed over time from an approach that paralleled English-style separation to one that became more like the Spanish attempt to incorporate Indians.

On the other major issue distinguishing Spanish and English colonial rule—the degree to which Indian regulation was centralized—the state governments took a consistent position: they argued in favor of decentralization of most regulation of Indians. Over the decades following American independence, the states were increasingly successful in implementing decentralized governance. Although the U.S. assertion of centralized national Indian policy emulated the Spanish colonial approach rather than the decentralized method applied in the English colonies, the formal centralized arrangement did not reflect the actual situation. Despite the federal government's formal claims of exclusive authority over Indian tribes, it was not the only American government to exercise power over Indians. Because of long experience of considerable autonomy and self-government by the individual English colonies, resistance to consolidated national regulation of Indians was evident in British-derived areas of the United States during the early national and antebellum periods. In practice, as is explained in the following chapters, the states played a crucial role in governing and regulating Indians in post-Revolutionary America.

PART ONE
Sovereignty

~

CHAPTER ONE

Tribal Sovereignty and State Jurisdiction

∼

On May 3, 1821, Chaughquawtaugh, a Seneca Indian woman, was found dead near Buffalo Creek in western New York State. At an inquest held by the local New York coroner, the jurors determined that Chaughquawtaugh had died as a result of a slit throat; they concluded that murder charges should be brought against a Seneca Indian chief named Soonongise or Tommy Jemmy.[1] At his arraignment in the Erie County Court of Oyer and Terminer in Buffalo on July 19, Jemmy acknowledged killing Chaughquawtaugh in fulfillment of a Seneca council determination that she should be executed as a witch. The defendant's primary Indian advocate during his 1821 trial, prominent Seneca chief Sagoyewatha or Red Jacket, argued that the state of New York had no jurisdiction over an act committed by a Seneca in Seneca territory because the Senecas were an independent, sovereign people.[2]

Nine years later, the sheriff of Hall County, Georgia, arrested George Tassel, a Cherokee man, for murdering another Cherokee in a part of Cherokee Territory that the state had just annexed to Hall County.[3] The Cherokees protested Georgia's assertion of jurisdiction over the case, arguing that the state's laws did not apply within the boundaries of the Cherokee Nation and that any attempt to try a Cherokee for violating Georgia law in Cherokee Territory constituted a violation of Cherokee national sovereignty. Directing the defense of Tassel was the Cherokee Nation's principal chief, John Ross. Like Red Jacket, Ross was a vocal and eloquent advocate for tribal sovereignty in the face of state efforts to extend jurisdiction over Indians and Indian territory.[4]

The Jemmy and Tassel prosecutions and the debates surrounding the two cases provide useful windows into white and Indian views of tribal sovereignty and state jurisdiction in the early nineteenth century. The Senecas asserted not only the inapplicability of state laws to Indians but also the tribe's independence from American government. The Cherokees likewise rejected state jurisdiction and claimed the tribe's right to self-government. Thus the primary issue from the Indian perspective was tribal autonomy, especially the tribes' right to be free from outside interference. Since *Jemmy* and *Tassels* demonstrate well how the tribal sovereignty issue was dealt with in state tribunals, that issue is the focus of this chapter, leaving for later chapters the other two major concerns of whites that affected how the cases unfolded: states' rights (discussed in chapter 2) and race (chapters 3, 4, and 5).

In *Jemmy* and *Tassels*, different positions on tribal sovereignty were expressed as the proceedings unfolded. Though white Americans hardly questioned the European rejection of Indian tribal autonomy, they did grapple with the two competing political paradigms displayed by the English and the Spanish during the colonial period: the Spanish model of incorporation versus the English model of separation. By extending their laws over Indians, both New York and Georgia officially promoted Indian policy that appeared to embrace the colonial Spanish model, which fit some Americans' abstract belief that Indians could and should merge into American society. Yet the rhetoric of the time in the two states, as well as the actual unfolding of events in the wake of the cases, evidence how strongly committed many Anglo-Americans were to the English model of separation.

In the end, both New York and Georgia rejected the notion that tribal sovereignty could override state criminal jurisdiction. They both argued that a state must have authority over all the land and people within its territorial limits. As will be seen, judicial decisions supporting assertive state government policies on Indians had lasting consequences in the two states. In the wake of the court cases, both New York and Georgia implemented legislation that solidified state control over Indian lands and people and, subsequently, encouraged or forced many Indian residents to move outside state boundaries altogether.

"TRIBAL SOVEREIGNTY"

Unlike most court cases dealing with Indian-related issues, *Jemmy* and *Tassels* involved Indian parties, which provided both an opportunity for Indians to express their views as part of the trial proceedings and an incentive for them to communicate their opinions outside the courtroom. Accurately comprehending those views at that time was complicated, however, and it remains so today. As Harry Robie has pointed out, scholars "must be extremely wary of documents purporting to be records of actual Indian speech events."[5] In the New York case, although Tommy Jemmy and other Senecas had a voice, everything the Indians said was filtered through a white interpreter before reaching non-Indian participants, decision makers, and commentators. Because extant documents are in English, and since no actual trial record currently exists, historians writing about the trial are largely dependent on the interpreter's version as presented in white-owned newspapers. Furthermore, the Indians' opportunities to speak in court, their form of expression, and the content of their arguments were constrained by the formalities of the legal process and narrowed by judges' definitions of what lines of reasoning would be deemed relevant. In addition, white lawyers played a prominent role in presenting Tommy Jemmy's defense and characterizing Seneca Indians' positions. Despite these factors, though, we can get a sense of the Senecas' views by studying the written record. In George Tassel's case, the absence of an official trial record makes it difficult to know what Tassel or other Cherokees might have said in court. However, the case took place in the context of a vigorous Cherokee challenge to Georgia's authority over Indians, and there are printed documents articulating the Cherokees' position. Though the authors of those documents may have been influenced by lawyers, missionaries, teachers, and others from the white community, and the content of some documents was crafted to appeal to white readers, they nevertheless powerfully convey the Cherokees' position with regard to the attempt to engulf them within state jurisdiction.

One could summarize the Indian perspective expressed in the *Jemmy* and *Tassels* cases by saying that they exemplify Seneca and Cherokee resistance to incorporation by the states, efforts to redefine the conditions for separation, and demands for white recognition of tribal sovereignty. However, because the debates at the time were framed by a European-American legal process and were translated and interpreted by whites, even these broad conclusions about the Indians' positions remove them from the actual Indian perspective. In particular, as used by whites, the word "sovereignty" not only failed to capture the Indian standpoint but also became a vehicle for erasing from white discourse the original Indian perception of how to govern their own societies and how to structure their relationship to whites. That the ambiguous word "sovereignty" had different meanings in different contexts made it easier to actually change the realm of what it was possible to argue in Indian dialogues with whites and within whites' conversations with each other.

21

If "sovereignty" means complete autonomy, self-government, self-determination, and freedom from external interference, then "tribal sovereignty" should have meant that the Indian tribes were entirely independent of both the United States and the individual states. It should have meant that the tribes had full and exclusive jurisdiction with regard to their own members and territory. If "sovereignty" means true nationhood, then "tribal sovereignty" should have meant that, at the very least, Americans would treat the tribes as foreign nations. Yet the notion of Indian tribes as wholly separate from the American governing structure was not accepted by most whites in the early national period. Even if Indians intended to convey their expectation of, or demand for, such total autonomy, their arguments came to be translated by whites to mean limited jurisdiction and partial self-government within—and subject to the higher authority of—the larger American political structure.

Whites' interpreting Indian claims to sovereignty in this way was consistent with their own application of the word "sovereignty" to the retained power of the states in the federal organization of the United States. "State sovereignty" referred to the states' retention of certain attributes of sovereignty after they delegated the enumerated powers to the federal government in ratifying the Constitution. During the early national period the exact extent of the states' "sovereign" powers was contested, but it was agreed that the individual states were not entirely independent of the federal government, which had authority to govern certain matters on behalf of the people of all of the states. At the national level, the notion of state sovereignty thus provided a paradigm for imagining the status of Indian tribes, even while, at the state level, it also became a tool for restricting or eliminating recognition of tribal sovereignty.

When whites used the term "tribal sovereignty" in the early Republic, even when they claimed to be translating the words and ideas of Indians, they most often were presuming a form of limited Indian sovereignty, not full and exclusive sovereignty. But whites' use of the word "sovereignty" did not remain constant; one can detect subtle changes in meaning over time. White writers' earliest uses of "sovereignty" when referring to the Indians' own positions could be seen as possibly reflecting an understanding that Indians meant to assert their total independence of both the state and the United States. However, the use of the word soon shifted meaning, and it became clear by the 1820s and 1830s that Indian independence of whites in areas of white settlement was no longer accepted (by whites) as a plausible argument.

Present-day Indian writings make it clear that the evolution of the definition of tribal sovereignty early in American history had a lasting effect. Because of the meaning whites came to give the phrase, some Indian authors do not consider tribal sovereignty to be a worthy ultimate goal for indigenous people. Criticisms of whites' limited notion of "tribal sovereignty"—which tends to center only on "internal self-determination" and is inclined to presume the United States' paramount authority to govern tribes as "domestic dependent nations"—have, for example, been presented in different ways by Vine Deloria (for example, in "Self-Determination and the Concept of Sovereignty"), Deloria and Clifford Lytle (in *The Nations Within: The Past and Future of American Indian Sovereignty*), David Wilkins (in *American Indian Sovereignty and the Supreme Court: The Masking of Justice*), Glenn Morris (in "Vine Deloria, Jr., and the Development of a Decolonizing Critique of Indigenous Peoples and International Relations"), Robert A. Williams (in "The Algebra of Federal Indian Law"), and Taiaiake Alfred (in the essay "Sovereignty").[6]

In this chapter, the word "sovereignty" does not have a more limited meaning when it is preceded by the word "tribal" than when it stands alone. That is, except in primary source quotations or in references to "state sovereignty," the terms "sovereignty" and "tribal sovereignty" refer to full autonomy and freedom from external control, not mere self-governance subject to the will of a higher sovereign.

THE SENECAS AND NEW YORK STATE

At the end of the Revolutionary War, most of present-day New York State was occupied by independent, self-governing Iroquois Indian nations. After the war, presuming that the state's authority nevertheless extended west to Lake Erie and the Niagara River, New York's leaders asserted the state's jurisdiction in western areas as much as possible. They met resistance on the part of the Iroquois, who continued to assert their own sovereignty in the territory they held. The Senecas, one of the six Iroquois Nations, became the strongest barriers to New Yorkers' western ambitions, and the Senecas' most powerful spokesman between 1790 and 1830 was Red Jacket. An eloquent orator, Red Jacket argued forcefully in support of Seneca land rights, cultural traditions, and sovereignty.[7] In various contexts, he spoke out against white efforts to acculturate the Senecas to the whites' way of life, maintaining that "the Great Spirit has made us all, but He has made a great difference between his white and red children." The

Great Spirit, who "knows what is best for his children," has "given us different complexions and different customs" and has made the two groups "for different purposes," Red Jacket asserted. Because whites and Indians were destined to remain distinct and the Senecas were meant to retain their own traditions and customs, it was wrong for whites to try to impose their religion and culture on the Senecas. On several occasions he also firmly informed New Yorkers that the Senecas would not sell their land.[8] And, most relevantly for this study, Red Jacket also challenged New York's right to include the Senecas and Seneca territory in its criminal jurisdiction.

Tommy Jemmy was not the first Seneca to be charged with murder and tried by New York's courts, nor was his case the only occasion on which Red Jacket zealously challenged the state's criminal jurisdiction over Indians. In 1803 Stiff-Armed George, a Seneca man, was accused of having killed John Hewitt on July 25, 1802, in the western New York town of Northampton. Witnesses for the prosecution explained how George had been scuffling with six white men, including the victim, immediately prior to the killing. The white witnesses—men armed with sticks, a club, and a brick—said they were merely trying to take George's knife away. In the course of the scuffle, they claimed, George wounded William Ward and then fatally stabbed Hewitt.[9]

George's act was quite different from Tommy Jemmy's in several ways: the victim was white, the killing was not alleged to have taken place on land reserved for Indians, and George did not claim to be acting under the authority of tribal law. Nevertheless, the Senecas refused to turn George over to state authorities. In a meeting of Seneca chiefs and white New Yorkers, Red Jacket contested the state's assertion that its laws covered the Senecas. He pointed out that the Senecas had never made a treaty with New York in which they agreed to submit to the state's laws. In fact, he said, the Senecas were "independent of the state of New-York" and had "different laws, habits and customs, from the white people." In short, he said, the Senecas were "determined that our brother shall not be tried by the laws of the state." When Stiff-Armed George was forced to stand trial in the Ontario County Court of Oyer and Terminer in Canandaigua, Red Jacket pleaded his case to the jury. Nevertheless, the twelve-man panel found George guilty of the murder on February 23, 1803, and he was sentenced to be executed on April 15. A local newspaper observed that the murder was not "a wanton and unprovoked one" and reported that the grand jury therefore unanimously signed a petition asking the legislature to pardon George. Judges Brockholst Livingston, Timothy Hosmer, and

Moses Atwater, along with Attorney General Ambrose Spencer, promptly recommended that George be pardoned. On March 5, Governor George Clinton conveyed Livingston's letter to the legislature. Noting the presence of both extenuating circumstances and "considerations of a political nature for extending the mercy of Government to the culprit," the governor expressed support for a pardon. The state's House and Senate debated the matter and, within a week, enacted a law to pardon Stiff-Armed George. Their only explanation for the law was that, based on the governor's message and the judge's report, it was "expedient" to issue the pardon.[10]

Eighteen years later, Red Jacket stepped forward again to defend a Seneca Indian in a New York state court. Tommy Jemmy was arraigned in Buffalo at the Erie County Court of Oyer and Terminer on July 10, 1821, and his trial took place before Judge Joseph C. Yates and a twelve-man jury on July 11. As the *Albany Argus* described the situation, Jemmy's alleged victim, Chaughquawtaugh, had been tried by a council of Seneca chiefs, found guilty of witchcraft, and sentenced to death. Speaking through an interpreter, Horatio Jones, Jemmy pleaded not guilty. He explained that when he executed Chaughquawtaugh, he had been acting as "a minister of justice" for the Senecas, "in compliance with their custom from time immemorial, sanctified to them by the traditions of their ancestors." It was necessary to avenge the deaths of several Senecas (including a relative of Jemmy's) caused by the accused witch. When some people in the courtroom questioned the legitimacy of the witchcraft accusation, Red Jacket provided a sharp response. He pointed out that white clergy had long warned against witchcraft and whites' laws had long punished it. The Seneca chiefs had done nothing that white officials had not done in the past. He firmly posed the question: "what crime has this man committed by executing in a summary way, the laws of his country and the injunctions of his God?" Red Jacket also described important aspects of Seneca customs, usages, and legal processes. He explained that among the Senecas it was the chiefs' job to determine the proper punishment for capital crimes. Compensation to the victim's family was a sufficient penalty for some kinds of criminal behavior, but in other cases—such as this one—the chiefs deemed execution to be the appropriate punishment.[11]

The core of Jemmy's defense was that New York did not have the right to try him. The *Geneva Palladium* presented the argument put forward by the defendant's lawyers: "[L]ong before the settlement of the late colony of New-York, and long before the state of New-York became a sovereign and independent state, the Seneca nation of Indians was a free and independent nation, possessing and exercising the rights and powers of sovereignty, among which they had hitherto always possessed and lawfully exercised the exclusive right to try and punish members of their own nation for offences committed against other members of the nation within their territory." Red Jacket and other Seneca witnesses testified to the fact that "the exercise of [those] powers . . . had never been disputed." From the context, it does not appear that Red Jacket conceded any attribute of the Senecas' sovereignty to either the states or the federal government; that is, he appears to have described the tribe as truly sovereign. That New Yorkers likewise viewed the Seneca position in the case as an assertion of complete sovereignty is indicated by the title of an article that appeared in the *New-York Journal* of New York City and that was reprinted in the Ithaca paper, the *American Journal*. In those papers, coverage of the trial fell under the headline "Imperium in Imperio, Or an independent State within an Independent civilized State." The defense lawyers maintained that Seneca sovereignty was not merely implicit but was explicit, since the United States had recognized Seneca national sovereignty in treaties made with the tribe. Since both Jemmy and Chaughquawtaugh were members of the Seneca nation, and the alleged crime had taken place in Seneca territory, the Court of Oyer and Terminer did not have jurisdiction over the matter, the Senecas argued. The jury agreed, rendering a verdict in favor of Jemmy.[12]

The prosecutor asked that the case be moved to the New York Supreme Court, which heard arguments on the jurisdiction issue in Albany a few weeks later, on July 30 and August 1. By the time the case came before the Supreme Court, the justices—and other New Yorkers and the Indians as well—would have been aware of another case that had unfolded at the same time. Just before the *Jemmy* trial, the Senecas had refused to turn over to New York authorities another Indian who had been accused of murder. New York had tried to get jurisdiction over Joseph Bigbag, who was thought to have killed his wife by drowning her in a creek on the Tonawanda Reservation. Instead of being tried in a New York court, however, Bigbag's case was considered by a council of forty-seven chiefs of the Six Nations who met on the Tonawanda Reservation. After investigating the matter for three days, the council found Bigbag innocent of the charge. The Six Nations' council's deliberations began on the same day that Jemmy was arraigned (July 10), and the chiefs rendered their decision on July 12, the day after Jemmy's trial and verdict. Accounts of the Seneca refusal to subject Bigbag to New York's jurisdiction and of his subsequent acquittal by the council appeared widely in newspapers around the time of the state's Supreme Court hearing in the *Jemmy* case.[13] The justices had to have been very aware of the Indian resistance to state criminal jurisdiction and also conscious of the alternative process that the Indians utilized in cases involving members of their own tribes. Recognizing the importance of the issue involved in the *Jemmy* appeal, both sides obtained the services of top lawyers in the state, and those lawyers presented incisive, forceful arguments before the Supreme Court.

The state's line of reasoning in *Jemmy*, presented by John Canfield Spencer (son of Ambrose) and New York attorney general Samuel A. Talcott, relied on the old European justifications for asserting control over Indians. They pointed out that "the earth belonged to the human race, and that those who clear and cultivate it, & thereby provide the means of sustenance, for greater numbers than can subsist on it in a savage state, are entitled to dominion over it." Therefore, by the law of nations, Europeans acquired a right of dominion over Indians and Indian lands. The Six Nations of Indians, including the Senecas, had acknowledged their subjection to Britain during the colonial period and to New York State since the Revolution. Indeed, the lawyers said that the Senecas "had not claimed or exercised sovereignty since 1620, that they had repeatedly and formally acknowledged the jurisdiction of the English government, and had, by a formal grant of 1726, transferred the whole of their territory to the British crown." Since the Senecas had sided with Britain during the war, they could now be treated as a conquered nation. By a right of conquest, Spencer and Talcott concluded, "we had an absolute and unlimited jurisdiction over their persons," and in various treaties since the war the Senecas had acknowledged both their conquest and their subjection.[14]

Jemmy's lawyer was Thomas Oakley, Talcott's predecessor as attorney general. He contended that the appellate court had no right to overturn the jury's findings that the Senecas were an independent nation and that New York lacked jurisdiction over one of their members for an alleged crime committed on Seneca territory. In case the Supreme Court rejected that argument, Oakley also addressed the law of nations issues directly. He distinguished between Europeans' dominion over territory and their jurisdiction over people living there: "though the objects of civilization justified them [Europeans] in making settlements here, and though it should even be conceded that the possessions they took, drew after them a general territorial jurisdiction over the whole extent of the country; yet they had no right entirely to deprive the natives of the soil; they [Native peoples] were justly entitled to retain as much as was necessary for their subsistence, and that they also retained the right to govern themselves by their own laws and customs." Oakley asserted that the Senecas had consistently "claimed and exercised the right of managing their own internal concerns by their own tribunals, and agreeable to their own laws and customs." Colonial era governors had respected Seneca independence. Although the Senecas had been conquered during the American Revolution, both the state and the federal government had subsequently signaled continued recognition of Seneca sovereignty by dealing with the tribe through treaties, the same mechanism used to make arrangements with other independent foreign powers. Finally, Oakley noted that New York had always refrained from exercising criminal jurisdiction over the Senecas in the past and, further, that they did not forfeit all right of self-governance just because they were not entirely independent of the state: "A dependence for protection was not inconsistent with their retaining to themselves the right of being governed in their internal concerns solely by their own laws, and their entire exemption from responsibility to the judicial tribunals of the country affording them such protection."[15]

The states' attorneys countered Oakley's arguments with two assertions. First, they said that the jury in this case only had the right to decide matters of fact, not matters of law, so the Supreme Court was not bound by the jury's determination on the jurisdictional issue. Second, the treaties made with the Senecas were not evidence of their independent status. The language of those treaties actually supported the inference that the Senecas were signing the documents as a conquered people. In any case, the Senecas had been dealt with through treaties "not because they were Independent nations, but from motives of policy, and as the easiest and best mode of governing them."[16]

After hearing two days of arguments on the Jemmy case on July 31 and August 1, the New York Supreme Court ordered that the defendant be allowed to go free on bail while they considered the issues, which they acknowledged to be very difficult.[17] In fact, the Court never issued a formal opinion. Instead, the state legislature took up the matter. Again as a matter of "expediency," the legislature pardoned Tommy Jemmy on April 12, 1822. This time, however, rather than just pardoning the accused Indian, the legislature stated explicitly that in the future the state intended to assert jurisdiction over such crimes and to carry through with punishment of convicted Indian criminals.[18]

Other states routinely used their criminal courts to try Indians who were charged with committing crimes against whites on or outside of reservation territory. A few months after the Tommy Jemmy trial, for example, a Chippewa Indian defendant in the Michigan Territory, Ketaukah, used the *Jemmy* case to justify a claim of tribal sovereignty that would preclude criminal proceedings by local white juries. Ketaukah was charged with murdering a white doctor on Winnebago Indian land during the summer of 1821. The Detroit court rejected the *Jemmy*-based jurisdictional challenge. Ketaukah was convicted of murder in October 1821 and was executed two months later.[19] Although, like Michigan Territory, other states and territories freely extended jurisdiction over Indian crimes against whites and over Indian crimes outside of reservation territory,[20] New York went further in that it explicitly extended its jurisdiction over inter-Indian crimes on Indian reservations.

New York justified its criminal jurisdiction over Indians by pointing to the need to eliminate what whites characterized as barbarous Indian practices, such as Tommy Jemmy's "horridly revolting" execution of Chaughquawtaugh. They argued that tribal sovereignty had to give way to "higher" values, and that it was legitimate to use state law as a tool for promoting order, furthering white principles of morality, and controlling and directing Indians' behavior. Specifically, in the 1822 statute, the New York legislature expressed dismay that the state's Indian tribes "have assumed the power and authority of trying and punishing, and in some cases capitally, members of their respective tribes, for supposed crimes by them done and committed in their respective reservations, and within this state"; and the legislature asserted that "the sole and exclusive cognizance of all crimes and offences committed within this state, belongs of right to courts holden under the constitution and laws thereof, as a necessary attribute of sovereignty, except only crimes and offences cognizable in the courts deriving jurisdiction under the constitution and laws of the United States." In order "as well to protect the said Indian tribes, as to assert and maintain the jurisdiction of the courts of this state," the legislature enacted a statute declaring that the state courts had "sole and exclusive jurisdiction" over crimes committed within the state, other than crimes covered by federal law.[21] Thus the New York statute asserted state criminal jurisdiction in place of tribal jurisdiction.

Although the New York Supreme Court declined to decide the *Jemmy* case, the case came up in the court's decision in another case a year after the justices heard arguments in Jemmy. In *Goodell v. Jackson*, the court was asked to determine the validity of a 1797 deed from an Oneida Indian,

William Sagoharase, to a white land speculator, Peter Smith. In 1791 the property in question had been granted to William's father, John Sagoharase, for military services rendered during the Revolutionary War. William claimed title to the property by right of inheritance. The case prompted state judges to address the question of Indian sovereignty and citizenship.

New York's Supreme Court of Judicature based its analysis on the principle that aliens had no right to inherit land. To that court, the validity of the deed from Sagoharase to Smith depended on whether Sagoharase was a citizen or an alien. In a decision issued in 1822, Chief Justice Ambrose Spencer concluded that William Sagoharase's deed to Peter Smith was valid because Indians are citizens who are subject to New York law. In his decision, Spencer referred to the recent law pardoning Tommy Jemmy and asserting the state's sole and exclusive criminal jurisdiction over all crimes within the state (except those covered by federal law) as evidence of Indian citizenship. He noted: "This statute not only asserts the exclusive jurisdiction of this state over all crimes or offences committed within the Indian reservations, but it expressly negates any jurisdiction to the Indian tribes, to take cognizance of offences committed therein, even by those of their own tribes." He continued: "If, then, our jurisdiction exclusively reaches them, if they have no right to punish offences, if they receive protection from our government, are subject to our legislation, being born within the State, they must owe to this government a permanent allegiance, and they cannot be aliens." The ways in which the Indians were treated differently than whites by the state government—that is, the fact that New York did not tax them or require militia service from them—were not relevant to the citizenship issue. Such exemptions were, he wrote, "a mere indulgence arising from their peculiar situation." Spencer acknowledged that New York's Indians had not necessarily always been citizens of the state. But he asserted that the Indians' "condition has been gradually changing, until they have lost every attribute of sovereignty, and become entirely dependent upon, and subject to our government." For years, he pointed out, New York had regulated Indians' property and contracts. Either the state or the Indian tribes had the exclusive right to regulate Indians; the authority could not be divided. Putting it another way, either New York had the right to regulate Indians in every way, or else New York had no authority at all over Indians on Indian lands in the state. There is, he wrote, "no half-way doctrine on this subject."[22]

When *Goodell v. Jackson* was appealed to New York's Court for the Trial of Impeachments and the Correction of Errors, Chancellor James

Kent reversed the Supreme Court's decision, holding in 1823 that William Sagoharase's deed was invalid. Kent ruled that the language of the land patent (which the legislature treated as legitimate) actually did allow William Sagoharase to acquire title to the land regardless of his citizenship status, but nevertheless Sagoharase could not legally convey the land to Smith for other reasons. Although Kent did not deem the citizenship issue to be crucial to determining the case, he nonetheless discussed it at length. He concluded that Indians were not citizens of New York but were instead distinct tribes or nations. Because he apparently did not exempt the tribes from ultimate regulation by the federal government, his opinion stopped short of concluding that New York's Indians retained full tribal sovereignty. However, Chancellor Kent provided strikingly supportive language on tribes' considerable independence and right to govern themselves.[23]

Echoing arguments made by Red Jacket and others at Tommy Jemmy's trial, Chancellor Kent's *Goodell v. Jackson* opinion recognized that the Indian tribes were separate and largely self-regulating. To justify his conclusion that the Oneida Indians retained a significant degree of independence, he pointed out that the white government had consistently negotiated with the sachems as leaders of their nations and that tribe members were born into allegiance to their tribal nation rather than to New York or the United States. Furthermore, tribal Indians had not become completely incorporated into the body politic of New York State: New York's laws did not permit them to enjoy full political and civil privileges such as voting and jury service, did not require them perform the duties of citizenship such as taxes and militia service, did not charge them with treason when they made war on whites, and did not impose on them the full range of whites' general social regulations such as those pertaining to religion or family. In all these regards, Kent said, the Indian tribes were alien communities.[24]

Kent acknowledged that the Oneidas and other Iroquois tribes were dependent on the United States and New York, and he said they still required the protection of white governments and could be regulated as necessary to protect public safety. However, depending on the protection of another nation did not automatically mean that the tribes forfeited all attributes of sovereignty. Citing the scholarship of leading law of nations expert Emmerich de Vattel, Kent explained, "Though a weak state, in order to provide for its safety, should place itself under the protection of a more powerful one, yet . . . if it reserves to itself the right of governing its own body, it ought to be considered as an independent State." Moreover, he pointed out, if New York claimed all Indians within its boundaries to be citizens, then consistency of principle would require that all Indians in federal territories be deemed U.S. citizens, but clearly the federal government did not regard them as American citizens.

The *Jemmy* case and the subsequent 1822 statute came up in arguments before the Court of Errors, but the case was used against the principle of Indian citizenship. Most notably, lawyer Abraham Van Vechten pointed out that the 1822 statute would have been unnecessary if Jemmy had been a citizen. Chancellor Kent, too, felt obliged to comment on the 1822 statute, given the weight Chief Justice Spencer had given to it. Since the statute did not destroy the political existence of the tribes, Kent did not think the statute affected the citizenship status of William Sagoharase. He believed that extending criminal jurisdiction over Indians within the state was not inconsistent with their "distinct national character." He pointed out that the United States also punished the subjects of other countries without the consent of their governments (e.g., if they were carrying on an illegal slave trade). In addition, he observed, it was appropriate for the state, as the guardians and protectors of the Indians, to prevent "foul executions" which were "shocking to humanity" and could not be tolerated "in the neighborhood, and under the eye of a civilized and Christian people."

If white writers' use of the term "sovereignty" when referring to the Indians' position in the *Tommy Jemmy* case of 1821 could be seen as possibly reflecting an understanding that Indians meant to assert their total independence of both the state and the United States, one can see evidence already in Kent's 1823 decision that the word's meaning to whites was shifting. "Tribal sovereignty" came to be seen as a more limited notion, subject to the higher authority of white government officials. Specifically, Kent envisioned that New York naturally would serve as a "guardian" for Indians and that the state's "protective" role included punishing Indians' criminal behavior, as the 1822 statute provided. Despite his patronizing comments about the Senecas, though, Kent's opinion was the strongest argument in favor of significant tribal autonomy made in a majority decision by any state justice in this era.[25]

When later courts in New York referred to *Goodell v. Jackson*, however, they tended not to cite Kent's opinion or its language supportive of a semi-independent tribal status. Instead, they tended to cite to the earlier lower court decision, where the judges focused on the ways in which New York's Indians had lost meaningful attributes of sovereignty. For example, in the 1845 case *Strong and Gordon, Chiefs of the Seneca Nation of Indians v. Waterman*, the court cited the 1822 decision to support its assertion that "[t]he laws of this state do not recognize the different tribes of indians, within our bounds, as independent nations, but as citizens merely, owing allegiance to the state government; subject to its laws, and entitled to its protection as such citizens."[26] Thirty years later, a federal district court in New York explained that a presumption of Indian citizenship could be extended back to 1843. Since the defendant was an Oneida, the judge in *United States v. Elm* focused part of his analysis specifically on the Oneidas, pointing out that, since they no longer existed as a separate community in New York and their tribal government had ceased in the state, the defendant was born into the jurisdiction of the United States and New York and therefore was a citizen. However, Judge Wallace also came to the broad conclusion that all individual Indians in New York should be regarded as citizens of the state, not by operation of the Fourteenth Amendment but based on Indians' actual legal condition in New York, as evidenced in two statutes pertaining to Indians that were enacted in 1843. As the judge noted, the period between the *Goodell v. Jackson* decision and the 1843 statutes witnessed significant changes in both the status of the Indian tribes and the Indians' political relationship with the state.[27] As discussed in the next section, those legal developments were fundamentally unilateral.

NEW YORK STATE'S REGULATION OF INDIANS

The 1843 statutes, which the *Elm* court deemed to be decisive in determining Indian citizenship, reflected changes in New York's relationship with Indians that occurred over the two decades following *Jemmy* and *Goodell*. During the 1820s and 1830s, it became increasingly clear in New York that Indian independence of whites in areas of white settlement would not be regarded by whites as an acceptable arrangement. Correlated with the shift toward increased monitoring of Indian conduct, during the two decades following the *Tommy Jemmy* case, New York steadily—and unilaterally—expanded its regulatory authority over Indians, implementing legislation that governed economic interactions between Indians and whites, drew Indian-white disputes into an Anglo-American legal system that would apply whites' standards, and solidified state control of Indian lands and people. By the end of the 1840s, a series of state statutes advanced New Yorkers' goal of incorporating Indians into the state's jurisdiction in order to enhance state management of Indians and their lands.

Specifically, in addition to extending their criminal jurisdiction to include Indians, over the course of the early national and antebellum periods New York increasingly regulated Indians within its borders in five ways. Early legislation in the first two categories—regulation of Indian land sales and Indians' contractual and litigation rights—may initially have provided some small degree of protection for the integrity of tribal territory, but later legislation on these two subjects served to draw Indians into the state land market and broader economic orbit, posing a challenge to the maintenance of tribal solidarity and communal landholding. Legislation in the last three categories—laws pertaining to tribes' governing structure, taxation, and family matters—emerged gradually during the antebellum period and significantly intruded on tribal sovereignty in a direct manner.

The first category of legislation regulating Indians was laws governing Indians' right to sell land to whites, as well as whites' right to purchase land from Indians. The New York legislature was particularly active in this regard, continuing colonial and Confederation era practices even after ratification of the U.S. Constitution. The early New York state constitution and laws echoed the federal restraints on private purchases and sales of Indian land. Most notably, in the 1821 constitution was a provision that "[n]o purchase or contract for the sale of lands in this State, made since the fourteenth day of October one thousand seven hundred and seventy five; or which may hereafter be made, of, or with the Indians, shall be valid, unless made under the authority, and with the consent of the Legislature."[28]

At the same time as private conveyances of land were prohibited, however, the state limited its protection of Indian lands (and contradicted federal laws) by authorizing commissioners or governors to purchase Indian lands. Laws of 1793, 1794, and 1795 appointed agents to meet with Indians of the Oneida, Onondaga, and Cayuga nations to make agreements with the tribes regarding their lands. If the tribes were inclined to dispose of the lands that had been appropriated for their use, the agents would make arrangements for them to receive perpetual annuities and (as specified in 1795) a plot for each family to farm. Once lands had been allocated to each Indian family, residual lands would be divided into lots and offered for sale to whites at public auction. Later in the decade, the legislature gave the governor authority to acquire Indian lands as he deemed appropriate. Statutes authorized the governor to appoint commissioners to negotiate or "treat" with Indian tribes to extinguish their rights to their lands in exchange for annuities, or allowed the governor himself to conduct such negotiations or make such treaties. For example, a 1798 New York law provided that it was "lawful" for the governor to appoint commissioners to "treat . . . with the chiefs of the Oneida tribe of Indians for the extinguishment of their claim to such part of the lands reserved for their use as may be convenient for public roads and suitable settlements and accomodations." New York negotiated a number of treaties with Indian tribes pursuant to these provisions.[29]

By the mid-nineteenth century, however, New York had completely changed its approach to acquiring Indian lands. An 1843 statute provided that "[a]ny native Indian may, after the passage of this act, purchase, take, hold and convey lands and real estate in this state, in the same manner as a citizen." Allowing "any Indian" to buy and sell land signaled that the state no longer relied solely on official negotiations to acquire Indian land. Moreover, in 1849 New York authorized Indian tribes to divide up their communally owned reservation land and distribute lots to individual Indian owners. Although those lots would be inalienable for twenty years, the allotment law provided that they would be held "in severalty and in fee simple," which appeared to lay the groundwork for the landowners later to be treated as freeholders who were subject to state laws and taxes.[30]

The second category of legislation affected Indians' ability to make enforceable contracts or participate in litigation. These laws, too, evolved and changed over time. During the early national period, New York's law simply mirrored the provisions of federal law. An act of 1790 stated that "no person shall sue, prosecute or maintain an action arising on a bond, bill, note, promise or other contract whatsoever, hereafter to be executed or made against any Indian residing on the lands reserved to the Oneida's, Onondaga's or Cayuga's." A few years later, the state explicitly voided contracts between Indians relating to New Stockbridge lands. By the antebellum period, however, New York's legislature was enacting statutes permitting Indians to make contracts enforceable in state courts. Most notably, an 1843 law asserted that "Any native Indian . . . whenever he shall have become a freeholder, to the value of one hundred dollars, he shall be liable on contracts, and subject . . . to the civil jurisdiction of the courts of law and equity of this state, in the same manner and to the same extent as a citizen hereof." Several years later, the legislature provided that Seneca Indians with substantial claims against other Indians could sue them in state courts "in the same manner and with the like effect as between white citizens."[31]

The third, fourth, and fifth categories of state legislation intruded the most into the internal affairs of the tribes. New York established a structure for tribes' internal governance, asserted the power to tax Indian land under certain circumstances, and made some Indians subject to the state's general laws on such matters as marriage, divorce, and inheritance. A New York State statute of 1845, for example, presumed to dictate the political organization of the Seneca Nation; three years later the legislature established the dates for elections on the reservations. On the issue of taxation, an 1843 New York law provided that any Indian who was a freeholder owning property in the state worth one hundred dollars would be "subject to taxation . . . in the same manner and to the same extent as a citizen thereof." Even before 1843, the state had required Indians to pay the cost of constructing roads through their reservations, but an 1842 treaty had protected them from such highway assessments. New York also enacted laws regulating Indian inheritance and marriage. In 1801, the state mandated that, upon the death of any Brotherton Indian land owner, the land would be equally divided among the decedent's children, the children of any deceased child of the decedent would divide the child's share, and the decedent's widow would be entitled to stay in the marital house. Finally, in 1849 New York simply extended its statutes pertaining to husband and wife over "all Indians residing within the state of New-York, with the same force and effect as if they were citizens of this state." The act further provided that "the same courts having jurisdiction under those laws in cases of citizens, shall have jurisdiction in like cases in which one or more Indians may be concerned."[32]

New York's regulations enacted in the 1840s solidified Indians' status as citizens of the state who were fully subject to the jurisdiction of New York.[33] Most pertinent were the statutes of 1843, which allowed Indians to buy and sell land, declared them liable on contracts and subject to the civil jurisdiction of state courts, and allowed taxation of land owned in freehold by Indians. Another 1840s law, which applied state marriage laws to Indians, further supplemented the 1843 provisions. By the end of the 1840s, Chancellor Kent's 1823 list of evidence for New York's lack of authority over Indians had been seriously undermined. The broad prohibition on Indians selling land was gone, as was Indian immunity from civil court enforcement of contracts. Kent could no longer point to the fact that Indians were exempt from New York taxation and from the application of general social laws, such as laws of marriage. Although the exclusion of Indians from political and civil privileges such as the suffrage and jury service continued, such exclusion was not seen as contradicting Indian citizenship. Much had changed since 1823. The expansion of settlement and transportation lines—and the laws that helped secure that development—created different conditions for western New York's Indians by the 1840s. The result was a declared end to tribal autonomy and independence in New York, achieved through a series of unilateral enactments by the state legislature.

New York's statutes did not, however, destroy the Senecas' own perception of themselves as a separate community, nor did they break up communal ownership of land on the reservations. Therefore, New York's progress toward subjecting Indians to state laws and criminal jurisdiction was accompanied by an effort to persuade them to sell their lands and move west. In the late 1830s, the Ogden Land Company, which held an option to buy Seneca reservation land, was particularly eager to dislodge the Senecas living on the Buffalo Creek Reservation—the remaining sections of the Seneca domain where Tommy Jemmy had been arrested for murder a decade and a half earlier. With the backing of a number of powerful New Yorkers, the company pushed for the removal of the Senecas. Those efforts culminated in the fraudulently induced Treaty of Buffalo Creek of 1838, under which the Senecas purportedly agreed to sell almost all of their lands to the Ogden Land Company and to move to an area west of Missouri (an area later known as Kansas) within five years. The treaty likewise provided for the removal of the other New York tribes, including the Oneidas, Onondagas, Cayugas, Tuscaroras, Stockbridges, Munsees, Brothertons, and St. Regis Indians. The Senecas, who in fact overwhelmingly opposed the treaty, lobbied against its implementation.[34]

By the early 1840s, the consensus in New York—as well as in the new Whig-dominated presidential administration in Washington—had swung against the whole removal policy. In 1842, the 1838 treaty was modified to return some of the territory to the Senecas. Because of the importance of the rising city of Buffalo and the presence of numerous white settlers there already, white negotiators made sure they held onto the Buffalo Creek lands, however, and the Senecas were all ousted from that reservation within seven years. But the Supplemental Treaty of Buffalo Creek at least made removal to the west voluntary. The legislature even requested that President Polk move New York's Indians back to the state from western areas where they were languishing.[35] In large part because of Red Jacket's persistence in speaking out to defend Indian land rights, the Senecas were to retain a home in New York. Despite the shift in white opinion, and despite Seneca relief that the provisions of the 1838 treaty had been modified and removal was no longer state policy, the Senecas still sought acknowledgment of their national sovereignty and had no interest in merging into New York society.

It is no coincidence that the Supplemental Treaty was drafted by the prosecutor in the *Tommy Jemmy* case of 1821, John C. Spencer, along with the chief justice who wrote the 1822 *Goodell v. Jackson* decision in favor of Indian citizenship, Ambrose Spencer. As historian Laurence M. Hauptman has explained, the father-and-son team saw the new treaty as a way to further a policy of incorporating Indians more fully into the state's jurisdiction while also advancing other Whig Party goals, such as developing the city of Buffalo and promoting construction of transportation lines to further economic development in the state. The Spencers and their Quaker allies opposed Indian removal but also rejected the notion of tribal sovereignty. Instead they advocated civilizing Senecas as part of a plan to absorb them into American society.[36] Not all whites agreed with the full assimilation model. For example, a legislative committee firmly expressed the common skepticism in 1845: "Past experience has abundantly proved," the committee wrote, "that the native Indian and Anglo-American, cannot, or will not, unite by assimilation into one social community."[37] Although many whites remained doubtful about the desirability of social amalgamation, however, New Yorkers overwhelming supported the state's authority to regulate Indians. By the end of the 1840s, a series of state statutes helped them achieve the goal of incorporating Indians into the state's jurisdiction.

THE CHEROKEES AND THE STATE OF GEORGIA

Although Indian removal from New York ended up being formally voluntary rather than militarily coerced, the legal precedents established in 1820s New York buttressed the successful compulsory emigration of Indians from Georgia and other southeastern states. Even though Red Jacket's compelling speeches from that earlier era were also cited and quoted during the debate over southeastern removal, New York's success in attaining jurisdiction over Iroquois Indians provided the more influential model for state and federal policy during the 1830s. By 1830, the issue of Indian status had simmered in the Southeast for years, with the white governments consistently hostile to the Indian tribes in their midst, coveting their land, and agitating for their expulsion. In Georgia, white clamor for Cherokee lands intensified in the 1820s as the white population grew rapidly, access to the Tennessee River through Cherokee Territory became more desirable, and the discovery of gold further increased the numbers of whites intruding on—and even settling in—Cherokee territory. The Cherokee Nation constitution of 1827, which proclaimed the Nation's existence as an independent, self-governing entity, alarmed and angered many whites.

Georgians' reaction to developments in the Cherokee community was certainly affected by racism (discussed in chapters 3, 4, and 5) and by a desire to protect states' rights (chapter 2), but the issue of tribal sovereignty was also crucial. Georgian leaders' resistance to Cherokee national independence within Georgia was theoretically grounded in their claim that, based on "state sovereignty," they held a superior right to govern all the territory—including tribal territory—within their borders. From the time of statehood, they argued, the states had inherited the power over land and people that the colonial European countries had asserted. Borrowing the old European argument that whites' more productive use of American land justified their superior title and that their more advanced civilization validated their authority over Indians, Georgians asserted vociferously that Indians could not rightfully keep whites out of their underutilized soil. Georgians were unwilling to acknowledge the possibility of an independent Indian enclave within the state nor to concede exclusive control of desirable land and resources to the Cherokees.[38] Since the people of the states and territories were on the front lines in relationships with Indians, and there were many more of them than there were federal Indian agents, soldiers, and missionaries, they were the ones who determined much of the reality of white-Indian relations.

In 1827, the Georgia legislature issued a resolution stating that the Indians were mere tenants at will, that Georgia held ultimate title to their lands, that the state could end their tenancy and take possession of their lands at any time, and that Georgia had "the right to extend her authority and laws over her whole territory, and to coerce obedience to them from all descriptions of people, be them white, red or black, who may reside within her limits."[39] Georgia soon began passing legislation to prevent the Cherokee Nation from functioning as an autonomous government within state borders, force dissolution of tribal organization, absorb Cherokee land into the state's control, and pressure the Indians to leave the state. Laws enacted in 1828 and 1829 (effective in 1830) extended full state jurisdiction over Cherokee Territory, providing that "all the laws both civil and criminal of this State be, and the same are hereby extended over [the Territory lying within the chartered limits of Georgia and now in the occupancy of the Cherokee Indians] . . . and all persons whatever residing within the same, shall . . . be subject and liable to the operation of said laws, in the same manner as other citizens of this State." Those statutes also nullified Cherokee laws, prohibited Indians from testifying in cases involving a white party, and punished anyone who interfered with Cherokees' emigration or land cessions. Four statutes of 1830 established a special guard of up to sixty men to protect the mines and to enforce the law in Cherokee Territory, described how the territory would be surveyed and allotted to whites by lottery, and required that whites (including missionaries) could not reside in the Cherokee Territory unless they took an oath to uphold the state's laws. In 1831 the legislature provided for the surveying of land to begin and authorized the governor to start the lottery process. An 1832 law ordered that the Indians be protected from trespass and other violations of their legal rights while they continued to occupy land in Georgia, but the dispossession process continued. The next year, the legislature authorized the governor to issue land grants when the lots drawn in the lottery lay within the lands of Cherokees who had taken individual allotments under the treaties of 1817 and 1819, presumably based on the assumption that such reservees had severed membership in the Cherokee Nation and forfeited their right to own land within Cherokee Territory. The law further forbade Cherokees from employing as laborers any whites, slaves, or persons who were not of Indian descent. An 1834 law allowed individual Cherokees to appeal their dispossession from land, but only if they signed an oath "admitting the right of the State of Georgia to pass the law." The early laws were intended to make it difficult for the Cherokees to remain in the East and to intimidate them into agreeing to a treaty of land cession and removal; by 1835 the legislature was on the verge of actually dispossessing all the Cherokees.[40]

The Cherokees protested the Georgia government's actions. Prior to passage of the Indian Removal Act of 1830, the tribe had pursued political (rather than judicial) avenues of resisting Georgia's state policies on Indians for over a decade. As Georgians had pressed the Cherokees to turn their lands over to the state and leave, the Cherokees had consolidated their government in centralized institutions that governed the Cherokees as a separate people, and in 1827 they formalized the arrangement, and firmly proclaimed their autonomy, in a written constitution. They rebuffed Georgia's efforts to gain land cessions from the tribe, enacted laws prohibiting the individual sale of Cherokee land, and sent delegations to Washington to demand that the federal government stand behind U.S. treaty obligations by protecting the Cherokees from state encroachments.[41]

The Cherokees also protested in numerous written documents addressed to whites. Principal Chief John Ross was particularly active in this manner, vehemently objecting to the Georgia extension law in letters to Congress, the president, the secretary of war, Indian agents, and various northern supporters. To Massachusetts reformer David L. Child he firmly declared that the Cherokees "*never will live in vassalage to Georgia*, but like their ancestors, should the last dire extremity come, *they can* and *will live* and *die as freemen*." More specifically responding to passage of the extension statute in a memorial to Congress, Ross, joined by the Cherokee National Council, pointed out that the "right of regulating our own internal affairs is a right which we have inherited from the Author of our existence, which we have always exercised, and have never surrendered." Therefore, Ross and his colleagues asserted, "[w]e cannot admit that Georgia has the right to extend her jurisdiction over our territory, nor are the Cherokee people prepared to submit to her persecuting edict. We would therefore respectfully and solemnly protest, in behalf of the Cherokee nation, before your honorable bodies, against the extension of the laws of Georgia over any part of our Territory."[42]

Ross used his annual message to the Cherokee people in 1828 to elaborate further on arguments against the state statutes. He and co-chief William Hicks confronted each of Georgia's justifications for claiming authority over Cherokee lands. In turn they explained why the principles of discovery, conquest, and compact were groundless, even "preposterous," justifications. The king of England had no power, under the principle of right of discovery, to grant to colonists the land that Cherokees had inhabited from time immemorial, they noted. Furthermore, the Cherokees had never been conquered by the United States. Since the Cherokees had been allies, not subjects, of Britain, the losing power in the Revolutionary War did not have the power to convey to the United States any rights over the Cherokees or their lands. The United States demonstrated its recognition of the reality of Cherokee national independence when it negotiated separately with the Cherokees and worked out terms of peace in treaties. Those treaties, Ross and Hicks observed, never forfeited Cherokee ownership of their lands not ceded; in fact, in the treaties the United States had guaranteed Cherokee title to their territory. Finally, they pointed out, any commitment that the federal government had made to Georgia in the Compact of 1802 imposed no legal obligations on the Cherokees, who were not parties to that agreement.[43] Like Red Jacket, John Ross here made a claim to genuine tribal sovereignty.

Ross also had a response to the American argument that the Cherokees could not remain as an autonomous nation in Georgia because the U.S. Constitution did not permit any states to be formed within already exist- ing states. After Secretary of War John C. Calhoun made the argument during a meeting with Ross and other Cherokee leaders, they boldly point- ed out that the Cherokees had been living in the territory long before the arrival of the Anglo-Americans and that it was the Americans who were foreigners in Cherokee Territory. They reminded the Madison adminis- tration that "the Cherokee are not foreigners but original inhabitants of America, and that they now inhabit and stand on the soil of their own ter- ritory and that the limits of this territory are defined by the treaties which they have made with the government of the United States, and that the states by which they are now surrounded have been created out of land which was once theirs, and that they cannot recognize the sovereignty of any state within the limits of their territory."[44] Moreover, on the issue of citizenship, when Americans informed Ross and the other leaders that the Cherokees would become citizens of the United States when the president declared them so, Ross and the others demurred, explaining that, instead, it would be up to the Cherokees to decide when (and whether) they would apply for citizenship and that until that time they remained members of their own independent nation.[45]

In an 1830 letter to the federally appointed Cherokee agent, Hugh Montgomery, Ross echoed Thomas Oakley's argument on behalf of Tommy Jemmy in New York and even borrowed from the final *Goodell v. Jackson* decision to support his argument for Cherokee sovereignty. Ross quoted a sentence from Chancellor Kent's opinion: "One community may be bound to another by a very unequal alliance and still be a *sovereign State*. Though a weak State, in order to provide for its safety, *should place itself under the protection of a more powerful one*, yet, according to Vatell . . . *it reserves to itself, the right of governing its own body in order to be consid- ered an Independent State*." In arguing that Cherokee sovereignty was not destroyed by the fact of the tribe's having placed itself under the protection of the United States, Ross was in fact not merely expressing a Vatellian idea. Rather than being just a European notion, the concept was at the heart of Indians' own understanding of what a treaty relationship demanded. As legal scholar Robert Williams points out, American Indians had long viewed treaties as creating a relationship of sacred trust and embodying a promise of mutual protection. If the United States had become a stron- ger party, it had all the more obligation to protect the weaker party—for example, against the people of Georgia—and Cherokee acceptance of U.S. protection did not undermine the extent of Cherokee sovereignty.[46]

Furthermore, Ross noted, treaties between the Cherokee Nation and the United States acknowledged that Cherokee territory was not within the jurisdiction of any state, and allowing a state to assert jurisdiction over the Cherokee domain would be contrary to the provisions of the treaties. He concluded that since "the territory of the Cherokees is not within the jurisdiction of Georgia, but within the sole and exclusive jurisdiction of the Cherokee nation . . . consequently the State of Georgia has no right to extend her laws over this territory—that the law of Georgia extending jurisdiction is unconstitutional and void."[47]

Ross and other Jacksonian-era Cherokees bluntly challenged Americans to live up to their own ideals of liberty, rights, sovereignty, and rule of law. They were able to make such arguments adroitly because familiarity with the American mentality led them to express their arguments in terms of the American political, cultural, and religious framework and to appeal to Americans' sense of national identity. Thus, as historian Andrew Denson has pointed out, the Cherokees argued that, in addition to illegally violating treaties and effectively ending the civilization experiment, the removal proposal would betray America's founding principles, set the country on an un-Christian and anti-republican path away from virtue and morality, and demolish the relationship of trust and friendship between Americans and Cherokees.[48] Yet, notwithstanding the eloquence of Cherokee appeals, Congress passed the Removal Bill, which provided for an "exchange of lands" with the eastern Indians. The Cherokees (and other tribes) would be persuaded to give up territory lying within state borders in exchange for land west of the Mississippi River; the federal government would also provide compensation to the Indians for the value of improvements they had made to their land, as well as aid and assistance to help them move west.[49] In setting national policy, it was considered more important to foster white westward expansion than to protect Indians or abide by treaties.

Despite the removal law, John Ross did not give up. Observing little support in the executive or legislative branches of the state or the federal government, the Cherokees decided that the courts would provide their most promising option for protection. But the state judiciary did not have a promising record. In each of the southeastern states, judges ignored Indian objections and provided support for legislative and executive branch policies on Indians. Weighing in on the jurisdictional issue in cases arising from criminal charges against Indians, southern judges discussed the issue of tribal sovereignty, cited the *Tommy Jemmy* case and *Goodell v. Jackson*, upheld state criminal jurisdiction over all territory and persons within state boundaries, and reinforced progress toward removal of Indians. The case of George Tassel, also known as Corn Tassel, provides a good example of such a criminal case.

Tassel was arrested in the summer of 1830 and was accused of murdering another Cherokee man, Cornelius Dougherty, in Cherokee Territory. Tassel's lawyer, William H. Underwood, immediately challenged Georgia's jurisdiction over the defendant. The trial court judge, Augustin S. Clayton, agreed to allow Tassel to appeal the legal issue of jurisdiction to the state's Convention of Judges, an appellate tribunal that preceded the existence of a state supreme court. The Convention of Judges ruled against Tassel. They noted that the fundamental principle of the "right of discovery," by which the European nations claimed dominion over the Americas, meant that the tribes lost aspects of their sovereignty upon the arrival of Europeans. The convention went on to explain how the United States had accepted and continued this principle since its founding; as evidence of the enduring adherence to the principle, the judges pointed out that Congress regulated trade with Indian tribes differently from the way it regulated trade with foreign nations, and, moreover, Congress never formally declared any of the wars waged against Indians because Indian tribes were not sovereign nations. Georgia became heir to whatever rights England held over the Indians, the judges concluded. Those rights included fee title to all land within the borders of the state, including soil occupied by Cherokees. Being seized in fee of a territory necessarily meant having jurisdiction over that territory and its inhabitants. The judges pointed out that nobody objected when New York extended criminal jurisdiction over Indians in 1822; nor was there any justification for challenging Georgia's equivalent jurisdiction. The Convention of Judges ended by rejecting the challenge to Georgia's extension statute and sending the case back to the superior court for trial. George Tassel's trial on November 22 ended in a guilty verdict. Tassel was sentenced to death by hanging, scheduled for December 24.[50]

In the face of the failure of the state judiciary to protect Cherokee rights, the Cherokees turned to the U.S. Supreme Court. Prior to Tassel's arrest, the leaders and their lawyers lacked an irrefutable argument to justify their legal standing in that court. As historian Tim Alan Garrison has explained, the Cherokee leadership hoped *Tassels* would provide them with an opportunity to escape dependence on state tribunals and to challenge the constitutionality of Georgia's extension laws in the U.S. Supreme Court. They anticipated that this criminal case would solve the standing issue and would serve as a test case allowing them to mount a federal court challenge to the state's actions. Following Tassel's conviction, his lawyers successfully obtained a writ of error from the U.S. Supreme Court and on December 20 delivered to the governor a notice of appeal and a subpoena to appear before the Court in January. At an emergency session on December 22, the state legislature agreed on a resolution asserting their rejection of the Supreme Court's order, and the governor ordered the execution to proceed. Tassel was hanged on December 24.[51]

Three days later, lawyers for the Cherokees initiated *Cherokee Nation v. State of Georgia* in the U.S. Supreme Court. Since Tassel had been executed, the Cherokees could no longer base a test case on Tassel's appeal. The lawyers therefore now argued instead that, because the Cherokee Nation was a foreign state, the Court had original jurisdiction over the matter under Article III of the Constitution, which generally included in federal court jurisdiction cases "between a State, or the Citizens thereof, and foreign States, Citizens, or Subjects" and specifically provided that such cases could be initiated in the Supreme Court (rather than the lower courts) whenever a state was a party. The suit requested an injunction to restrain Georgia from enforcing its extension laws that subjected Cherokees to state laws, destroyed Cherokee political and judicial institutions, and seized Cherokee property. The Court declined to accept jurisdiction of the Cherokee case, rejecting the argument that the Cherokees constituted a "foreign State." This could be seen as representing an official rejection of the view of tribal sovereignty expressed by some whites at the time of the *Jemmy* and *Goodell* cases a decade earlier. As Vine Deloria and Clifford Lytle point out, by defining the Cherokees as a "domestic dependent nation," Chief Justice John Marshall formalized a limited perception of "tribal sovereignty." Since that time, Deloria and Lytle observe, the debate between Indians and whites about tribal sovereignty has focused on the degree to which tribes retained rights of self-government within—rather than independent of—the American polity.[52]

The year after it rendered the *Cherokee Nation* decision, the Supreme Court accepted jurisdiction of another case that questioned Georgia's laws. In their defense in *Worcester v. State of Georgia*, white missionaries disputed the constitutionality of provisions of Georgia's extension laws that prohibited whites from residing in the Cherokee domain unless they obtained a license from the state and took an oath to uphold state laws. In its decision, the Court declared that Georgia had acted unconstitutionally when it extended its laws over the Cherokees and their territory.[53]

Often viewed as one of the most important court cases pertaining to

American Indians, *Worcester* has been discussed thoroughly by numerous scholars, and detailed analysis of the Supreme Court decision can be found in those other scholars' works.[54] Although the formal outcome of *Worcester* should have been positive for the Cherokees, what is most relevant about the case for purposes of this study of the situation at the state level is that Georgia ignored the Supreme Court's refutation of its theoretical justification for regulating Cherokees and refused to abide by the Court's ruling that the extension laws were unconstitutional. As Sidney Harring concluded, "[t]he language of John Marshall in *Worcester* was largely irrelevant to Indians confronted with the power of the states in the nineteenth century."[55] Historian Tim Garrison found that in the six years following *Worcester*, the southeastern states repudiated *Worcester* by asserting jurisdiction over the criminal cases of dozens of Indians, notwithstanding the U.S. Supreme Court's voiding of the extension laws. As Garrison concluded from his extensive study of the judicial record, state supreme court decisions in Georgia, Tennessee, and Alabama effectively "displaced the Supreme Court's decision in *Worcester*," making "southern removal ideology . . . the law of the land" in spite of the Supreme Court's opposition to its legal foundation.[56] Notwithstanding the Court's official recognition of Cherokee sovereignty, in 1838 almost 17,000 eastern Cherokees were forced to move to Indian Country west of the Mississippi River; Russell Thornton estimates that over 8,000 of the Cherokees may have died as a result of the removal. Tens of thousands of other Indians similarly were relocated west during Jackson's terms as president, leaving about 100 million acres of Indian land that was turned over to whites. By the end of the 1840s, President Polk announced that the goal of removing eastern Indians and obtaining title to their lands had been achieved; only a small number of Indians remained east of the Mississippi River, he said, and they were deemed to be subject to state jurisdiction.[57]

State legislation and state judicial opinions provided the main foundation for the mass expulsion. After the Georgia Supreme Court decided the *Tassels* case, the other southeastern states' opinions used similar justifications for rejecting tribal sovereignty and upholding state extension laws. They concluded that the tribes were not sovereign nations and that the states had jurisdiction over tribal members. In the aftermath of *Tassels*, the two southeastern cases that discussed the tribal sovereignty issue most extensively were *State of Tennessee v. Forman* and *Caldwell v. State of Alabama*. Both cases involved a murder allegedly committed in Indian Territory, in both cases the state claimed jurisdiction under its criminal extension law, and in both cases the state court rejected tribal sovereignty and upheld state jurisdiction. In *Forman*, the Supreme Court of Tennessee asserted that the Europeans' conquest of the Americas gave them the right to govern the Native peoples found there, and those peoples had no political rights that the conquerors had to respect. In *Caldwell* the Alabama Supreme Court discussed the tribal sovereignty issue at length. The judges pointed out that neither Europeans nor Americans ever considered the Indian tribes to be distinct and independent sovereignties because they lacked an established governmental structure, clear geographical boundaries, permanent homes, an agricultural foundation, and a civilized lifestyle.[58]

Southern courts of the early 1830s addressed the issue of tribal sovereignty more directly and fully than did the judiciary of any other region. Two of the state statutes under review in the southern extension law cases (Georgia's and Alabama's) explicitly rejected the tribal sovereignty asserted in the Cherokee constitution of 1827; those statutes not only extended state criminal and civil jurisdiction over the Cherokees but also nullified the laws of the Cherokee and Creek Nations. Because the issue of tribal sovereignty was thus prominent and obvious, the southern state courts addressed the issue in a way that judges did not often do elsewhere. However, in the years after the southern extension law cases, the tribal sovereignty issue did come up in some state courts outside the Southeast.

State of Wisconsin v. Doxtater, in which the defendant was an Oneida Indian accused of committing adultery in his home on the Oneida reservation, provides a good example. The defendant argued that the Oneidas—descendants of people who had been displaced from New York earlier in the century—were a self-governing sovereign nation separate from the states and not subject to state laws. The Wisconsin Supreme Court rejected this argument, though without much original or serious analysis. In dealing with the issue, the court relied heavily on lengthy quotations from selected federal cases indicating that the tribes in Indian Country were not independent nations, were subject to U.S. laws, and had the right to self-government only if and when the federal government explicitly granted them that right.[59]

Taxation of Indian lands also raised tribal sovereignty issues. In the Kansas case *Blue-Jacket v. Commissioners of Johnson County*, an Indian party, Charles Blue-Jacket, had the opportunity to testify directly on the tribal sovereignty issue. The 1865 case involved the Shawnees, who were originally an Ohio tribe, displaced to Kansas in the 1820s. Soon after Kansas became a state in 1861, the legislature began discussing strategies for removing the

Shawnees. In 1864 the state imposed taxes on land allotted to Indians. In the *Blue-Jacket* case, the Shawnees reacted to that legislative move by challenging Johnson County's taxation of the tribe's land. Head chief Blue-Jacket testified that the Shawnees had an established elected government that enacted regulations governing the tribe and had its own method for punishing criminals and for resolving contractual disagreements, inheritance matters, and other disputes among members. The lawyer for the Shawnees further argued that the tribe was an independent nation, had never given up its right to self-government, and owed no allegiance to Kansas or to the United States other than as agreed to in treaties. The Supreme Court of Kansas rejected these arguments. Chief Justice Robert Crozier explained that "[t]he Shawnees do not hold their lands in common, nor are they contiguously located" and observed that "[i]t is difficult to conceive of a national existence without a national domain upon which to maintain it." He concluded that the tribe did not have sovereign rights over the individually owned land in question, leaving it within the state's jurisdiction to govern and to tax. Even though the U.S. Supreme Court later overturned the state court's opinion, within four years after *Blue-Jacket* the Shawnees had left Kansas; once again moving out of the way of expanding white settlement, by the end of the 1860s the Shawnees had made a new home in the area that was to become Oklahoma.[60]

At times, state courts did allow some degree of tribal self-governance on internal matters. For example, a number of courts recognized marriages entered into or dissolved in accordance with tribal customs, even if they did not meet the requirements of the state's marriage and divorce laws.[61] Decisions of this kind did not broaden recognition of tribal authority beyond such internal matters, however. In general, although state courts paid some attention to tribal sovereignty issues, they rarely acknowledged such sovereignty if it conflicted with their own interests. When it came down to it, state legislatures enjoyed judicial support when they eliminated or nullified tribal authority. Overwhelmingly, when state judges evaluated the issue of tribal sovereignty, they tended to rule against the tribes. And often they did not even consider the issue.

While criminal jurisdiction cases were likely to involve Indian parties directly, most other kinds of cases raising issues about states' authority to govern relations with Indians did not involve Indian litigants. This was partly owing to the presence of a variety of barriers to Indian initiation of, or voluntary participation in, civil litigation, but it was also a result of the different nature of other kinds of state statutes pertaining to Indians. The prohibitions on activities relating to commercial exchanges (land sales, contracts, lawsuits) most often targeted whites' behavior rather than Indians', and cases involving violations of those prohibitions typically involved white defendants. Furthermore, such prohibitions could be seen as ways to keep whites and Indians from interacting in order to allow Indian tribes to retain both their land base and their character as separate political entities. In a sense, then, those prohibitions, unlike the criminal extension statutes, were not fully in conflict with tribal autonomy. In any event, cases without Indian parties rarely prompted discussion of tribal sovereignty. This was in part because in the absence of Indian parties, judges typically did not hear Indian voices or take into account Indian interests.

In part, though, state judges gave only limited attention to tribal sovereignty because, even in the extension cases, state judges were primarily concerned with the federal government's (rather than the tribes') constraints on states' actions. More than the issue of tribal sovereignty, the state judiciary was interested in discussing the federalism issue—that is, the question of when the federal government's authority to govern Indians gave way to a state's power. Even when state judges wrote about tribal sovereignty, they were doing so in order to assert the propriety of the state's— as opposed to the federal government's—preeminent right to regulate Indians, because, from the states' perspective, the tribal sovereignty issue was inexorably intertwined with the issue of states' rights. They believed that tribal sovereignty within the states was incompatible with state sovereignty. Therefore, any federal government action that might reinforce tribal sovereignty was seen as a threat to states' rights. The states resisted that potential threat by extending their jurisdiction over Indians within their borders.

New York, which set a pattern for other states, began its campaign to incorporate Indians into state jurisdiction soon after the Treaty of Paris ended the Revolutionary War. The policy of the mid-1780s was to try to make Indians "Members of the State." The Articles of Confederation granted Congress authority to manage relations with "Indians not members of any of the States." In a letter to James Monroe, James Madison explained that the phrase "members of any of the States" referred to Indians "who do not live within the body of the Society, or whose Persons or property form no objects of its laws."[62] Thus, making Indians subject to New York's criminal jurisdiction and to various other state laws was an attempt not only to counter Indian assertions of tribal autonomy but also to defy the federal government's efforts to control Indian policy. As this chapter has illustrated, all but a few European Americans in New York and Georgia courts and legislatures simply presumed that Indians had no sovereign rights that precluded regulation by Americans. Considering it a given that Americans had the right to govern Indians, the remaining question for state government officials was *which* Americans were authorized to exercise that right. As shown in the next chapter, the resounding answer of state court judges was: the states.

CHAPTER TWO

The State Sovereignty Argument for Local Regulation

From the perspective of state government officials, the primary legal challenge to states' authority to regulate Indians came from the federal government, not the tribes. Accordingly, the main legal issue in state cases, including *Jemmy, Goodell, Tassels, Forman,* and *Caldwell,* was not tribal sovereignty but states' rights in a federal political structure. Typically side-stepping the issue of tribal sovereignty, state courts reviewing legislation pertaining to Indians tended to focus primarily on the conflict between federal and state authority over Indians.

Constitutional provisions seemed to define regulation of Indians as exclusively a federal matter. In Article I, section 8, the U.S. Constitution granted Congress the power to "regulate Commerce . . . with the Indian Tribes." Other major sources of authority for federal regulation of Indians were the treaties clause in Article II, section 2 (giving the president the "Power, by and with the Advice and Consent of the Senate, to make Treaties"), and the property clause in Article IV, section 3 (giving Congress the "Power to dispose of and make all needful Rules and Regulations respecting the Territory or other Property belonging to the United States"). Because the United States claimed a property interest in Indian lands based on the doctrine of discovery, government officials regarded the property clause as providing a plausible foundation for the federal government's assertion of authority over Indians.

Federal statutes ostensibly further constrained state authority over Indians. Implementing its commerce clause powers, Congress enacted a series of trade and intercourse acts that nullified all purchases and leases of Indian land—whether by individuals or by states—except those accomplished pursuant to federal treaties; voided all executory contracts made by Indians for the payment of money or goods; prohibited everyone from negotiating treaties with Indian tribes outside of federal government-sponsored negotiations; and punished people who, in Indian territory, traded with Indians without a federal license, intruded or settled on Indian land, committed crimes against Indians, or sold liquor to Indians.[1] Yet, as this chapter shows, the formal allocation of power over Indian affairs to the federal government did not preclude extensive local involvement in Indian matters, justified largely by using state sovereignty arguments.

STATE REGULATION OF INDIANS

Despite the fact that the federal government had asserted authority over Americans' interactions with Indians as early as 1790, the states nonetheless claimed the right to enact their own legislation governing relations with Indians inside their borders. Between 1790 and 1880, state legislatures across the country enacted the same kinds of statutes that New York passed, as described in chapter 1. Like state legislatures, territorial legislatures were local in nature and they regulated Indians in similar ways.[2]

Historian Sidney Harring, author of an in-depth study of *Crow Dog's Case*, points out how difficult it is to determine with any certainty which states actually applied state criminal laws to Indians. States might have exercised such jurisdiction over Indians without formally enacting a statute declaring their authority to do so; they may have just presumed that their general criminal laws applied equally to Indians as to non-Indians within state boundaries. Moreover, the absence of any printed judicial decision explaining or justifying a state's authority to try Indians also does not mean that it did not subject them to criminal laws. Harring observes that few nineteenth-century Indians were in a position to raise jurisdictional issues. That is, most Indian criminal defendants lacked money, lawyers, and knowledge of American legal practices. They were tried in local courts, were quickly sentenced and punished, and often had no opportunity to raise a jurisdictional defense nor to appeal the issue of the state's jurisdiction to a higher tribunal that would have left printed reports of its decisions. Therefore, Harring writes, "if a state was silent on the matter of jurisdiction over Indians, in the absence of cases we cannot know whether this means the state claimed or did not claim jurisdiction over Indians within its boundaries." Based on his study of Indian criminal cases, Harring judges that "[m]ost states with substantial Indian populations" claimed criminal jurisdiction over tribes.[3]

Close examination of state legislation enacted between 1790 and 1880 supports Harring's conclusion regarding the pervasiveness of state imposition of criminal jurisdiction over Indians, especially in the eastern part of the country, but also in the West. That criminal and civil regulations were often applied to reservation Indians as well as Indians who were merged with the white population is evidenced by Commissioner of Indian Affairs Charles E. Mix's 1858 call for California to allow the federal trade and intercourse laws to apply to reservations in the state, rather than insisting on retaining state jurisdiction over those reservations.[4]

Overall, study of the legislation in the thirty-eight states that were admitted by 1880 uncovered evidence that at least three-quarters (twenty-eight) of them asserted criminal jurisdiction at least over Indian defendants accused of committing crimes outside of their reservations or white defendants accused of committing crimes within Indian reservations; a number of those states extended criminal jurisdiction over all Indians and whites anywhere in the state. Likewise, statutory records reveal that at least three-quarters (twenty-nine) of the states also regulated Indians' right to sell land, trade in goods, make enforceable contracts, and litigate in court. These results do not necessarily mean that the other nine or ten states declined to apply criminal and civil laws to Indians, however. The survey could have missed some statutes, and, furthermore, some states might have regulated Indians without explicitly mentioning them in laws or appellate judicial opinions. The absence of language expressly making statutes applicable to Indians was especially likely in states either where Indians were not viewed as members of a group whose unique status warranted explicit mention in laws of general application or where Indians' presence was not visible to whites (either because of ignorance or because of a myth that Indians had "vanished").

It is easiest to get accurate information about states that reported a high population of Indians, since they were most likely to make explicit mention of Indians in their statutes. A survey of the statutes in those states, in combination with analysis of judicial opinions, provides a fairly clear assessment of the situation. Table 1 below shows the extent of such regulation between 1790 and 1880 in the eight states with the highest population of Indians in 1860.[5] Examples of statutes from these and other states are in the appendix.[6] As is evident in the chart, California, Minnesota, Michigan, Kansas, New York, Wisconsin, and North Carolina had statutes expressly regulating Indians and subjecting Indians to criminal courts, but Oregon appears not to have had any such statutes during its statehood years before

TABLE 1. State laws pertaining to Indians in states with the largest populations of Indians in 1860 (1790–1880)

	Year State Admitted to Union	"Civilized" Indians, 1860	"Unenu- merated" Indians, 1860	Total Indians, 1860	Criminal Jurisdiction*	Civil Regulation of Indians**
California	1850	17,798	13,540	31,338	X	X
Minnesota	1858	2,369	17,900	20,269	X	X
Michigan	1837	6,172	7,777	13,949	X	X
Kansas	1861	180	8,189	8,369	X	X
Oregon	1859	177	7,000	7,177		
New York	1788	140	3,785	3,925	X	X
Wisconsin	1848	1,017	2,833	3,850	X	X
North Carolina	1789	1,158	1,499	2,657	X	X

*State laws asserting at least jurisdiction over Indian defendants outside of any reservation or jurisdiction over white defendants on a reservation. "X" indicates existence of at least one such law in the state.

**State laws regulating land sales, trades, contracts, or lawsuits of Indians. "X" indicates existence of at least one such law in the state.

1880. However, in December 1882, the state tried and convicted a Grand Ronde Indian, Tom Gilbert, of having murdered two other Indians, Dave Yatskawa and a woman named Pononapa, on the reservation in November 1882. Hearing the case on appeal in May 1883, the Supreme Court of Oregon made no jurisdictional objection, though it overturned the case on a legal technicality and ordered a new trial.[7] This case suggests that, at least by 1882, in practice Oregon did exercise criminal jurisdiction over Indians, even if it had no law expressly asserting that authority.

In terms of federalism, the states' regulation of Indian land sales, trading, and executory contracts was controversial because Congress covered these subjects in the federal trade and intercourse acts, and the normal rule was that if the federal government had acted on a subject falling within its constitutional powers, the states were precluded from legislating on the same topic.[8] In addition, whenever the states negotiated treaties with tribes in order to purchase Indian lands, they arguably came in conflict not only with federal laws asserting exclusive federal control of treaty making with Indians but also with section 10 of Article I of the U.S. Constitution, which provides that "No State shall enter into any Treaty."

State laws that punished and removed white intruders or settlers on Indian land, as well as statutes regulating the sale of liquor to Indians, were likewise questioned because of the existence of federal laws on the same subject that provided similar remedies. In the territory of New Mexico, for example, a particularly astute Indian agent questioned the legislature's power to enact anti-liquor legislation, "inasmuch as no state can, constitutionally, legislate upon any subject which has received congressional action; that where 'Congress has exercised their powers upon any given subject, the States cannot enter upon the same ground' and provide for same or different objects; much less can the Territorial Legislature."[9] New Mexico, like other territories and the states, overcame any hesitation about venturing into federal turf and went ahead to pass anti-liquor and anti-trespass legislation.

Finally, the states' legislating the form of tribal government structure and extending their criminal jurisdiction, tax laws, and marriage and inheritance rules over Indians was perceived by some as directly conflicting with federal treaty provisions that guaranteed tribal self-governance or as interfering with matters properly handled by the federal government. As a basic principle articulated in the supremacy clause (Article VI of the Constitution), the states were normally required to yield to federal laws and treaties. Thus, the states' regulation of Indians raised a number of difficult issues.

The federal government was not precise about linking its own exercise of power to its constitutional sources of authority, however. The U.S. Supreme Court cases between 1790 and 1880 that have traditionally been viewed as the major statements of federal authority regarding Indians—*Johnson v. McIntosh, Cherokee Nation v. Georgia*, and *Worcester v. Georgia*—failed to provide clear and consistent constitutionally based rules, and a decision (*United States v. Kagama*) discussing federal authority immediately following the close of the period under study exhibited the continuing ambiguity in the late nineteenth century.[10] The federal government's lack of precision meant that the states were freer to be vague in explaining why they were permitted to act as they did. Thus state courts often analyzed constitutional issues of federalism without referring to specific provisions of the Constitution. Furthermore, they often came to conclusions about the meaning of federal statutes without even explicitly naming, much less describing the language of, those statutes. The fact that so many provisions of the federal laws were ambiguous left the states a fair amount of room for vague interpretation, and the states took advantage of that by repeatedly upholding their Indian legislation. As judges had pushed aside tribal claims of autonomy, so they played a key role in easing the states' way past the potential obstacles of the U.S. Constitution and federal laws.

By the early national period, many Indians had already been dispossessed from northeastern states, and those who remained were left under state jurisdiction. The premise that Massachusetts, Connecticut, Rhode Island, New Jersey, and Pennsylvania would continue to have the same authority over Indians that they had exercised as colonies met with no serious challenge and created an expectation on the part of other states that they would enjoy similar power. New York was the first state to exhibit success in gaining jurisdiction over Indians who, prior to the Revolution, were neither governed by nor under the control of the colonial government. When the state asserted control over those Indians during the early national period, state judges upheld the state's regulations. New York courts provided early judicial precedents asserting states' rights to regulate Indians, and its success in obtaining authority over relations with the Iroquois served as a model for other states. Subsequently, courts in southern and midwestern states frequently pointed to New York's exercise of authority over Indians to justify their own power to act similarly. In Georgia, Tennessee, Alabama, and Florida, state courts provided the foundation for complete state jurisdiction over Indians. And in Indiana, Illinois, Michigan, Wisconsin, Minnesota, Iowa, Kansas, Nebraska, and Arkansas, state courts reinforced state authority over Indians in many contexts. Even the far western states and territories of California, New Mexico, and Washington found ways to regulate Indians, with judicial support.

This chapter examines the role of state courts in justifying state regulation of Indians between 1790 and 1880. As historian Tim Alan Garrison noted in his insightful study of the southern judiciary and Indian removal, scholars have tended to focus on the federal courts' role in defining "Indian law," giving little attention to the influence of state judges.[11] Yet state courts played an important role in furthering white control of Indians, and their arguments were different than those dominating federal court decisions. While federal judges frequently focused on the question of federal authority versus tribal authority, state courts most often framed their analysis around principles of federalism.[12]

In state cases, judges implicitly left it to the federal government, as part of its rationale for federal control, to make the argument that the tribes were distinct political bodies. Where the federal government failed to make a persuasive argument for federal authority by successfully asserting tribal distinctiveness, the states stepped in. The federal government commonly had no incentive to defend tribal rights vigorously. Since the federal government in fact shared more goals in common with the states than with the tribes, it offered little resistance to state assertions of authority over Indians. With the support of state courts, state legislatures often were left free to regulate Indians however they wished.

Although few state courts presented full, accurate, clear, specific explanations for decisions upholding state regulation of Indians in the face of apparent federal authority over relations with Indians, the rationales that were utilized fit into a discernible pattern. In analyzing federalism issues raised by state legislation pertaining to Indians, state judges presented justifications that fell into two categories. First, state judges focused on the nature of the law in question, arguing that the subject of regulation was outside of federal constitutional powers and was appropriately a state matter. These opinions were based on broad principles of state sovereignty and police powers. Second, the courts examined the objects of the regulation in question, that is, the regulated Indians. In these cases, the judges argued that the states could regulate particular Indians because their distinctive status, condition, or location exempted them from federal Indian laws altogether.

JUDICIAL ARGUMENTS BASED ON THE SUBJECT MATTER OF LEGISLATION

The first category of justifications for state regulation of Indians analyzed the subject matter of legislation and primarily relied on principles of state sovereignty and state police powers to explain state authority. State judges based their arguments on the principle that the U.S. Constitution created a federal government with limited powers. The federal government had only the powers delegated to it by the Constitution; authority over all other subjects was reserved to the states by the Tenth Amendment. Since Congress most often justified its regulation of Indians by pointing to its authority to regulate commerce with the Indian tribes, state challenges to federal authority over Indians frequently were founded on an assertion that the subject of regulation was not "commerce." There was a body of federal cases providing standards for interpreting the interstate commerce clause during this period, so state courts had a substantial foundation for making their arguments regarding the Indian commerce clause. If governance of Indians was necessary beyond the regulation of commerce, state judges argued, that governance constitutionally was left for the states to exercise under their police powers. In these cases, judges asserted a broad jurisdiction over all Indians within their borders, basing that jurisdiction on American principles of state sovereignty and states' reserved police powers to promote and protect the health, safety, and welfare of their citizens. Those principles were applied to justify both state regulation of Indians' contracts, land sales, and litigation and state removal of whites from Indian land and also state laws extending criminal jurisdiction over Indians.

Most courts in states where significant numbers of Indians remained in the nineteenth century, including courts in New York, the Southeast, the Midwest, and the Far West, upheld state legislative decisions on whether to allow Indians to sell land, make contracts, or sue in court, and whether to punish or remove whites who intruded on Indian lands. Perhaps it was natural that this important issue of federalism would have been so extensively addressed in New York, the locus of the events leading to the famous *Gibbons v. Ogden* case of 1824. To counter the argument that the commerce power was exclusive in Congress, the lawyer for the appellant in *Gibbons* used the regulation of Indians as an example of an area where there was a clear need for a concurrent commerce power in the states. Because New York had long legislated on issues relating to commerce with Indians (e.g., prohibiting the purchase of land from Indians or the sale of certain kinds of goods to Indians), the lawyer said it would cause havoc in state Indian laws if the commerce power were not deemed to be concurrent. The Supreme Court, however, issued a strongly nationalistic opinion. The Court, led by Chief Justice John Marshall, vigorously rejected New York's attempted regulation of steamboat traffic on the Hudson River, holding that navigation was part of "commerce" and that the federal government had superior jurisdiction over commerce that was interstate.[13]

By 1837 New York's lawyers had a more favorable Supreme Court precedent to rely on when they made commerce clause arguments. In *New York v. Miln*, the Court upheld the constitutionality of an 1824 state law requiring, among other things, masters of ships arriving in the port of New York to report certain information about all passengers and to post security for indigent passengers. The Court, now led by new chief justice Roger Taney, rejected the argument that the law constituted a regulation of interstate and foreign commerce and thus intruded on an exclusive federal government sphere of authority. Instead, the justices concluded that the statute fell within the state's internal police powers. That is, the state's right and duty to protect the health, safety, and welfare of its citizens encompassed this regulation enacted to protect New Yorkers against the financial burden and "moral pestilence" of paupers and vagabonds.[14]

Analyzing the validity of state regulation of Indians in the era of *Gibbons* and *Miln*, New York judges concluded that state laws pertaining to Indians did not constitute regulation of "commerce" with the Indian tribes and therefore did not fall within the commerce clause or the *Gibbons* ruling. Sometimes the judges went even further, finding ways of justifying the state's actions even when they directly conflicted with federal regulations. Rather than merely defending state laws as internal police regulations, they aggressively challenged the constitutionality of certain provisions of the federal trade and intercourse acts. They argued that Congress's power to regulate commerce did not authorize provisions of the acts that prohibited Indians from selling land or litigating in court, voided Indians' executory contracts, and prohibited whites from intruding upon Indian lands. Since regulations on such subjects were not within Congress's enumerated powers, the judges concluded, such regulations were left under the state's domain, within the powers of state sovereignty.

New York's cases on this subject came up in two different ways. Some state statutes permitted an action that federal law prohibited, and the court had to decide which law had precedence. Other state statutes prohibited an action that federal law also prohibited, and the court had to decide whether the state could regulate on a matter already being regulated by the federal government. In both situations, the underlying constitutional question was whether the commerce clause gave Congress exclusive authority to regulate on the particular subject or whether the matter was properly within the state's police powers by operation of the Tenth Amendment.

New York's Supreme Court of Judicature addressed the issue directly in an 1837 case where the legitimacy of an Indian's deed of 1809 was in question. Deciding *Murray v. Wooden* eight months after the U.S. Supreme Court rendered its opinion in *New York v. Miln*, the New York court rejected an attorney's argument that the commerce clause nullified the state's constitutional provision and statutes governing Indians' sale of their lands. In his opinion for the court, Chief Justice Samuel Nelson ruled that Congress's power to regulate commerce did not extend to the disposition of Indian lands by individuals. "It would seem to be carrying the power simply 'to regulate commerce with the Indian tribes,' to an extent beyond the legitimate and common meaning of the terms themselves, or in the connection in which they are used," he wrote. Given the fact that the commerce clause referred to "Indian tribes" rather than more generally to "Indians," this was a plausible constitutional argument. The court concluded that since Congress did not have the power to regulate Indians' sale of land, the Tenth Amendment reserved that power to the states. Since New York law at the time of the deed permitted this type of conveyance, the court upheld the Indian's deed as valid despite the federal restraint on alienation of Indian land.[15] Other New York cases upheld the state's power to prohibit the enforcement of Indians' contracts[16] and to bar Indians from suing or being sued in state courts.[17]

Two decades after *Murray v. Wooden*, another New York case became the focus of intense debate over the extent of the commerce power. *People of New York ex rel. Cutler v. Dibble* involved a challenge to the state's summary removal of whites intruding on Tonawanda Indian lands. After removal proceedings before Genesee County judge Edgar Dibble in 1853, lawyers for Asa Cutler and the other white settlers appealed the judge's ruling to the New York Supreme Court of Judicature. After that court upheld the constitutionality of the 1821 state statute regarding white intruders on Indian lands in 1854, Cutler unsuccessfully appealed to the New York Court of Appeals (1857) and then to the U.S. Supreme Court (1858). At each judicial level, Cutler's lawyers made a vigorous argument regarding the exclusivity of the federal commerce power. They asserted that New York's law was repugnant to the federal trade and intercourse acts and not justified because of the terms of the treaty with the Tonawandas; the state must give way to the federal Constitution, laws, and treaties. In the Court of Appeals, Cutler's lawyers had the support of Justice Hiram Denio, who dissented to the majority's decision. Denio wrote that the provisions of the federal trade and intercourse acts were "well warranted" by the commerce clause. He said the term "commerce" properly applied "to all transactions, respecting money or property, between an Indian tribe and the white citizens." In contrast, Dibble's lawyers argued that the commerce clause power and the trade and intercourse acts did not apply to New York Indians, who had always been governed by the police regulations—that is, the protective laws—of the colony and then of the state. The New York courts (with the later endorsement of the U.S. Supreme Court) ruled that there was no conflict between New York's action and the U.S. Constitution, federal laws, or the treaty, and they allowed the state's removal of the white settlers.[18]

As the courts further established in *Cutler v. Dibble*, federalism required that states must retain their proper police powers, especially their power to preserve peace within their borders and to protect incompetent people. Justice Richard Pratt Marvin of the New York Supreme Court pointed out that at the time of the 1821 statute for removing whites from Indian lands, "[t]he indians were but partially civilized, easily excited, and liable to resort to violence; they were liable to be imposed upon, and, in short, considerations of justice and policy required that the state should interfere and protect the lands of the indians from intrusion. The peace of society required this, the danger of strife and bloodshedding prompted to the passage of this and other laws." In sum, the statute fell squarely within the state's police powers because "[t]he object of the law, with various other laws of the state, was to protect the indians, to quiet them and render them secure." In the New York Court of Appeals, Justice John W. Brown further commented on the fact that the state had to take responsibility for removing intruders on Indian lands because the Indians were too weak to protect themselves. He observed that Indians were "both collectively and individually, feeble and helpless compared with the whites, and therefore needing constantly the protection and paternal care of the government." The Indians' "inability and utter incapacity to deal with the superior knowledge and sagacity of the whites is a recognized fact in our policy," he wrote, "and they have constantly occupied towards the government the same relations of pupilage and subjection that children and wards occupy towards their parents and guardians."[19]

In other cases, New York's judges further elaborated on the states' general police powers reserved to them by the Tenth Amendment, focusing especially on the same two powers mentioned in *Cutler v. Dibble*: the power to protect the safety of New York's citizens and the power to protect the welfare of Indians. Sometimes laws pertaining to Indians were deemed necessary for preserving public safety by maintaining peace with the Indians. For example, in *Jackson ex dem. Tewahangarahkan v. Sharp* (1817), the court said that the purpose of Article 37 of the state constitution and statutes that prohibited whites from making contracts with Indians and barred Indians from selling their land was to ensure "peace and amity" with the Indians by preventing fraud. Often, however, New York courts justified the states' actions by emphasizing not the peace of the state but the weakness and incompetence of the Indians. Judges argued that the state had the responsibility to exercise its police powers so as to protect incompetent people by limiting their rights. They resorted to patronizing and paternalistic language in explaining why Indians were similar to other incapacitated groups and needed special protections. In *Goodell v. Jackson*, Chancellor James Kent noted that protective federal laws implied "a state of dependence and imbecility on the part of the Indians, and that correspondent claim upon us for protection arising out of the superiority of our condition"; he referred to Indians as "a feeble and a degraded race, who stood in need of the arm of government constantly thrown around them"; and he observed that the statutory prohibitions on contracts with Indians "showed the sense of the Legislature, that an Indian, in his individual capacity, was, in a great degree, *inops consilii*, and unfit to make contracts."[20] Elsewhere, Indians were labeled weak and dependent and "notoriously unfit to make a contract" (*Hastings v. Farmer and Ellis*), and incapacitated by their "mental debasement" to sell land or to contract (*Jackson ex dem. Van Dyke v. Reynolds*). In a number of New York cases, Indians were placed in the same category as children, married women, insane persons, and other groups who were by law deemed to have a limited capacity.[21] Such analogies to "incompetent" people were presumed to justify protective regulations.[22]

Outside of New York, other state courts also supported state legislative regulations of Indians' contracts, land sales, and litigation and rejected the applicability of potentially conflicting federal laws based on arguments similar to those articulated in New York. In the Far West, the Supreme Court of California exercised its power to protect the welfare of Indians by holding that Indians could not convey land. The court determined that the Mexican Constitution, statutes, and decrees making Indians citizens did not eliminate restraints on alienation. The judge noted that a contract involving an Indian was similar to a contract with a small child (*un niño*) or a mentally deficient person (*un demente*). "Infants, idiots, lunatics, spendthrifts and married women, are also Mexican citizens," the court explained, "yet it can scarcely be claimed that those constitutional provisions were intended to remove all disabilities, under which they are placed by law, and enable them to contract and alienate their property without the intervention of tutor or curator, committee or guardian. So with the Indians." The judge concluded that treating the Indians differently was not abhorrent because the prohibition was intended to protect the Indians rather than to oppress them: "the object of the disability under consideration, was not to create an invidious distinction or impose a useless burden, but, in part at least, to favor the native inhabitants by shielding them from the impositions of the superior races." In the Midwest, the Supreme Court of Indiana made a similar argument in *Lafontaine v. Avaline*. In analyzing statutory prohibitions on Miami Indians selling land, the court acknowledged that the law imposed a disability on Indians in that it placed "serious obstacles in the way of the Indian who wishes to dispose of his lands." But, the court noted, the law was legitimate because "these obstacles are designed for the Indian's benefit;" the statute was for "the protection and relief of the Indians," to "shield them from the wiles and fraudulent practices of their more intelligent neighbors."[23]

In the South, Arkansas made a direct commerce clause challenge to the federal government: the court upheld a contract made by Ewhartonah, an Indian, as enforceable despite the federal prohibition, asserting that the commerce clause did not give Congress constitutional power to invalidate contracts entered into within the limits of a sovereign state. The "completely internal commerce of a State," is reserved to the state and does not fall within the commerce clause, the judge wrote, and in any case "commerce" does not include "ordinary business transactions occurring between individuals," such as Ewhartonah and his white colleague. In other cases, too, various state courts ruled that Indians' contracts and debts were enforceable in state courts despite the federal law voiding contracts by Indians. Specifically, they held that a Cherokee partner (Drew) in the merchant team of Drew and Scales could be held responsible for fulfilling the partnership's contractual obligations (Arkansas); that John Rubideaux, a Miami Indian chief, was liable to be sued in state court for nonpayment of money owed on a promissory note (Kansas); and the state had authority over the estate of the deceased Creek chief Samuel Hawkins (Alabama).[24]

State courts also addressed the issue of the constitutionality of extending criminal jurisdiction over Indians.[25] Southern courts were particularly concerned with the extension issue in the 1830s, but other regions also cared deeply about this subject. In *Tennessee v. Forman*, the defendant James Foreman was a Cherokee Indian accused of murdering another Cherokee, John Walker Jr., within the Cherokee Nation. The Tennessee Supreme Court pointed out that the federal government's "general punishment of crime" was not a regulation of commerce and therefore was not authorized by the commerce clause. If the Indian commerce clause authorized federal criminal jurisdiction over Indians, Justice John Catron observed for the court, then the interstate commerce clause would have to authorize such jurisdiction over the people of the states, which would be intolerable and inconsistent with the principles of federalism. In *Caldwell v. Alabama*, the defendant, James Caldwell, was a white man who was accused of murdering a Creek man named Fushatchee Yoholo in a part of the Creek Nation over which Alabama had recently extended its jurisdiction. The Alabama Supreme Court ruled that the commerce clause was no barrier to the state's asserting its authority over the Creeks. As Justice Reuben Saffold explained, Congress's power to regulate commerce with the Indian tribes extended no further than its power to regulate commerce with foreign nations or commerce among the states. With regard to the three-part commerce clause, Justice Saffold asked, "would it not be a strange heresy to maintain, that it confers authority, to exercise general municipal powers; or even to punish crimes and misdemeanors? If such be its effect," he observed, "it can not fail to annihilate the sovereignty of every State in the Union; and also of Europe, could it be enforced." *Wisconsin v. Doxtater* involved an Oneida Indian defendant who was accused of committing adultery (with a non-Indian woman) in his own house on the Oneida reservation. In that case, the Wisconsin Supreme Court held that Indians on reservations were subject to the criminal jurisdiction of the state's courts because once an area was admitted as a state Congress could only regulate commerce with the tribes; all other powers with regard to the Indians were reserved to the states by the Tenth Amendment. Finally, in explaining his holding that an executory contract between the Indian Ewhartonah and a white man was valid and enforceable, Justice Henry Massey Rector of the Arkansas Supreme Court pointed out in *Hicks v. Ewhartonah* that if the federal government had the power to invalidate agreements that a citizen made in his own state—regardless of whether the other party was another citizen of the state, a citizen of another state, an alien, or an Indian—it would be a serious infringement on state sovereignty. The commerce clause did not justify such regulation, since "commerce" did not include "ordinary business transactions occurring between individuals."[26]

In *Forman* the Tennessee Supreme Court also raised another constitutional issue when it asserted that in denying state criminal jurisdiction throughout Tennessee the U.S. government would effectively be ceding away part of a state to a group of people who were independent of the state. The Constitution (Article IV, section 3) provided that no new state could be erected within an existing state, the judges pointed out; it was even more abhorrent to consider the creation of a foreign and independent government within a state. In fact, the judges said, that foreign territory within the state would be not only independent but also lawless. Other than the state of Tennessee, there was no other source of law and order in Cherokee Territory, they said. If the state did not assume jurisdiction, Justice Catron warned, "then there will be, within the bounds of this Union, a lawless territory, where sanctuary is found for the murderer, the robber and the thief, free from molestation." In *Georgia v. Tassels*—the case discussed in chapter 1, where the Cherokee Indian George Tassel was accused of murdering another Cherokee in a part of Cherokee Territory that the state had just annexed—the Georgia Supreme Court had earlier taken a similar position. The judges concluded that no state should have to tolerate the existence of another sovereign independent nation within its borders. How can a state hold territory in fee and yet not have jurisdiction over that territory, they asked rhetorically.[27]

In support of the argument that states had the right to extend criminal jurisdiction over Indians within their boundaries, state courts also argued that the states existed before the United States was formed under the Constitution, and they never surrendered their sovereign power over Indians to the federal government. As the Georgia Supreme Court explained in *Tassels*, "[w]hatever right Great Britain possessed over the Indian tribes, is vested in the State of Georgia, and may be rightfully exercised." No federal statute or treaty could take that away from the state; the federal government did not have the right to make treaties with the Cherokees.[28] The judges in *Caldwell* were also attentive to this argument. In separate opinions, Chief Justice Abner Smith Lipscomb, Justice Saffold, and Justice John M. Taylor each explained the argument. Before the American Revolution, the British had complete dominion over the Indians. After independence, that sovereignty vested in the individual states with regard to land within their own boundaries; that is, after the Revolution, the individual states had the same powers and prerogatives with regard to the Indians as the British (and other European powers) had during the colonial period. In consenting to the Constitution, the states had not surrendered or delegated to the federal government general municipal authority over the Indians within the states. Before the Constitution, the states had authority to govern their Indians as wards, and that jurisdiction over the Indians had never been relinquished. The commerce clause delegated only the power to regulate trade with Indians; it did not delegate from states to the federal government all rights with regard to Indians, and specifically did not include criminal jurisdiction. As Justice Taylor put it, "the states had no more intention to surrender their sovereignty over those tribes, than they had to divest foreign nations of jurisdiction within their own territories by placing in the hands of the federal government the power to regulate commerce over them." Nor did the states delegate the right of jurisdiction over Indians in the apportionment provision of Article I, section 2, or in the treaty power in Article I, section 10 (which covered only agreements with independent sovereign nations, not agreements with Indian tribes). Since the state's jurisdiction over the Indians was not delegated to the federal government, the justices concluded, it was reserved to the states according to the Tenth Amendment. The Supreme Court of Tennessee made a similar argument in its extension case, *Tennessee v. Forman*.

New states formed after the first thirteen, such as Tennessee, Alabama, Georgia, and Kansas, argued that they were entitled to the same degree of sovereignty as that enjoyed by the original states. Since the old states could regulate Indians, so could the new states, which were admitted on an equal basis. In *Forman*, Justice Catron pointed out that "[t]here is no constitutional, conventional, or legal provision, which allows [new states] less power over the Indians within their borders, than is possessed by Maine or New York" and then asked rhetorically: "[w]ould the people of Maine permit the Penobscot tribe to erect an independent government within their State?" In *Caldwell*, Justice Saffold analogized the situation in Alabama to that in New York, where the state's regulation of and jurisdiction over its six thousand Indians had been upheld by the judiciary. Justice Taylor asked, "Is not Alabama as sovereign as New York, and do not the Creeks occupy to this state, the same situation which the Senecas do to that?" He pointed out that Georgia's articles of cession in 1802 provided that the ceded territory (later Alabama) would be a state "on the same conditions" as provided in the Northwest Ordinance, which guaranteed "equal footing" for new states. Furthermore, in 1819, Congress admitted Alabama as a state "on an equal footing," and that act described the boundaries of Alabama to include the territory occupied by the Creeks. "If Alabama is sovereign at all," Justice Taylor concluded, "she is so throughout her whole territory, and she can not be sovereign unless she has the right of jurisdiction." *United States v. Ward* similarly established the principle that Kansas was entitled to be admitted on the same terms as the original states. If Kansas was to be on equal footing with other states, the judges maintained, it must be able to enforce its own laws to protect its own citizens. Therefore, the court concluded, Kansas (not the United States) had criminal jurisdiction over a white man charged with murdering another white man on reservation land.[29]

In *Tassels* the Georgia Supreme Court suggested that northerners were biased against southerners and were hypocritical to complain about southern efforts to govern their people as they chose. For example, the court noted, other states, such as New York, had extended criminal jurisdiction over Indians with no problem, yet as soon as Georgia tried to do the same thing, "a hue and cry is raised against her." The Georgia court asserted that all states should be treated equally. Underlying this contention was an awareness of sectional differences. In the same time period as these arguments were being advanced regarding equal state sovereignty in matters pertaining to Indians, southern states were making a parallel argument that new states being admitted from western territories were entitled to the same control over slavery policy as older states enjoyed. Equal treatment of all states limited the federal government's constitutional authority to restrict slavery in new states, slaveholders claimed.[30] Like the equal-footing argument, the other states' rights theories used to justify state regulation of Indians also had counterparts that were used to guard against federal interference with slavery in the states and territories. The use of parallel arguments did not mean that the states' rights position with regard to Indians was presented merely to bolster the institution of slavery, however. Rather, states' rights theories, which were put forward by northern as well as southern states, genuinely addressed a pressing concern about control over Indians within state borders.

In summary, judges devoted considerable attention to states' rights arguments, the most powerful of which was (1) that Congress's power to regulate Indians under the commerce clause was limited to matters of commercial intercourse and did not authorize federal regulation of Indians' right to contract, sue, or sell property, leaving such matters to the states to regulate. Other arguments based on the states' police powers and state sovereignty were (2) a state had the power to preserve peace and order within its borders, (3) it had the power to protect incompetent people, including all Indians, by limiting their rights, (4) it had the power to extend criminal jurisdiction throughout the state because the Constitution forbade any separate government to be erected within an existing state, (5) the original states existed before the United States and never surrendered their sovereign power over Indians to the federal government, and (6) since the old states could regulate Indians, so could the new states, which were admitted to the Union on an equal basis.

JUDICIAL ARGUMENTS BASED ON THE STATUS,
CONDITION, AND LOCATION OF INDIANS

The second category of state court justifications was evident in cases that focused on the status, condition, or location of the Indians being regulated. In these cases, judges acknowledged that most Indians in the United States were properly governed by the federal government but argued that nevertheless there was room for state regulation of certain Indian tribes or individual Indians whose status, condition, or location distinguished them from federally controlled Indians. Unfortunately, in comparison to the judicial opinions centering on states' rights, judicial opinions analyzing the status, condition, or location of Indians addressed constitutional issues more obliquely. The judges' conclusions in these cases were often implicitly based on the absence of federal authority under the treaty clause or the property clause, but they tended not to explicitly mention the Constitution. If they referred to any texts at all, rather than grounding these arguments in any specific constitutional provisions, they were apt to focus their analysis on statutory interpretation or assessment of the terms of treaties. Frequently, however, discussion of relevant federal statutes and treaties, like analysis of constitutional issues, was entirely omitted from the judicial opinions.

Since state judges tended to assume state authority in the absence of federal authority, the *status* of a tribe as not federally recognized provided one of the simplest justifications for state regulation. A tribe was deemed to be federally recognized if it had a treaty relationship with the federal government, if it received annuities from the government, if the government had appointed an Indian agent for it, and if it had an intact political structure through which the government dealt with the tribe. To state judges, it was evidently obvious that if a tribe did not have this kind of relationship with the federal government, it was appropriate for the states to regulate the tribe. Thus, as early as 1801, New York's Supreme Court ruled in a murder case that the defendant, George Peters, a Brotherton Indian, was subject to the civil and criminal jurisdiction of the state's courts because the Brothertons did not constitute a distinct, federally recognized tribe. By 1871, the Massachusetts Supreme Court treated this point of law as an obvious and longstanding principle; in a case relating to the division of lands of the Herring Pond Indians, the court summarily endorsed the legality of state regulation of Indians in the commonwealth, asserting as a truism that the state could regulate remnants of tribes not recognized by the United States as independent political communities.[31]

The status of individual Indians also could subject them to state regulation, even if they were members of a federally recognized tribe. Indians who attained the status of U.S. citizens—usually pursuant to the terms of a treaty—were often subjected to state laws regardless of past or present membership status in a tribe. The principle is well illustrated in *Clark v.*

Libbey, a case involving an Ottawa Indian's conflicting deeds for the same property. The Kansas Supreme Court held that the sale of land by the Ottawa, William Hurr, before he became a citizen under federal treaties was void, but the sale that took place after he became a citizen was valid.[32]

State courts also looked to the *condition* of a tribe when determining whether an exception to federal control was justified. Specifically, if a tribe had a small reservation, held only scattered pieces of land, did not own its land in common, or had a small population, judges tended to support state jurisdiction over the tribe. Though state courts did not mention the property clause of the Constitution explicitly in connection with this justification, a plausible underlying constitutional argument was that the land base of tribes in such condition was not sufficient, or not sufficiently contiguous, to justify its being treated as U.S. "territory or other property."

In 1832 Justice Saffold of the Alabama Supreme Court pointed out that the 1802 trade and intercourse act acknowledged state authority over Indians who were surrounded by settlements of whites. He concluded that although the Creek Indians might not have fallen into that category in 1802, their situation had changed since then: their territory had been reduced by cessions of land, emigration had reduced their population, and they were now surrounded by settlements of U.S. citizens. Therefore, he argued, the condition of the Creeks was now similar to that of tribes remaining in New York and other states, which had long been subject to state jurisdiction. In the same case, Chief Justice Lipscomb added that it had always been assumed that states, rather than the federal government, had jurisdiction over small tribes within state boundaries. He explained that the federal government's power to regulate Indians was only intended to apply to relations with the "numerous and barbarous tribes of Indians" who lived outside state territorial limits.[33]

State courts continued to apply the same approach to tribes whose population and territory had dwindled over time, even after the 1802 trade and intercourse act was superseded by later statutes. Following the U.S. acquisition of the Louisiana Purchase lands in 1803, new trade and intercourse acts applied to tribes residing west of the Mississippi River and contained no reference to an exception for Indians surrounded by whites. Yet in *Hicks v. Ewhartonah*, the Supreme Court of Arkansas held that federal statutory provisions voiding contracts between Indians and whites were not applicable to Arkansas Indians who were surrounded by a white population. Instead, state laws governed, and the contract in question was enforceable.

Despite the protests of Shawnee Chief Charles Blue-Jacket, in *Blue-Jacket v. Commissioners of Johnson County*, the Kansas Supreme Court upheld state taxation of Shawnee land based on the fact that the Indians' lands were "widely scattered," "interspersed with the lands and settlements of white persons," and owned by individual Shawnees rather than held in common by the tribe. The court maintained that the trade and intercourse laws applied only to tribes that existed "as a distinct race, owning and governing a particular district of country"; since the Shawnees did not fall within that category the states were free to regulate them and tax their patented land.[34] Because the "surrounded by settlements" provision excepted only "trade and intercourse" with Indians who were surrounded by whites, there was some question about whether or not it applied to criminal jurisdiction, prohibitions on Indian contracts, or taxation, the subjects of the state statutes at stake in *Caldwell*, *Hicks*, and *Blue-Jacket*, respectively. The courts did not address this issue directly in these cases, but the ambiguity gave them room to decide in the states' favor.[35]

In *Hicks v. Ewhartonah* the court also made another argument for excepting Indians from federal control based on the condition of Indians. The judges asserted that because the Arkansas Indians were capable and civilized, they could and should be subject to the same laws as whites. This assertion appears to have called for boundaries on the U.S. protective guardianship power, a power that was sometimes vaguely connected to the property clause but sometimes viewed as entirely extra-constitutional.[36] More specifically, the Arkansas court explained that the Indians in the state "have, for many years past been an educated and intelligent people, many of them the owners of large estates, having a local government of their own, carrying on a foreign and internal trade with citizens from all parts of the Union, and having as much need for credit, and the validation of their pecuniary engagements as any other class of persons." These factors apparently justified excluding these Indians from federal guardianship. The court concluded that it was appropriate to apply state law to their transactions.[37]

State court justices also argued that the application of federal laws regarding Indians depended to some extent on the *location* of those tribes or individual Indians. If there was a constitutional foundation for these justifications, it was presumably that the property clause only authorized federal regulation of Indians on land owned by the United States, but that premise was never articulated by the judges in these cases. Often there was also a statutory foundation for a justification based on location. For example, in the trade and intercourse acts of 1834 and 1847, certain provisions applied only in "Indian country": the provisions applying U.S. criminal law and those prohibiting whites from trading with any Indian without a license, selling liquor to an Indian, or intruding on lands. In addition, whites were barred from settling on lands "belonging, secured, or granted by treaty with the United States to any Indian tribe." State judges did not, however, always cite to the relevant statutory provision as part of their explanation. Furthermore, two major provisions of the statutes—the prohibition on Indian land sales and the nullification of Indians' executory contracts—provided no geographic requirement; they were not limited to Indian Country.

There were three different judicial rationales based on the location of Indians. The first was based most directly on statutory interpretation: the trade and intercourse laws were deemed not to apply when a tribe was situated outside of "Indian country." This could have been presented as a constitutional principle (that land outside of Indian Country was not U.S. "territory or other property") but in practice was typically based on the language of the federal laws. The definition of "Indian country" in the trade and intercourse acts left room for some ambiguity, especially as to parts of the United States west of the Mississippi River. Although only the states of Missouri and Louisiana and the territory of Arkansas were explicitly excluded from coverage, other states and territories also claimed that they were exempt in the absence of explicit inclusion. Thus, judges concluded that there could be no prosecution for violations of the federal trade and intercourse acts in Nevada, Alaska, Oregon, and New Mexico because they had not been designated part of Indian Country. Indians in those jurisdictions were therefore left to be regulated by the state or territorial legislatures.[38]

The second rationale based on location was closely related to the first. State courts in the West, the Midwest, and the South argued that individual Indians who lived among whites or who were temporarily off their reservation were subject to state jurisdiction unless a federal law explicitly provided otherwise. When applied to criminal jurisdiction, this justification appears to have some basis in the language of the trade and intercourse acts, though both that connection and the connection to the property clause of the Constitution were usually left unarticulated. In *People of California v. Antonio* the California Supreme Court held that Juan Antonio, an Indian who lived among whites, was subject to the same laws as whites.

The court ruled that a state statute providing for different treatment of Indians accused of crimes was "obviously intended to be applied to Indians in tribes, or when living in separate communities or companies, and not to a case where an Indian has been living, as in this case, for years among white men." In *Hunt v. Kansas* the high court in Kansas analogized off-reservation Indians to aliens. In the case of George Hunt, a Wea Indian who was accused of killing another Wea Indian named Mah-cah-tah-chin-quah outside the reservation, the court held that Indians, like all foreigners, were bound to observe local laws; just as a French man would be subject to Kansas law while he was in the state, so was an Indian. Thus the murder case was appropriately tried in state court. Seven years later, in *Rubideaux v. Vallie*, the Kansas court extended the principle and came to the same conclusion with regard to a civil matter—a matter that had no locational limitation in federal laws. In the case of John Rubideaux, a Miami Indian who was being sued for payment on a promissory note given in exchange for land, the court found that the state had jurisdiction over Indian transactions taking place off the reservation and that it could enforce an executory contract by Rubideaux. The court explained that every person in Kansas was subject to the state's laws, whether citizen, alien, or Indian. Indians and Indian property might be exempted only when on reservations. An Indian who bought land in the state had to follow through on his contractual obligation to pay for that land. The Arkansas Supreme Court came to a similar conclusion in *Taylor v. Drew*, where Cherokee Indian Drew's contract made outside of Cherokee territory was held to be enforceable despite the fact that federal law nullified executory contracts by "any Indian" (i.e., not only Indian contracts made in Indian Country).[39]

Third, several courts maintained that it mattered whether a tribe was located in a territory or in a state. Even if federal laws applied to tribes located in a federal territory, once that territory was admitted to the Union as a state, it was argued, state jurisdiction supplanted federal jurisdiction unless a treaty or federal law explicitly reserved jurisdiction in the federal government. This argument was the most removed from the actual language of the trade and intercourse acts, and its foundation in those statutes was never adequately explained. By being unspecific about federal statutory language or by analyzing that language in a sloppy manner, courts in southern and midwestern states managed to expand the exclusion.

One might expect judges to have mentioned the property clause in support of their conclusion that Congress had less authority over Indians in states than in territories, but they did not. In the *Caldwell* case, Justice

Saffold of the Alabama Supreme Court explained the reason for the distinction without mentioning that constitutional provision: federal statutes properly governed relations with Indian tribes in areas under a territorial form of government, "which, from their recent organization, sparce population, and subjection to, and dependence on the general government, were incompetent to the efficient exercise of full sovereignty." And if the federal laws and treaties were to apply to Indians in the states, that could only be so "for a limited time, during the infancy of the states; or while any particular tribe should remain so savage, fierce, or formidable, as to render it impracticable, or inexpedient, to subject them to state empire. Such," he found, "is not the relative condition of this state and the Creeks." Nor did any treaty or federal statute limit the extent of the state's jurisdiction. In Alabama, Saffold concluded, guardianship over the Creeks shifted from the federal government to the state government as soon as the territory became a state in 1819.[40]

In *Wisconsin v. Doxtater*, a case involving an Oneida Indian, Doxtater, accused of committing a crime within the Oneida reservation, the Supreme Court of Wisconsin addressed the specific language of the trade and intercourse acts. Although the court ostensibly placed its decision in the context of the 1834 federal act, however, the decision nevertheless depended on fuzzy analysis that glossed over ambiguities in statutory meaning. Without showing how Indian land title in Wisconsin had been extinguished (and, further, without explaining exactly how the 1834 act applied east of the Mississippi, given the proviso in section 29), the court argued that the federal government could only pass laws for the government of tribes "not within any state." The judges concluded that even though the federal government had jurisdiction over the Wisconsin Indians when Wisconsin was a territory, it lost such general jurisdiction as soon as Wisconsin became a state in 1848: all land within the new state's boundaries was excluded from Indian Country, excluded from coverage of federal Indian laws, and included in the state's jurisdiction. The state's criminal laws applied to all persons within the state, including Indians, and therefore criminal trials of Indians would take place in state courts.[41]

Judges in states west of the Mississippi River relied on similar arguments, despite the distinctions in the 1834 act between lands east and west of the river. Soon after their transformation from territories to states, neighbors Kansas (admitted 1861) and Nebraska (admitted 1867) both obtained judicial endorsement of their jurisdiction over crimes previously assigned to federal courts by the trade and intercourse acts. The Kansas case *United States v. Ward* involved a white man charged with murdering another white man on reservation land, whereas the Nebraska case *United States v. Sa-Coo-Da-Cot* involved Pawnee Indian defendants accused of murdering a non-Indian outside of the Pawnee reservation. The courts upheld state jurisdiction in both cases. Clearly both the Kansas Territory and the Nebraska Territory had fallen within Indian Country before statehood, but the judiciary ruled that once a territory was admitted as a state its status under the Indian laws changed.

In the Kansas case the court maintained that, in defining coverage of the trade and intercourse acts, Congress intended that once states were admitted to the Union the land within state boundaries would no longer be part of Indian Country unless expressly designated as such. No treaty, constitution, or law declared that the lands of the Kansas Indians were in Indian Country: the treaties between the Kansas Indians and the United States included no guarantee that their lands would never be subject to the jurisdiction of the state, and the act admitting Kansas to the Union excluded from the jurisdiction of the state only Indian lands that were subject to such treaty guarantees. Since Kansas was entitled to be admitted on the same footing as the original states, the justices asserted, it must be able to enforce its own laws to protect its own citizens. Thus, Kansas state courts could exercise jurisdiction over a crime on an Indian reservation. The judges in the Nebraska case, explaining that the legal issue at stake was "whether the general government or the state, has legislative control" over the Pawnees, also examined public documents to see if there was any official document reserving jurisdiction to the federal government. They noted that neither the state's constitution nor the admitting act excluded the Pawnee reservation or Pawnee Indians from the jurisdiction of the new state, and the 1857 treaty with the Pawnees that reserved the land to them did not specify who had jurisdiction over that land or the Indians who lived there. Therefore, the court concluded, the trade and intercourse act of 1834 "ceased to be operative within the limits of Nebraska the moment when the latter was admitted into the Union as a state, upon an equal footing with the original states." The state of Nebraska could not be denied "the power to make her ordinary criminal statutes coextensive with the state limits, and enforce them against all persons living or found therein." Five years later, the Nebraska Supreme Court made it clear that its criminal jurisdiction applied to crimes committed within an Indian reservation, as well as to those occurring outside the reservations; this time the accused man was a member of the Omahas, the only original Nebraska tribe to successfully retain reservation land in the state.[42] These cases basing authority to govern Indians on the tribes' location in states rather than territories clearly also fitted squarely into the category of justifications discussed in the preceding section, because at their core they were grounded in state sovereignty.

Thus, in the period from 1790 to 1880, state courts upheld state legislative regulations of Indians and argued against exclusive federal control of Indians based on a diverse range of principles. In addition to the six arguments based on state sovereignty, certain Indians were deemed exempt from federal regulations because of their status, condition, or location based on the following arguments: (1) the state appropriately regulated Indians who were not members of federally recognized tribes that had treaties with the United States, (2) Indians who were citizens were subject to state laws, (3) states had jurisdiction over Indians on a small reservation that was surrounded by whites, (4) individual Indians who were capable and civilized could and should be subject to the same laws as whites, (5) states could regulate individual Indians who were temporarily off their reservation, (6) an Indian who lived among whites was subject to the same laws as whites, (7) states could regulate Indians outside of "Indian country," and (8) federal laws regarding Indians applied only to tribes in the territories, not to Indians living within state boundaries (except as reserved by treaty or the act admitting the state to the Union).

STATE INITIATIVES AND NATIONAL GOALS

It is sometimes said that nineteenth-century capital investors preferred conflicts to be resolved by the national judiciary because it was remote from local interests that could interfere with the marketability of land and other resources.[43] But that was not the case in most legal matters relating to Indians, where local (i.e., non-Indian local) regulation was preferred. From the perspective of potential white speculators, federal Indian policy often obstructed the marketability of land because of governmental commitments and obligations to Indian tribes. The federal trade and intercourse acts technically made much of Indian land legally unavailable to whites.[44] The states, though, often found ways around federal statutes, effectively making more land marketable. As long as the states were able to maintain social order and peace with Indians in their borders, the federal government usually acquiesced when states took authority upon themselves to regulate Indians.

When states made Indians subject to state court civil jurisdiction and allowed them to sell lands, they effectively brought Indians and their land into the American economic orbit. Specifically, during the period from 1790 to 1880, state actions increased the amount of Indian land available to investors for transportation lines, cotton plantations, and mining operations. Such land was also made more available to white settlers, who were seen as spreading civilization and securing American political control of more remote regions. More generally, states' actions expanded white jurisdictional authority over Indians.

When the states tried to incorporate Indians into white society or insisted upon their complete removal from state territory, the federal government made only weak gestures toward meeting its treaty obligations to protect Indian tribes and mounted no serious effort to defend federal constitutional prerogatives on matters relating to Indians. The states usually met with little federal resistance because their actions furthered the development of a strong national economy, helped strengthen the security of U.S. borders, and increased white control of Native peoples.

Well established at the time the federal government was created, New York ignored the provisions of federal trade and intercourse acts and acted to regulate Indian land sales and to make treaties with Indian tribes during the early national period and the antebellum period. Because this state policy furthered national interests by improving security along the Canadian border and by connecting the Atlantic Ocean to the Great Lakes and the Mississippi River with canals and roads through Iroquois territories, the federal government had little incentive to interfere.[45] As described in chapter 1, early New York statutes forbade the same activities barred by the trade and intercourse acts, but later laws explicitly permitted activities that federal law prohibited. The state also extended criminal jurisdiction over Indians and ultimately even applied ordinary civil laws (marriage, inheritance, taxation, etc.) to many Indians. State courts endorsed these developments. By the late nineteenth century, all of the Iroquois Indians either were subject to regulation by New York or, with the assistance of the federal government, had been relocated to the west, out of New York State to Wisconsin and Kansas.

Likewise, in the South and the Midwest, the federal government tended to acquiesce on Indian matters. Although in 1832 the U.S. Supreme Court held that Georgia's extending criminal jurisdiction over Cherokee territory was an illegal interference with Cherokee sovereignty, the decision lacked support elsewhere in the federal government and was successfully ignored by the southern states. As described in the preceding chapter, with strong backing by President Andrew Jackson and U.S. troops, Georgia was able to crush the political institutions of the Cherokees and assert control over them and their lands, and Tennessee and Alabama followed suit. Eventually, the tribes of the south—the Cherokees, Creeks, Choctaws, Chickasaws, Seminoles—were removed west, opening up their lands for white settlement and cotton plantations. Congress endorsed the removals after the fact, when it effectively excluded the southern states from the definition of Indian Country in the trade and intercourse act of 1834. Similarly, states in the Old Northwest and those in the region just west of the Mississippi asserted the right to regulate Indians that eastern states exercised and, with the help of the federal government, eventually managed to squeeze Indians out of land coveted for white settlement. Thus state initiatives played an important role in advancing national goals.

Despite the fact that states' actions regarding Indians promoted national goals and apparently were not perceived as a real threat to federal authority, when those actions were challenged in state court, judges nevertheless tended to frame the issue in such cases as a jurisdictional conflict between the state and the federal government. Consequently, they focused their analysis on the question of when states' rights and police powers properly took precedence over federal powers. Only rarely did the courts focus directly on the real issues: the authority of whites to govern Indians, the nature of tribal sovereignty, and the meaning of U.S. treaty obligations.

State sovereignty arguments provided a convenient counterweight to assertions of tribal authority and entitlements under treaties. The federal government owed certain duties to Indians, but federalism and state sovereignty, which were regarded as basic to the American constitutional structure and to the protection of Americans' rights, were treated as more highly valued principles. Accordingly, the courts repeatedly ruled in favor of the states. Framing the issue as one of conflicting federal versus state authority helped further shared goals, which were being promoted more effectively and practically by the states than by the U.S. government.

Linking state sovereignty arguments to discussion of police powers protecting the welfare of "vulnerable people" within state boundaries further diverted judicial focus from addressing issues of Indian rights. Judges' endorsement of protective prohibitions reinforced the belief that Indians lacked capacity to make legal decisions and were unable to govern themselves, which undermined any notion that tribal sovereignty was realistic. Presumed Indian incapacity had the effect of silencing Indians in official forums, so the real issues were less likely to be heard in court. Consequently, state courts were able to brush aside issues that truly were central to any determination of states' authority to regulate Indians.

The primary focus of the courts should have been the legitimacy of state authority over Indians in the face of tribal sovereignty and treaty rights; instead judges most often examined how the states' actions fit with federalism's division of powers between the federal and state governments. Full, fair, and proper legal analysis would have required state courts to confront directly the question of tribal sovereignty rather than skirting the problem. They evaded honest discussion of the issue by dwelling on such factors as Indians' federal status, condition, or location, presuming their own authority whenever federal authority had not been asserted or was deemed to be impractical. And they even more vigorously avoided serious analysis of tribal sovereignty by loudly claiming rights of state sovereignty. Yet the fourteen justifications for state regulation of Indians that are described in this chapter were irrelevant if the tribes were, in fact, distinct political entities with the sovereign right to govern themselves. It suited both the federal and the state governments to frame the issue in terms of federalism, however, because doing so allowed them to ignore the rights of Indians.

States' arguments in favor of their own sovereignty in cases relating to Indians bolstered states' rights arguments and therefore were sometimes seen as furthering interests that the states had in other kinds of regulations. Most notably, as mentioned above, southern state courts' decisions on jurisdiction over Indians reinforced their assertions of exclusive authority over slaves. Thus, between federal and state governments there were genuine jurisdictional conflicts unrelated to Indians that sometimes underlay arguments made with regard to Indians. But it was disingenuous to present the federal and state governments as having conflicting interests when it came to Indians.

The common goal of the state and federal governments with regard to Indians was control of Indians and Indian lands. By the end of the nineteenth century, the federal government had abandoned any idea of genuine recognition of tribal sovereignty and set about to destroy tribal political structures, cultures, and landholding practices. But well before the decision to stop making treaties with Indian tribes, and well before the General Allotment Act and the Major Crimes Act, the federal government's support for tribal sovereignty lacked sincere commitment. Although the federal government had signed treaties with Indian nations, throughout the century the government found various pretexts for commencing wars against the tribes in order to pressure them to give up lands guaranteed them by the treaties.

The federal government and the state governments shared an end goal, and they acted in tandem to achieve that goal. By presenting itself as the protector of Indians against the states and aggressive, land-hungry individuals, the federal government was able to squeeze more concessions from the Indians. It is doubtful that federal government officials envisioned sharing territory with truly autonomous Indian nations. The expectation and the plan was that wherever Indians lived in land coveted by whites, the Indians would either move out of the way or assimilate into American culture and society. By successfully asserting their authority to regulate Indians in a range of ways between 1790 and 1880, the states furthered that plan. The states pressured Indians to leave their lands and increasingly exerted various degrees of direct rule over the Indians in order to further the colonization process.

After about 1880 the federal government began taking a more active role in extending direct rule over Indians, no longer leaving that effort primarily to the states. Post-1880 federal policies aimed at breaking up the tribes and absorbing individual Indians into American society. Those policies were built on a foundation established over the preceding century, however. Between 1790 and 1880 the states played an important role in the process of incorporating Indians, and the support, the explanations, and the justifications provided by the state judiciary were crucial to the states' Indian policies.

PART TWO
Race

CHAPTER THREE

Slavery, the Law of Nations, and Racial Classification

༄

English settlers first established themselves in what became the American South in 1607, and the first Africans were brought to this early English colony in the Chesapeake in 1619. By the end of the seventeenth century, local legislation severely restricted the rights of Africans and their descendants, and a race-based institution of slavery was well established in Virginia.[1] Over the course of the colonial period, maintenance of the institution increasingly depended on slaves being readily identifiable by such indicators of race as skin color, hair, and facial features. Thus a clearly visible line between "black" and "white" became crucial to the institution of slavery. By the early nineteenth century, the color line had become fully entrenched and even more essential. In 1820, there were 1.5 million slaves in the United States, and in some counties 95 percent of the population was enslaved. Tight control of slaves depended on brutal punishments and constraints and, just as importantly, on maintaining clear physical markers of slave and free status.

The presence of a third group of people on the continent, the Native Americans, complicated this theoretically clean racial divide. Indeed, America was never merely a biracial world of black and white. The question of where Indians fit in the racial structure of America was an issue that whites grappled with for centuries. Early in the colonial period, the English perceived Indians as being different from themselves based on environmentally determined cultural traits, rather than race. Explorers and settlers frequently referred to the Natives disdainfully as "heathens" and "savages," owing to their different religious beliefs and social customs. Yet the English often expressed admiration for Indians' physical attributes and thought it possible that, after proper instruction, Indians (unlike Africans) could be assimilated into white culture. From the Indian perspective, although it was beneficial to borrow some English practices, most had no interest in totally abandoning their core belief systems. The colonists, in turn, became disillusioned by the failure of their efforts to transform Indians into Europeans and came to question their original premises. It seemed to the English that there had to be something defective about the Indians' basic character if they were unable or unwilling to become civilized. By the end of the colonial period, many of the colonists came to define Indians as a separate, nonwhite race.[2] Cultural differences—reflected in the "heathen" and "savage" labels—became less important in distinguishing Indians from European migrants, while race became more important. By the early nineteenth century, the Enlightenment standpoint that differences associated with race were shaped by environment and could be changed through education had given way to a new viewpoint based on racial determinism. Indians could not become civilized, many Americans came to believe, because their savagery was racially innate.[3]

Thus, state governments normally treated Indians as racially distinct from whites and placed Native Americans and African Americans into the same category, as inferior races and legally degraded people. Nonetheless, two factors—inherited colonial-era classifications of Indians as ineligible for slavery and jurisdictional dilemmas resulting from Indians' association in tribes—led to occasional exceptions. While chapter 4 discusses the ways in which state law discriminated against Indians on the basis of race and chapter 5 evaluates how racialist ideology affected the way whites talked about the status and rights of Indians, this chapter analyzes the exceptional contexts in which Indians legally had a racial advantage over blacks.

INDIAN SLAVERY AND THE LAW OF NATIONS

Some jurisdictions prohibited the enslavement of Europeans and Indians while permitting enslavement of Africans. In such jurisdictions, courts presumed members of the first two groups to be free and members of the last group to be slaves. Theoretically, in those states, enslaved people who could trace an unbroken line of maternal ancestry to an Indian could bring lawsuits to establish their free status. Where an Indian's suit for freedom did have a legislative basis, it was usually in a colonial-era law rather than a statute enacted in the early national or antebellum period; typically, however, the privilege was not clearly and explicitly laid out in legislation. Among English colonial laws, the Georgia and South Carolina statutes exempting "free Indians in amity with this government" from the general presumption that "every negro, Indian, mulatto and mustizo, is a slave" probably came the closest to articulating a principle that could later be used by a descendent of a "friendly" Indian to gain his or her freedom. More often, the statutory basis was vague, and the right to freedom had to be developed through judicial analysis. Despite reigning racial views that accepted Indians as inferior people in the nineteenth century, judges were eager to display meticulous adherence to the rule of law in suits for freedom, as they often were in other trials involving slaves. Therefore, they were willing to find a foundation to support Indians' lawsuits. For example, Virginia courts concluded that a colonial statutory provision authorizing the inhabitants to trade freely with any Indian effectively repealed the states' laws permitting Indian slavery. There was some debate as to whether the pertinent language first appeared in 1691 or in 1705, but that dispute did not affect the resolution of many Indian suits for freedom: most plaintiffs were successful.[4]

The legal issues were even more complicated in states that had previously been part of the Spanish or French colonial empire, such as Louisiana. Louisiana was a French colony until it was turned over to Spain by a treaty in 1763. In 1800 France reacquired the territory and then sold it to the United States in 1803. American judges faced an ambiguous situation when they confronted the issue of Indian slaves, since Spanish law formally prohibited Indian slavery but French law tolerated it.[5] When questions arose regarding the status of Indians in nineteenth-century Louisiana, state courts had to grapple with the issue of how to treat the old Spanish laws that apparently conflicted not only with French laws that previously governed the territory but also with the practice in some American states that had formerly been part of English colonies. Such questions most often arose in the context of enslaved Indians' suits for freedom. The plaintiffs in such suits claimed that they should enjoy free status because they were descended from Indians who had been illegally enslaved in Louisiana during the Spanish period. In order to resolve the issue, state courts were drawn into discussions of the applicability of the law of nations, a topic normally handled in federal courts. Louisiana courts faced this issue in the *Séville v. Chrétien* case.[6]

In the mid-1760s an Indian trader named Duchêne purchased an Indian prisoner of war known as Angélie and later sold Angélie to Joseph Chrétien. After Chrétien's death, several of Angélie's descendants brought a suit for freedom against their new owners, including Joseph's son Gérard

Chrétien, claiming that their maternal Indian lineage made them free.[7] The Louisiana Supreme Court focused much of its discussion on the question of which nation's law regarding Indian slavery should apply. The relevant principle of the law of nations was that when a nation conquered a territory, rights to property owned at the time of conquest were determined by the law that was in place at the time the property was acquired. This principle was articulated by courts of states and territories that were formally part of New Spain or New France, such as California (*Hart v. Burnett* and *Ferris v. Coover*), New Mexico (*United States v. Lucero*), and Missouri (*Charlotte v. Chouteau*).[8] The Louisiana Supreme Court expressed the idea in *Séville* as follows: "it is an incontrovertible principle of the laws of nations, that in cases of the cession of any part of the dominions of one sovereign power to another, the inhabitants of the part ceded, retain their ancient municipal regulations, until they are abrogated by some act of their new sovereign." Thus, the question facing the court in *Séville v. Chrétien* was whether the decision should be rendered in accordance with the colonial laws of Spain, which formally prohibited Indian slavery, or the colonial laws of France, which permitted Indian slavery. This was a particularly thorny question when applied to slaves purchased after the Spanish acquired Louisiana by treaty in 1763 and prior to both the French reacquisition of the territory in 1800 and the U.S. Louisiana Purchase in 1803. It was not clear whether the Spanish law prohibiting Indian slavery applied while Louisiana was a part of New Spain. Naturally the plaintiff, Séville, argued that Spanish law applied, while the defendant, Chrétien, claimed that French law pertained.

Based on testimony of people who had lived in Louisiana in the 1760s, the court found that although the treaty of cession between France and Spain was made in 1763, Spain did not actually take "effectual possession" of the territory until Governor Alejandro O'Reilly arrived there in 1769. Consequently, the court concluded, under the law of nations French laws were still in effect when Angélie was enslaved in 1765 or 1766. Since French law allowed Indian slavery, and since Indians were in fact enslaved in French colonies, Angélie's enslavement was lawful. Governor O'Reilly declared Indian slavery to be against Spanish law, the court said, but he also allowed slave owners to remain in possession of their Indian slaves until the king actually forbade the practice. The court concluded that no royal proclamation freed Indian slaves prior to the French reacquisition in 1800. The treaty by which the United States obtained Louisiana from France obligated the United States to recognize the inhabitants' property rights. Those property rights included the right of ownership in Indian slaves, which had continued uninterrupted for over forty years from before 1763. Thus the court decided that French law applied, and Séville and the others were lawful slaves.

Even after the conclusion of the *Séville* case, the Louisiana Supreme Court continued to grapple with the question of which Indians could be slaves. In the 1820s the court ruled in favor of freedom for the descendents of an Indian woman who was enslaved during the Spanish period.[9]

Other states that were drawn from the Louisiana Purchase lands also had to deal with the Spanish and French heritage, and they did not always interpret the documents the same way the Louisiana court did. When an Indian suit for freedom reached the Missouri Supreme Court, the judges there disagreed with the *Séville* conclusion.[10] The slave Marguerite brought her action against Pierre Chouteau, claiming that she was entitled to her freedom because her maternal grandmother had been an Indian of the Natchez nation. The grandmother had been sold into slavery while Louisiana was under the control of the French, yet in 1834 the court still ruled in favor of Marguerite's right to assert her freedom on the basis of her Indian ancestry.

Confronting the contrary *Séville* decision directly, the Missouri court held that the Louisiana case was founded on a misinterpretation of French law. The judges in *Marguerite v. Chouteau* agreed with the Louisiana court that the law of nations required a new sovereign to respect the property rights of the inhabitants of ceded or conquered territory, and they agreed that French colonial law determined the status of enslaved descendants of Indian women sold into slavery in Louisiana during the period of French rule (i.e., before 1769). They were not convinced by the historical evidence that France officially approved the enslavement of Indians, however, and therefore they concluded that self-proclaimed owners of Indian slaves in the eighteenth and nineteenth centuries had no lawful property rights in those slaves that had to be protected. Specifically, Judge George Tompkins, writing for the court, took issue with the *Séville* court's conclusion that Governor O'Reilly's 1769 statement recognized Louisianans' right to own Indian slaves. In fact, Tompkins pointed out, O'Reilly not only forbade the inhabitants from acquiring Indian slaves in the future but also prohibited slave owners from selling their Indian slaves and required them to register the names of all such slaves, orders that under the law of nations were inconsistent with recognition of property rights in the Indian slaves. O'Reilly, on behalf of the Spanish government, did not approve of Indian slave ownership and intended to free the Indian slaves.

Judge Tompkins concluded that because France's policy was to protect Indians, not to enslave them, "[a] French subject . . . never could have enslaved an Indian but by the express permission of his sovereign," and no such permission was ever given in the form of either written or unwritten law. In French Louisiana the enslavement of Indians was unlawful, Tompkins wrote, and therefore U.S. courts were required to recognize the principle that slave status acquired no justification from the enslavement of female Indian ancestors during the French period. The slave Marguerite was declared a free woman.[11]

Missouri was later the source of the most famous suit for freedom in American history, the *Dred Scott* case. Although Dred Scott and his family members were African Americans, when the case was finally decided by the Supreme Court in 1857, Chief Justice Roger Taney inserted some comments about the status of Native Americans, illustrating that in some regards blacks and Indians continued to be placed in different categories. The situation of descendents of Africans, he wrote, was "altogether unlike that of the Indian race." Given Indians' history as "a free and independent people," they were, unlike blacks, eligible for citizenship through naturalization by Congress. Thus, they could be entitled to a variety of rights and privileges—presumably including access to federal courts—that were denied to blacks.[12]

THE PROBLEM OF RACIAL CLASSIFICATION

All courts that permitted slaves to obtain their freedom upon proof of Indian or white racial identity had to confront the problem of racial classification. Since written documentation of ancestry was rarely available, such plaintiffs had to present witnesses who could testify that their appearance, behavior, perceived status, and reputation in the community were consistent with their Indian or white race. Indians most often had to buttress oral evidence of their Indian pedigree with physical evidence of that racial classification. Thus the success of their lawsuits depended on their displaying their own bodies—or those of their mothers and grandmothers—as evidence of their right to freedom. In many freedom trials, testimony focused on witnesses' descriptions of visible markers of race. It was assumed that race could be determined visually, and slave or free status was thus read on the bodies of litigants and their families. The 1820s Louisiana case *Ulzère v. Poeyfarré* provides a good example of how trial courts identified people's race in suits for freedom.[13]

In 1777, during the American Revolution, a soldier from Louisiana seized a number of Indians after successfully taking the British fort at Natchez. Among the Indians was a Chickasaw woman who came to be known as Marianne. Upon the soldier's return to New Orleans, he sold Marianne; after a series of further sales, she ended up as a slave on the plantation of Manette Songi in the parish of St. Jacques. Marianne subsequently had two children, Françoise and Ulzère, who were also held by Manette Songi as slaves. In the late 1780s Marianne left the plantation and went to New Orleans to try to obtain a certificate of her right to liberty and freedom. At Songi's request, Marianne left her two children on Songi's plantation. The commandant general of the province, the Baron de Carondelet, apparently granted Marianne the certificate of freedom, and she lived for about six years as a free woman, dying in New Orleans in 1794. In St. Jacques parish, Songi died in 1804, and Jean Baptiste Poeyfarré of New Orleans inherited her slaves, including Françoise and Ulzère. In 1807, Françoise had a daughter, Marie Thérèse, and the next year she had a son, Casimir. On March 5, 1812, Ulzère, Françoise, Marie Thérèse, and Casimir brought a suit for their freedom in the city court for New Orleans. Their "nearest friend," Louis Matin—who was referred to as a "free man of colour"—signed the papers (with his mark) on their behalf. Thomas Gales was appointed to represent the plaintiffs, who were released on $3,000 bail in December 1813. After many years of delays, the case finally went to trial in February 1820.

The slave or free status of Ulzère and Françoise depended on their proving that their mother, Marianne, was an Indian. It should be noted that Ulzère and Françoise's father's race was not an issue in determining whether they were free. According to the testimony of Joseph St. Fabre, Ulzère and Françoise were the children of a black slave named Étienne. Even though Étienne was one of Jean Baptiste Poeyfarré's slaves, Poeyfarré appears never to have relied on that fact to assert his rightful ownership of Ulzère and Françoise as slaves. He accepted the principle that the slave or free status of children followed the status of their mother.

Since written documentation of Marianne's ancestry was not available, and the plaintiffs had only hearsay oral evidence of her seizure from the Chickasaw tribe, they had to rely primarily on testimony about her physical appearance to make their case. Thus Marianne's body itself was crucial evidence in this case; her body was rhetorically on display before the jurors.

Interrogation of witnesses took place in French. Several different words were used to refer to Marianne's race. The standard question presented to each witness asked whether they knew "une sauvagesse ou femme de couleur" (a savage or woman of color) who lived with Songi. In response to this question, almost every witness referred to Marianne as a "sauvagesse." None categorized her simply as a "femme de couleur." And nobody used the word "indienne." One witness, Joseph St. Fabre, used a more generic word: he said he knew that at Songi's house there were "many mestizoes ('mestiques'), but he did not know whether they were savages or women of color."

The nineteen witnesses were asked to describe visible markers of race evident in Marianne's appearance. More specifically, they were asked what color Marianne was ("quelle etait sa couleur [son tient]") and what kind of hair ("quels espèces de cheveux") she had. Among the twelve who had known Marianne, there was a variety of ways of describing her skin color. None labeled her either white or black. Only two witnesses, Jean Marie Malard and Jacques Cantrelle, categorized her as "red." Pierre Bourgeois, Auguste Gravois, Olivier Bourgeois, and Joseph St. Fabre called her "reddish" or "a little reddish" ("un peu rougâtre"). François Courneaux thought she was "red bordering on yellow" ("rouge tirant sur le jaune"), while Bonaventure Gaudin and Jean Baptiste Picou called her "yellowish" ("jaunâtre"). Two witnesses, Madame Joseph Caittet and François Croizet, declared that Marianne was "more white than red."

There was more consensus on Marianne's hair. Everyone agreed that her hair was black. Beyond hair color, everyone seemed to understand from the question that they were being asked whether Marianne's hair was straight or kinky—i.e., more like a Native American's hair or more like an African American's hair. Olivier Bourgeois and Joseph St. Fabre said they did not know whether her hair was "lisses ou crépus," but ten other witnesses testified that her hair was "smooth" or "straight": Courneaux, Croizet, Gravois, Malard, Gaudin, Caittet, Pierre Bourgeois, and Pauline Matis categorized her hair as "lisses," Picou called it "plats," and Cantrelle called it "droits."

Apparently the jury was satisfied that Marianne's skin color and hair were consistent with Native American heritage. Having found that Marianne's physical characteristics showed her to be of Indian origin, they brought back a verdict in the plaintiffs' favor: because their mother/ grandmother had been an Indian, the plaintiffs were held to be free. The court accordingly issued a judgment in favor of Ulzère, Françoise, Marie Thérèse, and Casimir. Poeyfarré appealed the judgment to the Supreme Court of Louisiana.

In May 1820 the Louisiana Supreme Court found that it had been improper for the lower court to have admitted evidence of Marianne's efforts to assert her freedom in the 1780s because that lawsuit was *res inter alios acta*. That is, because none of the parties to *Ulzère v. Poeyfarré* were parties to Marianne's lawsuit, that suit was irrelevant to this case. Ulzère, Françoise, Marie Thérèse, and Casimir had to establish their own case independent of their mother/grandmother's. The Supreme Court also found that the parish court had inappropriately allowed the jury to determine matters that should have been left up to the judges.[14] The Louisiana Supreme Court reversed the decision of the parish court and remanded the case back for a new trial.

In 1824 the parish court of New Orleans conducted a new trial in accordance with the Supreme Court's guidelines. This time the parties waived their right to jury trial, leaving the verdict up to the judges. The parish court judges took into account the factual findings of the jury in the first trial and took note of certain matters of law that were within their prerogatives. At the end of the trial, the court issued a judgment in favor of the plaintiffs. Also in 1824 the Louisiana Supreme Court sustained the lower court's judgment and held that because Marianne had been an Indian, the defendant had no legal right to hold her descendents, the plaintiffs, as slaves.

The suit for freedom was a common context in which the problem of classifying people as either white/Indian or black arose in the antebellum period.[15] The basic nature of the claim to freedom based on race crossed colonial boundaries, as those cases appeared in states that had been English, Spanish, and French colonies. Although most studies of suits for freedom do not mention the fact, typically plaintiffs had to display their own bodies or those of their ancestors, and they had to put the determination of their race into litigation. The *Ulzère v. Poeyfarré* case exemplifies the ways in which race was socially constructed in the nineteenth-century courtroom: lawsuits played a major role in fashioning the cultural understanding of race. In the antebellum South, such fashioning was done in such a way as to support and maintain the all-important color line between slave and free. Since it was essential for the maintenance of the institution of American plantation slavery that this line be clearly visible, resolution of disputes over slave status relied primarily on physical markers on plaintiffs' bodies. In sum, such cases depended on juries' ability to "see race."

Courts also had to determine Indian racial identity in other situations where they had to draw a line between privileged whites and Indians on the one hand and nonprivileged blacks on the other. Louisiana courts tended to categorize Indians with whites. For example, in an 1842 case in which the plaintiff accused the defendant of slander for saying that the plaintiff's family was not white, the state supreme court described the plaintiff's witnesses who expressed the opinion that the plaintiff's mother had no "negro blood" but rather "was white, or at least of Indian descent, and that she kept company with white ladies." Four years later, in a dispute over whether a steamship owner could be charged with illegally transporting a slave, the defendants' witnesses asserted that the person who was being transported could not have been a slave because he "was to all appearance a white man." His complexion suggested that he "might have some Indian blood or be of Spanish descent," one witness noted, "but no one could suppose he had any African blood; he would pass any where for a white man, and a great many white creoles have a darker complexion than he has." Thus judges seemed to accept the distinction made by the people of Louisiana between Africans on the one hand and whites and Indians on the other.[16]

Outside of Louisiana, other state courts also grappled with the issue of racial distinctions. Although Louisiana laws often classified Indians with whites, other states more often classified Indians with (or as) blacks.[17] As the numbers of mixed-race individuals increased, more jurisdictions found it expedient to drop the distinction between African and Indian ancestry in such individuals. As other scholars have reported, even during the colonial period the term "mulatto" often applied to any person of mixed racial ancestry, including the offspring of European-Indian and African-Indian couples as well as the children of European-African pairs. By the end of the eighteenth century, some jurisdictions started to use the terms "person of color" or "negro" in place of "mulatto."[18] In one English colony, a law defined the term "mulatto" to include "the child of an Indian"; in another colony the law required slave owners to categorize all mixed-blood slaves as "negroes" for purposes of taxation.[19] By the nineteenth century, both the slave and the free population of "colored," "mulatto," and "negro" persons included many people of Indian descent even if they had no African ancestry at all, as evidenced by local tax rolls and federal census records.[20] In early national and antebellum America most people who were categorized as Indians were presumed not to be slaves, and most slave laws no longer explicitly mentioned Indians as slaves.[21] Yet many people of Indian descent were not categorized as Indians. Most notably, there still existed large numbers of slaves who had Indian ancestry because the descendents of Indians who had been enslaved in accordance with colonial laws typically continued to hold slave status well into the nineteenth century. Plantation owners in the southeastern states ordinarily would categorize such slaves as "Africans," "negroes," or "blacks" regardless of their actual ancestry, and such designations were difficult to challenge in court.[22] Moreover, in states that officially recognized Indian slavery, suits for freedom based on Indian descent raised no need to distinguish between African and Indian ancestry.[23] Except for Virginia, there were few suits for freedom based on Indian ancestry in states derived from English colonies. Consequently, the issue of racial classification typically involved free people rather than slaves.

Judicial determination of parties' and witnesses' race was necessary in a variety of contexts where statutes treated people differently on the basis of race. Indians in court were most likely to present evidence of their racial affiliation when laws gave Indians a racial advantage over blacks, such as laws that prohibited Negroes, but not Indians, from carrying weapons, making contracts, and conducting other activities. The question of whether a person was an Indian was also raised by people claiming the benefits of white status in the face of statutes discriminating against Indians. There was no uniform rule for determining a person's racial classification. Although some state courts examined the person's appearance, behavior, associations, and reputation, others based their classification on a determination of the "preponderance of blood."

Some states allowed racial classification to be based on appearance but only accepted "experts'" judgments. In a dispute over whether a defendant had violated the prohibition on free Negroes carrying firearms, the state of North Carolina introduced testimony by a man who, based on his twelve-year experience as the owner and manager of slaves, claimed expertise in classifying people as white, Negro, or Indian. The witness, who admitted that he knew nothing about the defendant's ancestors, assessed the appearance of the defendant and concluded that he was not white or Indian but, rather, "a mulatto —that is, half African and half white." Since North Carolina law defined a "free negro" to be one who was "descended from negro ancestors to the fourth generation inclusive," the defendant fitted the category of "free negro." The state supreme court rejected the defendant's challenge to the witness's qualifications to testify as an expert. The court explained: "The effect of the intermixture of the blood of different races of people, is surely a matter of science, and may be learned by observation and study. Nor does it require a distinguished comparative anatomist to detect the admixture of the African or Indian with the pure blood of the white race." Although a "common observer" could tell whether a person had some African ancestry, only an expert could determine blood quantum of less than one-quarter. It was a scientific question whether a person had "only a sixteenth part of African blood in his veins" (the cut-off point in the statute), but a longtime slave owner who had "an eye rendered keen, by observation and practice," such as the witness, was fully capable of making such a scientific determination as an expert.[24]

Reputation in the community was a very important criterion in some states.[25] In *Bryan v. Walton*, a decedent's racial status would determine whether he had had the right to make a contract that was disputed after his death. If Joseph Nunez was a "negro," he did not have the right to make the contract, but if he was part white and part Indian, he was empowered to contract. The Georgia Supreme Court admitted evidence of general reputation and public rumor as to the racial identification of both the decedent and his family. For example, Mary Rogers testified that the decedent's father, Jim Nunez, was not a "negro" but "was of mixed Indian and white blood." Rogers stated that Nunez had the appearance of an Indian and "was always treated and regarded in the neighborhood as not a negro, or having any negro blood in his veins, but as a respectable Indian and white blooded man," and that he "kept as good company as anybody in the neighborhood." She recalled that Nunez "was always among respectable white people in the neighborhood in their dances, parties, &c., and was received by them as on a footing with whites," whereas she did not "remember of a free negro ever having been received and treated in that way by the neighborhood." Stephen Newman and Mary Harrel agreed that Nunez was of mixed Indian and white ancestry. They based their conclusions on the man's appearance, his graceful style of dancing, the fact that "he never kept low, trifling or rakish company" but, rather, "associated with respectable whites in the neighborhood" and "was often at their balls and parties, assemblies and little gatherings, where no free negro was allowed to associate with the whites, and dined with the whites just the same as any gentleman would have done." In the end, however, perhaps because of a lack of evidence that Joseph and Jim Nunez had actually exercised the political and legal rights of white men, Joseph Nunez was determined to have been a man of color who therefore did not have the right to make a contract.[26]

Other states did not permit racial classifications based on appearance alone and, rather than relying on evidence of reputation, required consideration of a person's racial ancestry. Statutory rules of racial classification based on blood quantum were sometimes a relevant factor in such determinations. Yet although many states provided a legal measure for who would be classified as a "negro" or "colored person" based on percentage of

African ancestry, not all provided a clear definition of who was an "Indian." Some states that did have definitions distinguishing between "Indians" and "colored" people made sure to exclude people of African descent from the definition of "Indian" and then typically required that people be defined as "Indians" if they had one Indian grandparent (or, sometimes, one Indian parent). An example is Virginia, where an 1866 statute provided that anyone who had "one-fourth or more of negro blood, shall be deemed a colored person, and every person, not a colored person, having one-fourth or more of Indian blood, shall be deemed an Indian." Other states, such as California, apparently did not see the categories "Indian" and "mulatto" as mutually exclusive, allowing a person to be defined as both an "Indian" and a "mulatto." Although California's law pertaining to witnesses deemed anyone "having one-half of Indian blood" to be Indian, the state's definition of "mulatto" meant that any "Indian" who had "one-eighth or more of negro blood" would also be labeled a mulatto.[27] Thus the legal definitions were not always clear-cut. In any case, racial classification in the courtroom more often came down to juries' determinations based on their understanding of racial identity.

In the 1860s the Michigan Supreme Court ruled that boards of voter registration could not disqualify a man from voting based only on personal inspection. In one case the court held that where the defendant, William Dean, alleged that he satisfied the whiteness requirement for the franchise because his ancestry was less than one thirty-second Indian and the rest was white, the board could not summarily reject him as a legal voter based on mere inspection. In a second case, the court ruled that a board was required to allow the petitioner, O. S. Ward, to offer testimony showing that, since his father was half Indian and his mother was a "mulatto," he did not have more than one-quarter African ancestry and therefore was a "white male" entitled to the right to vote. Interestingly, in neither the November 1866 case nor the October 1868 case did the state court consider the possibility that either the Civil Rights Act or the Fourteenth Amendment might nullify the state constitution's racial qualifications for the suffrage altogether, making clear the need for the Fifteenth Amendment.[28]

An Indiana case took into account a blood quantum calculation as well as behavioral and reputational evidence in determining whether a person was an Indian subject to the statutory prohibition on Indians devising land without legislative consent. The judges concluded that Catherine Lasselle was an Indian under the statute because she was always recognized by the state, the federal government, and tribal leaders as a member of the Miami tribe; because "her birth, education, and language" further signaled her classification as a Miami Indian; and because she had three-eighths Indian blood.[29] In antebellum Ohio the state judiciary weighed blood quantum even more decisively. Ohio judges determined that the category "free white citizen" included any person who had "a predominance of white blood," even if he or she also had Indian (or black) ancestors. Thus, for example, the court declared that a plaintiff who was the son of a white man and a woman of mixed white and Indian parentage was a lawful voter.[30]

Where insufficient evidence of Indian ancestry or appearance was presented in court, judges sometimes declined to presume that a person was Indian based on social or political roles or affiliations alone. An example is an Indiana ejectment suit in which the court had to apply a law prohibiting Indians from testifying for or against whites. When one of the parties challenged the competence of a witness named Richardville, who was described in a treaty as "principal chief of the Miami nation of Indians," the Indiana Supreme Court justices found there was no evidence that the witness was, in fact, an Indian. Since a white man could be chief of an Indian tribe and since the witness had been allowed to testify at the trial in the lower court, the justices would not presume that the witness was an Indian and therefore would not exclude his testimony pursuant to the state's law limiting Indian witnesses.[31] Other cases make it clear that the receipt of Indian entitlements also was not definitive evidence of Indian racial classification. For example, to the Tennessee Supreme Court deciding cases involving the allocation of reservation land, race apparently did not limit who could be considered the "head of an Indian family." In the *Morgan v. Fowler* case, the court assessed the status of a white man who was married to a Cherokee woman and who was regarded as a member of the Cherokee nation. The court concluded that he was the head of an Indian family within the meaning of the 1817 and 1819 treaties made with the tribe and therefore was not precluded from being allotted a life estate in reserved land under those treaties. Similarly, in *Tuten v. Martin*, the same court was willing to treat a white man as an Indian entitled to an allocation of reservation land under federal treaties when he had married an Indian woman, lived among Indians, and was enrolled as a member of a tribe.[32]

RACE, STATUS, AND SOVEREIGNTY

Although, as discussed in chapter 1, state courts usually rejected (or completely ignored) claims of tribal sovereignty, they sometimes allowed tribal customs to prevail where such customs did not constitute a significant threat to the state's own claims of sovereignty. Such respect for Indians' status as members of semi-autonomous tribes led to their being treated differently from both blacks and whites. That different treatment sometimes reflected recognition of the validity of certain Indian customs that had legal consequences where there was no parallel official acceptance of African customs conflicting with state laws. In these situations, the different treatment of Indians was a result of the convergence of consideration of race, status, and sovereignty.[33]

An example is state recognition of marriages between Indians living in tribal territory and under tribal jurisdiction. In 1844 the Supreme Court of Tennessee ruled that marriages entered into in accordance with Cherokee customs prior to the date when Tennessee laws were extended over the Indians within its borders would be recognized equally with a marriage pursuant to the laws of a foreign country; thus the court recognized as valid a marriage entered into by Gideon Morgan and Margaret Sevier in 1813 in Tennessee's Cherokee Territory in accordance with the "forms and ceremonies" of the Cherokees.[34] The Alabama Supreme Court went further and explicitly held that the state's law extending jurisdiction over the Choctaws did not supersede Choctaw marriage usages and customs. In *Wall v. Williamson*, the court recognized a marriage between two Choctaw Indians, David and Delila Wall, in accordance with the laws of the tribe but also recognized the termination of the marriage by the act of the husband pursuant to those same tribal laws.[35]

Acknowledging the legality of Indian marriages placed them in a different position than marriages performed in accordance with African customs, but such acknowledgment did not preclude state regulation of the marriages. A New York statute of 1849 explicitly granted recognition of Indian marriages, providing that "[a]ll Indians who heretofore contracted or shall hereafter contract marriage, according to the Indian custom or usage, and shall cohabit as husband and wife, are and shall be deemed and held to be lawfully married, and their children legitimate." Although peace makers were empowered to substitute for justices of the peace in solemnizing Indian marriages in tribal areas, however, the statute also provided that state laws respecting husbands and wives would apply to all Indians in the state.[36] Therefore, the overall benefit to Indian autonomy was limited.

State and territorial courts were somewhat less eager to honor marriages between whites and Indians that were formalized on Indian land in accordance with tribal rituals, but occasionally they extended recognition to such marriages, as exemplified in two Missouri cases. In *Johnson v. Johnson's Administrator*, the Missouri Supreme Court upheld the legitimacy of the 1812 marriage between a white man and an Indian woman where the couple cohabitated together for several years in Indian Country outside of any state (at a military post at Prairie du Chien) and had three children whom the man treated as his legitimate daughters even after he separated from the woman and married another.[37] Missouri's recognition of white-Indian marriages solemnized by Indian customs continued through the Reconstruction era. In *Boyer and Charley v. Dively, Donnelly, and Black*, the Missouri Supreme Court recognized the marriage of a white man, William Gilliss, and a Piankeshaw Indian woman, Kahketoqua, in accordance with the Indian tribe's customs. Although the marriage took place within the boundaries of Missouri, it was never formalized under state law. Instead, the marriage followed tribal customs in that a messenger from Gilliss contacted Kahketoqua's parents to propose the marriage, the parents approved, Gilliss brought presents to the parents, the parents accompanied Kahketoqua when Gilliss brought her to the trading post where he resided among the Delaware Indians, and Gilliss and Kahketoqua subsequently lived together as husband and wife at the trading post. At the time of the marriage (1830), most Piankeshaw and Delaware Indians had been removed from Missouri, but remnant Indians in the state, including Kahketoqua's family, were still managed by an agent of the federal government; they were not subject to state laws of marriage and inheritance but, rather, followed tribal customs on those matters. Consequently, the court ruled that the grandchildren of Gilliss and Kahketoqua were their legitimate heirs and were entitled to inherit their mother's one-third share of the real and personal property in Gillis's estate.[38]

The law of husband and wife covered matters beyond the legitimacy of a marriage and the issue of inheritance. The *Fisher v. Allen* case in Mississippi raised the issue of whether John Allen's creditor could collect a debt from property that Allen's wife, Betsy Love, had brought to the marriage. Love was a member of the Chickasaw tribe who was married to Allen according to Chickasaw customs. Since Mississippi's extension law explicitly provided that marriages entered into by virtue of Choctaw or Chickasaw usages would be deemed valid, the state's Supreme Court easily concluded that John Allen and Betsy Love were married to each other. The trickier issue was raised by the fact that Chickasaw customs did not give a husband any rights in his wife's separate property. The court concluded that Indian customs regarding property rights applied to property Love had brought to the marriage, making that property unavailable to Allen's creditor, John Fisher.[39]

Some states went beyond the issue of marriage and recognized and honored other Indian customs and practices. In a pre-removal (1823) case, the Tennessee Supreme Court held that a Cherokee innkeeper in Cherokee country, Elizabeth Pack, could not be sued under Tennessee laws for damages arising from her failure to care properly for a guest's horse. Instead, the court concluded, the laws of the Cherokee Nation applied. As Judge John Haywood explained, the Cherokees are "an independent nation, subject to laws both civil and criminal, made by themselves, for the regulation of their internal affairs and exterior relations."[40] Other southern courts also recognized a degree of tribal sovereignty even after their legislatures had extended criminal jurisdiction over Indian tribes within their boundaries. As the Texas Supreme Court pointed out in 1847 in *Jones v. Laney*, "[t]he right of those Indian nations residing within the limits of a State to regulate their own civil polity has never been questioned, at least until the State authority has, by some affirmative act, claimed jurisdiction that would be incompatible with the existence of such rights in the nation of Indians. Their laws and customs regulating property, contracts, and the relations between husband and wife, have been respected, when drawn into controversy, in the courts of the State and of the United States." In this Texas case, the court upheld the emancipation of slaves by a Chickasaw Indian, James Gunn, but only because there appeared to be no Chickasaw law prohibiting manumission.[41]

Although *Duval v. Marshall* arose well after Arkansas extended criminal jurisdiction over Indian territory and tribes, the state's supreme court recognized the separate nationhood of the Creek nation at least with regard to civil matters. The case involved a dispute over the estate of an intestate Creek Indian, Ben Marshall. Upon Marshall's death, the Creeks recognized his son George W. Marshall, also a member of the Creek Nation, as administrator of the estate, while the state of Arkansas appointed as administrator another man, by the name of Whitesides. In the Arkansas Supreme Court's decision, Justice David Walker observed that the court could neither impose Arkansas inheritance laws on people and property within the Creek Nation nor treat the Creek Nation as if it were simply another state of the United States. Instead, he treated the Creek Nation as a foreign jurisdiction. He recognized the Creek Nation as Ben Marshall's domicile and consequently George W. Marshall as the primary administrator of property located there; administration in Arkansas, with Whitesides as administrator of the property located outside Creek territory, was "auxiliary" or "ancillary" to the primary administration in the Creek Nation.[42]

Although the United States negotiated treaties with Indian nations as it did with other countries, and Indian nations were sometimes specifically referred to as foreign countries, as in the Arkansas case just discussed, it was rare for recognition of tribal sovereignty to go so far as to lead Americans to let the law of nations limit them in their dealings with Indian tribes. State courts applied principles of the law of nations when the resolution of Indians' suits for freedom necessitated the application of European colonial law, and they sometimes considered the possible application of the law of nations to their domestic, internal policies (such as policies governing slavery), but state judges rarely had occasion to apply the law of nations to their relations with Indian tribes. Since the Constitution allocated responsibility for foreign affairs to the federal government, state courts would have been challenging the principles of federalism too directly if they had encroached on the federal sphere by openly deciding on matters of international conflict.

A law of nations issue involving Indians did arise in a Texas case of 1844. It would be a year before the Lone Star Republic became a part of the United States, but in hope and anticipation of annexation, Texans had written a constitution similar to the U.S. Constitution and applied many of the same legal principles. The *Herbert v. Moore* case raised the issue of whether the law of nations principle of postliminy applied to property taken during a skirmish between Anglo-Texans and Indians. The rule of postliminy determined who would legally own property that was taken by an enemy during a time of war. If moveable property was recovered within twenty-four hours of its seizure, then title would revert to the original owner, but if it was recovered after twenty-four hours had elapsed, title went to the person who recovered the property. In this case, the horses and mules taken from the plaintiff were found and retaken from the Indians by the defendant two days after they were initially stolen. Thus if the law of postliminy applied, the defendant would be the legal owner of the animals. The court, however, ruled in favor of the plaintiff's right to the property, concluding that postliminy rules did not apply because there was no state of war. Citing U.S. Chief Justice John Marshall's opinion in *Cherokee Nation v. Georgia* on the status of American Indians, the judges in *Herbert v. Moore* explained that because Indian tribes were not nations, violent conflicts with Indians did not constitute "war." In fact, the tribes' lack of status as nations meant that international law and the law of nations did not apply at all to Texas's relations with Indians.[43]

Although states were reluctant to recognize tribal sovereignty when it interfered with their own interests—whether their need to keep order, their desire to maintain a predictable commercial economy where contractual obligations were enforced, their craving to acquire land and resources, or their determination to avoid giving the federal government any pretext for undermining a state's authority within its own borders—they often did not mind allowing tribes to regulate internal matters that had only a minimal effect on whites, such as Indian marriages. When states left room for tribal self-regulation, they were in effect granting Native Americans privileges that were not offered to African Americans. Although black separatism was usually tolerated (or even required) in social contexts, such as churches, schools, and benevolent associations,[44] blacks were not permitted to extract themselves from coverage of general state laws; Africans in America could claim no special separate status equivalent to the Indian tribe. It was state government officials, not blacks themselves, who had the privilege of deciding when blacks would have to abide by different laws than those obeyed by whites. Unfortunately for Indians, when they were regulated as part of the state community—outside of their tribes—they, too, often were treated as an inferior class and were subject to discriminatory laws, as discussed in the next chapter.

CHAPTER FOUR

Indians and Racial Discrimination

Although one of the most basic principles of early American democracy was that general laws were to be uniform in application, the precept did not require laws to apply in exactly the same way to every person in the jurisdiction. Instead, as explained in an 1869 California case, it simply mandated that the laws operate "in the same manner upon all persons who stand in the same category, that is to say, upon all persons who stand in the same relation to the law, in respect to the privileges and immunities conferred by it, or the acts which it prohibits."[1] Both before and after ratification of the Fourteenth Amendment, this concept was used to justify disparate treatment of people in different racial groups.

Specifically, the idea that it was reasonable and constitutional to treat Native Americans differently from European Americans was widely accepted by legislators and judges alike. In the case quoted above, *Ex parte Smith*, which assessed the constitutionality of a city ordinance that classified people on the basis of sex, the California Supreme Court used the prohibition on the sale of liquor to Indians as an example of appropriate class-based legislation. The New York Court of Appeals took a similar position in *Wynehamer v. People of New York*, observing that because Indians were reasonably categorized with minors and habitual drunkards, it was not impermissible to prohibit the sale of liquor to Indians. Similar reasoning was used to reject challenges to other forms of discriminatory legislation. In the *Murphy and Glover Test Oath Cases*, the Missouri Supreme Court explained that excluding Indians (as well as Negroes, minors, and women) from political powers was "plainly founded upon natural, inherent and permanent incapacities, and looks only to the first necessities of good government."[2]

Such racist presumptions on the part of judges and legislators led to various forms of discrimination against Indians during the period from

1790 to 1880. Most notoriously, during the antebellum period, racism led to state efforts to expel Indians. Moreover, numerous antebellum state statutes and constitutions categorized Indians with blacks and discriminated against both groups on racial grounds. After the Civil War, some states continued to discriminate against Indians, either because they did not interpret the Reconstruction Amendments as impediments to certain categories of racially discriminatory state legislation affecting blacks and Indians alike, or because they persisted in viewing Indians as lying outside the political community, even while they asserted regulatory power over them.

It is not within the purview of this study to examine in detail the underlying causes of the racist belief system that underlay such discriminatory policies. But it is apparent that racism itself was not merely a psychological response driven by irrational gut instinct, nor solely a collective symbolic construction to define American whiteness, nor simply an abstract ideological position compelled by pseudo-scientific conceptions of the time. Both the pronouncements of intellectuals and collective and individual psychology may have influenced racial sentiment, but it is important to keep in mind that racism also served the tangible and intangible economic and political interests of whites in various ways. As other historians have shown, racializing relationships between people categorized as "white" and "nonwhite" in the United States helped justify appropriation of nonwhites' land and labor in the nineteenth century, and racialization also helped bond whites together, buttressing poor whites' loyalty to economic and political elites at a time of increasingly sharp class differences. Thus, both national expansion and national identity were interconnected with racial constructions.[3] Regardless of the underlying explanatory foundation for white Americans' racism in the nineteenth century—psychological, ideological, economic, political, religious, or scientific—their belief in white superiority and Indian inferiority was real. Racism genuinely motivated the unequal treatment of Indians under state governments and the efforts to remove them from white society, and it served to justify and legitimize those actions to whites throughout the country.

RACISM AND CHEROKEE REMOVAL

Georgia's rejection of tribal sovereignty and unwillingness to allow the Cherokee Nation to function as an autonomous government within state borders was a major factor shaping state government policy on the Cherokees in the 1820s and 1830s, as discussed in chapter 1. Also influential was Georgians' defensive posture based on assertions of states' rights, described in chapter 2. But neither the denial of tribal sovereignty nor claims of state sovereignty actually required expelling Cherokees from Georgia. Both principles could have been satisfied by the forced dissolution of tribal organization and absorption of Cherokee land and individual Indians into the state (i.e., if it had been possible to impose such a solution on the Cherokees). Yet Georgia chose instead to seize Cherokee land and pressure the Indians to leave the state. Clearly, Indian removal promised to do more than just strengthen states' rights claims and destroy tribal sovereignty within Georgia. In a purely economic sense, removal also helped whites by satisfying their intense desire to obtain Indian lands. But that goal, too, cannot stand on its own. In the absence of a perception of racial differences, white Georgians presumably would not have perceived Indian possession of lands as unjustifiable obstacles to white possession of those lands, nor would they have felt entitled to flout rule of law and resort to violence in order to press their alleged superior claim to those lands. Racism significantly determined Georgia's actions. White racism made absorption of Cherokees into the state as individuals unpalatable to Georgia government officials. White Georgians maintained that Indians could not be merged into white society because they were racially inferior—superior to people of African ancestry, they conceded, but inferior to whites. Moreover, Georgians argued, there was no prospect that Indians could be taught civilized behavior, because their inherent racial inferiority could not be overcome.

It is evident that Georgians held this view of Indians long before it became the dominant belief in the country and came to shape official federal government policy. In this regard, Georgians shared the outlook of many other whites on the frontier, the edge of European and American settlement where there was the most contact between whites and Indians. Settled in the eighteenth century, much of Georgia was still frontier country at the end of the American Revolution, so Georgians had more in common with western settlers than with easterners up the coast from the Carolinas to Massachusetts. Reginald Horsman has explained that as the frontier moved west, a disparity emerged between the eastern seaboard region that Europeans had first colonized in the seventeenth century and inland regions that they settled later. White inhabitants of the former area, no longer experiencing regular conflict with Indians, took on a detached, theoretical attitude about Indians and argued optimistically in favor of a continued commitment to the civilization program. Meanwhile, frontier whites, who were more likely to clash with Indians in their daily lives as they pressed against Indian territory, generally harbored more aggressively hostile views of Indians, were impatient with talk of extended efforts to help them acclimate to European-American ways, were unwilling to tolerate the continued presence of Indians on lands abutting the frontier, presumed it to be inevitable that whites would naturally displace innately inferior peoples, viewed Indians as obstacles to the progress of civilization, and interpreted Indian resistance to white advances as evidence of Indians' savagery. In a sense, as Elise Marienstras has argued, seeing Indians as savage and innately different helped reinforce Indians' symbolic utility in defining American national identity in the early Republic.[4]

In the early nineteenth century the long-held beliefs of frontier whites gained an intellectual foundation in new racial theories. Enlightenment ideas of the eighteenth century had supported the belief that racial differences were caused by environmental and educational factors, which helped sustain the view that those differences could be eliminated and people of different races, including Indians, could be assimilated through instruction and good example. However, in the early nineteenth century intellectuals replaced older theories with the notion that racial differences were biological, innate, and immutable. Furthermore, it was widely believed that each race had its own distinctive social, political, and ethical characteristics. By the antebellum period, the racial theory dominant among whites assumed that whiteness embodied inherently different cultural qualities that could not be transferred to Indians.[5]

Attempting to civilize Cherokees in Georgia was, according to this theory, bound to be fruitless. It might appear that the Cherokees had made some progress toward civilization, but full transformation was not possible. Cherokees, it was alleged, could not possibly attain the level of civilization that would justify their retaining lands that could be more profitably utilized by white owners. The awkward fact that there were striking similarities between the lifestyles of leading Cherokees and whites led Georgians to play down or ignore cultural factors. As Daniel Richter has explained, in general, whites' notion of the differences between themselves and Indians was blindly constructed out of conceptual misinterpretations, yet those perceived differences were construed as fundamental racial distinctions. Race became the primary justification for limiting Cherokees' civil rights and subsequently for pressing for their removal. As historian Theda Perdue observes, Cherokees were excluded from equal membership in the state community "not because they were 'savages' or 'heathens,' but because they were Indians." It was deemed necessary to create a new "geography of race," James Ronda explains, a "tidy geography of division" between two peoples who were so "intrinsically different" that they could not live together in the same space.[6]

Once Georgia had extended its jurisdiction over Cherokee Territory, stepped up harassment and intimidation of Cherokees, and encouraged squatters to enter Cherokee lands, some members of the Cherokee leadership saw that remaining in the state was not feasible. The Cherokees had never wanted to be absorbed into Georgia as individuals anyway, since they had a keen sense of tribal identity and distinct cultural practices that they did not want to give up. But those who signed the Treaty of New Echota also understood that incorporation into the Georgia community as equals was not possible.

As Mary Young has pointed out, Principal Chief John Ross was lighter skinned than John Ridge or Elias Boudinot, two prominent Cherokee leaders who had vehemently opposed removal before the 1830s but ended up signing the Treaty of New Echota in 1835. Because of his light complexion, Young observed, Ross had not experienced the same level of racism in white society and may not have fully comprehended the racial barriers to equal treatment in Georgia that the Cherokees would face if they agreed to disband the Nation and submit fully to the state's jurisdiction. Having encountered blatant racism in their own interactions with whites—e.g., on the occasions of their marriages to white women—Ridge and Boudinot knew that remaining in Georgia was no longer a realistic option.[7] Following a council of pro-treaty Cherokees held at John Ridge's home, Running Waters, in November 1834, Ridge and Boudinot expressed their deep skepticism about assimilation in a memorial: with "all the unrelenting prejudices against our language and color in full force," they wrote, "we must believe that the scheme of *amalgamation* with our oppressors is too horrid for a serious contemplation. . . . Without law in the States, we are not more favored than the poor African."[8] Ridge and Boudinot understood that state law would not protect their rights and that they would end up being legally categorized with blacks. Thus they knew that racism precluded incorporation of Indians in Georgia.

The Cherokees' own view of race—like that of whites'—was complicated. Anthropologist Circe Sturm explains that prior to contact with Europeans, Cherokees defined community based on kinship and cultural commonalities, but by the end of the eighteenth century they also came to see race as a defining characteristic of peoples and nations. Absorbing

European-American views of racial difference, they included a sense of racial identity in their self-definition as they centralized the Cherokee political structure in the early nineteenth century. Appropriating their white neighbors' policy toward African Americans, Cherokees also institutionalized racial discrimination against blacks by recognizing black enslavement, prohibiting marriage between Cherokees and "Colored Persons," and barring people of African descent from public office in the Cherokee Nation. Though the Cherokees may have hoped that such laws would help persuade whites that Cherokees were civilized and also that they had an identity distinct from blacks, the laws failed to convince Georgians to treat Cherokees as equals or to allow the Cherokees to stay on their lands. John Ridge and Elias Boudinot understood white conceptions of race well, and by 1835 it was clear to them that Cherokees could not avoid second-class status in white society if they remained on land claimed by Georgia.[9]

In many regards Indians were categorized with blacks (as discussed later in this chapter), but their unique position in the United States resulted in their having a somewhat different experience. One important distinction was that people of African descent provided labor, which required that they remain a part of American society. That blacks were not also removed from the South was attributable to plantation owners' dependence on slave labor. They may have liked the idea of creating an all-white Republic, but they were not willing to give up their supply of field workers, nor would they gain any additional land by expelling blacks. Thus, although "colonization" programs for free people of color were widely discussed, there was little support for applying such programs to slaves. Indians were in a different position, however. Though many Indians did in fact work for whites, white Americans viewed Indians primarily as sources of property rather than labor. Since land could not be obtained from Indians as long as they occupied it, many whites concluded that they had the most to gain from expelling Indians rather than from integrating them. In a sense, because of the perceived link between widespread white land ownership and republican values, one could argue that the concept of white democracy was as dependent on removing Indians from territory coveted by whites as it was on enslaving blacks to extract their labor. Indian removal not only helped racially "purify" the Republic but also made room for white expansion onto new lands.[10]

Blatant about rejecting the notion of Cherokees as equal neighbors, Georgia successfully pressured the Cherokees—and the Creeks as well—to leave the state. That the final expulsion did not take place until 1838 was not because white Georgians were patient, nor was it only because it took some time for the vanguard of the frontier settlement line to reach Cherokee Territory. Rather, the delay is in large part attributable to the fact that Georgia was waiting for the federal government either to make land-cession-and-removal treaties with the Cherokees or otherwise to fulfill its 1802 pledge to clear the state of Indians. The federal officials' reluctance to do so was chiefly because, as Reginald Horsman has pointed out, until 1829 the federal government was dominated by an eastern elite that believed acculturated Indians could be absorbed as part of an expanding United States. But throughout the early national period, those leaders' standpoint differed sharply from that of the people of the states, that is, the masses of white Americans who had long viewed Indians as irredeemable savages who could never be equal to whites. The federal barrier to Georgia's expulsion project evaporated with the election of a westerner to the White House.[11]

In addition to Georgia, the removal of people deemed racially unsuited to citizenship also occurred in other southeastern states, including Mississippi, Alabama, Tennessee, and Florida. Additionally, many northern Indians were pushed to give up their lands and move to remote locations. Between the 1810s and the 1850s, Indians ceded land and left large areas of New York, Ohio, Indiana, Illinois, Michigan, Wisconsin, Minnesota, and Iowa. Thus, racism affected not only Indians who were part of white society but also those who remained separate and were never given a genuine option of assimilating. In one of the more extreme acts of racism against Indians, vast numbers of them were simply removed from the states entirely.

RACIAL DISCRIMINATION BEFORE THE CIVIL WAR

Considering the extensive evidence of racial discrimination against Indians in the Southeast and throughout the rest of the United States in 1835, John Ridge and Elias Boudinot were realistic to doubt their chances of being admitted to the Georgia community as equals. And the situation did not improve significantly for the rest of the antebellum period.

Even without mentioning Indians, many laws discriminated against people of Indian ancestry in practice by including them within broad racially defined groups that held a diminished status in American society. Some Indian-descended people were covered by legislation pertaining to "free colored persons" and were subject to wide-ranging limitations on their liberty and rights, including common exclusion from skilled occupations and comfortable residential neighborhoods, and segregation in public transportation, hotels, and restaurants.[12] Others occupied the most degraded position as slaves. Although after the American Revolution it became rare for free Indians to be newly enslaved, the nineteenth-century slave population included people descended from the many Indians who had been enslaved during the colonial period, as noted in chapter 3. The tendency of nineteenth-century plantation owners to classify all their slaves as "negro" or "African" regardless of their actual racial ancestry masked the extent to which Indians served as slaves right through the end of the Civil War. It is not clear how many nineteenth-century slaves had Indian ancestry, but whatever their numbers, all of those enslaved people would have been subject to general state laws regulating slaves.[13] Because there was a vast number of laws and cases pertaining to slaves, and because there is an extensive pertinent literature on the subject of slavery, such laws will not be discussed here. Instead, this section focuses on legislation that expressly applied to Indians.

State laws throughout the country explicitly discriminated against Indians on the basis of race during the early national and the antebellum periods. Such legislation, which often had roots in the colonial era, distinguished between whites and Indians in a variety of contexts, including marriage, crime, trials, juries, and voting. None of these laws could reasonably have been seen as protecting Indians, as the statutes prohibiting Indians from selling land or making enforceable contracts were justified at the time. Rationales based on Indian sovereignty were also unpersuasive rationales for most of these laws. Although the separate and distinct political status of Indian tribes might have served as the original rationale for laws excluding Indians from voting and serving on juries, by the nineteenth century the exclusion often was applied indiscriminately both to Indians who retained a tribal affiliation and to those who did not, signaling clearly the underlying racial reason. Similarly, although early rules prohibiting Indians from testifying in court might have been based formally on the fact that, as non-Christians, they were perceived as unable to take an oath, the laws did not make any exception for Christian Indians even after many Indians had converted. That Indians were excluded along with other disfavored racial groups, such as Chinese and African Americans, further indicates that exclusion from lists of jurors, witnesses, and voters was a form of racial discrimination. Finally, prohibiting interracial marriage and imposing harsher criminal penalties on Indians than on whites could only have been motivated by racism. Consequently, all of these categories of legislation—marriage, crime, and political rights—must be interpreted as forms of racial discrimination.

Most states proscribed *intermarriage* between whites and Indians, as they prohibited whites and blacks to intermarry. In large part, interracial marriage was restricted because it threatened to blur racial boundaries and thereby complicate race-based policies, especially the institution of slavery. Because miscegenation laws sent the message that whites degraded themselves if they had intimate relations with nonwhites, such statutes had the effect of reinforcing whites' sense of their own superiority and the corresponding inferiority of racial groups defined as "other."[14] When Indians were included among the groups who could not marry whites, their status in white society was tainted. Consequently, the miscegenation laws mattered not only to individual Indians who might have wished to have their—or their parents'—interracial relationships recognized by law but also to all Indians who wanted to find a place in the white community and to be treated equally there.

Prohibitions on Indian-white interracial marriage had their origin in the colonial period. For example, during the second decade of the eighteenth century, legislation in North Carolina provided that "no White man or woman shall intermarry with any Negro, Mulatto or Indyan Man or Woman"; the white man or woman who violated this law, as well as the person who performed the illegal interracial ceremony, was to be fined fifty pounds. The legislature clarified the statute in 1741 by specifying that the prohibition applied to "any Person of Mixed Blood, to the Third Generation." A mid-nineteenth-century statute expressed the prohibition in more ambiguous language but specified explicitly the consequences of interracial marriages: an 1838 law declared it unlawful for "any free negro or free person of color to marry a white person" and declared any such marriage to be null and void. Nullifying the marriage left the interracial couple open to prosecution for fornication or adultery if they cohabitated. Although the 1838 miscegenation statute did not define racial classification, courts applied the blood quantum requirement provided for in the miscegenation statute of 1836. In an 1852 prosecution of a white woman and a man of Indian descent who lived together as husband and wife, the North Carolina Supreme Court ruled that where the degree to which the man was removed from his Indian ancestor was not known, it could not be presumed that he was within three generations. Since the marriage in question could not be declared illegal on the evidence provided, there could be no conviction for fornication, but it seemed to be assumed that the law would have prohibited the marriage if the man had been shown to be Indian.[15]

Other states also attacked intermarriage between whites and Indians. In Massachusetts a 1786 statute proscribed marriage between a white person and "any Negro, Indian or Mulatto."[16] Two other New England states, Rhode Island and Maine, had similar laws, enacted in 1798 and 1821, respectively. While the Massachusetts statute was repealed in 1843, Rhode Island and Maine did not repeal their laws until after the Civil War. Far western states and southern states, too, enacted legislation intended to prevent interracial marriages. Nevada (in 1861), Oregon (in 1866), Virginia (in 1691), and Tennessee (1821) specifically included Indians in their laws. Altogether, of the thirty-eight states admitted to the Union by 1880, thirty enacted a law punishing or nullifying interracial marriage at some point, and nine of those states explicitly applied those penalties to white-Indian intermarriages.[17] Other states left the application of the prohibition to Indians ambiguous by barring intermarriage between whites and "mulattoes" or "persons of color." Typically, states that did not make express reference to Indians in their marriage laws categorized them as "persons of color" or "mulattoes" and thus may have prohibited white-Indian marriage in practice. That not all jurisdictions prohibited marriages between Indians and whites is evidenced by the existence of some interracial couples. A most prominent example is Kit Carson, the famous trapper, military scout, and New Mexico Indian agent, who married an Arapaho woman, Waa-nibe, and then a Cheyenne woman, Making-Out-Road. He was fortunate to live in the Territory of New Mexico, which had liberal policies on marriage.[18]

Criminal laws sometimes explicitly categorized Indians with blacks when defining crimes and punishments. Normally in such laws, the race of both the victim and the accused criminal mattered in establishing whether a prosecutable crime had occurred and determining what the punishment would be. Like African Americans, Indians experienced the lethal combination of unequal protection and discriminatory enforcement of criminal laws: they were more likely than whites to be charged with criminal behavior and less likely to be protected by criminal laws. Thus Indians shared with African Americans what Randall Kennedy has called "racially selective underprotection." Furthermore, criminal laws forced on Indians, as on blacks, what Kennedy has referred to as a "stigmatizing code of conduct . . . that demanded exhibitions of servility."[19]

Laws of Kentucky and Mississippi provide good examples. A Kentucky law of the early national period punished with thirty lashes any "negro, mulatto, or Indian, bond or free [who] shall at any time lift his or her hand in opposition to" any white person, yet the state's legislation provided no parallel punishment for whites striking Negroes, mulattos, or Indians, nor any punishment for Negroes, mulattos, or Indians lifting their hand against other Negroes, mulattos, or Indians. This law was a continuation of an earlier Virginia colonial law to the same effect, which remained in force in Kentucky under the state's 1792 constitution. Clearly, Indians had to show proper deference to white people. Other Kentucky laws of that time period meted out the death penalty to any slave who raped or attempted to rape a white woman but mentioned no punishment for raping an Indian or black woman.[20] Similarly, a Mississippi statute of 1852 punished Negro or mulatto men who raped or attempted to rape a white woman but did not provide any punishment for the rape or attempted rape of an Indian or a black woman. Six years later, the legislature amended the law to provide punishment also for rapes of Indian women, but there was still no punishment if the victim was black. Although Indian women were thus included in the statute, the form of punishment for rape depended on whether the victim was white or Indian. The convicted rapist was automatically subjected to the death penalty if the victim was white, but in cases where the victim was Indian a severe whipping could substitute for execution, at the jury's discretion. Furthermore, the 1858 law treated statutory rape (consensual sex with a girl under the age of fourteen) the same as forcible rape if the victim was white but not if the victim was Indian.[21]

Throughout the South, most states followed Kentucky's model of rape law rather than Mississippi's. State laws typically only punished the rape of white women, impliedly excluding Indian women as well as black women. Such discriminatory laws of rape that recognized only white victims made Indian women and girls more vulnerable to sexual violence than white women were. Failing to punish men who raped Indian women, or punishing them less severely than those who raped whites, also sent the message that Indian women were not "ladies" who shared white women's presumed purity.[22] The law of rape thus reinforced the notion of the inferiority of persons of color, including Indians.

Other laws punished nonviolent illegal behavior of Indians. For example, in 1803 and 1807, territorial Indiana enacted laws that prohibited Indians, along with Negroes and mulattoes, from purchasing any white servant but allowing members of each group to own servants "of their own complexion."[23] The clear message of these acts was that no white person could be made subordinate to a nonwhite person. The laws, like those relating to violent crime, signaled the inferior status of Indians and other people regarded as nonwhite and helped ensure the continuity and stability of the established racial hierarchy.

Once charged with violating a state law, Indians encountered substantial barriers to proving their innocence. Lawyers, jurors, witnesses, and judges were all likely to be white, owing to racial restrictions on legal and political rights that routinely excluded Indians and other racial minorities from every role in a criminal trial other than defendant. The most widespread explicit exclusions focused on Indians as witnesses and as jurors.

State laws often prohibited nonwhites from testifying as witnesses in court against whites. Many of those proscriptions explicitly included *Indian testimony* along with that of Negroes, mulattoes, and (in the western states) Chinese. For example, an 1818 Virginia law provided that "No negro, mulatto or Indian, shall be admitted to give evidence but against, or between negroes, mulattoes or Indians." As late as February 1866, Virginia had slightly broadened the opportunity for "colored persons and Indians" to testify. In civil cases they could be witnesses in cases "in which a colored person or an Indian is a party, or may be directly benefitted or injured by the result," while in criminal proceedings they could testify if a colored person or Indian was either a victim or a defendant (even if a co-defendant with a white person). Legislation specified that a person who was not "colored" would be classified as "Indian" if he or she had "one-fourth or more of Indian blood."[24] Georgia's law barring Cherokee or Creek Indian testimony against whites made an exception for a white person who lived within the Indian nation's territory. Other southern states explicitly prohibiting Indians from testifying against whites, or in cases involving whites, include Maryland, North Carolina, and Texas.[25]

Interestingly, southern states that were in the process of extending their jurisdiction over Indian land or expelling Indians tended to allow Indian testimony. Because Mississippi's extension laws granted Indians the same rights as white inhabitants, the state's supreme court concluded that Indians and whites were equally competent to testify in court. Similarly, in 1832, when the land surrounding the "remnant" of Cherokee Indians in Georgia was about to be granted to and settled by whites, the state enacted a statute to protect the Indians from "depredations of lawless and dissolute white men"; in order to make the protection of Cherokee and their property meaningful, the statute, "for these special purposes," made an exception to the usual rule—re-issued as recently as 1829, in the extension statute—that "the oaths of the Indians, are not admitted in our courts of law."[26]

States outside the Southeast also had racial qualifications for witnesses. In 1850 California provided that "[n]o black, or mulatto person, or Indian, shall be permitted to give evidence in any action to which a white person is a party, in any Court in this State"; the legislature included as "Indians" people who had "one half Indian blood." Reinforcing the same principle, another statute enacted the same day asserted explicitly that in no case before the justices of the peace "shall a white man be convicted of any offence upon the testimony of an Indian, or Indians." A few years later, the legislature reiterated its rule that "Indians or persons having one half or more of Indian blood" could not be witnesses in any actions or proceedings in which a white person was a party. But in 1855 the 1850 statute pertaining to Indians and justices of the peace was amended to allow Indians to be competent witnesses in cases arising from complaints to the justices of the peace, with the Indians' "credibility being left with the jury." In *People v. Hall* (1854), the exclusion of black, mulatto, and Indian witnesses was interpreted to cover Chinese people as well. In 1863 the legislature amended the witness statute to explicitly exclude "Mongolian" and "Chinese" people, along with Indians, from testifying in cases involving white parties.[27] Other western states barring Indians from testifying in certain cases include Oregon and Nevada. The Nevada law allowed blacks and mulattoes to serve as witnesses in any case but prohibited Indians and Chinese from giving evidence either for or against a white person. The exclusion of Indian witnesses extended to "persons having one-half or more of Indian blood."[28]

Midwestern states similarly limited Indian testimony. States that explicitly prohibited Indians from testifying in court against whites or in cases in which whites were parties include Indiana and Illinois. Nebraska's prohibition broadened between 1855 and 1857. The 1855 law stated that "an indian, a negro, or mulatto or black person shall not be allowed to give testimony in any cause wherein a white person is a party," but two years later the last seven words were omitted from the provision. Thus Nebraska legislation formally prohibited Indians (and other racial minorities) from testifying in any trial, whether or not the case involved whites.[29] Although stated law does not always reflect what happens in practice, the cases show that Indians were in fact customarily prohibited from testifying in court.[30]

State laws further restricted Indians' participation in legal processes by excluding them from *juries*. Typically only men who had the right to vote were eligible to serve on juries, and racial limitations on the suffrage were widespread. The qualifications for jury eligibility usually appeared in state constitutions or statutes, but even the common law was viewed as providing an adequate foundation for racial restrictions on jury service. The Supreme Court of Virginia found that common law provided the basis for excluding Indian jurors where there was no statute explicitly providing a racial qualification. Indians, like minors, free Negroes, and women were not "*liberi et legales homines*" (i.e., not in the same category as "free and lawful men") and were therefore automatically disqualified from jury service regardless of the absence of any exclusion in positive law.[31]

RACIAL QUALIFICATIONS FOR POLITICAL RIGHTS IN THE ANTEBELLUM PERIOD

Every state also had racial qualifications for exercising political rights, such as the *elective franchise*. Because political rights often correlated with citizenship, state politicians sometimes felt they had to explain how their determining who could exercise such rights was consistent with the U.S. Constitution. To justify their authority over the franchise, they pointed out that the Constitution assigned to the states the power to decide who would have the right to vote for members of the House of Representatives and for president. They noted that although the U.S. Constitution gave Congress the power to "establish an uniform Rule of naturalization" throughout the country, it also provided that the electors who chose a state's representatives to the U.S. House of Representatives were to have "the Qualifications requisite for Electors of the most numerous Branch of the State Legislature" and that each state's electors for the presidential election would be appointed "In such Manner as the Legislature thereof may direct."[32]

In states where they wanted to restrict the suffrage to white men, antebellum legislators denied that the privileges and immunities clause in Article IV of the U.S. Constitution presented an obstacle. Whatever weaknesses their argument might have had when applied to African-American men (prior to *Dred Scott*), it was considerably more persuasive when applied to most Indians. As the Tennessee Supreme Court held in *Tennessee v. Claiborne* (1838), the privileges and immunities clause did not apply to Indians who were not citizens.[33] Some states went further, claiming that it was their prerogative to determine that certain Indians were not citizens even when U.S. treaty provisions seemed to accord them citizenship status. In 1847, for example, the Alabama Supreme Court ruled that Choctaw Indians falling within the terms of the Treaty of Dancing Rabbit Creek—which provided that Indians who remained in the state would receive a land patent and become citizens—were in fact not "citizens" but only "inhabitants" or "residents" of the state. The court dismissed the treaty's reference to Indian "citizens" as an "inaccurate use of a word." By identifying Indians as mere "inhabitants," the judges were clearly signaling the second-class status of Indians. Emmerich de Vattel, a leading Swiss expert on the law of nations, had defined "inhabitants" as people "of an inferior order," like Jews or gypsies, who were not entitled to all the benefits of the society. The Alabama judges pondered the question of whether the state's laws permitted "Indians to participate equally with us in our civil and political privileges," and concluded that they would not as long as the Indians constituted a "distinct and independent community."[34]

Even renunciation of tribal affiliation and membership in the state's community did not guarantee acceptance to citizenship status, however. In 1822 the Kentucky Supreme Court explained that while some people in the state were "citizens," others were mere "subjects" not entitled to the same full array of rights.[35] Moreover, even citizen Indians could be barred from voting, based on the argument that citizenship did not guarantee suffrage. As the Kansas Supreme Court pointed out two years after Kansas was admitted as a state, citizenship and the elective franchise were two very different rights. Someone could be a citizen and yet lack the right to vote, while another person could have the right to vote even in the absence of citizenship status.[36] Thus, there were a number of explanations offered to justify denying the suffrage to nonwhite men in general or to Indians specifically.

Typically, state constitutional provisions on the elective franchise extended the suffrage only to "white" men, which effectively excluded most Indians. Some states, however, explicitly excluded Indians from voting. Kentucky's 1799 constitution excepted "Negroes, Mulattoes, and Indians" from its general provision that every free male citizen could vote, while Rhode Island's 1842 constitution excluded members of the Narragansett tribe. A few states permitted some Indians to vote or at least theoretically made it possible that some Indians might be able to vote. California's 1849 constitution gave the legislature the discretion to admit some Indians to the suffrage in special cases. Maine's (drafted 1819, in effect 1820) and Texas's (1845) exclusion of "Indians not taxed" impliedly left room for voting by nontribal Indians who were citizens. However, the minute numbers of nonreservation Indians in Maine made the language inconsequential;

even as late as 1860 (the first year when Indians were listed in the census), the census listed only three "civilized" male Indians in the state, and they may not have been U.S. citizens, may not have been taxpayers, and may not even have been old enough to vote.[37] Michigan (1850), Minnesota (1857), and Wisconsin (1848) all allowed "civilized Indians" to vote. The antebellum state constitutions of Alabama, Arkansas, Connecticut, Delaware, Florida, Illinois, Indiana, Iowa, Louisiana, Maryland, Mississippi, Missouri, New Jersey, North Carolina, Ohio, Pennsylvania, South Carolina, Tennessee, and Virginia retained the provision that only "white" men could vote and offered no explicit exceptions that might enfranchise some Indians. Georgia's 1789 and 1798 constitutions included no racial requirement for the suffrage but allowed only citizens of the state to vote; in practice, only a handful of Indians were permitted to become state citizens. New York allowed a "man of color" to vote only if he met certain residency and property qualifications. On the eve of the Civil War, only Massachusetts (1780), New Hampshire (1784), and Vermont (1777) had permanently eliminated the "whiteness" requirement for voting and had no exceptions for classes of Indians or people of color in their constitutions.[38]

In sum, in the period from 1790 to 1860 most of the states exhibited a pattern of discrimination under their laws. By the 1850s, most white Americans had, through their state legislation, made it clear that they did not and would not accept Indians as equal citizens. The discriminatory statutes fell into three categories. They either excluded Native Americans from certain rights in the states—such as the elective franchise or the right to testify in court—or exempted them from civic obligations that were markers of citizenship—such as jury service—or kept them separated from whites—for example, through marriage laws.

Unfortunately, the discrimination was persistent and consistent. There is little evidence of improvement over time, though there were a few positive developments, namely Massachusetts's repeal of its miscegenation law in 1843 and some Indians gaining the right of suffrage in Michigan, Wisconsin, and Minnesota between the 1830s and the 1850s.

In some ways, conditions in the Northeast and Midwest were better than they were in the South. Northeastern states began with fewer racial restrictions at the start of the early national period, most notably reflected in the absence of miscegenation laws in most northeastern states; the lack of a "whiteness" requirement for voting in several early New England state constitutions; and the non-existence of formal prohibitions on Indian testimony in northern courts. Midwestern states imposed more racial disabilities on Indians than New Englanders did but were more likely than southerners were to allow Indians to vote and to intermarry with whites. Southern legislation embodied the worst discrimination against Indians and other "persons of color." Southern states' constitutional provisions and laws involving those groups prohibited intermarriage with whites, punished violent crimes more harshly, disallowed trial testimony in cases with white parties, barred jury service, and withheld the franchise. The existence of all these disabilities in Georgia's laws shows that John Ridge and Elias Boudinot were, sadly, correct in their assessment of the dismal prospects for Indians in antebellum Georgia.

INDIANS AND THE RECONSTRUCTION AMENDMENTS

In the wake of the Civil War, the Thirteenth Amendment to the U.S. Constitution abolished slavery in 1865. The Civil Rights Act of 1866 declared that "all persons born in the United States and not subject to any foreign power, excluding Indians not taxed" were citizens of the United States, and the 1866 law further provided that citizens of every race and color had the same right "to make and enforce contracts, to sue, be parties, and give evidence, to inherit, purchase, lease, sell, hold, and convey real and personal property, and to full and equal benefit of all laws and proceedings for the security of person and property as is enjoyed by white citizens, and shall be subject to like punishment, pains, and penalties, and to none other." The Fourteenth Amendment, ratified two years later, provided that "[a]ll persons born or naturalized in the United States, and subject to the jurisdiction thereof" were U.S. citizens and citizens of the state where they resided, and no state could "deny to any person within its jurisdiction the equal protection of the laws." Finally, the Fifteenth Amendment, prohibiting states from denying any U.S. citizen the right to vote on the basis of race or color, became a part of the Constitution in 1870. These dramatic new guarantees seemed to restrict the states' capacity to treat American Indians differently from other residents.

The Fourteenth Amendment's equal protection clause led some states to repeal their race-based laws. Many states, however, found justifications for retaining racially discriminatory legislation. An extensive historical literature describes judicial interpretation of how the Fourteenth Amendment affected the rights of African Americans in the nineteenth century.[39] In the first decade after ratification of the amendment, most state and lower federal courts held that the amendment did not prohibit a wide range of statutes that classified people on the basis of race, including miscegenation statutes as well as laws providing for segregation in schools and in public accommodations. Although the Fifteenth Amendment (1870) made it unconstitutional to deny anyone the right to vote on the basis of race, and *Strauder v. West Virginia* (1880) and the Civil Rights Act of 1875 established that blacks could not be excluded from juries on racial grounds, those prohibitions were effectively evaded and ignored by the states in the late nineteenth century.

Native Americans' situation was somewhat different from that of African Americans. Before they could claim that their rights were shielded by the Fourteenth Amendment, Indians had to establish that they were entitled to such constitutional protections. Some states justified continuing discriminatory treatment of Indians based on the argument that Indians owed primary allegiance to their tribes rather than to the United States and were therefore not within U.S. jurisdiction. Since the Fourteenth Amendment only guaranteed citizenship to people who were "subject to the jurisdiction" of the United States, only barred a state from abridging the privileges and immunities of citizens, and only prohibited a state from denying equal protection to people who were "within its jurisdiction," many state officials presumed that Indians were not encompassed in those guarantees. Their interpretation received some support in late 1870 by a report of the Senate Committee on the Judiciary, which concluded that tribal Indians did not become citizens through section 1 of the Fourteenth Amendment.[40] The report was ambiguous about the status of Indians who were not members of any tribe, however. State courts consequently had to grapple with the issue in a variety of contexts.

Determining which Indians might enjoy the protections of the constitutional amendments and civil rights laws was tricky. Some courts looked to section 2 of the Fourteenth Amendment for tangible guidance as to the coverage of section 1. Section 2 excluded "Indians not taxed" from the population count that would determine the number of representatives from each state. A federal court decision in 1877 laid out one approach to drawing a line between Indians who were and were not covered by federal constitutional and statutory guarantees against discrimination. The court ruled that Indians who were taxed by the state of New York were included in the grant of citizenship under the Civil Rights Act. Furthermore, the court found in *United States v. Elm*, Indians in New York whose tribe had "disintegrated," who had abandoned any tribal relationship, who individually held land among whites, and who were taxed by the state were "subject to the jurisdiction" of the United States and therefore were protected by the equal protection clause of the Fourteenth Amendment. The court acknowledged, however, that Indians who still retained their tribal relationship were members of distinct sovereign communities. Such Indians were not subject to U.S. jurisdiction, not made citizens by the Fourteenth Amendment, and not protected by the equal protection clause.[41]

Although most jurisdictions concluded that tribe-affiliated Indians— or "Indians not taxed"—were not citizens through operation of the Civil Rights Act or the Fourteenth Amendment, and most seemed to accept that Indians whose tribes had been dissolved by federal treaties were U.S. citizens, uncertainty about the status of Indians who had individually severed their tribal membership and moved off the tribe's reservation to live among whites continued for over a decade and a half after ratification of the Fourteenth Amendment. In *Standing Bear v. Crook* a federal district court in Omaha ruled that a Ponca Indian, Standing Bear, could withdraw from his tribe and thus from management by federal agents as well as from the requirement that he move to Indian Territory.[42] But that case did not settle the citizenship question as it pertained to Indians who had severed ties with their tribe. Finally, the U.S. Supreme Court weighed in on the issue in 1884. In *Elk v. Wilkins*, the Court held that such Indians were not U.S. citizens, which meant the Fifteenth Amendment did not protect their right to vote and the Civil Rights Act did not apply to them. Moreover, despite the extensive regulation of Indians by the federal and state governments, the vast majority of them were categorized as persons not subject to the jurisdiction of the United States and not within the jurisdiction of the states. Consequently, they were not covered by the broad protective language of the Fourteenth Amendment, leaving them vulnerable to discriminatory state statutes.[43]

INDIAN TESTIMONY, INTERRACIAL MARRIAGE, AND SCHOOL SEGREGATION

Even Indians who were deemed to be eligible for Fourteenth Amendment protections did not consistently find the amendment to be a barrier to discrimination. Indians, like others who were considered to be nonwhite, continued to be subjected to racial discrimination under state law. An example is the continuing prohibition on *Indian testimony* in some states. In *California v. Brady* (1870), the California Supreme Court ruled that the statutory prohibition on Indians, Mongolians, and Chinese people serving as witnesses in cases involving a white party did not violate the Fourteenth Amendment. The court concluded that rules of evidence in state courts—including rules identifying which groups of people were competent to testify truthfully, intelligently, and reliably in court—were matters for the state itself to decide and were not subject to supervision by the federal government. Allowing federal interference in state evidentiary policies, the court said, would seriously undermine the state's sovereignty by depriving it of independent authority over matters within its reserved powers.[44]

Also, in 1867 the Kentucky Supreme Court upheld the state's racially based rules on witness eligibility despite the passage of the federal Civil Rights Act. Kentucky's prohibition on nonwhite witnesses in cases involving a white party had been reissued as recently as 1866. Justice George Robertson wrote the opinion of the court, ruling that the Thirteenth Amendment did not give Congress authority to interfere in domestic matters of the individual states, such as local decisions on rules of evidence in state courts. A concurring opinion by Justice Rufus K. Williams elaborated on the issue of states' rights in a federalist system. As support for his argument that the federal government could not intrude on the state's proper sphere of governance, Williams cited the *New York v. Dibble* case, in which the U.S. Supreme Court ruled that the state of New York retained sovereign power over the persons and property of Indians within its borders, despite the special relationship between Indian tribes and the national government.[45]

After the Civil War some states introduced limited exceptions to their prohibition on Indian testimony. An 1877 Nevada law declared Indians to be competent witnesses for or against any person charged with violating the ban on selling liquor to Indians. The 1866 code of Nebraska, which had previously included a blanket prohibition on Indian testimony in any case with a white party, began allowing Indians to testify under certain circumstances. The language of the law indicated that the bias against Indian testimony continued, however. While the law stated the broad principle that "[e]very human being of sufficient capacity to understand the obligation of an oath, is a competent witness in all cases, civil and criminal," it also specified that incompetent witnesses included not only the racially neutral category "persons of unsound mind" but also the racially specific category "Indians and negroes who appear incapable of receiving just impressions of the facts respecting which they are examined, or of relating them intelligently and truly."[46]

Owing to vague or complex statutory language, an Indian's eligibility to testify sometimes had to be decided by the state supreme court. In an 1880 decision the Nebraska Supreme Court found that the prosecutor had failed to establish the competency of an Indian witness, Holly Scott, who testified against two other Indians charged with murdering a white man on the Winnebago reservation. Chief Justice Samuel Maxwell explained that only people who understood the obligations of an oath were competent witnesses, that it was particularly important to establish such understanding on the part of someone who "was still a member of a tribe," and that the word "oath" meant "an outward pledge given by the person taking it, that his attestation or promise is made under an immediate sense of his responsibility to God." Since the trial record showed Scott did not understand that "God the Great Spirit would be displeased if [he] should tell a lie," the justice concluded that Scott did not "show his capacity to understand the obligations of an oath" and therefore had not demonstrated competence to testify. In contrast, the Supreme Court of Kansas upheld a trial court's decision to allow an Indian to testify even though he did not understand the nature of an oath. Chief Justice Samuel A. Kingman declared it would have been constitutionally inappropriate for the trial court judge to ask the witness whether he believed that he would be punished in the afterlife, but he concluded the Indian was a competent witness because he understood that it was wrong to lie and that he might be hanged as punishment for lying.[47]

Other states legislatively repealed their prohibition on Indians testifying against whites in court. Indiana took an initial (though very limited) step toward eliminating racial discrimination in trial testimony in December 1865, when a statute provided that all persons, "without distinction as to color or blood," were competent witnesses, except for Negroes or mulattoes who came into the state in violation of section 13 of the state constitution. Finally, an 1867 Indiana law provided that every person of competent age could testify as a witness in court. Like Indiana, Texas admitted Indian witnesses in two stages. The 1866 Texas statute that declared the Alabama, Coshattie, and Muscogee Indians subject to Texas laws "as if they were citizens of this State" also granted those Indians the right to testify in any case "involving the right of, injury to, or crime against any of them." Statutory law evidently did not permit Indians to testify in matters involving only non-Indian parties, even though the constitution of 1866 did not completely prohibit Africans and their descendants from testifying. Finally in 1871 the state eliminated the restriction on Indian testimony, declaring broadly that "in the courts of this State there shall be no exclusion of any witness on account of color." North Carolina addressed the Indian witness issue directly, providing in 1861 that "in all cases whatever, Indians shall be competent witnesses." In 1866, the Reconstruction government of Tennessee declared that "persons of African and Indian descent" were competent witnesses in the state's courts. Minnesota repealed its prohibition on Indian testimony in 1868.[48]

Most states did not view Reconstruction-era congressional acts or constitutional amendments as requiring them to dismantle their system of prohibitions on *interracial marriage*. In most state court cases on miscegenation, the prohibitions were upheld in the face of challenges based on the Fourteenth Amendment; courts throughout the South and West ruled that the laws did not violate the equal protection guarantee because they treated people of all races equally. Only eight of the thirty states with such prohibitions repealed them before 1900. During the two decades following passage of the Civil Rights Act of 1866 and ratification of the Fourteenth Amendment, four states—Illinois, Rhode Island, Maine, and Michigan—permanently abolished their prohibitions on interracial marriage. Three states—Pennsylvania, Massachusetts, and Iowa—had already repealed such prohibitions before the Civil War, and eight states had never enacted any such prohibition.[49]

After the Civil War many states instituted new *school segregation* statutes, and some of those statutes included Indians. Because western states contained a higher population of Indians, their school segregation statutes tended to mention Indians explicitly, and the courts customarily upheld the constitutionality of those laws. California's 1870 general school act provided that "[t]he education of children of African descent, and Indian children, shall be provided for in separate schools." In 1874 the Supreme Court of California ruled that that law did not violate the privileges and immunities clause of the newly enacted Fourteenth Amendment because the privilege of attending public school was not a privilege or immunity held by a U.S. citizen. Moreover, the court concluded, being denied the right to attend a particular school did not deprive a person of life, liberty, or property, and excluding nonwhites from schools designated for whites did not violate the equal protection clause as long as the state provided nonwhite children with an alternative public school education "upon equal terms" in another facility.[50] An 1867 Nevada statute provided that "Negroes, Mongolians, and Indians shall not be admitted into the Public Schools, but the Board of Trustees may establish a separate school for their education." Examining the constitutionality of the statute in 1872, the state supreme court ruled that although trustees of a public school could not constitutionally exclude Negroes from the public schools altogether, they could constitutionally send Negroes and whites to separate schools.[51] Other state courts, too, continued to uphold laws permitting or mandating segregated schools after 1868.[52] During the Reconstruction era, several states—including Georgia (1877), Missouri (1865 and 1875), North Carolina (1876), Texas (1866), and West Virginia (1870)—placed their school segregation provisions directly into their state constitutions, making it impossible to mount state constitutional challenges to segregation.

INDIAN SUFFRAGE AFTER THE CIVIL WAR

Furthermore, neither the Fourteenth nor the Fifteenth Amendment effectively guaranteed the *elective franchise* to Indian men who were subject to U.S. jurisdiction. The Fourteenth Amendment was seen by many as giving Congress exclusive power to determine citizenship status.[53] Although by the end of Reconstruction most state officials might have recognized that the federal government had control over citizenship status, they saw no reason to concede authority to define eligibility for the suffrage, which they had long claimed as within the state's prerogative. State courts made it clear that states retained the right to determine who would be entitled to the elective franchise; just because the U.S. Constitution, a federal treaty, or a congressional law recognized someone as a citizen did not mean the state had to allow the person to vote. Since eligibility as an elector was customarily also a requirement for the exercise of other rights and privileges—such as public office holding and jury service—exclusion from the franchise had a broad effect on political rights.

Several jurisdictions that eliminated the whiteness requirement for voting explicitly excluded from the elective franchise all "Indians not taxed." While Texas eliminated its exception for "Indians not taxed" in its 1870 constitution, Maine retained its exclusion. Mississippi added the exclusion in 1868. Several states that joined the Union after 1880 also excluded "Indians not taxed" from the suffrage or included only Indians who had severed tribal relations. Idaho (constitution of 1889), Washington (1889), and New Mexico (1910) are examples of the former; North Dakota (1889) falls in the latter category. Other conditions on the right of suffrage that did not mention Indians nevertheless had a disparate impact on Indians owing to their political status. For example, when South Dakota became a state, its new constitution allowed male citizens to vote and included no explicit exclusion of Native Americans, but a provision that "[n]o person under guardianship shall be qualified to vote at any election" had the effect of excluding many tribal Indians, even if they were citizens. Similar clauses appeared in the constitutions of other states entering the Union at the same time, including North Dakota, Idaho, and Montana.[54] Neither the Fifteenth Amendment nor the Fourteenth Amendment protected Indians against differential treatment on these bases.

A few years after ratification of the Fourteenth Amendment, the California Supreme Court—in a case dealing with the women's suffrage issue—observed that there was a distinction between political and civil rights. While every citizen was entitled to civil rights, only certain classes of citizens were entitled to political privileges such as the right to vote and to hold office.[55] In another case, the same court observed that the Treaty of Guadalupe Hidalgo, which guaranteed U.S. citizenship to those who had been citizens of Mexico, did not mandate that Indians have the right to vote in California even though Indians in the Republic of Mexico had been recognized as citizens and were permitted to vote. Since "[t]he possession of all political rights is not essential to citizenship," California was entitled to decide which among its citizens would be permitted to vote. Therefore, the state's constitution, which limited the suffrage to white male citizens, did not unconstitutionally conflict with the treaty.[56] The court's finding was consistent with the conclusions of the delegates to California's state constitutional convention in 1849. A few delegates, pointing out that the supremacy clause of the U.S. Constitution required adherence to federal treaties, initially expressed concern that a state constitutional provision excluding Indians from the suffrage would violate the guarantees of the treaty. Other delegates, mostly lawyers, assured the others that although the treaty described who were citizens, it remained within the state's prerogative to decide which inhabitants could vote. Subsequently the convention agreed to allow only white male citizens to vote but left room for the legislature to admit some Indians to the right of suffrage in special cases.[57]

In the wake of the Civil War and Reconstruction Amendments, however, most state constitutions did eliminate official racial qualifications for voting. As shown in table 2 below, some of the states that reported the highest population of Indians went further and formally enfranchised some Indians within their borders.[58] These eight states not only included the highest total number of Indians but also contained relatively high numbers of Indians living among whites. As a result, they were more likely than other states to specifically mention Indians in their constitutions.

TABLE 2. State constitutions and the right of suffrage in states with the largest populations of Indians in 1860 (1787–1880)

	Year State Admitted to Union	Year when the state constitution specifically mentioned that all or some Indians could vote	Whiteness requirement for the right of suffrage at the time of the Fifteenth Amendment
California	1850	1849*	Yes
Minnesota	1858	1857**	No
Michigan	1837	1850	Yes
Kansas	1861		Yes
Oregon	1859		Yes
New York	1788		No
Wisconsin	1848	1848	Yes
North Carolina	1789		Yes

*California's 1849 constitution, which went into effect when the state was admitted to the Union the following year, did not explicitly grant Indians suffrage but authorized the legislature to enfranchise Indians at its discretion.

**Minnesota's constitution went into effect in 1858, with statehood.

Throughout the period from 1790 to 1880, whatever abstract principles underlay the federal government's Indian policies, it was actions on the state level that established what it would mean in practice for Indians to be incorporated into American society. In most states, the actuality was that incorporation meant second-class status. Racially discriminatory statutes undergirded assimilated Indians' low position. Even the addition of an equal protection guarantee to the Constitution did not hinder the employment of such laws.

Although explicit racial barriers to suffrage rights were abolished after the Civil War in new and revised state constitutions or by operation of the Fifteenth Amendment, in practice various tactics prevented most African American and Native American men from voting. As has been described by other scholars, African Americans were effectively disfranchised in the late nineteenth century through the use of fraud and intimidation, combined with facially race-neutral statutory and constitutional conditions for voting, such as poll taxes, literacy tests, and grandfather clauses.[59] Similar devices were also applied to Indians who were U.S. citizens.[60]

Thus, despite the new civil rights laws and Reconstruction amendments to the U.S. Constitution, many states continued to discriminate against

Indians on the basis of race in the realms of politics, court trials, education, and marriage. Throughout the rest of the nineteenth century and well into the twentieth, Indians were commonly excluded from voting privileges, public office, jury pools, trial witness lists, all-white schools, and interracial marriages. Incorporating Indians into American society, it turned out, did not mean according them equal status or granting them access to all the privileges of full membership. Indians who had once been members of nations lying outside state jurisdiction came to be treated as inferior racial minorities within state communities. How white leaders rationalized differential treatment of Indians is the subject of the next chapter, which takes an in-depth look at nineteenth-century constitutional convention discussions of Indian voting rights and militia duties in two midwestern states.

CHAPTER FIVE

Debating Race, Culture, and Political Status

∾

The statutes described in the preceding chapter provide irrefutable evidence of discrimination against Native Americans. However, examining the language of the laws alone does not reveal white Americans' reasons for treating Indians differently from whites. This chapter examines the mentality that underlay decisions about Indians' legal rights, concentrating especially on the issue of race. Specifically, the chapter analyzes debates about Indians in the four constitutional conventions held in Michigan and Minnesota between 1835 and 1867. The convention debates provide considerable information about how the delegates viewed Indians, how they understood the issue of race, and how they went about defining which Indians were qualified for inclusion in the state community. Since most of the discriminatory laws described in the preceding chapter either excluded Native Americans from certain rights or exempted them from civic obligations, this study examines one issue in each category: the analysis centers primarily on discussions about qualifications for the elective franchise and also looks at debates about eligibility for service in the militia.

The convention debates in Michigan (admitted as a state in 1837) and Minnesota (admitted in 1858) provide good examples of the language used to argue for and against Indian suffrage and militia duty. A number of Indian tribes inhabited the region. The Santee Sioux (Dakotas[1]) were the four eastern-most bands of the seven-tribe Sioux confederation: the Sissetons and Wahpatons (known as the upper tribes, because of their position on the Minnesota River) and the Wahpekutes and Mdewakantons (the lower tribes). Also speaking a Siouan dialect in the region were the Winnebagos (Ho-Chunks). The Chippewas (Ojibwes), an Algonquian tribe, occupied territory to the north and east of the Santee Sioux. They were allied with two other Algonquian tribes in the area, the Ottawas and the Potawatomis; this "Council of Three Fires" often clashed with the

Sioux (and also with the Iroquois to the east). In the Great Lakes region, these Indian tribes developed a fur-trading relationship with the French during the seventeenth century and subsequently also traded furs with the British and then the Americans. The U.S.-sponsored Treaty of Prairie du Chien (1825) drew a boundary line between the Chippewa and Sioux territories. Federal treaties during this era also obtained Indian cessions of large tracts of land, concentrated Indians on a small portion of their former lands, and removed whole tribes to the west. By 1860 Chippewa, Potawatomi, and Ottawa Indians had relinquished most of their Michigan land to the United States in treaties of 1819, 1821, and 1836. Meanwhile, in Minnesota the Santee Sioux had ceded almost all their land in 1851 and 1858, the Winnebagos lost land in an 1855 treaty, and the Chippewas gave up territory in several treaties, most notably in 1837, 1854, and 1855.[2]

Despite all the land cessions, by the mid-nineteenth century, both Michigan and Minnesota still had a relatively large population of Indians, ranking third and second, respectively, among all the states reported in the census of 1860, the first census that enumerated Indians as a separate group. The 1860 census reported 6,172 "civilized" Indians and 7,777 other ("unenumerated") Indians living in Michigan, whereas 2,369 civilized Indians and 17,900 other Indians were recorded in Minnesota.[3] The treaties did not always articulate clearly what status should be accorded to these Indians who continued to live in increasingly white-dominated Michigan and Minnesota. However, one of the treaties allowed individual Indians from the Sisseton and Wahpaton bands of the Sioux in Minnesota to become U.S. citizens if they dissolved their tribal connection and moved off the reservation, thus raising the issue of what rights the state would grant them.[4] To those Indians, and potentially to a select few others who satisfied certain state criteria, the leadership of Michigan and Minnesota offered a form of membership in the political community. Suffrage was the primary privilege offered to those Indians, but in both states it was offered only after extensive debate about the Indians' qualifications.

Although there are a number of fine published studies of the history of Michigan and Minnesota, as well as on the history of Indians in the Midwest, the coverage of Indians in constitutional convention debates has received no focused scholarly attention.[5] Yet the debates are very revealing of white attitudes. As the debates in Michigan and Minnesota illustrate, the question of which Native Americans should be offered the privileges held by European Americans raised complicated issues of race, culture, political status, tribal sovereignty, and the nature of citizenship in the United

States. A convention delegate's stance on Indians was affected by such factors as whether he viewed Indian tribes as constituting separate nations, whether he saw Indians as prepared to participate in the political system, and whether he categorized Indians as white or nonwhite. A man's position was also usually strongly affected by his party affiliation. As a general rule, Jeffersonians (during the early national period) and Democrats (during the antebellum and Reconstruction eras) were more likely than Federalists, Whigs, Know-Nothings, and Republicans to support extending the right to vote to aliens but less likely to support enfranchisement of African Americans.[6] American Indians were variously seen as analogous to aliens, African Americans, or European Americans; how a delegate classified Indians affected his judgment as to what rights they should have.

Delegates to the conventions considered not only whether Indians were "white" but also whether they could plausibly be a part of the European-American community and whether they shared its "civilized" culture. The primary focus of debate shifted over time. Antebellum debates centered primarily on racial differences. "Race" clearly meant more than just color and other physical characteristics, however. The convention delegates' concept of race often enfolded cultural factors. The link between race and culture grew out of a change in white intellectuals' perspective on race. In the early nineteenth century, behavioral characteristics that had once been thought malleable came to be viewed as intrinsically tied to race. Consequently, it was natural that racial and cultural factors would be intertwined in antebellum constitutional convention debates. Peggy Pascoe argues that to nineteenth-century "racialists," "the important point was not that biology determined culture (indeed, the split between the two was only dimly perceived), but that race, understood as an indivisible essence that included not only biology but also culture, morality, and intelligence, was a compellingly significant factor in history and society."[7] The way discussions of race were connected to references to culture in the antebellum Michigan and Minnesota debates is consistent with Pascoe's characterization of nineteenth-century racialist ideology.

In the Michigan convention held after the Civil War, however, delegates said little about race in the course of their discussion of Indian suffrage and militia service. Both Michigan and Minnesota had fought on the side of the Union during the Civil War. After the war, Republicans from victorious Union states pressed for national constitutional protections against racial discrimination in the granting of political privileges. Perhaps it was natural, therefore, that when people in Michigan and Minnesota discussed the rights of Indians in the postwar period, they would not focus on racial difference. Nevertheless, neither state was willing to open the doors to full political participation by all Indians. It seems evident, therefore, that racialist concerns had not disappeared, but they were no longer determinative of Indians' official position under state law. Instead of focusing on race, political leaders in the two states devoted increased attention to Indians' political status as defined by federal laws and treaties. This chapter examines the rhetoric used to analyze the position of Indians in the state community, addressing particularly the ways in which the delegates' concerns, and their way of expressing those concerns, changed over time from a focus on race to a concentration on status.

DEBATING RACE IN ANTEBELLUM MICHIGAN

In 1835 most delegates to the constitutional convention in Michigan supported the disfranchisement of blacks, which meant that the suffrage clause in the state constitution would make whiteness a necessary qualification for voting. More hotly debated were the criteria for classifying someone as white and the question of which categories of white people should be allowed to vote. Discussion of the suffrage provision focused primarily on the latter question, especially on the question of whether a state could allow noncitizen inhabitants to vote and, if so, whether Michigan should implement alien suffrage as a matter of policy. Some delegates questioned whether, given exclusive federal power over naturalization, the state had the authority to extend the franchise, which was normally regarded as a privilege of citizenship, to noncitizens, but after extensive discussion of the subject the majority decided that it was up to the state to decide who qualified as electors.[8] Michigan's interest in extending the suffrage to noncitizens was understandable, since the state was eager to attract settlers. The issue of Indian suffrage, like that of alien suffrage, focused on analysis of whether or not Indians were legitimately part of the civil society of Michigan who had a stake in the community and were knowledgeable enough to participate in elections; but unlike the discussion of aliens, the debate over Indians addressed the question of whether they were "white" and whether they were civilized enough to vote.

When delegate Ross Wilkins proposed deleting the word "white" from the draft suffrage provision in order to allow blacks and Indians to vote, hostility to the concept of black enfranchisement led to the prompt defeat of the motion. Sympathy for Indian suffrage then led John McDonnell to seek alternative language that would allow some Indians to vote. It apparently was clear that not all Indians should be eligible for the franchise; the problem was how to define which Indians could vote. Traces of an argument that would later become central are evident in McDonnell's attempt to identify Indians who were part of Michigan society and over whom the state exercised authority, using the proxy of tax payment. He suggested explicitly including "Indians paying a State, County or Township tax" in the "white male inhabitants" who were eligible to vote. The delegates rejected this approach, partly because of discomfort with the idea of injecting into the constitution any tax-based qualification for suffrage—even one that screened for jurisdictional authority rather than financial status—at a time when property qualifications were being abolished across the country and when new states could not afford to deter possible new immigrants of any economic class.[9]

The delegates' larger concern with McDonnell's proposal was that it did not fit their racial views. The president of the convention, John Biddle, questioned McDonnell's motion on the ground that it presumed Indians were included in the word "white." To clarify the issue, he inquired whether McDonnell meant that Indians could be regarded as a subset of "white male inhabitants." McDonnell answered in the affirmative, explaining that "the word white was used in contradistinction to the black alone, and though the Indian was copper-colored, he was not to be classed among the latter." In other words, people who were not "black" were "white." Other delegates took issue with the idea that all Indians were white. They seemed more comfortable with the formulation of John Norvell, who explained that if a descendent of Indians had any white ancestors, he was "entitled to be treated as a white man." In response to the objections raised, McDonnell proposed a new amendment that offered privileges to Indians who had some white parentage. He suggested adding a proviso "that nothing herein contained shall be so construed as to exclude such halfbreed Indians as may be domiciliated and have fixed abodes within said state, and claiming to be citizens thereof," but this amendment, too, was rejected.[10]

Later in the convention, McDonnell again stepped forward to propose language giving Indians certain political rights. This time he conceded that Indians—even Indians of mixed racial lineage—would not be treated as a subset of the category "white"; furthermore, he also took into account a point raised earlier by John R. Williams, who had expressed willingness to support enfranchisement of Indians whose mode of living was like that of whites. McDonnell moved to amend the suffrage section by adding that "Indians who are, in their habits and customs, domiciliated according to the usages of the white population, and claiming to be citizens of the United States, shall enjoy the civil and political rights, privileges, and capacities of the white inhabitants of the state." Convention delegates declined to include the proposed language in the final document, however; the 1835 constitution made no reference to Indians in the paragraph on qualifications of electors.[11]

A few years after the convention, the legislature took an important step toward bringing Michigan Indians into the state's commercial and legal systems by making them eligible to sue and be sued in court beginning in 1841. Since many of Michigan's antebellum settlers came from New York, where state officials presumed that their authority to regulate Indians was well established, it is not surprising that during its first few years of statehood Michigan enacted Indian legislation similar to New York's.[12] The 1841 statute made it safer for whites to sell goods to Indians on credit, knowing that they would have judicial recourse if the debts were not repaid. Since the 1836 federal treaty with the Ottawas and Chippewas had set aside $300,000 to cover Indians' debts, whites could be confident that there would be funds available to repay loans. A decade after enactment of the statute, a joint resolution by the state senate and house of representatives directed at the state's U.S. congressmen, noting Indian liability for debts under the law, requested that funds still remaining after the payment of pre-treaty debts be applied to debts contracted with whites after the treaty was signed.[13] While avoiding the citizenship label, Michigan officials continued their effort to incorporate Indians—or at least selected Indians—into the state community.

That the people of Michigan continued to view formal citizenship status as a federal matter is indicated by a joint resolution adopted by the state senate and house in 1844. Apparently in response to a petition from a group of Ottawa Indians who lived along Lake Michigan, the legislature instructed the Michigan senators and representatives in Congress to try to obtain citizenship rights for those Indians.[14] Six years later, constitutional convention delegates described their understanding of the line between state and federal authority on citizenship. Ebenezer Raynale asserted that "[n]o gentleman will deny our right to decide who shall be electors in our own State." Joseph R. Williams noted that, like Michigan, other new states in the region, such as Wisconsin and Illinois, had asserted the right to determine liberally who was eligible to vote in the state without feeling bound to limit the franchise to "citizens," and Congress had not regarded such state decisions as inconsistent with its exclusive constitutional power to enact uniform laws of naturalization. As Williams explained, "[w]e make men electors within our own borders—not citizens beyond our borders. We make them electors for State purposes, not citizens for national purposes."[15]

When delegates met in 1850 to revise the state's constitution, they once again debated the issue of Indian suffrage. Despite petitions from "sundry civilized Indians, praying the rights of American citizenship," the franchise provision drafted by the committee on the elective franchise made no mention of Indians. In the end, however, delegates to the convention took it upon themselves to modify the draft so as to grant the most important political right, suffrage, to "every civilized male inhabitant of Indian descent, a native of the United States and not a member of any tribe." The initial motion proposing addition of the language on suffrage came from William Norman McLeod, who categorized such men as "white to all intents and purposes, except they had descent from Indian parents." Although his proposed amendment made no explicit reference to different racial categories among Indians, McLeod's use of the phrase "inhabitant of Indian descent" rather than "Indian inhabitant" might have implied that he intended the clause to apply only to men who had some white ancestry. Indeed, McLeod himself specified that his comments referred to the mixed-race sons of intermarriage between "the French and Indian races" in the northern regions of the state. Thus, he appeared to have been presuming that "civilized" Indians had at least one white parent, most often a trader father. In any case, he pointed out that such Métis men encountered difficulties at election time. Their rights had been discussed "at almost every meeting of our boards of inspectors"; while some boards had allowed those Indians to vote, others did not. In some counties civilized men of Indian descent even served as justices of the peace, judges, and other positions of "trust and honor," he observed. McLeod's proposed amendment was adopted without much debate. Although civilized Indians were described as "white to all intents and purposes," however, the fact that they had to be mentioned specifically in the suffrage provision (which already allowed all "white" men to vote) meant that in fact they were not legally presumed to be included in the term "white."[16]

Continuing ambivalence about the worthiness of Indians to take on certain responsibilities, as well as the relevance of racial classification in determining Indians' position under the law, is evidenced in the discussion of militia service and the right to bear arms. The original draft of the militia provision restricted service to "able bodied white male citizens." When Dewitt C. Leach moved to delete the word "white," the amendment was not approved. The fact that "white" was presumed not to include Indians was suggested by the related debate on the bill of rights provision regarding the right to bear arms. The original draft provided that "[e]very person has a right to bear arms for the defence of himself and the State." Joseph H. Bagg moved that the right be limited to "white" people. He said his proposal was motivated by the general principle that although nonwhite people should be eligible for various "benefits and charity," he did not want to "let them come into our civil, political, social, conjugal or connubial relations." To make it clearer which groups he excluded from the category "white," he explained more specifically that "[c]olored people, negroes and Indians should not be allowed to bear arms with us. It will be made a pretext with them to get into other circles. I am for keeping them where they are, believing them to be a species at least one link beneath us. The moment you let them into the political circle, you open the social and every other circle." He concluded, "I trust the Convention will never leave out the word 'white' in the organic law." Jerry G. Cornell objected that depriving a man of the right to bear arms "would take away his natural rights, the right of self-defence, which has never been given up." McLeod responded more personally, noting acidly, "I know many, both among the Indians and negroes, who, in point of intelligence, virtue and personal appearance, in all that elevates the man above the brute, are at least equal to the delegate from Wayne" (i.e., Bagg). After Bagg's amendment was subsequently voted down, he followed up by proposing the deletion of the words "and the State." It was one thing to allow nonwhite individuals to own weapons to defend themselves and their property, but quite another thing to suggest that they would be expected to help defend the state. Bagg was "opposed to obliging them to do military duty, and thus insinuate themselves among us." The convention rejected Bagg's second amendment. The final draft of the constitution left the right to bear arms in broad language, without any racial qualification, but it limited the militia obligation to white men.[17]

Left unstated publicly during the convention debates were the delegates' personal political and economic interests that often affected the positions they took on various issues, especially on Indian suffrage. A delegate who had a large number of potential Indian voters in his jurisdiction, one who wanted Indian territory to be part of the Michigan land market and the state's tax base, one who wanted access to sources of copper or timber on Indian territory, one to whom Indians owed money, or one who sought to profit from allocating money and provisions as a federally appointed Indian agent might find that his position on Indian suffrage was affected by more than just his views on the race and culture of Indians. For example, delegate McLeod, who initially proposed the suffrage amendment, was from Mackinac County, which, according to the 1860 census, had the second largest population of Indians among the sixty-two counties in Michigan. McLeod thus might have benefited politically from the position he took in the convention. More generally, individual ownership of land was one of the main criteria for measuring whether an Indian was "civilized," yet as historian Charles E. Cleland has pointed out, whenever Michigan Indians owned individual allotments of land they tended to lose that land to white speculators, settlers, and loggers.[18] Pressure to make Indian territory available for white use and settlement—based on a continuation of the colonial-era assumption that productive whites had the right to take over underdeveloped land—played an important role in delegates' decisions regarding the political and legal status of Indians, as is discussed further in chapters 6 and 7. For purposes of this section, the rhetorical use of racial language as the foundation of arguments for or against Indian rights is of most interest, but it must be kept in mind that delegates were influenced by factors other than those explicitly expressed during the convention.

DEBATING RACE IN ANTEBELLUM MINNESOTA

Racial discourse played an even more visible role in the Minnesota constitutional conventions, which took place just a few years after the Kansas-Nebraska Act controversy, the violence of "bleeding Kansas," and the formation of a new political party committed to the ideal of protecting the territories as free soil. The *Dred Scott* decision had been issued just months before the Minnesota convention was to meet in the summer of 1857, further heating up the political environment. As a result, tensions between the Republicans and Democrats were so powerful that elected delegates from the two parties were unable to meet together. Instead, they held separate conventions to draft a constitution for the new state. In the Republican convention the initial draft provision prepared by the committee on the elective franchise restricted the suffrage to white males and did not mention Indians.[19] In contrast, the committee draft in the Democratic convention included among legal voters both white men and Indians who had "adopted the customs and habits of civilization."[20] By October the parties and the voters of Minnesota had agreed on a constitution that, on the issue of suffrage, was closer to the Democrats' draft.

The Republicans hotly debated the issue of whether or not to include the whiteness requirement for the right to vote; in fact, as delegate Frank Mantor observed, discussion of that question caused the most "feeling and anxiety" in the convention. Much of the suffrage debate focused on the question of whether blacks and Indians should have the same rights or be treated differently. A number of Republican delegates simply believed that there should be no racial qualifications for voting and that blacks and Indians alike should be enfranchised. In the end, however, the majority of Republican delegates were reluctant to provide for black enfranchisement. Their proposed compromise position was to submit the question as a referendum to the legal voters of Minnesota, allowing them to decide whether or not to delete the whiteness qualification. Meanwhile, there was no serious debate in the Democratic convention about whether blacks in Minnesota should be enfranchised, and the Democrats' discussion on the issue of Indian suffrage was not bundled with arguments about black enfranchisement. While the Republicans tended to see the racial debate about blacks' political rights as relevant to the voting rights of Indians, most Democrats did not see a decision on black suffrage as being germane to the issue of Indian suffrage. Instead, the Democratic delegates were more likely to argue about whether Indians should be treated the same as white foreigners, who were to be allowed to vote if they had declared their intention to become citizens.[21]

Although the tenor of the debate on the "whiteness" requirement for the suffrage differed in the two conventions, Democrats and Republicans actually shared a common understanding regarding Indians. To delegates from both parties, assessing the whiteness of individual Indians required a cultural judgment as well as a racial one. This concept was expressed most directly during the conventions by Joseph R. Brown, a prominent fur trader who was married to a Sioux woman, and Henry Sibley, an active fur trader and treaty negotiator. During the debate about Indian suffrage, Brown observed that among Minnesota's Indians were many who were "thoroughly in their manners and feelings, white men." If "manners and feelings" could make someone "white," then clearly whiteness was about more than color. In connection with discussion of the militia provision, Sibley urged the delegates to clarify the ambiguous word "white" by making explicit that there were cultural, as well as biological, criteria for membership in the "whiteness" category. He proposed adding to the constitution a provision that "the word white where it occurs in this section, shall be construed to include those persons of pure and mixed Indian and white blood who have adopted the customs and manners of the whites." The effect of Sibley's definition, which he was willing to apply to the entire constitution, would have been to classify as white every person of Indian descent who was perceived as living according to white "customs and manners," even if he or she had no white ancestors at all.[22] Sibley did not address the point, but he presumably would have excluded from the "white" category any person of Indian descent who also had African ancestors, even if he or she also had white ancestors.[23] In any case, other delegates would not accept racial classification that was entirely independent of color, but they did agree that with regard to Indians, culture was one marker of race.

What were considered to be the cultural measures of whiteness? Republican delegate S. A. D. Balcombe was willing to include in the political community those Indians who owned property, could read and write, and were able to understand political issues. Republican Thomas Foster elaborated, recommending Indians he knew who owned large tracts of land and "magnificent" homes and who were "high-minded" men of the "highest culture." Democrat Charles E. Flandrau pointed out that the Sioux Indian community represented by those who petitioned the convention satisfied important criteria of civilized (i.e., white) men: they had developed a regular system for governing themselves and for transacting business, they could read and write, they had built a church, and they were intelligent, educated men.[24] Although Republicans and Democrats agreed on the general indicators of civilized life, they were not entirely confident that they could articulate a clear, enforceable line between civilized Indians who should be classified as white and uncivilized Indians who should be treated as nonwhite. Delegates' uncertainties about whether their definition could be subject to abuse and lead to election fraud were well conveyed by lawyer Thomas Wilson, who expressed concern about voting qualifications that were based on an assessment of how "civilized" a prospective voter was. Specifically, he worried about "[t]his putting a coat upon one Indian, and when he has voted, stripping it off and putting it on another, and thus running them up to the polls by hundreds."[25] Apparently it was too easy to feign whiteness. Minnesotans encountered this problem of identifying who was civilized in another context as well. Historian Gary Anderson points out that because Indian agents selectively distributed annuities and food only to Indians who were adopting white customs, many Sioux men cut their hair and began wearing white clothing; yet some of those men periodically changed back into traditional Sioux attire in order to participate in Sioux religious and cultural activities, indicating the incomplete nature of their conversion.[26] When performing whiteness brought tangible benefits, visual clues could not necessarily be trusted as indicators of genuine commitment to civilized living.

Because it was so tricky to decide who was civilized, some proposals intended to prevent fraud included not only cultural criteria but also status conditions, such as tribal affiliation, that correlated with the standards of civilization but were deemed easier to assess than purely cultural factors. Proposals by Republicans Lewis McKune and Amos Coggswell suggested admitting to the suffrage only Indians who satisfied basic cultural criteria and who also rejected tribal membership and renounced government annuities.[27] Most Democrats did not see the necessity of such requirements, however. Charles E. Flandrau noted that an Indian could be well qualified to vote even if he received an annuity, while Joseph Brown pointed out that many Indians depended upon the annuity payments for their subsistence.[28] To some extent, party concerns and economic interests of the delegates underlay this discussion of Indian suffrage. A number of major fur traders who dealt regularly with Sioux Indians, including delegates Henry Sibley, Joseph Rolette, and Joseph R. Brown, were Democrats. Given their close ties with trading Indians and the support they received from those Indians, it was natural that Sibley, Brown, and other party members would support acculturated Indians' right to vote in the new state.[29] Furthermore, since maintaining Indians' right to annuities was essential to preserving Indian resources for paying debts to fur traders, the trader delegates clearly had a strong self-interest in protecting Indian annuity rights.[30]

What is particularly notable about the references to tribal relations and annuities is that they were typically framed as ways of further measuring the extent to which individual Indians lived like whites. Only one delegate, Lafayette Emmett—the attorney general of the Minnesota Territory objected to the enfranchisement of reservation Indians on the ground that they were outside the state's jurisdiction and not subject to state taxes. Any man who "pays nothing for the support of our government," he asserted, "has no right to vote" because "[t]axation and the elective franchise ought always to go together."[31] Emmett's line of reasoning would become the primary argument against Indian suffrage after the Civil War. In the prewar period, however, constitutional convention delegates focused more on racial discourse, though it was a complicated racial discourse that enveloped cultural and status factors as well as questions of color. Given the climate of 1857, it was natural that the delegates would view the Indian question through the lens of race, even framing cultural and status arguments in terms of race or as elements of racial difference.

For most Democrats and Republicans in antebellum Minnesota, cultural issues pertaining to Indians were typically considered only in conjunction with race. This was clearest when delegates distinguished between "mixed blood" and "full blood" Indians in their analysis. For example, the distinction was repeatedly made when delegates described past behavior or entitlements of Indians that warranted suffrage. Democrat George L. Becker maintained that in deciding who would enjoy the rights of citizenship, it would be "monstrous" to treat "half-breed" Indians differently from foreigners, considering that many such Indians had fought to help protect white settlements in Minnesota and had rescued whites who had been captured by hostile Indians.[32] Republican Foster noted that many "half-breeds" were already voting in territorial elections, and "it would be great injustice to that class of people, after having enjoyed the privilege of voting for so long a time, to refuse them that privilege, now or hereafter, simply because we cannot extend to another race, against whom people have great prejudices, the same privilege."[33] Republican B. F. Messer pointed out that there were hundreds of "halfbreeds" in the territory years before any significant white settlement, and such people should not be disfranchised.[34] Democratic delegate Emmett argued that "if a person of mixed blood is a civilized member of society, he should be allowed to participate in the privileges of citizenship, whether he holds tribal relations or not" (presuming that he did not live on a reservation).[35]

Even more emphatically, delegates distinguished between "mixed blood" and "full blood" Indians when they evaluated the evidence that should be required to prove that an Indian was acculturated enough for the franchise. Republicans and Democrats alike perceived that most civilized Indians had some white ancestry. Despite his earlier proposed amendment that made no distinction between "full blood" and "mixed blood" Indians, Henry Sibley was among those who agreed that most civilized Indians were of "mixed blood."[36] Some delegates' views of "mixed bloods" were certainly influenced by their particularly close connections with that portion of Sioux society; those connections were both economic and biological—as in the case of Joseph Brown and Henry Sibley, both of whom had children with Sioux women.[37] Close links to "mixed bloods" reinforced a desire to draw them away from reservations and into white society.[38] But the delegates were not just influenced by their own personal relationships. Their presumption that white "blood" conveyed a natural propensity for civilization was a common view in antebellum America. As Theda Perdue points out in her study of "mixed-blood" Indians of the early South, Americans tended to presume people with both white and Indian ancestry to be genetically and culturally superior to (i.e., more civilized than) those who were solely of Indian descent and thus presumed them more capable of conducting themselves like white people. Consequently, compared to "full bloods," "mixed bloods" could be offered more privileges and required fewer safeguards and prerequisites.[39]

In its elective franchise provision, the final constitution reflected Minnesotans' understanding of such racial distinctions by imposing different requirements on "full blood" and "mixed blood" Indians, as well as different requirements for white foreigners and Indians. Men who had mixed white and Indian ancestry merely had to have "adopted the customs and habits of civilization" in order to vote, whereas those who were solely of Indian ancestry enjoyed the elective franchise only if they had "adopted the language, customs and habits of civilization" and if they had obtained a certificate from a district court stating that they were "capable of enjoying the rights of citizenship within the State." The 1857 constitution contained no requirement that the Indians have severed relations with their tribe, nor that they forego annuities from the federal government. Foreign white males only had to declare their intention to become citizens in order to be entitled to vote, whereas white male citizens had the right to vote without qualifications or conditions beyond age and residence.[40]

Closely tied to the suffrage debate in the Minnesota convention of 1857 was discussion about another duty and privilege of citizenship: service in the militia. On this issue, too, racial discussion predominated. In the Democratic convention, the initial report of the committee on the militia proposed that the state militia consist of "all free, able-bodied male persons" who met the residence and age requirements, "Negroes and Mulattoes excepted." Convention delegates quickly agreed with Michael E. Ames's motion to insert the qualification that only "white" males be part of the militia, but the ensuing complex discussion about race, culture, and citizenship left the delegates stymied about how to resolve the issue of militia service.

Henry N. Setzer's inquiry about whether "Indian half breeds" would be included under the word "white" in Ames's motion led to another discussion about how Indians were racially classified. Ames responded that he thought "they would legally be included under the word 'white'" and that therefore mixed blood Indians would be eligible for militia service even if the word "white" were inserted into the state's constitution. But Charles E. Flandrau (a future state supreme court judge), Henry Sibley, and B. B. Meeker expressed concern that the use of the word "white," as judicially interpreted, would have the undesirable effect of disqualifying from militia service "worthy" and "valuable" men of mixed Indian and white descent, men who had done "[t]he greatest portion of the fighting upon the part of the Territory lying on the frontier." In response to Flandrau's, Meeker's, and Sibley's concerns, Ames conceded that "the decisions of the Courts have not, by any means, been uniform in their construction of the word 'white,' as applied to persons of mixed white and Indian blood." He agreed to lawyer George L. Becker's suggestion that the delegates delete the word "white" in the militia provision and substitute the word "citizens" for the word "persons," which led to a debate over whether Indians were or could be citizens. Uncertainty on the issue among the delegates led Becker to suggest that they replace the word "citizens" with a provision that would include in the militia all male inhabitants who were qualified to vote. Explicitly tying militia service to the suffrage also did not satisfy the majority of delegates, however. In the end, they settled on a constitution that simply left it up to the legislature to pass laws relating to the militia "as may be deemed necessary."[41]

The Civil War broke out four years after Minnesota's constitutional convention. The war years were a time of great tension between whites and Indians in Minnesota. The most significant developments in Indian-white relations during the early 1860s, focused on in contemporary accounts and more recent histories alike, were the stepped-up efforts to confine Minnesota's Indians to reservations, the increased availability of land to white settlers as a result of Indian cessions of nearly all of the land in the state between 1851 and 1863, the Santee Sioux conflict that erupted in 1862, and the resulting expulsion of most Sioux—as well as Winnebagos—from the state.[42] The rhetoric of the delegates reveals their racist thinking to some extent, but their actions outside the convention convey even more unambiguously how they really viewed the American Indians. Although convention delegates in Minnesota supported the idea of including some Indians in the European-American community—even to the extent of offering voting rights—their preferred approach to Indians was expulsion, echoing the old colonial English policy of displacing rather than incorporating Indians.[43]

Race, Culture, and Political Status

Michigan held a third constitutional convention two years after the end of the Civil War. Although the voters ultimately rejected the draft constitution, the record of the proceedings illustrates shifts in the focus of debate regarding Indian suffrage. Most notably, fitting the climate and the political realities of postwar America, the rhetoric on Indian issues in the convention shifted away from race toward more of a focus on culture and, especially, status. Although delegates' continued use of the term "whites" in a way that clearly distinguished that group from "Indians" makes it clear that they did not universally classify Indians as white, their arguments did not concentrate on race. They had adjusted to new political realities. In the immediate post–Civil War environment, convention delegates in a Republican state were naturally much less likely than before the war to discuss official racial classifications in an overt way. The language of debate in 1867 fit prevailing northern postwar political values. Instead of focusing on racial distinctions between Indians and whites, delegates concentrated on issues of Indians' formal status under federal law, which they saw as increasingly pertinent to their own concern about the scope of state authority over Indians.

Convention delegates agreed that, given the provisions of the recently enacted Civil Rights Act and the pending Fourteenth Amendment, it was time to delete the "whiteness" requirement from the suffrage provision in the constitution, thus allowing black men to vote. Some delegates argued that the same principles warranting black male suffrage also mandated Indian enfranchisement. Speaking most directly to the issue, Jonathan Shearer reminded the delegates of the fundamental American principles of liberty and equal justice to all. Delegates Jacob Van Valkenburgh, William S. Farmer, Thaddeus G. Smith, and P. Dean Warner warned that categorically excluding Indians from the franchise, while allowing black and white men to vote, or describing qualifying tests (such as literacy or English language competency) that were applied only to Indians and not "to other races in the community," would constitute unfair "class legislation" and would be making "invidious distinctions" based on race. It would be best not to have any distinctions with regard to color in the state's constitution, they said. Supporters like Leach and Omar D. Conger observed that hundreds of Indians had already been voting for seventeen years, which had not harmed the political system. Conger, Van Valkenburgh, Shearer, and Smith also pointed out that the Indians were the original owners of the soil in Michigan and therefore were entitled to some rights in the state.

Furthermore, Conger and John Q. McKernan argued, Indians should have the right to vote because many of them had served as "first-rate" soldiers for the Union in the Civil War.[44]

Opponents of broad Indian suffrage rejected the rights arguments on various grounds. The main counterarguments relied on familiar assertions that Indians should not enjoy the franchise because they were not equal to whites or blacks in degree of civilization or because they were not equally attached to the Michigan or U.S. government owing to their tribal allegiance. Norris revealed his discomfort with the whole notion of equality when he warned that conceding political equality to Indians also conceded social equality to them. Several delegates went beyond those cultural and political arguments to criticize the notion of Indian "rights" and to mock the "poor Indian" arguments made by others. Henry H. Coolidge disagreed with the contention that whites owed Indians the right to vote because of how whites had treated Indians in the past. He said it did not make sense to enfranchise Indians in order to compensate them for past seizures of land. Besides, he said, whites had not taken anything that the Indians rightfully claimed. He reverted back to the old colonial-era justification for settlement of land in the Americas: "I have never felt very much the force of the argument that because there were a few Indians on this great continent, therefore they were the rightful owners of all the land; land to which they never attached a particle of value, except for the game that they found in the forests." In other words, since Indians were not really using the land much before the arrival of whites, they could not claim to be its rightful owners.[45]

Most delegates took neither of the extreme positions: few rejected all Indian rights outright, and only a handful endorsed the notion—put forward by the subcommittee on elections—that all male Indians should enjoy the suffrage. Most were comfortable with the concept of enfranchising some Indians, but there was considerable debate about how to define which Indians should be allowed to vote. The delegates split on whether the subcommittee's proposed Indian suffrage provision—which suggested enfranchising "[a]ll male Indians, natives of the United States"—should be more restrictive or should be eliminated completely. To restrict the provision, various delegates proposed requiring that Indian voters must be "civilized," that they be capable of speaking English, that they must not be "members of any tribe," and that they must not receive an annuity from the federal government. The first two restrictions focused on cultural issues, while the last two addressed concerns about Indians' political status. Although the delegates argued heatedly during the convention, they in fact agreed on the underlying premises of state Indian policy.

Those who argued that all or some Indians in the state should be allowed to vote because they were civilized used familiar criteria for measuring degree of civilization. They maintained that Indians had certain positive personal characteristics (intelligence, industriousness, honesty, virtue) that made them worthy of the vote and pointed to the civilized style of living (dressing like whites, living in houses, sleeping on beds, eating at tables, sitting on chairs, and cultivating crops on farms) exhibited by Michigan Indians.[46] It was further argued that enfranchisement of Indians would "stimulate them to further efforts in civilization" and would elevate their moral condition.[47] Those who opposed broad Indian enfranchisement on the ground that some or all Michigan Indians were "uncivilized" attributed to them a litany of negative and threatening characteristics (degraded, sullen, treacherous, beastly), primitive style of life (that they were "vagabonds" who roamed "as savages through the woods," had "no particular home," and were "clad in sheep-skins and goat-skins"), eagerness to sell their votes in exchange for whiskey, and inability to vote responsibly because of limited English language capability and ignorance of political issues. Opponents further argued that granting Indians the suffrage too early would take away their motivation to become civilized.[48]

The Indian suffrage discussion included debate not only about the level of cultural development of Michigan's Indians but also about their political status under the terms of federal treaties, about which the delegates were uncertain. Treaties signed in 1855 stated that "[t]he tribal organization of said Ottawa and Chippewa Indians, except so far as may be necessary for the purpose of carrying into effect the provisions of this agreement, is hereby dissolved." There was, however, no obligation described in the treaties that clearly could only be carried out by a tribal organization.[49] Furthermore, at the time of the constitutional convention in 1867, both the ten-year land trust period and the ten-year annuity period described in the 1855 treaties should have expired for most Indians. Nevertheless, some delegates to the 1867 convention expressed concern that tribal relations and annuities, as well as Indian immunity from state laws and taxes, continued.

Delegate Henry R. Lovell, the most vocal opponent of Indian suffrage, contrasted the Chippewas and Ottawas with European immigrants in Michigan who were enfranchised once they had declared the intention to become U.S. citizens: whereas the latter foreswore allegiance to their mother countries, the former continued to respect the authority of their chiefs and to maintain allegiance to their tribes, he claimed. Delegates Perley Bills and William S. Utley shared Lovell's concern that the Indians continued to be members of their tribes and acknowledged no allegiance to Michigan's government. To deal with this problem, Perry H. Estee moved to amend the draft of the constitution to provide that only Indians who were "not members of any tribe" could vote. The problem was not just a question of allegiance, however. Opponents of Indian suffrage objected to the prospect of enfranchising those who received annuities from the United States; mistaking the yearly disbursements as charity rather than as they were presented in the treaties, as payment for land ceded, these opponents scorned the recipients as dependent, rather than self-supporting, men. Utley, who moved to make it explicit in the constitution that Indians who received an annuity from the government were not eligible electors, argued that an Indian should gain the franchise only when he was in the same position as other freemen and "ceases to be a pensioner upon the government." Furthermore, those who wanted to add conditions to Indian suffrage complained that Indians were not subject to state laws, their lands were not taxable by the state, and state residents could not collect debts from them in Michigan courts. As Estee explained, Indians should not enjoy privileges without assuming responsibilities.[50]

Supporters of broad Indian suffrage pointed out the factual errors underlying the opponents' arguments. Dewitt Leach, who had previously served as an Indian agent for four years, authoritatively declared that people could and did collect debts from Indians in Michigan courts, that state courts had conducted criminal prosecutions of Indians, that all personal and real property purchased by Indians was taxable, and that land allotted to them by the federal government would be taxable as soon as the U.S. issued the patents in accordance with the treaty. Van Valkenburgh and Conger echoed Leach's assertion that Indians were "subject to the laws of the State, precisely as white men are." Even Leach acknowledged, however, that the Chippewa and Ottawa tribal organizations were only "partially dissolved."[51]

The delegates' arguments over factual issues at the 1867 convention masks their agreement on a basic principle of state Indian policy: they appear to have agreed that Indians over whom the state had authority could safely enjoy the rights of citizens, including the suffrage. The impassioned comments on the question of whether Michigan Indians were civilized, the complicated arguments about whether they maintained tribal relations, and the conflicting opinions as to whether they were subject to state laws and courts addressed only narrow factual issues that did not need to be resolved at the convention.

As established in chapters 1 and 2, state courts had already firmly established the principle that states had full authority over certain Indians within their borders, including all Indians over whom the federal government did not have lawful authority. Though it was not an indisputably established rule, many argued that once an Indian was civilized, there was no longer any justification for federal authority over that Indian, and the state therefore acquired authority over him or her. More consistently recognized was the concept that a state had authority over an Indian within its borders when the federal government relinquished its own power over the person and recognized him or her as a U.S. citizen independent of any tribe. Consequently, the question of the extent of state power underlay the convention debates about whether Michigan's Indians were civilized and whether they owed allegiance to a tribe or a chief. This issue was addressed most directly when delegates pondered whether state laws and state taxation applied to Indians. Indeed, this was the primary concern. Neither proponents nor opponents of Indian suffrage wanted to have voters who were not subject to state criminal and civil laws. Thus the two groups were not disagreeing about whether voting rights should depend on state authority over Indians. Instead, they disagreed about whether the state had sufficient authority over Indians to justify their participating in the political process.

Not only did proponents and opponents agree that there was a necessary correlation between franchise rights and state jurisdiction, but in the end a majority of both groups also agreed on how to phrase the suffrage provision of the draft constitution: they would not mention Indians at all. Early in the convention, some of the Indians' strongest supporters argued that the constitution needed no explicit reference to Indians. William S. Farmer and James Birney explained that it was not necessary for convention delegates to struggle over the question of how to describe which Indians could vote; the proposed clause relating to Indian suffrage was dispensable because the Civil Rights Act enacted the previous year already defined who were citizens. The law made all Indians citizens except those who were not liable to taxation, Birney pointed out. And as soon as the Fourteenth Amendment was ratified by the states, he expected, it would make all Indians citizens. Indians should not and need not be categorized separately from other citizens, he concluded. P. Dean Warner moved to strike the entire provision relating to Indian suffrage on the grounds that the federal law and the pending amendment rendered the provision mere "surplusage." Indians would be covered by the general provision that every "male citizen" could vote, he said. As evidence that it was not necessary to mention Indians in the elective franchise provision, Warner pointed out that most other states did not mention Indians in their constitutions, including some, like New York, that contained a significant Indian population. The delegates rejected Warner's motion by a 23–28 vote on July 22. When the convention took up the issue later in the summer, however, the notion of striking out the clause enfranchising Indians drew support from men who had been frustrated by their colleagues' rejection of proposals (the exclusion of Indians who could not speak English or who received an annuity) that would have defined more clearly which Indians could vote. Three weeks after Warner's motion was defeated, Martin P. Stockwell— who was fearful about Michigan's "opening the door [to the suffrage] so wide as to extend it to Indians"—put the motion forward again. This time it passed by a 38–31 vote. Consequently, although delegates had conflicting reasons for supporting Stockwell's motion, the proposed constitution of 1867 did not mention Indians at all in Article 3's description of qualifications for the elective franchise.[52]

Omitting any reference to Indians in the suffrage provision meant that the line between voting and nonvoting Indians lay in the general requirement that an elector be a "male citizen of the United States." This solution satisfied both sides in the debate over Indian suffrage because it recognized the political reality that it was now the federal government that would determine which Indians the states could regulate, prosecute, and tax. Ambiguities would emerge later, when the U.S. Supreme Court ruled that citizenship was not incompatible with continued U.S. guardianship and federal regulation.[53] But in 1867 it seemed apparent that state taxes and laws applied to anyone whom the federal government recognized as a U.S. citizen. Thus the delegates' primary concern was satisfied, regardless of which side of the culture and status lines they thought Michigan's Indians fell.

The white electorate's rejection of the proposed 1867 constitution (by a 110,582 to 71,333 vote) showed that voters were still nervous about the possible impact of enfranchising blacks in the state. Soon after ratification of the Fifteenth Amendment to the U.S. Constitution, however, Michigan's electorate voted in support of amending the state constitution to permit black suffrage. The 1870 Michigan amendment deleted the word "white" in the state constitution's description of eligible electors.[54] The status of Indians in Michigan remained ambiguous, however. The 1870 constitutional amendments made no changes in the description of Indians eligible to vote, which remained as it had been framed twenty years before: "every civilized male inhabitant of Indian descent, a native of the United States and not a member of any tribe." Thus the Indian suffrage provision remained through the end of the nineteenth century.

MINNESOTA IN THE LATE NINETEENTH CENTURY—AND BEYOND

Minnesota did not hold another constitutional convention during the nineteenth century, but the government found the 1857 constitution flexible enough to accommodate changes in Indian suffrage policy paralleling those emerging in Michigan during the Reconstruction period.[55] The post–Civil War climate led to a decreased focus on racial bases for excluding Indians from political privileges. By the end of Reconstruction, even cultural measures declined in importance, despite the fact that they were embodied in the franchise provision of the 1857 constitution that enfranchised Indians who had "adopted the customs and habits of civilization." Instead, an Indian's relationship with his tribe came to be viewed as a more important indicator of readiness for the suffrage, even though there was no constitutional provision explicitly making relinquishment of tribal relations a condition for enfranchisement. As suffrage requirements were applied in the late nineteenth century, Indians who maintained tribal relations were not deemed to have adequately "adopted the customs and habits of civilization." Affiliation now mattered more than race or culture.[56]

Several decades after Reconstruction, this practice was endorsed by the Minnesota Supreme Court when it held that tribal Indians could not vote even if they had adopted the habits and customs of civilization to a considerable extent.[57] Specifically, in his opinion on behalf of the court, Justice Andrew Holt acknowledged that the Indians in question "live in separate dwellings, constructed and furnished after the manner of the surrounding white settlers. Most of them can understand and speak English and even write their names, are members of Christian churches, and make a living much the same way as people in the vicinity of the reservation." Thus, it seems that the Indians met the basic cultural criteria discussed in the constitutional convention. The court deemed it more pertinent, however, that the men in question were tribal Indians under federal government guardianship. "Can it be said," Justice Holt inquired rhetorically, "that persons so situated have adopted the customs and habits of civilization within the meaning of the constitutional provision quoted?" Justice Holt acknowledged that at the time of the constitutional convention debates "it was not . . . deemed necessary that Indians and mixed bloods sever their tribal relation in order to become qualified voters." Nevertheless, the court thought it had become a necessary condition. The opinion made it clear that the state's main concern was a jurisdictional one: a member of a tribe that was under federal jurisdiction could not also be under state jurisdiction, and, the judges determined, no person could vote who was not within the state's jurisdiction.

Minnesota's evolving position on the issue of Indian suffrage in the late nineteenth century was affected by changes in Indian policy at the national level. State constitutional provisions and laws, like those of Minnesota, that attempted to incorporate civilized Indians into the state's political community were effectively mooted when the U.S. Supreme Court denied the power of individual Indians to acquire citizenship by moving off reservations, severing ties to tribes, and taking on the habits and customs of "civilized life."[58] In an unprecedented manner, the federal government asserted its authority to decide when Indians could become citizens, and the states yielded. But the states were not merely bowing to a stronger authority; the conditions had changed. The states' incentive to enfranchise noncitizen Indians diminished once the Supreme Court ruled definitively that such Indians owed no allegiance to the states and the states had no authority over them.[59] If the states could not regulate those Indians, could not tax all their land, and could not prosecute them for Indian-on-Indian crimes committed on reservations nor judicially enforce their land sales or contracts made within reservation territory, the states perceived that they had nothing material to gain by admitting those Indians to political privileges.

Thus, in *Opsahl v. Johnson* the Minnesota Supreme Court disregarded the constitutional provision that permitted Indians to vote if they met certain cultural criteria. Instead, the court bluntly denied the suffrage to any Indian who was not subject to the state's laws and taxes. As Justice Holt explained, "[i]t cannot for a moment be considered that the framers of the Constitution intended to grant the right of suffrage to persons who were under no obligation to obey the laws enacted as a result of such grant. . . . No one should participate in the making of laws which he need not obey." The court concluded that no Indian would be deemed to have adopted the "customs and habits of civilization" unless he had been released from federal guardianship and submitted to state laws.

MICHIGAN AND MINNESOTA OVER THE
COURSE OF THE CENTURY

Examining the rhetoric on Indians used in Michigan and Minnesota from the antebellum period through the late nineteenth century makes evident the changes that took place over time. The first of the two to enter statehood, Michigan, immediately accepted the principle that had already been established in the East: states had authority to regulate Indians in their interactions with whites within the state. In their first constitutional convention, in 1835, in order to exclude African Americans from the elective franchise, the delegates required that, to be a voter, a man had to be white. Inserting a whiteness requirement for the suffrage prompted two questions with regard to Indians: whether Indians were white, and, if not, whether an exception to the racial qualification should be made for Indians. The delegates answered both questions in the negative, resulting in a state constitution that did not explicitly enfranchise Indians. Fifteen years later, however, it evidently seemed to most of the delegates that a certain portion of the Indian inhabitants were already a part of white society—some of them already even voting. Although the whiteness qualification for the suffrage remained, without much dissent the delegates decided to make an exception for civilized, detribalized Indians, who were granted the right to vote.

Seven years later, Minnesota's new state constitution also allowed civilized Indians to vote. There was broad agreement among the delegates to the 1857 convention that voters had to be white. As in Michigan, however, they concluded that civilized Indians who already lived like whites deserved to be in the same political category as whites. After considerable debate about how to define who was civilized, the delegates concluded that there should be different criteria for "full-bloods" and "mixed-bloods." Where Michigan representatives had merely suggested (and eventually rejected) the possibility of treating Indians differently depending on whether or not they had any white ancestry, Minnesota followed through on the concept. The 1857 constitution provided that mixed-race men merely had to have "adopted the customs and habits of civilization" in order to vote, while those who were solely of Indian ancestry only enjoyed the elective franchise if they had "adopted the language, customs, and habits of civilization" and if they had also obtained a certificate from a district court stating that they were "capable of enjoying the rights of citizenship within the State."

After the Civil War the focus of debate changed. In Michigan's 1867 constitutional convention, the delegates fairly easily agreed to delete the whiteness requirement for the franchise, but they debated the issue of Indian suffrage more extensively. Their main concern now was not how Indians should be categorized racially, nor did they primarily focus on determining which Indians were civilized. Now the question had become a matter of which Indians were under the full authority of the state. Delegates did not want to enfranchise anyone who would not be subject to state laws and taxes, which led to their reluctance to grant the suffrage to any Indian who was under federal government administration. They solved the dilemma by making citizenship, rather than race or lifestyle, the criterion for voting. Presuming that the state would have full jurisdiction over all Indian men who were U.S. citizens, they allowed such men to vote. Minnesota came to a similar conclusion. By judicial decision rather than by constitutional amendment, Minnesota determined that no matter how otherwise civilized an Indian was, he could vote in the state only if he had severed tribal relations. To Minnesotans, a detribalized Indian was no longer under federal jurisdiction, leaving him clearly subject to state laws and taxes and thus worthy of state franchise rights.

Thus, in constitutional conventions prior to the Civil War, delegates in both Michigan and Minnesota focused on the issue of race when discussing Indian rights; they also intertwined cultural issues with race, in keeping with the dominant antebellum belief in a link between race and behavior. After the Civil War, both states shifted from a focus on race to a focus on Indians' political status. By the end of the nineteenth century, Michigan and Minnesota admitted Indians to membership in the state community, but only to the extent that the federal government recognized them as subject to state authority. These states had taken incorporation of Indians as far as they would be allowed; the rest of the process would be under federal government control.

PART THREE

Citizenship

～

CHAPTER SIX

State Citizenship by Legislative Action

~

During the early national and antebellum periods, while the states regulated many Indians within their boundaries and quietly absorbed some individual Native Americans into their communities, they generally refrained from declaring all Indians to be citizens. This situation changed in many Northern states in the 1860s, with New England states leading the way. On the eve of the Civil War, New Englanders were concerned about protecting their prerogative to determine residents' citizenship status. Their assertion of their right to include free blacks as citizens in the late 1850s paved the way for legislation declaring resident Indians to be state citizens in the 1860s and 1870s. As a case study of legislative debates in Massachusetts shows, however, states' motivations for granting Indian citizenship, and Indians' reasons for supporting or opposing citizenship, were multifaceted. Defense of state authority and assertion of equal rights were not the only factors prompting states to make Indians citizens, and Indians were not primarily focused on demanding rights. Economics and gender also played an important role for both state legislators and Indians in debates over Indian citizenship. Finally, while many Indians were concerned about preserving their corporate identity, cultural values, and communal land base, the states' rationales for Indian citizenship included the desire to assimilate them and their land into the mainstream American culture, society, and economy.

FEDERALISM AND THE IDEOLOGY OF CITIZENSHIP

During the early years of American independence, individual states established naturalization procedures. Although in 1789 the U.S. Constitution granted Congress the power to establish a "uniform Rule of naturalization," it was initially unclear whether this was a grant of exclusive control over naturalization, and most states asserted a concurrent power to naturalize foreigners even after passage of the first federal statute on the subject in 1790. Five years later, Congress, in providing that naturalization could take place under conditions described in a new law "and not otherwise," more forcefully asserted federal control over naturalization, but not until 1817 did the U.S. Supreme Court firmly articulate the principle of exclusive federal government authority over the subject. A later Court decision upheld the federal government's collective conferring of U.S. citizenship on inhabitants of territories acquired by conquest or treaties. Left unsettled during the early national period was whether states could still confer "state citizenship" on foreigners and whether native-born individuals could be denied the rights of citizenship.[1]

Southern Jeffersonian Republicans of the early Republic and Southern Democrats of the Jacksonian era tended to oppose nationalist policies, including an exclusive national conception of citizenship, while they aggressively defended states' rights, including a notion of state-centered citizenship. Conceiving of the United States as a "white man's republic," they tended to favor gentle citizenship requirements for white immigrants and almost insuperable barriers to citizenship for nonwhites. Allowing the states to retain some control over citizenship would permit southern politicians to deny birthright citizenship to residents from certain racial groups. Although southern whites were most concerned about excluding essential laborers of African descent from the political community, they were also very aware of the many Indians living within their state boundaries. By the Jacksonian era, southerners were committed to pressuring Native peoples to leave the region altogether.

Federalists and then Whigs, who dominated in the Northeast, advocated a stronger federal government and took a more nationalistic view of citizenship. Convinced that Americanism was epitomized by the special intrinsic qualities of the American-born Protestant Anglo-Saxon, these northern-based parties advocated restrictive naturalization policies but came to be more open to egalitarian reform movements that promoted abolitionism and women's rights. In the Jacksonian period, although there were removal projects focused on Indians north of the Ohio River, many New Englanders protested Cherokee removal in the Southeast, many Whigs argued that eastern Indians could be "civilized" and then included in the political community, and old Federalist John Marshall issued a Supreme Court decision recognizing a degree of tribal sovereignty.[2]

For Indians, the outcome of southern civic ideology was removal from the Southeast to lands west of the Mississippi River, as discussed in chapters 1 and 4. In the wake of legislation extending state authority over Indians within state boundaries and establishing conditions making it difficult for Indians to remain in the Southeast, southern states allowed citizenship to a few Indians on an individual basis rather conferring collective citizenship on whole tribes. Such grants were not, however, assertions of states' authority over citizenship, since they were consistent with federal removal treaty provisions stating that some Indians could remain in the Southern states as citizens.[3] Furthermore, scholars of Indian removal have concluded that the land allotment provisions that accompanied the citizenship provisions in these treaties were not intended to incorporate Indians as citizens over the long term. Instead, they have argued, white treaty makers expected Indian allottees to sell their lots of land to whites and voluntarily move west, and in practice most southeastern Indians did lose their allotments to white speculators.[4]

Whatever the goal on the part of the states, they did declare some individual Indians to be citizens. Georgia passed several laws in the 1830s and 1840s granting the rights and privileges of citizenship to specifically named Indians, removing all legal disabilities that had previously been imposed on those Indians and compelling them to perform the duties of free white citizens. The Tennessee statute that extended the laws and jurisdiction of the state over the Cherokees in 1833 made it clear that the state legislature had already granted citizenship rights to some of the Indians and that others were expected to receive such rights in the future. Alabama also declared certain persons of Indian descent to be citizens. Finally, the Mississippi Constitution of 1832 gave the legislature authority "to admit to all the rights and privileges of free white citizens of this State, all such persons of the Choctaw and Chickasaw tribes of Indians as shall choose to remain in this State, upon such terms as the Legislature may from time to time deem proper."[5]

As in the southeastern states, federal treaties declared certain Indians in Kansas to be U.S. citizens. When the Kansas legislature subsequently declared those Indians who had received land patents from the federal government to be citizens of the Territory of Kansas and, later, the state of Kansas, it was therefore endorsing rather than challenging federal policy. The legislature provided, however, that citizenship status should not "be so construed as to confer the right of suffrage on any Indian." Although aliens who had declared an intention to become citizens were allowed to vote in Kansas, Indians were not. In addition, an 1858 treaty with the Sisseton and

Wahpaton bands of the Sioux permitted individual Indians in Minnesota to dissolve their tribal connection, move off the reservation, and become U.S. citizens. A few years later, Minnesota provided for state citizenship for selected "civilized" Indians. Both the Kansas and the Minnesota laws followed after treaties granting citizenship to Indians within the states' boundaries—and most of the Indians were removed from both states around the same time, as they had been removed from the southern states.[6] As in the Southeast, all of these grants of citizenship were both selective and elective, rather than collective and all-encompassing; citizenship was neither offered to, nor imposed on, all Indians in these states.

The circumstances of northeastern states' granting Indians citizenship were very different. Northern civic ideology had its greatest impact on Indians in New England a few decades after southern removal. The conflicts over state versus national citizenship, as well as over governmental authority to deny birthright citizenship, became especially acute in New England after the U.S. Supreme Court issued its opinion in *Dred Scott v. Sandford*, in which, among other things, Chief Justice Roger Taney declared that people of African descent could not be citizens of the United States. Presumably motivated by a desire to deny Congress authority to naturalize blacks born in the United States while dealing with the fact that past treaties had already naturalized some Indians, Taney distinguished between the two groups. He explained that Congress did have the authority to naturalize Indians. Though living under the pupilage of the United States, Indians were basically a free people whose governments were respected as "foreign Governments." Therefore, "they may, without doubt, like the subjects of any other foreign Government, be naturalized by the authority of Congress, and become citizens of a State, and of the United States."[7] Despite the distinction between Indians and blacks, however, Taney still maintained that it was the federal government's role to award citizenship. Northerners did not allow the decision to go unchallenged, and their actions ended up broadening state citizenship to include Indians.

The New England state legislatures responded negatively to *Dred Scott*, primarily because they feared that the decision could lead to the nationalization of slavery but also because they disagreed with its concept of citizenship. The Massachusetts legislature declared that the commonwealth would not be bound by any aspect of the decision that was not necessary to its determination and asserted that it would not allow the people's rights to be violated "by reason of any usurpations of political power" by the Supreme Court. The legislatures of Maine, New Hampshire, Vermont, and Massachusetts repudiated the *Dred Scott* decision as "alarming," "dangerous," "odious," "extra-judicial," "repugnant to the constitution," and "not binding." Those four states, as well as Connecticut, also asserted state authority over citizenship. Connecticut declared that every state was "sovereign and independent" and maintained that each state's right to determine the political status of inhabitants could be limited only to the extent required by federal constitutional provisions granting Congress authority to establish a uniform rule of naturalization and restricting the state's authority over escaped slaves and criminals. The statute proceeded to define who were deemed to be citizens of Connecticut: every person born in the state, children of state citizens temporarily absent from the state, and persons who moved to the state with the intent to reside permanently there as citizens (except "aliens, paupers, fugitives from justice and fugitives from service"). The Massachusetts legislature asserted that "all negroes, not aliens, domiciled within her limits, are citizens of Massachusetts," and "all citizens of Massachusetts are citizens of the United States"; the legislature also enacted a statute authorizing the secretary of the commonwealth to issue "to any citizen, whatever his color may be," a passport stating that the bearer was a citizen of the Commonwealth of Massachusetts. Maine claimed that "the independent right of each state to determine who shall be admitted to political franchise and citizenship within its own limits, is clear and indisputable"; New Hampshire resolved that "every person born within the limits of this State, and owing allegiance to no foreign government, is a citizen thereof"; and Vermont stated that "[n]either descent . . . from an African . . . nor color of skin or complexion, shall disqualify any person from being, or prevent any person from becoming, a citizen of this State."[8]

Northern state courts also addressed some of the issues raised by the *Dred Scott* case. In March of 1857, Maine's state Senate sent an inquiry to the Supreme Judicial Court asking for its opinion on the question of whether state residents who were "free colored persons, of African descent" were eligible to vote. The judges answered in the affirmative. Explaining that the *Dred Scott* decision was not binding upon the states on a question requiring interpretation of the state's constitution and that Taney's opinion did not determine how the state constitution's reference to a "citizen of the United States" should be interpreted, the court held that in Maine the term applied "as well to free colored persons of African descent as to persons descended from white ancestors." One of the judges, Judge Joshua W. Hathaway, expressed the contrary view that *Dred Scott* was legally conclusive of the question of U.S. citizenship and was binding upon the states; he believed *Scott* left room for free colored persons of African descent to be electors only if their ancestors were not brought into the United States and sold as slaves. Judges John Appleton and Woodbury Davis also issued separate opinions; while they concurred with the conclusion of their five colleagues who signed the majority decision, they both directly disagreed with Taney's decision in *Dred Scott*. Both judges argued that each sovereign state had the exclusive authority to determine for itself the civil status of its native-born inhabitants; that the federal government's constitutional authority over citizenship under the U.S. Constitution extended only to naturalization and treaties, leaving the states with the reserved power to govern citizenship derived from birth; and that all people who were recognized as citizens of Maine, including people of African descent, were necessarily also citizens of the United States pursuant to the privileges and immunities clause of Article 4 of the Constitution.[9]

Though the New England states' laws and judicial decisions were prompted by concern about the outcome of a case involving an African American, and though legislators and judges (including Justice Taney) recognized that tribal Indians were distinguishable from free blacks because the former had their own separate form of government, the statutes and court opinions also provided the constitutional foundation for citizenship of Indians born in the state. Northern commitment to the principle of birthright citizenship and advocacy of egalitarian reform movements reinforced the states' inclination to formalize resident Indians' status as citizens. Unlike the southern citizenship laws conferring citizenship on selected Indians, the northern laws were not enacted in accordance with federal arrangements with Indian tribes.[10] Thus the New England laws constituted assertions of state authority in the citizenship arena.

Massachusetts took the lead in granting citizenship rights to Indians. Just two years after the *Dred Scott* decision, the legislature announced its intention to confer political rights on Indians. Three years later, it placed most commonwealth Indians on the same legal footing as non-Indian residents, and in 1869 it declared all Indians within the commonwealth to be citizens.[11] The other New England states followed suit. Connecticut made all Mohegan Indians citizens in 1872 and did the same for Niantic Indians four years later. Those citizenship laws provided that the Indians would thereafter "form a part of the people of the state" and would be "entitled to all the rights, privileges and immunities, and subject to all the duties, obligations and liabilities of natural born citizens."[12] An 1880 law in Rhode

Island abolished the tribal authority, tribal relations, and tribal rights of the Narragansett tribe of Indians; every person who had been a member of the tribe immediately ceased being a member thereof and became instead a member of the state's civic community, "entitled to all the rights and privileges, and . . . subject to all the duties and liabilities to which they would have been entitled or subject had they never been members of said tribe."[13]

In order to examine in greater depth what led New Englanders to grant citizenship to Indians, the next section examines Indian policy in one state, Massachusetts. As will be seen, the Massachusetts story begins with a decline in Indians' rights immediately after the Revolution, followed in the mid-nineteenth century by a movement toward greater civil and political rights for Indians. The discussion of change over time in Massachusetts begins with a description of the history of legislation and judicial decisions pertaining to Indians in Massachusetts in the nineteenth century. It then focuses on the debate over Indian citizenship in the decade beginning in 1859, analyzing what motivated the legislature to declare all Indians in the Commonwealth to be citizens in 1869, evaluating the Indians' own perspective on the issue, and assessing what the legislature's action meant for the Natives.

FROM WARDS TO CITIZENS IN MASSACHUSETTS

As described in the introduction, Indians in colonial Massachusetts were subject to extensive regulation.[14] Although in the eighteenth century New Englanders grew to resent their own subordination to the British, at the same time they increased their control over the Natives in their midst. Even after they ended their own colonial status by obtaining independence from Britain, they continued to deny Indians both autonomy and equality. Although European Americans viewed themselves as having grown up, no longer children and no longer needing the king as a father, they continued to see the Indians as having a childlike nature that made them unprepared for independence or the rights of citizenship. Though Massachusetts asserted its right to naturalize foreign-born citizens after the Revolution,[15] it did not treat native-born Indians as citizens. Thus revolutionary rhetoric, which emphasized self-rule and individual rights, was not seen as applying to the Indians, and the American Revolution did not prompt any improvement in their situation.

As a legislative committee report observed in 1849, "[e]ven the Declaration of Independence, the Bill of Rights, our State Constitution, brought no deliverance from oppression, no recognition of unalienable rights, no constitutional guaranties to the poor Indian."[16] In fact, as early as the 1830s, two advocates for the Mashpees, one white and one Indian, argued that the Revolution only made things worse for the Indians. Benjamin Hallett concluded that the tribe "was much more unkindly dealt by *after* the Independence, than they were under the government of Great Britain," and William Apess, a Pequot Indian, noted more bluntly that from the time of the American Revolution "the Marshpee Indians were enslaved by the laws of Massachusetts, and deprived of every civil right which belongs to man."[17]

During the early national and antebellum periods the legislature not only reiterated colonial era prohibitory regulations but also reduced the Indians' legal situation even further. Notably, the Indians' claim to land was weakened. Although in the seventeenth and eighteenth centuries the language of the laws seemed to recognize that the Indians owned the land, by the antebellum period the laws seemed to be based on the assumption that title to the land was in the Commonwealth of Massachusetts, held in trust for the Indians. A 1652 statute acknowledged that the Indians had a "just right" to lands that they possessed and improved, and it further stated that the English had a right to other lands at "the invitation of the Indians." Moreover, a 1719 statute used the word "owned" in referring to the Indians' relationship to the land they occupied: the statute, which related to lands that creditors could seize to satisfy debts owed, provided that "nothing in this Act contained, shall Extend to the Lands owned by the Indian Natives of this Province." And a 1725 statute further acknowledged Indian title by providing that the English "may assist . . . Indians in building houses for them on their own lands."[18] In contrast, an 1840 statute provided that when any person trespassed upon land, "the title to which is in the Commonwealth, for the use of any tribe or body of Indians in the Commonwealth," that land could be recovered in an action commenced by the attorney general or district attorney in the county court of common pleas. In 1855 the provisions of the 1840 statute were extended to lands "the title of which is in trustees, guardians, or agents appointed by the Commonwealth for the use or benefit of any tribe or body of Indians, or any individuals of such tribe or body, or their descendants."[19]

Asserting the commonwealth's ultimate title to Indian lands paved the way for converting communal control of property by Indian tribes to ownership of subdivided lots by individual Indians or Indian families in the nineteenth century. At first, allocation of land to individual Indians was temporary, but later statutes provided for permanent allotment. For example, an 1810 statute empowered the guardians of the Chappaquiddick Indians to assign lots of land for a period of ten years, but an 1828 statute provided that portions of the Chappaquiddick lands would be partitioned and permanently granted to individuals and their heirs.[20] Some statutes specifically provided that the Indian allottee would hold fee simple title to the land, but nevertheless they were normally not allowed to sell that land to someone who was not a member of the tribe.[21]

Another form of decline in the Indians' situation after the Revolution was evident in the laws pertaining to governance of the Natives. Soon after the end of the war, the Massachusetts General Court repealed the 1763 statute that had given the Mashpees some degree of self-government. The 1788 law provided that there were to be three guardians appointed for the Mashpee Indians. Those guardians, all of whom were white, were empowered to perform the functions formerly handled by the overseers.[22] In the nineteenth century, white men appointed by the governor continued to serve for the Mashpees many of the functions that guardians served in other tribes.[23] And the opportunity for those other tribes to rule themselves declined during the same period as the guardians were given additional powers. During the antebellum period, guardians gained such new powers as the authority to (1) settle all controversies among the Indians, and between them and the neighboring whites, (2) administer punishments for various crimes and misdemeanors on the lands of the Indians, (3) bind out as servants or sailors anyone who was a habitual drunkard, vagabond, or idler, and (4) bind out poor children. In Chappaquiddick and Christiantown, the guardians were also jointly empowered with the overseers (who were chosen by the Indians) to regulate the police of the Indians, assess and levy taxes, and provide for schools.[24]

Thus, during the early decades after the Revolution, Indians in Massachusetts experienced reduced control over resources and constriction of autonomy and self-governance. Although these statutory changes indicate a decline in the legal status of Indians in Massachusetts, court cases illustrate the ambivalence and uncertainty that accompanied the legislative actions. Not everyone in the commonwealth accepted the premise that Indians should be treated differently under the law. For several decades before the citizenship statute, the courts periodically ignored protective laws that limited Indians' civil rights, demonstrating a willingness to treat Indians like members of the commonwealth community under certain circumstances. Judicial decisions show a lack of consistency in how Indians were treated in practice. In some cases the terms of laws regulating Indians were strictly upheld, but in other cases, where the facts were flexible enough to allow it, the courts demonstrated their eagerness to apply to the Indians the same basic principles governing contracts and property that were routinely applied to European Americans.

Examples of strict adherence to protective laws and firm acceptance of the distinct status of Indians include an 1816 case in which the Supreme Court of Massachusetts held that a town did not have to support Indian paupers living within town boundaries (as they would be obligated to support non-Indian paupers) because Indians who were under guardianship had no legal settlement in the town. In another nineteenth-century case, an Indian conveyance that had occurred in 1686 was found to have been void and invalid in the absence of approval of the General Court. Even as late as 1866 the court decided in another case that the 1811 statute barring actions against Indians for debts unless the agreement had been approved by their guardians prohibited William B. Mayhew from suing the Gay Head Indians or the District of Gay Head for payment for groceries and other goods sold and delivered to the Indians. And in 1871 the court confirmed that until the 1869 citizenship statute Indians were not "endowed with the ordinary civil and political rights of citizens, but were treated as the wards of the Commonwealth; the title in the lands occupied by their tribes was in the state, and could not be alienated by them without the consent of the legislature."[25]

In some pre-1869 cases, however, standard common law principles were applied in lawsuits involving Indians. In an 1837 property dispute between an Indian and a non-Indian, the Massachusetts Supreme Court applied normal rules of adverse possession (which presumed ownership of land by a longtime occupant), even when the challenger to the non-Indian's title was an Indian who claimed that her ancestor had had no legal right to sell the land to non-Indians.[26] In another case three years later, the court upheld an Indian's contractual arrangement, even in the absence of explicit approval by the guardian. The Supreme Court dismissed a lawsuit brought by the administrator of Samuel P. Goodridge, a deceased Chappaquiddick Indian, to collect the wages Goodridge had earned on a whaling voyage. The court determined that Goodridge's arrangement with the defendants providing that the defendants outfit him for the voyage as an advance upon his wages was enforceable, and since those sums advanced were more than the wages owed to Goodridge, the administrator could collect nothing.[27]

These cases suggest an eagerness to treat Indians the same as other people of Massachusetts, especially in matters relating to property and contracts. Although awarding greater rights to Indians would not revive lost elements of their autonomy and self-governance, at least it would allow them to be treated as members of the political community of the commonwealth.

During the antebellum period Massachusetts officials began to express concern about the treatment of Indians. In 1838 the legislature issued a resolution protesting the proposed forcible removal of the Cherokee nation from the Southeast. Later, the 1849 Report observed that the Mashpee Indians were not "domestic nations," as the U.S. Supreme Court had labeled the Cherokees. Consequently, the Mashpees were not aliens. Since all inhabitants of the commonwealth were presumed to be citizens, except for aliens, paupers, and persons under guardianship, the only barrier to Mashpee citizenship was the fact that the state exercised guardianship authority over them. The commissioners expressed regret that such guardianship unnecessarily perpetuated the Indians' subordinate, degraded status.[28]

Not everyone agreed with the commissioners that Indians should be citizens, however. For example, a Massachusetts newspaper article on the 1849 Report expressed the opinion that although the commissioners "propose a scheme for absorbing [the Indians] into the community," such a plan would "find a formidable obstacle in the mutual jealousy existing between the Indians and those with whom they are expected to associate." The article pointed out that Indians "dislike all connection with the town governments in their neighborhood, and the towns people equally dislike political connection with the Indians." None of the Indians complain that they are ineligible to vote, the article observed.[29]

Regardless of mixed feelings among the people of Massachusetts— white and Indian alike—in 1859 the legislature declared its intention of conferring civil and political rights on the Indians of the commonwealth. The statute provided that the governor should appoint a commissioner to study the condition of all Indians in Massachusetts so that the legislature could judge "whether they can, compatibly with their own good and that of the other inhabitants of the state, be placed immediately and completely, or only gradually and partially, on the same legal footing as the other inhabitants of the Commonwealth."[30] Pursuant to the 1859 law, the governor appointed John Milton Earle commissioner to study the conditions of the Indians. Earle submitted his 147-page report two years later, along with a 78-page census of the 1,610 Indians of the commonwealth.[31] Earle recommended (1) that no change be made in the political status of Indians residing on the reservations of the Chappaquiddick, Christiantown, Gay Head, Mashpee, Herring Pond, Fall River, and Dudley tribes or other Indians who were being supported by the state, except that any individual from any of those tribes who wished to become a citizen should be entitled to do so, (2) that all other Indians in Massachusetts—that is, those not residing on any of the above-named reservations nor supported by the state—be immediately placed on the same legal footing as other inhabitants of the state, and (3) that a single commissioner, with responsibility to supervise and watch over the interests of the Indians of the state, take the place of the treasurer of the Mashpee and Herring Pond tribes and the guardian of the Chappaquiddick and Christiantown tribes and have advisory powers in the Gay Head tribe.[32]

Earle recommended that Indians who had no reservation and resided among whites should be treated differently than other Indians because, he said, most of them lived as comfortably as their white neighbors and did not need special protections. In fact, some of them were already treated like regular citizens and had no legal disabilities, and the others were well prepared to handle the responsibilities of citizenship. Although Earle recommended that the present condition of other Indians—the 850 members of the Chappaquiddick, Christiantown, Gay Head, Mashpee, and Herring Pond tribes—should not be perpetuated indefinitely, he concluded that they should not immediately and completely be placed on the same footing as other inhabitants. Except for the appointment of a commissioner, no further change should be made with regard to these five tribes until the commissioner deemed that they were ready. Earle called for an effort to prepare those Indians for citizenship, led by the commissioner for the Indians and implemented especially by teachers and ministers. The goal was to place all of the Indians on a plane of legal and political equality with other inhabitants of Massachusetts as soon as they were ready to handle the responsibilities of citizenship.

The year after Earle issued his report, the Massachusetts legislature put his recommendations into effect. An 1862 law provided that "[a]ll Indians and descendants of Indians are hereby placed on the same legal footing as the other inhabitants of the Commonwealth, except such as are or have been supported in whole or in part by the state, and except also those residing on the Indian Plantations of the Chappequiddick, Christiantown, Gay Head, Marshpee, Herring Pond, Fall River and Dudley tribes." The legislature further provided that any Indian in those tribes who desired to possess the rights of citizenship could elect to become a citizen of Massachusetts. The law also incorporated the plantation of Gay Head into a district to be governed in the same way as Mashpee. The next year, the legislature empowered the Mashpee Indians to elect their treasurer; either a proprietor or a white person who was not a proprietor could be chosen, as the voters of Mashpee decided. The treasurer for the Herring Pond Indians would continue to be appointed by the governor. Finally, in 1869 the Massachusetts General Court passed a law declaring all Indians in the Commonwealth to be citizens.[33]

To understand the meaning of the citizenship law, and to determine its effect on the continuing colonial status of the Natives, one needs to examine the legislators' motivations. Fortunately, the extant documents from the 1860s citizenship debate include the report of a hearing at which Mashpee Indians had the opportunity to express their views. Because Massachusetts primary sources are available as a foundation for studying not only the white perspective but also a number of Indians' opinions on the issue of their status, Massachusetts is one of the few states whose nineteenth-century Indian citizenship policies have received previous scholarly attention. Most notably, Ann Marie Plane and Gregory Button's article on the enfranchisement act provides an excellent discussion that focuses especially on ethnicity issues in the citizenship debate. Plane and Button describe how the citizenship debate revealed conflict between insiders' and outsiders' definitions of Indian ethnic identity. While the self-identity of Massachusetts Indian tribes focused on shared practices and culture, they explain, whites tended to categorize the Indians in racial terms. Nevertheless, not all Indians took the same position on the citizenship issue, nor did all whites have the same opinion.[34] The next three sections of this chapter build on Plane and Button's findings by describing three different factors that appear to have motivated Massachusetts to declare all Indians in the commonwealth to be citizens.

INDIAN CITIZENSHIP AS A MATTER OF EQUAL RIGHTS

In addition to the interest in promoting sovereignty over people within state borders, many supporters of Indian citizenship appear to have been motivated by a sincere commitment to racial equality and civil rights. Certainly, they most often expressed their support in language consistent with such concepts. In the course of the Mashpee protest against their treatment under Massachusetts law in the 1830s, both Benjamin Hallett, a European American, and William Apess, a Pequot Indian, expressed their support for the Mashpee Indians in terms of their entitlement to equal rights.[35] Furthermore, the 1849 and 1861 reports on the condition of the Indians both lamented the fact that Indians were deprived of equal rights under Massachusetts law. The 1849 study noted that everyone else in Massachusetts could enjoy the privileges of American citizenship and that "[t]he Indian alone . . . is a vassal in the land of his fathers." That report went on to point out "[t]he inconsistency of our past and present treatment of the Indians, with the whole spirit, and, indeed, with the letter of our constitution." The three authors of the report concluded by writing: "We ask for the Indian a full share in the rights asserted in the Declaration of Independence, and our Bill of Rights, and guaranteed by our Constitution."[36] Earle's 1861 report said that the Chappaquiddick, Christiantown, Gay Head, Mashpee, and Herring Pond communities were "within the State, but not of it, subject to its laws, but having no part in their enactment; within the limits of local municipalities, yet not subject to their jurisdiction; and holding real estate in their own right, yet not suffered to dispose of it, except to each other." Not only were Indians deprived of the right to make contracts or buy and sell land without the consent of guardians, but they also were subject to punishment—even unusual and cruel punishment—by the guardian for a variety of petty offenses. This was a situation that should not continue for the long term, Earle opined. He knew that laws alone would not ensure racial equality. As he wrote, "[t]he disabilities under which they labor can be remedied, only in part, by legislative action. The bitter prejudice of color and caste, and social exclusion can be remedied only by a more liberal, just, humane, and Christian public sentiment, and a satisfactory change in this respect must necessarily be a work of time." He also knew, however, that changing the laws so they no longer imposed civil and legal disabilities was the right place to start. "That the Indians have an absolute *right* under our constitution to be citizens, few, probably, would deny." But he pointed out that the Indians had lived for so long under legal disabilities that it would not be appropriate or fair to suddenly remove those disabilities completely.[37]

Between the publication of Earle's report in 1861 and the legislature's action on the issue of Indian citizenship, the Civil War and early Reconstruction further shaped the language of the debate over the issue. Massachusetts played an important role in political developments of the 1860s, and in the federal government some of the most vocal supporters of African Americans' civil rights came from Massachusetts. In 1864 the

Massachusetts legislature struck out the word "white" from statutes relating to eligibility for military office; in 1865 the legislature passed a statute providing that "[n]o distinction, discrimination or restriction on account of color or race shall be lawful in any licensed inn, in any public place of amusement, public conveyance or public meeting in this Commonwealth"; and in March 1869 the legislature ratified the Fifteenth Amendment to the Constitution, which prohibited denying any citizen the right to vote on the basis of race.[38] By the late 1860s many leaders of the state government were arguing that now that African American men were acquiring rights of citizenship in the United States, Massachusetts could not continue to deny the franchise to Native Americans. The fact that many tribe members and spouses of tribe members had some African ancestry may have further spurred the state to take action, in the belief that people living on the reservations should be given the same "benefits" as "other non-whites." That whites tended to see the matter this way reflected their perception of reservation inhabitants as simply another part of the nonwhite population of the state, rather than as groups of people with distinct corporate identities.

In his opening speech to the legislature in January of 1869, Governor William Claflin took note of the equality argument, saying: "While calling upon the national government to guarantee equal civil and political rights to all citizens within its jurisdiction . . . it becomes us to remember that we have within our own borders a considerable number of persons to whom these rights and privileges are denied." The Indians, he observed, "are not paupers, nor slaves, and yet not citizens. They are treated as the wards of the Commonwealth, recipients of its charities, but debarred from all agency in making the laws by which they are governed." The governor declared that the Indians should be made citizens.[39]

A special joint committee of eight members of the house and three members of the senate was appointed as a Committee on Indians to discuss pertinent portions of Governor Claflin's address.[40] On June 3, 1869, Francis W. Bird presented the committee's report, accompanied by a proposed statute that would enfranchise the Indians of Massachusetts and make them citizens.[41] The report noted that the Indians were subject to "laws which they have no voice in framing; tried by juries upon which they are not drawn; sentenced by judges appointed by an executive for whom they cannot vote." The committee wrote: "We believe that Massachusetts is ready to-day,—has long been ready, to wipe out all distinctions of race and caste, and to place all her people on the broad platform of equality before the law." They concluded by saying that if the proposed citizenship statute were enacted, "[t]hese remnants of a long oppressed race will be brought within the declaration of our bill of rights: 'All men are born free and equal, and have certain natural, essential and unalienable rights, among which may be reckoned the right of enjoying and defending their lives and liberties; that of acquiring, possessing and protecting property; in fine, that of seeking and obtaining their safety and happiness.'"[42]

ECONOMIC ISSUES AND INDIAN CITIZENSHIP

Although many supporters of Indian citizenship genuinely believed in racial equality and civil rights, analysis of the record suggests that there were also two other reasons for changing the status of Indians in the commonwealth. First, to a significant extent, changes in the Indians' status under law were motivated by economic developments that called for increased privatization of property and predictability and uniformity of property and contract rights. Many Americans were eager to incorporate the Indians and their land into the individualist, capitalist economy.[43]

Not everyone believed that the Natives would benefit from incorporation into the European-American economic orbit, and indeed the history of the European American–Native American relationship provided foundation for concern. The reports of 1849 and 1861 described how many tribes had lost their land while they were living under the protection and supervision of white commissioners and guardians. The 1849 Report concluded that "[w]e have taken the management of their [the Indians'] property, and have allowed it to be squandered and lost."[44] In 1861, Earle detailed the partitions, allotments, and sales of tribal lands by guardians and the legislature more extensively. He described how the Chappaquiddick Indians lost "the better portion" of the land when their island was divided between them and the whites, leaving them with the most bleak and barren land; he expressed the opinion that the division of common lands into individual lots "proved disastrous to the interests of the Marshpee tribe"; he pointed out that that Natick, Dartmouth, and Middleborough Indians no longer held any common lands; he noted that the Punkapog tribe used to be proprietors of five thousand acres of land but "[n]one of this property now remains in their possession" because it had been sold off by the guardians; he recalled that the reservations that were set aside for the Hassanamisco Indians had been sold off with the permission of the legislature, leaving them with no common lands and only two and a half acres held by one individual member; and he observed that the Dudley Indians had recently been moved from their lands to a one-acre lot.[45] Earle warned that if outsiders were permitted to purchase the remaining tribal lands, all of those lands would be likely to be lost to whites. It would be disastrous for the tribes, for "they would become a prey to the unprincipled and unscrupulous." As the Natives themselves expressed their fear to Earle: they would become the victims of "shrewder and sharper men outside." Consequently, "the little property they possess would be wrested from them, and . . . they would be turned out, destitute, upon the cold charities of the world." Without tribal lands, their communities would be broken up and scattered. Earle reported that the Indians did not want to become citizens nor did they want to make their land available for sale in private markets.[46]

But the Committee on Indians took a different view: they focused on how deprived the Natives were in being excluded from the land market. The committee's report noted that no Indian could convey land to a non-Indian, or, in legal terms, the Natives' lands were "entailed."[47]

Thus, the 1869 Report pointed out, Indians were shut out of "the enterprise which is pushing the outside world ahead." Exclusion from economic opportunities left the Indians "to comparative thriftlessness and decay." Three years earlier, the white man serving as treasurer of the Mashpees, S. C. Howland, commented that as long as the land entailment existed, "not much can be done by way of enterprise among them on account of lack of capital necessary for business transactions." He observed that Mashpee District had several valuable streams, and "were it not for the entailment of their land prohibiting the sale to other than a proprietor, probably some of them, ere now, would have had manufactories on them, and made employment for them." White observers not only lamented the negative effects of entailment and the ownership of communal land but also raved about the economic benefits that accrued when the Indians were allowed to own and sell lands. For example, the 1849 Report described beneficial effects of land allotment among the Chappaquiddicks: "The result has been new incentives to industry and economy, arising from an assurance of their rewards, and a love of approbation, and self-respect, which are at once the fruits and the guarantees of progress."[48]

Wealthier, more market-oriented men living among the Indians—many of them non-Indians married to Indians—were eager to be free to profit from their ownership of land and natural resources. Ann Marie Plane and Gregory Button, who examined Mashpee petitions for and against the end of land entailment in December 1868, found that those supporting the change in land tenure to allow people to sell their land to whomever they pleased tended to be wealthier on average than those opposing the change.[49] At the hearing in Mashpee held by the Committee on Indians in February 1869, supporters of citizenship and the end of entailment also tended to be more successful financially.[50] For example, Solomon Attaquin and Matthias Amos, who supported the change, were both selectmen of Mashpee and both entrepreneurs. Eight years earlier, Earle's census reported that Attaquin held land and buildings worth $2,618 plus personal property worth $488, while Amos had real property worth $2,550 and personal property worth $265.[51] Two years before the hearing, the two of them, along with a third man, had incorporated the Marshpee Manufacturing Company for the purpose of manufacturing baskets, brooms, woodenware, and other articles in the Mashpee district.[52] At the hearing Amos acknowledged that he made "a good comfortable living." But he said he could not have made his money in Mashpee, "because my property was not worth anything. I could not go and mortgage my land for three or four hundred dollars and get money to work it with." In response to a question from a member of the Committee on Indians, Amos said he did not mind if other men (from outside the tribe) came in and bought the Mashpee land. Attaquin agreed: "I don't care a whit what becomes of the land, so long as it goes into better hands than it comes out of." Another supporter of the right to sell property, Mr. Sewell, who admitted owning a large share of the cranberry bog, testified that the Mashpee Indians were being held back by their inability to attract capital investment. The cranberry swamp could be improved, he asserted, if capitalists were allowed to come in and invest. In general, "[t]he property here can be made productive, if they will allow men of capital and genius to come among us."[53] Like the American colonists a century before, these men perceived the commonwealth's economic regulations as unduly limiting their freedom to use their property as they wished and to profit from it as much as possible. They chose individualism over traditional practices and collective community interests.

But other Mashpee Indians disagreed. According to the transcript of the hearing at Mashpee, Nathan S. Pocknett claimed it was "selfish motives" that drove those who supported the end of the entailment. Those men, he said, "want to raise a little money to pay off this bog-debt—sell a little land and raise four or five hundred dollars." Why should the entire community be forced to accept the end of legislative protection of their property, just to accomplish the business of the few wealthy who wanted to be able to sell land and make profits, he asked. "We shall all die paupers if this change is made," he said, "for our properties will go one after another." Fellow Mashpees William Simons, Joseph Amos, and John B. Brown agreed with Pocknett, expressing fear that if the entailment were ended, the Indians would end up losing their land. As Simons put it, "by taking the entailment off of the land, we shall be at the mercy of those who have got the money."[54] As was the case in New York in the 1820s and Georgia in the 1830s, these men, along with most other Mashpees, preferred to retain communal property ownership and tribal sovereignty. In the post–Civil War era, they held to this position even when the alternative was not removal but full incorporation.

However, the situation was different in 1860s Massachusetts than it had been decades earlier in New York and Georgia. Now there were men affiliated with a tribe who took a strong position in favor of absorption into the state. To the advocates for detribalization and citizenship, the Mashpees who resisted citizenship were clinging unnecessarily and irrationally to a disadvantageous and outdated status. As Sewell put it disdainfully during the hearing, "[w]e have Red Jackets growing up amongst us, that oppose civilization." His scornful reference to the Seneca leader who had been such a strong advocate of tribal sovereignty at the beginning of the century conveyed clearly how some Americanized Indians (or spouses of Indians, as in Sewell's case) viewed more traditional tribe members. Convinced of the higher value of individualism over communalism, they pressed for equal citizenship, willing to disband tribal affiliations.[55]

In the Massachusetts General Court, the arguments against change lost out to those in favor. As the region became increasingly individualistic, market oriented, entrepreneurial, and capitalistic, there must have been considerable discomfort with the presence of land and resources in the commonwealth that were off limits to developers and businessmen, as well as uneasiness with the presence of people who lived communally and were unavailable for private labor arrangements. Granting Indians citizenship erased those uncomfortable anomalies. Not surprisingly, the outcome of Indian citizenship in later years was further loss of Indian land to Americans, as well as forced assimilation of Natives into the European-American economy.[56]

GENDER ISSUES IN THE CITIZENSHIP DEBATE

In the debate over the Indian citizenship bill, there was a third factor that may have been just as important as concern about civil rights and eagerness for economic gain: gender. When American colonists presented arguments for independence in the late eighteenth century, they not only asserted their maturity as evidence of their preparedness for autonomy from the father-king but also stressed their male qualities as evidence of the strength and superiority of American character. They appealed to men by highlighting American/male "virtue" as contrasted with British/female frivolity and dependence on luxuries.[57] During the nineteenth century, increasing numbers of American men lost their economic autonomy as they left farms to work in factories, but they gained compensation in the form of expanded white male suffrage and money wages, which gave men increased power in the home over women, children, and property. Thus even if middle-class men now had to answer to others in the economic sphere, they were "equals" with other men politically and shared dominance over women. Reinforcement of gender divisions helped mask increasing class differences.

The situation on the reservations was problematic for many American men, because often real property was, by law, owned and controlled by Indian wives rather than by non-Indian husbands. Plane and Button observe that African American husbands of tribe members may have been particularly sensitive to this issue, since they expected postwar freedom to allow them to take on the position as heads of their families, as defined by the prescribed gender roles of the dominant white community. Daniel Mandell also notes that men of African descent who had married Indian women tended to support detribalization; their primary goal, he says, was "[p]atriarchal landholding in severalty." To white Americans, too, it seemed that granting Indians citizenship would bring an end to the anomalous situation of women as primary property owners and would make all Massachusetts men the bosses in their own families. Furthermore, Indian citizenship would extend to Indians male political prerogatives from which they had been excluded. As John Milton Earle pointed out, one of the major problems with the political arrangement with the Indians was that through no fault of their own, Indians had been "shorn of their manhood."[58] With citizenship status they would no longer be childish or feminine dependents; citizenship would make them real men.

The transcript of the hearing on the citizenship issue held in Mashpee in 1869 makes it clear that the Massachusetts legislators encouraged the Indians to frame their comments in terms of manhood—and also makes it evident that by "manhood" they did not simply mean "personhood." Committee members and wealthier, assimilated male members of the

Mashpee tribe asserted that citizenship would "make them men" and implied that only weak, unmanly Indian males would oppose citizenship. Solomon Attaquin and Matthias Amos were among those expressing the desire to become citizens in gender terms. Attaquin testified, "I want to see the day that I am a citizen and man, as well as other men," while Amos stated that he signed the petition in favor of citizenship because "[n]ow I feel as if I wanted to come out and be a man." Other Mashpees elaborated more on the subject. Sewell, an African American married to a Mashpee woman, objected that denying Indian males the right to vote and handle their own affairs forcibly infantilized them and did not allow them to become adult men. "You may take one of your sons and keep him in a dependent state all his life, and it will have the same effect upon him" as such a state had had on men of color. Treating Indian men as wards "is against all our common ideas of American republicanism," he argued. The Mashpee Indians were entitled to be organized as a regular town "so that it can be established that colored men can govern themselves, but I don't want you to establish a town *because* they are colored men, but because they are *men*." He said: "I don't want any less standing than Governor Claflin has, and if you give me anything else, I feel I am so much less the man." Sewell protested his "servile condition," noting: "I feel as though I am a man, every inch of me, and there is nothing, no reason why I should not have the privileges of a man." In short, he pleaded, "I ask you to make us men, and give us all the dignity of manhood."[59]

Samuel Godfrey, who was an African American married to a Mashpee woman, stated that it was wrong and illogical that he was entitled to the benefits of citizenship when he lived in Boston, Philadelphia, and Norfolk, but not in Mashpee. In his initial statement, he did not mention anything about being treated like a man or not, but in summarizing Godfrey's comments Nathaniel J. Holden, the white chair of the Committee on Indians, added the element of manhood: "you spoke of feeling that you are more of a man elsewhere than you are here." Holden's colleague Nathaniel Hinckley also summarized the feelings of the Indians in gender terms: "There is a strong feeling on the part of many intelligent persons in Marshpee to become, as they express it 'men;' to be citizens of the United States, and of the State, with the privileges that the white men enjoy. That is not strange. They are men with us. . . . They are our brethren." Hinckley asked: What could possibly explain the reluctance of some men of Mashpee to be granted citizenship? Do those opposed to citizenship "want to drive off all those men that feel as if they wanted to be men and leave only those who don't want to be men, if there are any such. I hardly think it." The gender-based plea for citizenship was stated most simply by Young Gouch (also a black man whose wife was a Mashpee): "I wish to be a man, with equal rights with every man."[60]

A number of the men supporting the petition requesting citizenship (including Sewell, Godfrey, and Gouch) were non-Indians who had married into the tribe. Because of laws limiting land ownership to tribe members, those "foreign" men did not have the right to own land. Instead, their Indian wives owned the land. These men spoke of the land as if it were naturally theirs and only through the perversion of wardship law owned by women. They argued that they paid the taxes on their wives' lands and contributed their labor to improve the land, and consequently they should get the rights and benefits of land ownership. When they testified in the hearing "I want to be a man," more than anything else they appeared to be saying that they wanted to be bosses in their own families. In short, one of the reasons Indians were granted citizenship in Massachusetts was to allow male Indians and male spouses of Indians to join the world of men, thus further reinforcing the gender line and empowering all men.

The political status of women in the Indian communities had been weakened by American legislation during the first half of the nineteenth century, though there seemed to be some variation among tribes. The 1849 Report stated that among the Chappaquiddick Indians "[t]he rights of woman are fully recognized, the females taking the same liberty of speech, and, when unmarried or in the absence of their husbands, enjoying the same right of voting with the men."[61] The 1834 law pertaining to the Mashpees, however, provided that only adult male proprietors of the district, including "such as may be proprietors in right of a wife," could vote for selectmen and other public officials. The provision meant that women born into the Mashpee tribe were denied the right to vote for tribal officials, a right enjoyed by their non-Indian husbands. This provision apparently trumped an earlier law that stated that a proprietor of Mashpee "must be a child or lineal descendant of some person who is now a proprietor," and "[i]n no other way or manner shall the rights of proprietorship be acquired."[62] Across Massachusetts, men were reluctant to grant women political rights. Throughout the 1869 legislative term, a separate special joint committee had been considering the question of women's suffrage. Between the first day of the term on January 6, 1869, to the last meeting on June 24, the Journal of the House of Representatives mentions 146 petitions in favor of female suffrage received by the house, most of them with multiple signatories. Despite all those petitions, and despite the rhetoric of civil rights used to explain granting Indians the right to vote, Massachusetts legislators could not bring themselves to extend the right of suffrage to women. One week before the granting of Indian citizenship, the house, by a vote of 84 to 111, rejected a bill that would have granted women the right to vote.[63] The legislators' rejection of the women's suffrage bill can be seen as entirely consistent with their support for the Indian citizenship act if the latter act was intended to bolster the power of men on Indian reservations, rectifying a perceived inappropriate power balance between men and women there. Thus, concern about gender issues, along with awareness of civil rights and economic issues, played a role in the debate over Indian citizenship.

AFTERMATH OF THE CITIZENSHIP ACT

After discussion in the Massachusetts House and Senate, the Indian citizenship bill was amended and then finally passed on June 23, 1869.[64] In its final form, the statute provided as follows: "All Indians . . . within this Commonwealth, are hereby made and declared to be citizens of the Commonwealth, and entitled to all the rights, privileges and immunities, and subject to all the duties and liabilities to which citizens of this Commonwealth are entitled or subject." Ending the land entailment, the law provided that "all Indians shall hereafter have the same rights as other citizens to take, hold, convey and transmit real estate." The statute also provided that land held by any individual Indian was thereafter to become the property of that person and his heirs in fee simple. The legal effect of these provisions can be seen in an 1880 case involving a dispute over land in Mashpee that used to be owned by an Indian proprietor, Mercy McGrego. One plaintiff claimed the land by descent from McGrego, and the other claimed it by an 1873 deed from another of McGrego's descendants. The defendant, in contrast, claimed the land based on McGrego's 1834 deed to the defendant's father, Jesse Webquish. The court ruled in favor of the plaintiffs because the deed to Jesse Webquish was made at a time when the law prohibited Indians from conveying land to nonproprietors. Since McGrego was incapable of making contracts or conveying land to Webquish, who was not a proprietor, the deed was void. Furthermore, neither the 1842 law under which Webquish became a proprietor nor the 1869 law that granted Indians citizenship rights had the effect of legitimizing the 1834 deed retroactively. Therefore the land remained in McGrego's estate when she died and passed to her descendants. By 1873, when McGrego's descendant conveyed the land, such a sale by an Indian proprietor was legal.[65]

The citizenship statute also provided that lands held in common by a tribe (other than Mashpee or Gay Head) could be partitioned and sold on order of the probate judge if any tribal member requested such action and if the judge, after a hearing, agreed that it was in the interest of the Indians. The Supreme Court of Massachusetts interpreted this provision to mean that every Indian in the tribes covered immediately acquired rights of ordinary tenants in common. Obtaining those rights meant that upon individual application, an Indian could have his share (or the proceeds from sale of his share) set off to him to be held individually. That right vested the moment the 1869 statute took effect.[66]

The year after it passed the Indian citizenship law, the legislature abolished the districts of Gay Head and Mashpee, incorporated the territories into towns by the name of Gay Head and Mashpee, respectively, and provided for judges to order the partition and sale of common lands. In Gay Head, such division and sale of land would be directed by the probate judge, upon application of the selectmen of the town or any ten resident owners of land therein, while in Mashpee it could be ordered by any justice of the superior court upon application of the selectmen of the town.[67] Thus, the situation for the Mashpee and Gay Head Indians who wanted to divide up the common lands was somewhat different from that of other tribes. In 1879 the Massachusetts Supreme Court upheld the constitutionality of the 1870 law and left it within the discretion of the local justice to determine how much of the common lands of the two tribes should be divided and sold. The court noted that the 1869 statute was not intended to give to the tribes or to individual Indians in the tribes "the absolute and unqualified control of common lands occupied by them." The court specifically noted that "[t]he guardianship of the State was thus to be exercised over . . . Indians . . . after they were declared to be citizens."[68]

In 1869 the Commonwealth of Massachusetts granted to Indians the civil and political rights they had been denied for two and a half centuries. Although the citizenship statute ended the limbo status of Indians in Massachusetts and formally granted them legal equality, Massachusetts continued to deny them the more desirable option of genuine autonomy, and the grant of rights came at a price. For a short time Mashpee and Gay Head lands continued to be treated differently from most land in the state, but the citizenship law otherwise meant the immediate elimination of the protections of tribal lands and Indians' distinct legal identity, which in turn led to the erosion of the Native land base, the further scattering of tribe members, and, for many, the weakening of communal bonds and traditional cultural practices during the late nineteenth and the twentieth centuries.

For European-Americans who sought to "civilize" and assimilate Indians, it was essential to lead the Natives to accept private property ownership, European-American-style rule of law, and patriarchy. The Massachusetts citizenship act of 1869 marked European-American success on all three grounds. First, the statute completed the partitioning and allotment of Indian lands and permitted Indians to participate in the land market by selling their property and resources; the result was privatized land ownership (mostly by non-Indians). Second, the law placed Indians under the same laws as Americans and allowed them access to courts. Third, the 1869 legislation removed wives from control of real property and confirmed women's lack of political roles, thus "masculinizing" the men.

Since Massachusetts played a leading role in the assertion of state-based Indian citizenship and land privatization, it is no surprise that Massachusetts men later took the cause of Indian citizenship to the federal level. Less than two decades after the Commonwealth enacted its citizenship law a U.S. senator from Massachusetts, Henry L. Dawes, drafted and spearheaded efforts to pass the federal General Allotment Act of 1887, which contained many of the same principles as those embodied in the Massachusetts Indian citizenship act.[69]

CHAPTER SEVEN
The Politics of Indian Citizenship

The debate about the appropriate status of Native peoples in the European-American political structure that began during the earliest years of European exploration and settlement in the Americas continued into the nineteenth century. As previous chapters illustrate, local jurisdictions unilaterally regulated Indians and Indian land during the early national and antebellum periods, typically without directly tackling the question of whether Indians were citizens, wards, or separate nations. By the mid-nineteenth century, many state and territorial governments were prepared to take on the citizenship issue, either by granting certain Indians the most important right of citizenship, the suffrage, or by explicitly awarding citizenship to Indians within their borders.

Chapter 6 analyzed the Mashpee Indians' conflicting responses to the various goals of white advocates for Indian citizenship in Massachusetts. That chapter discussed the arguments of Mashpee proponents and opponents of the proposed law. The present chapter focuses more on the nature of the debate between different categories of whites about Indian citizenship in another jurisdiction. Because local government officials had conflicting personal stakes in Native status, as well as varying views of Indians, the decision to grant Indian citizenship in a jurisdiction was preceded by heated political wrangling over the question of whether Indians should have a special "protected" status or, instead, should be regarded as members of the community who were equals under the law. Beneath intellectual discussions on that subject lay jurisdictional disputes, conflicts over economic benefits, and battles over cultural boundaries. This chapter examines those disputes, conflicts, and battles in New Mexico.

Although New Mexico remained a territory of the United States throughout the period under study, there were many parallels between its situation and that of the states, and authorities in the territory faced many of the same issues relating to Indian regulations as officials in the states confronted. New Mexico's legislators were elected from among local inhabitants; dealt with most of the same subjects handled by state legislatures, such as property, contracts, corporations, marriage, and crime; had the same inclination to regulate Indians as state lawmakers had; and faced similar questions about whether their enactments could be applied to Indians. Their constitutional position was different, however. Officials in a territory of the United States could not utilize state sovereignty or states' rights arguments to justify local regulation of Indians. Thus, in their effort to justify local authority over Indians, New Mexicans encountered complications beyond those confronting the states.

The characteristics of the Native peoples and the interests of the Americans living in New Mexico make the Indian citizenship debate there particularly revealing. The territory was home to a wide range of Indians, from those who were perceived as completely uncivilized to those seen as living in a fairly civilized manner, which led government officials to be more explicit about articulating cultural judgments and distinctions than they otherwise might have been. Furthermore, among the Americans living in New Mexico were both people who made their living from protecting Indian wards and people who stood to gain power and profit from Indian citizenship, making the jurisdictional and economic battles particularly impassioned.

The debate in New Mexico was also complicated by its history under Spanish and then Mexican rule, as well as by ambiguities in the treaty by which the territory became a part of the United States. The Treaty of Guadalupe Hidalgo, ending the Mexican-American War in 1848, provided all Mexican citizens in the territory acquired from Mexico with U.S. citizenship unless they declared their preference to remain Mexican citizens within one year of the treaty ratification. Unclear to the Americans was whether Indians—especially Pueblo Indians—were actually recognized and treated as Mexican citizens. Neither the Treaty of Guadalupe Hidalgo nor the Organic Law of 1850, which created the Territory of New Mexico, specifically addressed the issue of Pueblo Indian status. In the frontiers west of the Mississippi, the U.S. government was used to dealing with tribes that were (or were presumed to be) nomadic and hunting oriented, which it customarily treated as entities separate from the American body politick. The United States had no ready policy for agricultural Indians—such as the Pueblos—living in towns, nor did the government act quickly to clarify the Pueblo Indians' status. Remaining unclear for many years was whether the Pueblo Indians were to be treated the same as other U.S. Indians or were instead to have the rights of U.S. citizens.[1]

The debate over Pueblo Indian citizenship in the early territorial period focused on a handful of issues: the degree to which the Pueblo Indians were "civilized," the potential effect of withdrawing protection from them, the history of Pueblo Indian status under previous governments, the effect of the Treaty of Guadalupe Hidalgo on Indians, and the nature of Pueblo Indian title to land. Interestingly, there was little direct mention of racial issues throughout the debate. As in post–Civil War debates in Michigan and Minnesota, discussion in territorial New Mexico focused not on race but on the interrelationship of culture and status. The major participants in the New Mexico debate were Indian agents and lawyers. The agents, along with superintendents of Indian affairs, argued that Pueblo Indians were not ready for U.S. citizenship and needed the protection of the federal government. In contrast, lawyers and judges argued that these Indians were legally entitled to citizenship rights. By the late 1870s the decisive center of debate had shifted from the executive branch to the courts, and administrative authority had given way to the predominance of judicial authority. Concluding that the Pueblo Indians were civilized enough to be formally incorporated into the New Mexico community, territorial judges determined that those Indians were citizens.

ARGUMENTS OF INDIAN AGENTS AND SUPERINTENDENTS, 1850–1866

During the 1850s, the governors of New Mexico also served as the superintendents of Indian affairs. Indian policy was one of their biggest responsibilities, because of the large number of Indians in the territory. When the U.S. census of 1860 included the Indian population for the first time, it listed a total of 65,607 Indians, including 10,507 "civilized" Indians (mostly Pueblo Indians) and 55,100 other, "unenumerated" Indians (Navajos in the West, Apaches in the South, Utes in the Northwest, and Comanches in the Northeast).[2] Initially the governors, in their role as superintendents, assumed responsibility for managing relations with all of those Indians. Consequently the governors were actively involved in the debate over the status of the Pueblo Indians.

James S. Calhoun, who came to the territory as an Indian agent in 1849 and also served as governor and superintendent of Indian affairs from 1851 to 1852, tried to bring the Pueblo Indians into a protected position as wards of the U.S. government, and his successors and colleagues in the Indian service continued those efforts. Much of the debate about the status of the Pueblo Indians focused on the collective characteristics that distinguished them from other Indians. In New Mexico, government officials in the 1850s and 1860s most often characterized the Pueblo Indians as "half civilized," frequently noting that, unlike most other Indians, they lived a settled life in towns, supported themselves through agriculture rather than hunting, had a stable political structure, lived peacefully with their neighbors, and dressed and behaved in a decorous manner.[3] Despite the recognition of substantial differences between the Pueblo Indians and other Natives in New Mexico, government officials insisted that the Pueblo Indians still needed the special federal protections extended to other American Indians. The governors/superintendents and the agents therefore pressed the New Mexico territorial legislature and U.S. Congress to clarify the wardship status of the Pueblo Indians. They focused their efforts on three issues: the Pueblos' right to sue in U.S. courts, the apparent inapplicability of federal Indian laws to New Mexico, and legal uncertainty about the citizenship status of Pueblo Indians.

First, the governors and agents argued for the repeal of an 1847 statute that authorized Pueblo Indians to sue and defend collectively in lawsuits relating to their land.[4] This statute was perceived at the time as establishing the Pueblos as "quasi-corporations." Indeed, the statute contained much of the language that was typically used in the mid-nineteenth century to incorporate towns, private companies, and nonprofit associations. Unlike those laws, however, the New Mexico statute relating to the Pueblo Indians extended the right to sue and be sued only to actions brought to protect their title to land; other New Mexico incorporation statutes extended the right to sue and be sued to "all actions, pleas, and matters whatsoever" without the added qualification that the actions must relate to land. Furthermore, the other statutes uniformly granted the right to purchase and sell real estate, while the Pueblo statute omitted that power.[5]

Despite its limited scope, the governors and agents disapproved of the 1847 statute. They believed that the Pueblo Indians should not have to initiate litigation to protect their lands but should be able to depend on the federal government for protection of their property. In his address to members of the legislative assembly, Acting Governor and Superintendent William Watts Hart Davis (1855–1857) tried to persuade them to repeal the 1847 law for the welfare of the Pueblo Indians. When the assembly refused, Davis wrote the commissioner of Indian affairs to advocate congressional repeal as the only recourse. The 1847 act, he informed the commissioner, was "most mischievious in its tendency" and "working great wrong to this simple minded people." Governor and Superintendent David Meriwether (1853–1857) also recommended congressional repeal, because the Pueblo Indians were "ignorant and but little removed from a savage state," and "interested persons" encouraged "litigation between the different Pueblos and between the Mexican population and the Pueblos." If the possibility of suing the Pueblos were not eliminated through repeal of the law, he wrote, the expenses of litigation would be so high that many Pueblo villages would be "reduced to want and broken up." Abraham G. Mayers, agent to the Pueblo Indians, made a particularly forceful plea for Congress to repeal the 1847 law. He pointed out that "petty and frivolous" lawsuits were subjecting the Pueblo Indians to unnecessary legal costs. A better, and cheaper course, he said, would be granting the government's Indian agent the power to settle differences between the Pueblos.[6]

Governors and Indian agents also attempted to clarify the wardship status of the Pueblo Indians by convincing Congress to extend the federal trade and intercourse act of 1834 over them. The governors believed that the statute should be applied to the Pueblo Indians as it was to other Indian tribes in the United States. The object was to protect the Pueblos from abuses and encroachments by Anglos and Hispanos. The statute made Indians wards of the U.S. government and guaranteed federal protection to them and their property. Among other things, the law prohibited Americans from trading with Natives in Indian Country without a license, selling them liquor in Indian Country, or settling on any lands belonging to Native Americans or secured or granted to any Indian tribe by treaty with the United States. The statute also provided that conveyances of land from any Indian nation or tribe were invalid unless made by treaty.[7]

Federal policymakers and administrators doubted that the trade and intercourse act of 1834 applied to land acquired by the United States from Mexico and consequently to any Indians or any Indian lands in New Mexico. While serving as an Indian agent under the U.S. military government, and then as governor and Indian superintendent of the territory, Calhoun repeatedly urged Congress to amend the statute to make clear that it applied to all the Indians of New Mexico. He explained to the commissioner of Indian affairs in Washington DC that the Pueblo Indians had requested federal protection; he even negotiated with most of the Pueblos a treaty in which they agreed to be covered by the trade and intercourse act, but the document was never ratified by the Senate.[8] Calhoun also pressed the federal government to send Indian agents to the Pueblos for their protection, as was the practice with other Indian tribes. Finally, in 1852 Calhoun's successor appointed interpreter John Ward as special agent for the Pueblo Indians.[9] In the continuing debate over Pueblo Indian citizenship status, the argument that the federal government had never acted to place the Pueblos under wardship status was supported by two pieces of evidence: the fact that Indian agents to the Pueblos were appointed by the governor rather than explicitly by Congress and the fact that the Senate never approved the treaty placing Pueblos under the trade and intercourse act.

By a federal statute of 1851, the law regulating trade and intercourse with the Indian tribes was expanded to cover the Territory of New Mexico.[10] Because the terms of the trade and intercourse act applied to "Indian country," and because judges in New Mexico ruled that no part of New Mexico had been legally designated Indian Country, many New Mexicans doubted that the 1851 statute actually had the effect of extending the provisions of the 1834 act to cover any Indians in the territory. Governor Meriwether and Indian agent Edmund A. Graves urged Congress to clarify further the coverage by specifying which parts of New Mexico were and were not part of Indian Country.[11] Despite their repeated recommendation, applicability of the trade and intercourse act in the territory remained ambiguous.

Perhaps the biggest concern was whether the trade and intercourse laws authorized officials in New Mexico to prevent the sale of liquor to Indians in the territory. For example, in 1853 Indian agent J. M. Smith informed Governor Meriwether that New Mexicans were trading regularly with the Indians at a local farm. Smith was particularly concerned that the sale of whiskey from the farm increased disorder and violence but was not sure that he had the legal authority to do anything about it.[12] Concern about sales of liquor to Indians was so strong, and uncertainty about the applicability of the federal law so troubling, that the legislature of New Mexico enacted its own statute prohibiting the sale of liquor to Indians.[13] But as long as there existed ambiguity about the applicability of the federal law, the legitimacy of this local statute was problematic as well. As Indian agent Graves pointed out, if the 1834 federal statute did apply in New Mexico, the territorial statute would be void, "inasmuch as no state can, constitutionally, legislate upon any subject which has received congressional action; that where 'Congress has exercised their powers upon any given subject, the States cannot enter upon the same ground' and provide for same or different objects; much less can the Territorial Legislature."[14] Although the territories faced similar jurisdictional conflicts between federal and local legislation as the states confronted, territorial officials could not advance any equivalent to the states' rights or state sovereignty argument to justify passing legislation that paralleled or conflicted with federal law.

New Mexico's government officials had their strongest doubts about the applicability of the trade and intercourse act of 1834 to the Pueblo Indians. Indian agent Mayers asked Acting Governor Davis in late 1855 whether non-Indians could carry on trade with the Pueblo Indians without first having obtained a license to do so (as required by the trade and intercourse act). Davis replied that on this matter the Pueblo Indians were "in the same situation as those known as the wild tribes." But Governor Meriwether, then in the midst of a visit to Washington DC, expressed disagreement in a letter to the commissioner of Indian affairs. The situation of the Pueblo Indians—many of whom lived just a few miles from Santa Fe, and who regularly sold their surplus produce in that city—made it illogical to limit them to selling only to license-holding New Mexicans. In fact, he pointed out, the territorial act of 1853 allowed dealers in liquor to sell to Pueblo Indians in the same manner as they could sell to any other citizen of New Mexico. Furthermore, when the legislative assembly passed an enforcement law to implement the trade and intercourse act, it used the term "Savage Indian tribes" in the title of the law, which suggests that they did not believe the 1834 law applied to the Pueblo Indians.[15] Local assumptions were not determinative, however. Throughout the early territorial period, New Mexicans could not be sure whether the sale of liquor to Pueblo Indians was legal or not.

The other major issue was whether the trade and intercourse act prohibited Americans from settling on Indian lands—especially Pueblo lands—in New Mexico. In 1859 the territory's superintendent of Indian affairs, James Collins, asked the commissioner of Indian affairs whether the government had the authority to remove illegal squatters on Pueblo lands. Collins noted that if the lands granted to the Pueblo Indians by the Spanish were "to be considered as Indian Territory, then the authority exists in the intercourse act of 1834," but he needed the commissioner to provide instructions on the extent of Indian Territory in New Mexico. As late as 1866, the agent for the Pueblo Indians, John D. Henderson, reported to the commissioner that the Pueblos were still complaining of encroachments on their lands by "Americans and Mexicans" but observed that the ambiguity in federal Indian laws muddied the Pueblo Indians' land rights. He asked for specific instructions on the matter, noting that the new superintendent, A. Baldwin Norton, was unable to provide guidance.[16]

To some extent the application of the 1834 act and related questions were tied up with the third issue: citizenship. The governors who also served as superintendents all opposed Pueblo Indian citizenship. Calhoun argued against politically merging the Pueblo Indians with the rest of the population of New Mexico. The Mexicans and Pueblos had nothing in common and therefore could not be represented by the same elected officials and should not be subject to the same laws. In Calhoun's opinion, the Pueblo Indians should have the right to vote only for officers in their own pueblos; they should not vote in New Mexico elections.[17]

Calhoun's position—the exclusion of Pueblos from the suffrage—seemed to have the support of national legislation. Creating New Mexico Territory in 1850, the Organic Law explicitly mentioned Indians in section 5, which described the legislative assembly of the new territorial government. While providing for proportional representation of each district in the territory, the Organic Law excluded Indians from the population legally counted in each district. Furthermore, in that law Congress also specified that for the first election only free white male inhabitants of New Mexico over the age of twenty-one were entitled to vote. For subsequent elections the legislative assembly of the territory was to prescribe the qualifications of voters and officeholders. In statutes enacted during its first year, the legislative assembly continued the race-based restrictions on suffrage and officeholding.[18]

Calhoun informed the commissioner in early 1850 that some Indians from Taos had already been induced to vote by unscrupulous New Mexicans. Traveling to Taos Pueblo, Calhoun explained to the Indians that voting in territorial elections was inconsistent with their maintaining a Native community that was distinct and independent from the rest of New Mexico. They could participate fully in the political process and be citizens only if they abandoned their separate communities, relinquished all forms of self-government, and gave up the right to the protective umbrella of the federal government enjoyed by other Indian tribes. Calhoun advised them that such a trade would not be to their advantage, and the Taos Indians apparently agreed.[19]

Calhoun's successors and colleagues agreed that the Pueblo Indians were unprepared for citizenship. In 1854 Governor and Superintendent Meriwether contended that despite the semi-civilized status of the Pueblo Indians, they were still "buried in ignorance and superstition." Therefore, the Pueblo Indians should have "the protection and fostering hand of the government." In 1859 Superintendent of Indian Affairs James Collins concurred that the Pueblos were Indians "pretty well advanced in civilization, and yet not enough to make it proper to extend to them the rights of citizenship." In an address to the legislative assembly on 3 December 1855, Acting Governor and Superintendent Davis similarly acknowledged that the Pueblo Indians were different from other Indians but concluded that they needed government protection nevertheless. "It is true," he said, "that the Pueblo Indians occupy a position somewhat different from that presented by the wandering tribes, being permanently settled in villages, and enjoying a higher degree of civilization, but this is not sufficient to remove them from the immediate jurisdiction of the United States." In his 1857 memoir, Davis concluded that the Pueblo Indians shared the political status of the "wild Indians": they were not citizens. He pointed out that since the Republic of Mexico had treated Indians as wards rather than as citizens in practice, and since the Treaty of Guadalupe Hidalgo gave only "Mexicans" the right to become U.S. citizens, no Indians, Pueblos included, acquired U.S. citizenship through the treaty. Furthermore, he noted, it made no sense to grant New Mexico's Indians rights that other Indians in the United States did not enjoy. Governor David Meriwether agreed that the Pueblo Indians were not citizens.[20]

Indian agents were particularly eager for the issue of Pueblo citizenship to be firmly resolved. In 1852, 1853, and 1857, respectively, Agents Edward H. Wingfield, Edmund Graves, and Abraham G. Mayers unsuccessfully appealed to the commissioner of Indian affairs to settle the matter, noting that the Pueblo Indians' uncertain status left them without federal protection but also without citizenship rights. Mayers expressed frustration that when an agent tried to act on behalf of the Indians to defend their lands or other interests, he was frequently thwarted by claims that such matters could only be dealt with by the courts. Wingfield recommended that, as the Pueblos wished, they be officially categorized as "Indians." Graves directly asked the commissioner whether the Pueblo Indians held the same political status as former Mexicans, but Commissioner Manypenny's reply, issued two months later, dodged the question. Another Pueblo agent, Samuel M. Yost, believed that the Pueblo Indians had the potential to advance themselves adequately to justify making them citizens, but that raising them to a sufficiently high "degree of civilization" would take attentive "fostering care of the government."[21]

In practice, legislation pertaining to Pueblo citizenship remained ambiguous, with some statutes suggesting citizenship and others denying it. The territorial legislature tried to clarify the issue during Meriwether's administration. The *Santa Fe Weekly Gazette* reported that on January 3, 1854, in the territorial Senate "Mr Baca y Pino offered a joint resolution, requiring the Governor to summon all Captains of the several Pueblos, to appear before this body and declare their intention in relation to their citizenship." The implication was that Pueblo Indians could in fact become citizens of the United States. Later that winter, however, the legislature enacted a law excluding Pueblo Indians from the privilege of voting, except in elections for overseers of ditches and within their own pueblos. This provision was to remain in place until the Pueblo Indians should "be declared, by the Congress of the United States, to have the right" to vote. Two years later the Pueblo Indians were further marginalized by a law exempting them from a requirement that all adult males in New Mexico pay a tax to support education of youth in the Territory.[22]

Thus, by the late 1860s, Pueblo Indians were allowed to sue in American courts but not to vote in elections. The federal government recognized Pueblo title to their land but withheld the power to sell it. A federal government appointee had negotiated with the Pueblos a treaty that the Senate never ratified, and the territorial governor/superintendent, not Congress, had sent the Pueblos federal agents. The territorial prohibition on selling liquor to Indians did not apply to the Pueblo Indians, but the application of the federal trade and intercourse act of 1834 to the Pueblos was still uncertain. In short, after two decades of debate, the status of the Pueblo Indians remained ambiguous.

JUDICIAL DECISION MAKING, 1867–1877

For many years after New Mexico became part of the United States, the legal status of the Pueblo Indians remained a political discussion centered particularly in the executive and legislative branches of the territorial government. The governors, superintendents of Indian affairs, and Indian agents debated the issue on a regular basis. Meanwhile, the legislature periodically passed legislation that sent conflicting messages about Pueblo status. In the late 1860s, however, the judiciary stepped in assertively to resolve the issue.

The cases prompting judicial review involved alleged violations of the trade and intercourse act of 1834. The District Court of the First Judicial District of New Mexico ruled in 1867 that the statute did not apply to the Pueblo Indians. In *United States v. Ortiz*, the defendant (a non-Indian) had occupied land belonging to the Pueblo of Cochiti and was charged with trespass on Indian lands. The United States brought an action to collect the fine imposed by the 1834 act. In a decision written by Justice John N. Slough, the district court dismissed the suit. The issue of applicability of the trade and intercourse act to the Pueblo Indians reached the Supreme Court of New Mexico in 1869. Like *Ortiz*, *United States v. Lucero* was initiated in the District Court of the First Judicial District in 1867 and was an action to collect the fine from a non-Indian man who had settled on Pueblo lands. In a decision written by Chief Justice John S. Watts, the Supreme Court of the territory agreed with Justice Slough's reasoning in the lower court. In 1874 more challenges to the applicability of the trade and intercourse act to the Pueblo Indians came to the New Mexico Supreme Court, and in 1877, the decisions by Justices Warren Bristol and Hezekiah Johnson on this issue were endorsed by the U.S. Supreme Court in *United States v. Joseph.*[23]

These judicial opinions demonstrate that when justices addressed the status of Pueblo Indians in New Mexico, they based their decisions on many of the same criteria that authorities in the other two branches had used to argue their positions on the issue, but once they concluded that the Pueblo Indians were civilized, they shifted to generally applicable principles of law to decide on the Indians' position in New Mexico.

Like governors, superintendents of Indian affairs, and Indian agents, justices in New Mexico assessed the cultural characteristics of Pueblos, analyzing whether they were different from or similar to other Indians to determine whether they were "civilized" enough to be U.S. citizens. Justice Slough in *Ortiz* and Justice Watts in *Lucero* both concluded that the Pueblo Indians were civilized tribes. Because they were different from the "savage and uncivilized" Indian tribes of the United States, the trade and intercourse act was not intended to apply to them, leaving them to be regulated by local territorial officials rather than the federal government in Washington.

Once legal writers had determined that the Pueblo Indians were civilized, they set aside cultural issues and moved on to historical and legal arguments. As officials in the executive branch had done for twenty years, justices took note of the Spanish and Mexican history of New Mexico and evaluated whether the Treaty of Guadalupe Hidalgo necessarily made the Pueblo Indians citizens. Such a consideration fell squarely within appropriate judicial concerns, for it involved interpreting the language of the treaty in light of the legal circumstances in 1848. Justices Slough, Watts, and Bristol argued that Pueblo Indians were not covered by the trade and intercourse act because, having been citizens of Mexico, they became citizens of the United States by the terms of the Treaty of Guadalupe Hidalgo. Justices Watts and Bristol also pointed out that the United States had not treated the Pueblo Indians like Indian tribes. Watts noted that Congress had neither appointed agents for nor made treaties with any of the Pueblo Indians as it had done with other American Indian tribes, and Justice Bristol observed that the United States had treated Pueblo land claims in the same way that it handled other Spanish land-grant claims. The justices used these historical arguments as the basis for rights-based conclusions. Watts concluded that the court "does not consider it proper to assent to the withdrawal of eight thousand citizens of New Mexico from the operation of the laws, made to secure and maintain them in their liberty and property, and consign their liberty and property to a system of laws and trade made for wandering savages and administered by the agents of the Indian department." In *Ortiz* Justice Slough concluded, "[t]he federal Constitution guarantees to all citizens the same privileges and immunities and protection to life, liberty, and property. These rights are as much guaranteed to pueblo Indians as to any other class of citizens of the United States."

New Mexico territorial justices also raised certain legal issues that had not previously entered the political debate. In fact, the decisions made by the New Mexico Supreme Court during the 1870s incorporated a more predominantly legalistic focus than the court's 1860s decision had. In all of these Pueblo Indian cases, the issue was whether a non-Indian who settled on Pueblo land had violated the trade and intercourse act. In *Joseph* and its companion cases, the New Mexico Supreme Court kept its decisions more directly focused on that issue, declining to take on the broader issues of the Pueblo Indians' legal status, which the justices had tried to resolve in *Ortiz* and *Lucero*. The courts in *Joseph* concentrated especially on the nature of Pueblo Indian title to their land. The decisive fact was that unlike other Indian tribes (who held only the right to use the land they occupied, leaving ultimate ownership in the United States), the Pueblo Indians held full legal title to their land. The justices, therefore, gave two reasons for concluding that the trade and intercourse act was not applicable to Pueblo land. First, since the law by its own language prohibited non-Indian settlement only on Indian land acquired by *treaty* between Indians and the United States, it did not apply to Pueblo Indian land, which had been obtained by grants from the government of Spain (later confirmed by the U.S. government) rather than by treaty. Second, the purpose of the statutory provisions protecting land occupied by Indians was to protect the federal government's ultimate ownership of that land, yet that object was not advanced by applying the statute to land in which the United States had no ownership rights to protect. Based on these legal reasons, the courts decided that a non-Indian who settled on Taos Pueblo lands was not guilty of violating the trade and intercourse act, and any encroachment on Pueblo Indian lands was appropriately dealt with by commencing a trespass or ejectment action in the civil courts of New Mexico.

Not surprisingly, Indian agents and the superintendent were strongly critical of the district court decisions. One of their main concerns was that the judicial decisions would lead to the loss of Pueblo lands. As one government official explained in a letter criticizing the *Ortiz* decision as "erroneous," the Pueblo Indians "occupy some of the fairest portions of this territory . . . [and t]he white man naturally covets these fertile lands."[24] Superintendent of Indian Affairs Norton, Pueblo agent Henderson, special Pueblo agent John Ward, and Indian agent William F. M. Arny all warned of the dire consequences of the court decisions to the Pueblos: "Mexicans and Americans" would swindle the defenseless Indians out of their lands, and the previously self-supporting, civilized Pueblo Indians would become landless paupers and would return to a savage state. They argued that Pueblo Indians could not survive without the protection of the superintendent and the Indian agents.[25]

CONFLICTING VIEWS ON INDIAN CITIZENSHIP

As a general rule the Indian agents and superintendents of Indian affairs (including the governors, who also served as superintendents) tended to advocate clearly placing the Pueblo Indians into the same wardship status as that held by other Indian tribes in the United States and making them subject to the trade and intercourse act of 1834. Consistent with that broad position, they argued that the 1847 statute should be repealed, that Indian agents rather than courts should mediate disputes and controversies in the pueblos, that the federal government should actively protect Pueblo lands and supply provisions to support Pueblo members, and that Pueblo Indians should not participate in the territory's political process or otherwise exercise the rights of U.S. citizens. In contrast, lawyers and judges tended to advocate citizenship status for the Pueblo Indians. Thus, they argued that the Pueblo Indians should have the right to sell or lease their lands and should protect their own lands against encroachment by bringing complaints to court. Because the Pueblos could govern themselves, they had no need for Indian agents.

What explains the differences between positions taken by superintendents or agents and those advocated by judges? It is possible that because the superintendents and agents worked more closely with Indians, they understood, better than others did, the realities of the Pueblo Indians' lives and the exploitation and other disadvantages that would result if they were given no special protections and were treated as citizens. It is possible that lawyers and judges reached different conclusions because their training led them to rely more than anything else on legal precedent dating from the time of the Mexican Republic and official documents, particularly the Treaty of Guadalupe Hidalgo, to determine Pueblo Indian status. Thus, in a debate that posited reasonable, plausible arguments on both sides, the two groups could have taken opposing views as a natural result of their different training and experience. Also conceivable, however, is that both groups acted out of narrow self-interest.

The jobs of the Indian agents and superintendents depended on the Indians' falling within the scope of the trade and intercourse act and outside the boundaries of citizenship. Even those agents who did not work directly with the Pueblo Indians might have feared that exempting the Pueblos from the trade and intercourse laws would set a troubling precedent and put them out of a job. Field positions in the Bureau of Indian Affairs could be quite lucrative. The annual salary of an Indian agent was $1,500, while the superintendent of Indian affairs was given an annual salary of $2,000.[26] In the early territorial period, the average full-time blacksmith worked three years to earn $1,500, and a servant, a decade or more to collect that much.[27]

Furthermore, there is evidence to suggest that some agents derived benefits beyond their salaries. Indian agents and superintendents in New Mexico, like their bureau colleagues throughout the West, were charged with disbursing annually tens of thousands of dollars allocated by the federal government to cover the costs of supplying and serving the Indians of the territory.[28] Some people suspected that much of that money simply went into the pockets of the agents and their friends. Julius K. Graves, the special commissioner sent to evaluate Indian affairs in New Mexico in 1866, observed that "the present Agents have very many relatives and friends who hang on to the agencies and evidently appropriate a large share of the articles and food intended for the Indians." Specifically, he questioned whether there was any continuing need for an agent to the Pueblos and whether the Indians accrued any benefit whatever from the money allocated to support the agent and his work. In fact, he wrote, "the annual salary now paid the Pueblo Agent would under their [the Pueblo Indians'] economical and judicious management be productive of much good, whereas under present arrangements this expenditure results in little or no good to these Indians."[29]

New Mexico attorney and judge John Watts expressed even blunter, more negative views of government officials who dealt with the Indians in the territory. In a sixty-four-page letter addressed to the secretary of the interior in 1869, Watts claimed that statutes allocating money to pay for the subsistence of New Mexico Indians were routinely exploited for private profit. Influenced by half a dozen New York and Philadelphia mercantile businesses, the Indian Department, asserted Watts, allowed such funds to be used in New Mexico not for food but for shoddy blankets. And, most notably, the department purchased the blankets at "over double their real value," paying 60 percent over the going rate—nineteen rather than twelve cents per pound—for transporting the goods to New Mexico. According to Watts, profits from this misallocation of funds went into the hands of men in the "Indian ring." He pointed out that nationwide the government had brought in millions of dollars of profit by purchasing Indians' land at a price of two cents an acre and then reselling it at $1.25 to $2.50 per acre. Thus, as a general rule, declaring groups of Indians to be quasi-nations rather than citizens simply allowed the government "to monopolize the right to cheat them out of [their land]." Furthermore, the men appointed to hold office in New Mexico were typically lazy and ignorant of conditions in the territory and were there only to collect their salaries, not to serve the interests of the people of New Mexico. Watts argued that the profit to be made from contracts to supply the Indians, from the sale of Indian lands, and from placing cronies in office in New Mexico, motivated unscrupulous government officials to perpetuate the subjection of New Mexico's Indians to "the dependent vassalage of the Indian Department."[30]

Clearly evident was the potential for abuse of federal funds by Indian agents and superintendents, and complaints about the incompetence and corrupt practice of Indian agents were common in early territorial New Mexico. Coinciding with the territorial court decisions in the late 1860s was an effort to remove Pueblo agents Ward and Henderson. Whether from real concern about corruption or eagerness to eliminate genuine advocates for the Indians, their enemies sought their removal by accusing them of various forms of fraud. For example, in 1868 lawyer Charles P. Clever accused Henderson of submitting false vouchers and making fictitious disbursements.[31] Unclear in the historical record is whether Henderson was guilty, but New Mexico historian Marc Simmons has described the Indians of the territory in general as "the hapless prey of disinterested or dishonest agents, corrupt territorial officials, and thieving supply contractors."[32]

If Indian agents in New Mexico were corrupt, they were apparently not acting much differently from agents stationed in other parts of the country during this period. Reformers argued that many Indian agents throughout the United States were political spoilsmen eager to serve only for the sake of anticipated financial gain. Of all the deficiencies in the Indian service, the most blatant and urgent problem lay in the process by which annuities and supplies were provided to Indians. The agents, who were responsible for distributing money and for procuring and allocating goods, often profited enormously by defrauding both the Indians and the federal government.[33]

New Mexico's lawyers, too, had a personal interest in their position on Pueblo Indian citizenship, and the interests and perspectives of judges coincided for the most part with those of practicing attorneys.[34] Lawyers stood to gain in several ways from the inclusion of Pueblo Indians as citizens of the United States: (1) they wanted Pueblo Indian clients, (2) they wanted access to Pueblo Indian land and water, and (3) they wanted to establish legal precedents that would open non-Pueblo land to private ownership.

First, if the Pueblo Indians were federal wards, they had no right to bring or defend lawsuits in court, and the business of New Mexico's lawyers would decline. In 1854 lawyer Spruce Baird was paid a retainer of one thousand dollars for representing Acoma Pueblo in its various ongoing lawsuits over land, water, sheep, and other matters. At the same time he was not precluded from handling other legal business or engaging in other occupations.[35] The handsome fees lawyers received for their legal work on behalf of the Indians likely inspired many of New Mexico's attorneys actively to argue that the trade and intercourse acts did not apply to the Pueblo Indians and that they were free to sell land and litigate in court.[36]

Indian agents and superintendents in New Mexico eagerly pointed out this conflict of interest to the commissioner. They often accused lawyers of taking advantage of Pueblo Indians and claimed that the lawyers alone benefited from Pueblo Indian litigation. In 1857 Pueblo agent Mayers asserted that the "best reason" for repealing the 1847 act that allowed the Pueblo Indians to sue and be sued was "the fact that the lawyers and not the Indians are benifited by it." In 1866 Pueblo agent Henderson explained to the commissioner of Indian affairs that "Americans and Mexicans" were dragging the Pueblo Indians into biased local courts with legal claims to their land. The government needed to act to free Pueblo Indians from the burden of such "vexatious prosecutions." Governor and Superintendent of Indian Affairs Meriwether informed the commissioner in 1855 that lawyers were stirring up litigation among the Pueblos and were profiting immensely from doing so. "As an evidence of the extent to which the practice has obtained," he wrote, "I would mention the fact of the Pueblos of Acoma and Laguna having over twenty suits now pending between them, and when all these are decided I fear the lawyers engaged, and the officers of the Courts, will have claims for fees sufficient to cover all that the two Pueblos are worth."[37]

Second, the lawyers' interest in Pueblo Indian status was that citizenship would make the tribes' land and water available for purchase. Pueblo land was particularly attractive because of the easy access to water from the Rio Grande and its tributaries. In New Mexico, developers, farmers, and ranchers could use land for colonization, cultivation, or pasturage only if they also had control of water. Strategic purchases of land that had a water supply allowed the owner to determine the utilization of surrounding acres that were dependent on that source.[38] Thus, outsiders focused on obtaining rights to portions of Pueblo lands that included water or were, at least, irrigable. The evidence suggests that non-Indians were fairly successful: by the time of the *Sandoval* case (1913), which nullified all Pueblo land and water sales going back to 1848, non-Indian claims on Pueblo lands included almost all of the water on those lands.[39]

Third, lawyers knew that securing the marketability of Pueblo land might also increase the potential for private ownership of non-Pueblo lands. Lawyers wanted as much land as possible on the market both for their professional role as legal advocates of land occupants and for their personal role as land speculators. Consequently, they worked hard to persuade the surveyor general that a community land grant to a group of settlers was really a private grant to an individual. Successfully making Pueblo Indian lands alienable had the potential to open up other lands as well, if the lawyers could reinforce the parallel between the status of community grants to Hispanics and the status of collective grants to Pueblo tribes. The occupants of a community grant did not individually own and could not individually sell any part of the commons, which was used for pasturing livestock, collecting firewood, and hunting. In contrast, any part of a private grant could be sold by the owner. Thus, land lawyers litigated to undermine the concept of communally owned land in order to persuade judges that a few private individuals actually owned land occupied by many settlers. Gaining official approval of the principle that the grant of citizenship to the Pueblo Indians at the end of the Spanish colonial period had the effect of privatizing Spanish land grants to Pueblos contributed to the effort to portray Spanish and Mexican grants to non-Indians as private rather than community grants. Attacking Pueblo Indians' collective ownership not only made Pueblo land itself alienable but also potentially reinforced the legal view that Hispanics' land was privately owned.[40]

Making more land available in the market meant that owners would more likely need litigators to argue for confirmation of their claims and also meant that the land would be available to lawyers as a form of payment for attorneys' fees. As historians have pointed out, lawyers often took advantage of Indian and Hispano landowners' ignorance of Anglo-American law and the English language. After Congress established a method for confirmation of land titles in 1854, unscrupulous lawyers exaggerated the complexity of the process in order to persuade local landowners that they needed expert legal advice. Since most landowners lacked sufficient cash to cover the attorneys' bloated fees, they commonly paid the lawyers in land. Typically, the fee for obtaining a land-grant confirmation was one-third of the acreage, and sometimes attorneys received one-half for their services on behalf of the claimant. The consequence was that lawyers increasingly gained ownership of large portions of the Spanish and Mexican land grants.[41]

Of the seven New Mexico attorneys—Merrill Ashurst, Kirby Benedict, William Breeden, Stephen B. Elkins, Joab Houghton, Richard H. Tompkins, and Henry L. Waldo—who represented defendants in the trade and intercourse actions that led to *Ortiz*, *Lucero*, *Joseph*, and the companion cases, at least six were heavily involved in capital investments or legal work that depended on the marketability of land and the availability of water for their profitability.

Stephen B. Elkins, who served as Antonio Joseph's attorney before the U.S. Supreme Court in the 1870s, most clearly exemplifies lawyers' personal stake in land speculation. In the 1860s and 1870s Elkins was one of the most active speculators in New Mexico land, holding interests in some of the largest land grants, including the Maxwell Grant, Mora Grant, and Ortiz Grant. In addition to speculating in land, Elkins was involved in other enterprises, including a railroad company, a cattle company, a silver-mining company, and a bank. Elkins, Breeden, and Waldo were close political and economic allies, members of the infamous "Santa Fe Ring." According to many contemporary New Mexicans and some later historians, that infamous organization controlled land speculation, ranching, mining, rail-roads, politics, and the courts in territorial New Mexico. A fourth lawyer from the cases under study, Kirby Benedict, former justice and land-title expert, was thought to be a member of the ring as well. Another of the law-yers, Joab Houghton, represented twelve different land-grant claimants in efforts to secure title confirmation, and he held personal interest in several of the grants. The sixth New Mexico lawyer, Merrill Ashurst, also repre-sented a number of land-grant claimants in the decade and a half before he died in 1869. Thus, the only one of the seven lawyers who apparently did not take an active role in land speculation or in representing land specula-tors was Richard Tompkins. Furthermore, when the *Joseph* case was argued before the U.S. Supreme Court on April 20, 1877, the New Mexico lawyers were assisted by William M. Evarts, an influential New York lawyer and former U.S. attorney general who wrote the brief in support of Antonio Joseph. Evarts, an easterner, provided business and legal support for mem-bers of the Santa Fe Ring and played a continuing and important role in the capital development of New Mexico.[42]

Even the territorial judges—Bristol, Johnson, Slough, and Watts—who wrote judicial decisions advocating that the trade and intercourse act did not apply to Pueblo lands had an interest in land speculation. John Watts, a lawyer-judge, opposed application of the trade and intercourse acts to Pueblo Indians and was a strong critic of the Indian agents but also had his own personal interest in New Mexico's land. Watts, the judge who wrote the *Lucero* decision, was active in land acquisition and speculation in the 1850s and 1860s; Emlen Hall has referred to him as "one of New Mexico's earliest land speculators." In the late 1850s Watts's legal work included forty-three land-grant cases, and the payment for his legal services was often in land. Two of the other justices also had ties to land speculation or the Santa Fe Ring. When he died in late 1867, Slough was the president and business manager of a company organized to develop and sell lots of land in the proposed new mining town of Virginia City. During the violent unrest in Lincoln County in the late 1870s, Justice Bristol was accused of serving as a "tool" of the Santa Fe Ring.[43]

At the national level, there was a good deal of support for the position the courts took in *Joseph*. Many advocated assimilation of Indians into the American political and economic community. Furthermore, in the indi-vidualistic late nineteenth century, many Americans disapproved of and were uncomfortable with communal living and property. Privatizing land ownership in New Mexico was consistent with this general national ethos.

Allotment of Indian lands had long been accepted as a means to assimilate Indians into American society. In the mid-nineteenth century, Congress was providing for the allotment of some tribes' lands; a few years prior to the *Joseph* decision Congress had determined that the United States would no longer treat Indian tribes as independent nations with whom the country could make treaties; and a decade after the *Joseph* decision Congress authorized the allotment of all tribal lands, along with U.S. citizenship, to individual Indians.[44] The judicial interpretation in *Joseph* and the companion cases allowed Pueblo land and water to join the American land market, a measure that was consistent with Anglo-American eagerness to find profitable uses for natural resources. Parallels are seen in a number of other U.S. states and territories, where Indians were incorporated, assimilated, or removed in order to give Americans access to desirable lands and resources.[45]

The evidence thus suggests that in the debate over the legal and political status of the Pueblo Indians, the individual self-interest of some participants affected the positions they took. Both lawyers and Indian agents were accused of being rapacious and unscrupulous, and both were criticized for earning undue financial rewards from their dealings with the Indians. At the same time, important to keep in mind is that it really was not clear whether or not the Pueblo Indians would actually gain or lose from U.S. citizenship. There were legitimate and objective bases for the arguments on both sides. What is of particular interest here is the way in which government officials dealt with the issue, how they saw—and fought for—their own interests, and the language they used to talk about the subject.

Not only did the arguments presented by Indian agents and lawyers reflect their different professional backgrounds and the form of expression common to their particular occupations, but the language used by each side also helped support the group's own position in the jurisdictional clashes between administrative and judicial authority and the conflict between control from Washington and local management within the territory. As long as Pueblo Indians were treated as U.S. government wards, they fell under the federal agents' administrative authority, and New Mexico's lawyers and judges found their power, as well as their profits, diminished. On the other hand, declaring Pueblo Indians U.S. citizens removed Pueblo Indians and their lands from executive administrative control and placed them under court jurisdiction; naturally that relocation was a threat to the political power and economic interests of the Indian agents.

Although group economic interests prompted the positions of both

Indian agents and lawyers on Pueblo Indian status, the judicial decisions in *Joseph* and the related cases had an impact and a meaning that went beyond the economic interests of those two groups. First, because the decisions had ramifications for determining definitions of property and access to property, they affected other people as well, most notably the Pueblo Indians. Second, the decisions had deep cultural meaning. The very adjustment of the line between insiders and outsiders, and citizens and noncitizens, was based on Anglo Americans' sense of their own cultural identity. Thus, the jurisdictional conflict between Indian agents and lawyers had ramifications both for economic opportunities (or determining who would be positioned to gain property and make money) and for cultural boundary drawing (or designating who was inside and who was outside the political community).[46]

Together, the histories of Massachusetts and New Mexico in the nineteenth century show how states and territories unilaterally and collectively incorporated Indians as citizens where it was both advantageous and feasible to do so. The two accounts reveal some of the ways in which political, economic, social, and cultural factors affected people's positions on the Indian citizenship issue. The Mashpee hearing in Massachusetts shows that not everyone affiliated with a tribe opposed citizenship and land allotment, but it also suggests that Natives who had grown up with a tribe rather than marrying into it as adults may have been more likely to express a preference for retaining the corporate identity and collective landholding of the tribe. The alleged position of the Taos Pueblo Indians in New Mexico was consistent with such opposition to merging with the white population, though it is difficult to assess the accuracy of Governor Calhoun's account of what the Taos Indians wanted.

The New Mexico debate makes it clear that among whites there also was not complete agreement on the issue, though the Massachusetts experience, as well as the history of New York, Michigan, and Minnesota, indicates that overall most white Americans seem to have supported the idea of Indian citizenship. Where they did disagree, it was often because they had conflicting political or economic interests involved, as exemplified by the Indian agents' stake in Indians as wards as opposed to the tangible advantages to lawyers if Indians were citizens. Genuine commitment to principles of equal rights also led some Americans to advocate Indian citizenship. Finally, powerfully reinforcing white Americans' support on the citizenship issue were powerful cultural norms. Both the Massachusetts legislative decision and New Mexico's judicial opinions on Indian status reflected and expressed a strong sentiment in favor of advancing American individualism and expanding economic markets, promoting patriarchal social arrangements, and welcoming into the fold peoples who had demonstrated that their way of life and character were consistent with American values.

The underlying presumptions of the debates in Massachusetts and New Mexico were consistent with those inspiring the terms of the 1850s and 1860s constitutions in Michigan and Minnesota and set a national precedent. In her analysis of the writings of Lydia Maria Child and Lyman Abbott, Lucy Maddox describes the development of a presumed link between behavior and rights that had solidified nationally by the early twentieth century. Indianness and citizenship were thought to be incompatible. Consequently the 1924 federal law granting citizenship to the entire Indian population was possible only because Indians had by then shown that they were "capable of giving up [their] Indianness and behaving like real Americans, performing the signs of [their] entitlement."[47] Massachusetts' Indians and a portion of New Mexico's were considered to have already reached that stage in the late 1860s. As shown in chapter 5, the language of the franchise provisions in Michigan and Minnesota, too, demonstrated that "civilized performance" was seen as a condition for rights. In short, local jurisdictions—Massachusetts, New Mexico, Michigan, Minnesota, and other states and territories—set the standard over half a century before the federal citizenship law: Indians who surrendered their own culture, social and economic organization, and political structure were those deemed to be worthy of American citizenship and rights.

Conclusion

State Law and Direct Rule over Indians

The states led the way to incorporating Indians into American society between 1790 and 1880. During the nine decades following the ratification of the Constitution, the states applied their laws directly to Indians within state borders, brought Indians into the legal order by giving them access to law courts and including them in the states' criminal jurisdiction, and integrated many Indians into the political structure by granting them the right of suffrage and citizenship status. The underside of those developments was the states' disregard of tribal sovereignty, reliance on tenets of white racial superiority, and pervasive paternalistic posture toward Indians. State Indian policies were also influenced by other interests and goals, such as asserting state sovereignty, maintaining the racial foundation of the institution of slavery or—at a later time—promoting principles of civil rights, furthering pride in regional identity, reinforcing private property ownership and patriarchal values, and bringing land and resources into the market economy. With these motivations and attitudes shaping their legislative and judicial decisions, the states established a pattern of decentralized American Indian policy and created a model for extending direct rule over Indians.

THE STATES' ROLE IN INCORPORATING INDIANS

While federal government officials merely expressed the long-term goal of eventually integrating Indians after they had been acculturated, the states began the process of amalgamating Indians into their communities. Territorial governments followed a similar policy where possible. The first small step in integrating Indians was evident in the early national period, when states began regulating Native peoples as well as whites' interactions with Indians. To a large extent, this action was a natural result of the permeability of the barriers between whites and Indians. Whites were not willing to cede to Indians ultimate authority over tribe members who entered white areas or whites who traveled onto Indian lands. During the first few decades of the Republic, local white officials successfully asserted control over many aspects of Indian activities and over whites going into tribal territory. Moreover, they drew Indian-white disputes into the Anglo-American legal system. Nonetheless, there were limits to whites' willingness to absorb Indians in pre–Civil War America. Perceptions of Native Americans' insuperable racial differences meant most whites were hesitant to bring Indians fully into the states' civic communities during the antebellum era and even worked to encourage or force Indians to move outside state boundaries altogether. Removing Indians was sometimes regarded as a desirable alternative to incorporation, especially Indians who could otherwise reasonably be subject to federal, rather than state, authority because they retained their separate tribal identity.

The second stage of state incorporation of Indians took place in the Civil War era, when a number of northeastern states bestowed citizenship on all Indians remaining within state territorial limits, New Mexico determined that Pueblo Indians were citizens, and midwestern states offered the franchise to Indians on a selective basis. Racial theories had changed so as to make these new policies possible. Racist views, along with assumptions about racially determined cultural characteristics, dissipated significantly in northern states in the mid-nineteenth century. As a result, people who had once been considered racially unsuited to citizenship rights came to be seen as part of the state political community.

Yet eagerness to incorporate Indians in the states and territories was not solely indicative of greater openness or progressive sentiment. Though some whites viewed the extension of citizens' privileges to Indians as an essential part of a broader civil rights movement, others had more self-serving material and ideological purposes. Declaring Indians citizens and disbanding their tribes reinforced state sovereignty in the Northeast, and even the midwestern process of enfranchising eligible Indians extended state sovereignty there as far as was possible without encroaching on federal jurisdiction. Assimilating Indians eliminated what were seen as anomalous exceptions to the general rule that a state should have authority over all the land and people within its territorial limits. Incorporating Indians into the civil structure helped the states to manage both Indians and their lands. Furthermore, making Indians citizens was a welcome reinforcement of patriarchal family structure, individualism, and private property ownership, which were regarded as important American values. From east to west—in Massachusetts, Michigan, Minnesota, New Mexico, and elsewhere across the country—Indian citizenship was intended to lead to the conversion of communal land and resources to privately held property as well as the absorption of Indians into the white American culture and society. And in practice, citizenship did usually result in increased white access to Indian land and resources.

In the nineteenth century, extending legal jurisdiction over a previously excluded group of people and their land was a common method of paving the way for including that land and its products in the larger market economy. Parallels can be seen, for example, in British, French, and Portuguese colonial actions in India, Africa, and Australia. Laura Benton's comparative study of the nature of the colonial regimes in those regions revealed common patterns that are also evident in the United States. Most significantly, she describes the shift from legal pluralism (i.e., the existence and recognition of multiple legal systems in a territory) to a state-centered legal order (i.e., a system in which the colonizing power asserted legal hegemony).[1]

Another way to express the same shift that occurred whenever expansions of legal authority took place in colonies is to say that such jurisdictional expansion effectively marked a change from "indirect rule" to "direct rule." Political scientist Mahmood Mamdani describes these two concepts in clear and simple terms as they relate to the African context. He explains that European countries that governed their African colonies through indirect rule did not incorporate native people into their own legal order but, rather, allowed the continuance of separate native institutions. Colonial powers used native authorities to keep order in indigenous communities, to adjudicate indigenous people's internal matters, and to implement colonial policies. Since European colonizers did not wish to be ruled by native authorities themselves, Europeans in the colonies asserted the right to be ruled by European laws and courts. Thus, indirect rule was a system that created an environment of legal pluralism and separated nondominant colonized groups from members of the dominant, colonizing group. In contrast, colonial powers that governed through direct rule did not recognize separate indigenous legal orders but included colonizers and colonized alike in a unitary European-defined legal order. Everyone in the territory would be subject to the same law. Direct rule was a regime that assimilated the nondominant group into the legal and political structure of the dominant group. Mamdani points out that direct rule typically meant not only a weakening of native autonomy but also a breaking up of native people's communally held land and appropriation of that land by Europeans. Thus a shift from indirect to direct rule had significant economic and cultural effects as well as political impact. Furthermore, to present the situation in the other way, if a colonizing nation's primary goal was to acquire and settle on land occupied by indigenous people, that nation might find that direct rule of natives was the most effective governing strategy. In practice, colonial rule did not always fit neatly into one category or the other, but the conceptual models of direct and indirect rule nonetheless are useful.[2]

This book is hardly the first publication to suggest that there might be parallels between United States governance of Indians and Europeans' colonial rule elsewhere in the world. Many Native American writers today—including, for example, Robert A. Williams, Robert B. Porter, Devon A. Mihesuah, Carol Chiago Lujan, Gordon Adams, Waziyatawin Angela Wilson, Susan A. Miller, and Bonita Lawrence—portray the relationship between the United States and the Indian tribes as colonial in nature. Indeed, among Native scholars, the colonial character of U.S.-Indian relations is widely presumed, and many non-Indian authors have also addressed themes of colonization. As Elizabeth Cook-Lynn and James Riding In observe in their introductory comments to a special issue of the *Wicazo Sa Review* devoted to the Lewis and Clark expedition, "federal Indian policy is essentially colonial policy."[3] Historians who regard U.S. Indian policy as a form of colonial administration have described how the federal government began to make more concerted efforts to assimilate Indians both culturally and politically in the 1880s and 1890s. Such scholarship provides evidence of a late-nineteenth-century shift from indirect rule to direct rule.[4]

The precedent and model for the federal government's direct rule of Indians was set by earlier state Indian policy. Well before federal Indian administration came to be marked by direct rule, the states had shifted to that approach wherever possible. The reason for the states' preference for direct rule was clear: they lacked legal justification for indirect rule. Indirect rule presumes the continuation of separate indigenous communities and would require that the states recognize tribes and chiefs through whom state control could be exercised. Yet the very act of recognizing tribes and chiefs (and autonomous territory) would mean forfeiting state authority to the federal government, which claimed exclusive constitutional authority over Indian Territory and relations with Indian tribes. The states could justify their jurisdiction only to the extent that Indians were seen as members of the states. If Indian tribes were recognized as separate and even partially self-governing through their own chosen leaders, states would find it difficult to challenge federal power over those tribes. As discussed in chapter 3, when it posed no threat to state sovereignty, states did sometimes recognize Indian customs on marriage, divorce, and inheritance. But where such recognition might undermine the state's claim that it, rather than the federal government, had authority over Indians, the states were firm in undermining any suggestion of separate tribal governance, even in the area of family matters. On federalism grounds, most of the time the states could make the most effective argument for their own authority over Indians by portraying them as individuals, not as distinct, autonomous groups. In short, since the states had only two logical options regarding Indians remaining within state borders, direct rule over Indians or no authority at all, it was natural that the states would press for direct rule.

Furthermore, it was at the state level where it became apparent how a clearly delimited indirect rule by the federal government was difficult to maintain over the long term because there was rarely a distinct line between whites and Indians. Moreover, the boundaries were not stable, since rapid white population growth and intense demand for land led to a constant effort to move the line toward the Indians. Despite attempts to keep whites and Indians separate, the boundary between them was porous, even when Indians were assigned to reservations. Brad Asher effectively describes such a situation in Washington Territory;[5] that condition was replicated in states and territories across the country. In practice European-Americans and Indians interacted in many ways, giving rise to economic disputes, social conflicts, and criminal acts over which whites wanted jurisdiction in order to protect their own interests or values. They were not always successful in asserting their authority—sometimes indigenous laws and customs determined the outcome of intergroup problems. But Americans generally tried to gain control over such matters, and doing so constituted a shift to direct rule over Indians. New York's increasing application of its laws to Iroquois Indians, described in chapter 1, provides an example. State laws relating to land and contracts were prompted by the economic interactions between whites and Indians. The laws were crafted to ensure that white standards were applied to resolving disputes between Indians and whites. At the same time, law was used in New York as a tool for promoting order, furthering white principles of morality, and controlling and directing Indians' behavior. Thus, the state's criminal extension law was motivated at least in part by white disapproval of what they characterized as barbarous Indian practices (such as Tommy Jemmy's "horridly revolting" execution of Chaughquawtaugh). The law in New York was intended to play a crucial role in assimilating Indians.[6]

In addition to its role in monitoring Indian conduct and in regulating interactions between Indians and whites, law was also used as means of circumscribing the bounds of (white) civil society, determining who would be deemed a citizen and who would be regarded as a subject. In the nineteenth century, cultural factors were crucial in defining the border between insiders and outsiders in the United States, just as they were elsewhere. Lauren Benton describes how legal politics and cultural identities were intertwined in the colonial world. She explains that in European colonies in Africa and India, the colonizing nations' perception of cultural boundaries determined where they drew the line of legal jurisdiction. Thus, for example, when European powers were determining who should have access to their courts, be eligible for legal rights, and participate in legal processes (e.g., as witnesses), they restricted those privileges to people deemed to be civilized. Mahmood Mamdani likewise explains that even in a system of direct rule, only civilized people have access to citizenship and the political rights that may accompany citizenship status.[7]

Such line drawing is clearly evident in the New Mexico debate. As described in chapter 7, Pueblo Indians, who were considered civilized, had access to local courts, were subject to local legislation, and were officially treated as citizens. However, Indians in the same territory who were viewed as uncivilized, such as the Apaches, were excluded from the state's jurisdiction. The distinction is explicit in an 1884 case in the New Mexico Supreme Court, *United States v. Monte*, where the territorial court declined jurisdiction over Carpio Monte, a Mescalero Apache man who was accused of murdering a white man on reservation lands. The court distinguished between the proper jurisdiction of the territorial courts and that of the regular federal district courts. The decision meant that the federal government, pursuant to its paternalistic, guardianship function with regard to uncivilized reservation Indians, would handle the matter of the accused Apache; the local courts would take the cases only of Indians who were deemed worthy of being considered an integrated part of the New Mexico community.[8]

Culture was also prominent as a factor in boundary drawing in Michigan and Minnesota. Chapter 5 describes how both states explicitly tied voting rights to civilized lifestyle. In 1850 Michigan enfranchised "every civilized male inhabitant of Indian descent," as long as he was not affiliated with a tribe. Seven years later, Minnesota granted the suffrage to Indians who had "adopted the customs and habits of civilization." Constitutional convention delegates in both states struggled to identify suitable legal signifiers of civilization, however. Moreover, the language of the convention debates evidences how culture and race were sometimes conflated, resulting in a characterization of "whiteness" that ambiguously encompassed both behavior and physical characteristics. The states' treatment of mixed-race people also demonstrates how race and culture were seen as interconnected. The constitutional convention debates in Michigan and Minnesota show how many whites felt they shared a greater natural cultural affinity with Indians who had some European heritage than those whose heritage was solely Indian. Even the smallest degree of white ancestry was seen as making it more likely that an Indian would be civilized enough for political rights. Indeed, the suffrage provision of the Minnesota constitution formally recognized the presumed natural distinction between "mixed-blood" and "full-blood" Indians by establishing different criteria for measuring civilized behavior in the two groups.

At times Michigan and Minnesota convention delegates proposed that they simply decline to define a line between civilized and uncivilized Indians. The state would just assert jurisdiction over all Indians left unregulated by the federal government. This approach, which was adopted by both Michigan and Minnesota in the late nineteenth century, was not actually an abandonment of the critical degree-of-civilization factor, however, since the federal government based its own jurisdictional line on that same criterion. While federal government officials came to impose tight disciplinary and regulatory administration of uncivilized Indians toward the end of the nineteenth century, they were generally amenable to the states' taking jurisdiction of civilized Indians. In this sense, the federal and state governments were not actually in competition with one another. Despite all the rhetoric about federalism that suggested a keen rivalry between local and central officials, in practice those officials were often in agreement about the goals of their Indian policies.

Of course, the state and federal governments were not the only actors in the process of shaping Indian-white relations. As was shown in chapter 1, Native people were not simply passive victims of American rule. Not only did they resist militarily at times and, in other instances, negotiate the terms of intergovernment relations, but they also took advantage of opportunities to express their positions in white forums, including courts of law and legislative hearings. Indians spoke up during criminal proceedings to assert their own interests. Notably, at the end of their cases in New York, Tommy Jemmy and Stiff-Armed George were both freed. Thus the Senecas' arguments were successful in both cases. Indians also spoke out in legislative hearings, as shown by the Mashpees' active participation in Massachusetts's citizenship debate in the 1860s. Furthermore, Indians attempted wherever possible to exploit the jurisdictional conflict between state and federal authority. In state court cases they asserted the higher authority of the federal government and federal treaties, as exemplified by the actions of Cherokee principal chief John Ross in the 1830s. Ross demonstrated a sophisticated understanding of American legal and constitutional principles when he challenged Georgia's actions by appealing to the U.S. Supreme Court, pointing out that "Congress alone possesses the power to regulate commerce . . . with the Indian tribes," that treaties "compose a part of '*the supreme law of the land*,'" and that the federal government should not allow Georgia "to march across the line of her constitutional boundary to pass laws repugnant to [the] treaties and laws of the United States."[9]

To some extent, then, law was the outcome of various forms of negotiation between Indians and whites. This was not a one-sided history, in which Indians were inactive as they were taken advantage of by white settlers and policymakers. Instead, Indians played an active role in contesting the states' actions and in consistently asserting and defending their sovereignty. However, for most areas in the nineteenth century, whites and Indians were not equally strong parties in the process of working out how (or whether) they would live together. During the century following the Revolution, the disparity in power and population came to be so significant that in practice whites had more influence in shaping the conditions of the relationship. Over time, Indians increasingly came under direct rule by white authorities.

RACE

Although the states made major strides in incorporating Indians in the nineteenth century, assimilation was far from universally accepted. During the antebellum period, racism was a significant barrier to integration of Indians. When white racism was combined with Indian refusal to relinquish tribal relations and disinclination to amalgamate with state society (e.g., as in Georgia in the 1820s and 1830s) or exhibition of overt hostility to whites (as exemplified in violence in Minnesota in the 1850s and early 1860s), the states eventually advocated Indian expulsion.

In the antebellum South, a desire to maintain the racially based institution of slavery and to bridge the wide gap between slave-owning and non-slave-owning whites led to particularly firm adherence to strict racial boundaries (or at least as "strict" as was possible, given all the problems with racial classification, as described in chapter 3).[10] Native Americans as well as African Americans bore the brunt of whites' racial policies, as is evident in the discriminatory laws discussed in chapter 4. Even after the Civil War, racism continued to affect Indians' rights most obviously in the southern states, where there was the highest proportion of people categorized as nonwhite.

In addition to official state government actions, racially based vigilantism enforced white prerogatives and advanced white interests. Such violence was especially evident in frontier areas and could be seen throughout much of the West. Although New Mexicans integrated Pueblo Indians as citizens through court decisions of the 1860s and 1870s, frontier violence continued to mark the relationship between New Mexicans and other Indian tribes, such as Navajos and Apaches. Frequent violent skirmishes between Indians and non-Indians also occurred in California, Texas, Utah, and Washington. Brad Asher's analysis of the situation in Washington Territory is instructive as to the situation in western areas. He points out that white settlers in Washington Territory, who tended to share the political and racial views of southerners, believed that policing nonwhites was appropriately a private matter, that nonwhites were not entitled to the use of formal legal procedures. Therefore, he says, "[s]ettlers exercised a racial privilege to mete out private discipline for perceived offenses perpetrated by Indians." Only during the last quarter of the nineteenth century did white inhabitants give up vigilante justice and come to accept the notion of using the local court system to deal with their conflicts with Indians. Although Washington's Indians were incorporated into white society in the 1870s and 1880s, they were not accorded full equality. Instead, Asher concludes, they were brought into American society as a "subjugated people."[11]

Some aspects of the pattern evident in the South and the West—including Indian displacement from their lands as whites expanded their settlement area, Indian resistance, frontier violence and vigilantism, the need for lower-status whites to bolster their own position by emphasizing the inherent cultural and racial inferiority of nonwhites, a move to reject autonomous Native governance, a shift toward incorporating Native people into white society and subjecting them to white-dominated courts and laws, and continuing inequality after incorporation—have some parallels to the nineteenth-century British-controlled settler state in New South

Wales, as described by Benton. Certainly there are important differences between Australian history and American history, especially the presence in the United States of vast numbers of slaves descended from imported Africans. Nonetheless similarities are also apparent. Benton concludes that extending white law over Aborigines in New South Wales brought few benefits to Aboriginal people. Not only did white jurisdictional claims undermine Aboriginal autonomy, but "[t]he legal fiction of inclusiveness in fact provided a more permissive environment for brutality against Aborigines," and Aborigines continued to be disfranchised and denied equal rights in practice.[12]

Likewise, particularly in southern and western areas of the United States, nonwhite citizens—including Indians—were not granted full and equal membership in the community during the period following the Civil War. So, although racial obstacles to citizenship subsided, racism continued to limit Indians' rights in practice. Being subject to the same state laws as whites did not mean being treated equally under those laws, because statutes allowed for racial discrimination. Indians who took on white culture might be accepted into the local white community, but since many white-dominated communities were marked by strict racial classifications, Indians were bound to be treated as second-class citizens.[13] In short, even Indians who met the cultural and status criteria for inclusion in the states were still not necessarily incorporated as the peers of whites. Neither incorporation nor citizenship necessarily brought equality.

SECTIONAL NATIONALISM AND NORTHERN STATES' INCORPORATION OF INDIANS

Sectional nationalism provided a motivation for Massachusetts, Michigan, Minnesota, and other northern states to give the rights of citizenship to Indians within their borders. Such actions had to be initiated at the state (rather than the federal) level if they were to serve the purpose of highlighting regional differences and enhancing northern political and cultural power. New Englanders were particularly eager to have their values shape American identity, and in the nineteenth century other northerners came to identify with New England's vision for the nation in many regards. Principles of liberty, equality, rights, commercialism, and individualism became central to the ideological self-definition of the North. The northern states self-consciously acted to further their image in accordance with those precepts.

Other scholars, such as David Waldstreicher and Susan-Mary Grant, have described how New England's (and other northerners') sense of sectional identity during the early national and antebellum period was highly dependent on contrast with negative characteristics of the South.[14] More specifically relating to issues of race and morality, Joanne Pope Melish has explained that prior to the Civil War, New England solidified its sense of regional identity by developing a mythic historical narrative that diminished or even denied the role of slavery in New England's past. While such a re-visioning reinforced ideals of liberty, Melish says it also symbolically removed African Americans from New England's past and therefore from the (antebellum) present as well. This bolstered New Englanders' imagined view of their region as historically white, free, and morally pure, in sharp contrast to the South. By the time of the Civil War, Melish argues, other northern states had come to identify with this New England ideology, which articulated the foundation of northern superiority to southerners and provided moral justification for northerners' antipathy toward—and subsequent domination of—the South.[15]

Joshua David Bellin points out that the nineteenth-century construction of New England's past served to distance whites in the region not only from slavery but also from the uncomfortable fact of Indian dispossession. Antebellum New England literature described the noble and tireless efforts of seventeenth-century missionary John Eliot to save Indians from the extinction that they thought was otherwise sure to result from their encounter with the superior English culture. Eliot's role in establishing separate settlements ("Praying Towns") for Christian Indians as a necessary step on the way to assimilating them was portrayed as a benevolent way to protect Indians from complete annihilation. In the view of antebellum writers, that the Indians rejected civilization despite Eliot's efforts meant that they themselves were to blame for their resulting disappearance: it was lamentable that the Indians did not take advantage of the opportunity so generously and honorably offered to them and sad that they had almost died out completely in New England, but because of the Indians' inferiority, their extinction was part of a natural process that could not have been prevented. Further, in this view, it was inevitable (as well as morally desirable) that white America would expand and Indians would fade away because, as Massachusetts Congressman Edward Everett observed in 1835, "it was obviously the purpose of Providence, that [America] should become the abode of civilization, the arts, and Christianity," and it is to be expected that "as the civilized race rapidly multiplies, the native tribes will recede, sink into the wilderness, and disappear." In this fashioning of history, not only were white New Englanders blameless, but the Indians were vanishing.[16]

After the Civil War, Indian citizenship finished off the process of making New England's Indians symbolically "vanish." Jean O'Brien has described the means by which English colonists began the process of making New England Indians seem to disappear, thus allowing a myth of Indian extinction to emerge by the time of the American Revolution. Although whites gradually dispossessed Natick's Indians from their land, O'Brien explains, the Indians resisted, persisted, and survived. Yet, she points out, "European (and Euro-American) assumptions about Indian cultures as static and race as indelible, coupled with their notions that Indians are Indians only when their autonomy is secured through diplomatic relations with colonial powers and a recognized and unbroken land base, blinded them to Indian survival in New England."[17] After the Revolutionary War, the process of dispossession of Indians and regulation of their everyday lives continued through the early national and antebellum eras. Later, when Massachusetts and other states incorporated Indians by making them citizens after the Civil War, they were making Indians less visible. This in turn fortified the states' own amnesia about their history with Indians and reinforced the states' deafness to Indian voices in the present. The presence of Native Americans was more obvious when their separateness was recognized. Formally erasing Indians' separate corporate existence relieved whites of reminders of their problematic past and freed them from having their past violations of property rights and rule of law tainting their nineteenth-century self-image as the moral touchstone for the nation.

Accompanying Indian citizenship rights with a repudiation of legal race discrimination also allowed New England and other northern states to reinforce their sense of moral superiority over the South. Although northerners' commitment to civil rights in the immediate post- Civil War period was presumably genuine, it also served the interests of sectional nationalism. Northerners could be proud to proclaim that they had expunged blatant official racial discrimination from their states and consequently to see themselves as more virtuous than southerners. By the mid-1870s, however, with their sectional moral superiority firmly established in their own minds and with the federal government otherwise committed to their broad agenda for the country, northerners were willing to relax their insistence that white southerners protect the civil rights of African Americans in that region. Re-union with the white South was more important than nationwide racial equality.

In fact, it may be the case that official racial equality under law in the North was also more important than the actual conditions of racial minorities there. An absence of racially discriminatory laws did not mean equal treatment under law in practice. As Bruce A. Rubenstein has pointed out in his study of Indian-white relations in Michigan, racism on the part of trial participants, from jurors to judges, meant that Indians could not depend on a fair playing field when they entered a northern courtroom. More broadly, John Wood Sweet identifies the principle of "universal freedom but racial inequality" as the "northern model" developed over the colonial and early national periods, and he argues that that model came to be accepted nationwide after the Civil War. In any case, unofficial racism meant that Indians continued to be treated unequally as members of the states. Additionally, incorporation into the civic structure of the states did not entirely dislodge the old negative stereotypes or "expectations" of Indians in American popular culture, many of which, as Philip Deloria has shown, continued well into the twentieth century. "Inclusion" into American society did not bring with it an end to a common white perception of Indians as inferior.[18]

Furthermore, as laudable as the precept of equality was, when applied to Indians it ignored other principles. Defining the issue of Indians' status in northern society as a question of equal rights presumed that Indians would be incorporated into northern society and that incorporation was inconsistent with the retention of a collective tribal affiliation. Regarding the status of American Indians primarily as a matter of race discrimination failed to take into account the broader question of whether Indians should be subject to state laws at all, that is, whether Indians should only be answerable to their own laws and such other laws by which they consented to be bound. This is an issue of concern that has been discussed recently by Native writers. In their book *Tribes, Treaties, and Constitutional Tribulations*, Vine Deloria and David Wilkins question whether people can be declared citizens without their consent. While the context of their discussion is the Indian Citizenship Act of 1924, which granted United States citizenship to Indians, the same point could be made with regard to state declarations of Indian citizenship in the nineteenth century. Addressing the civil rights issue directly, legal scholar Robert Porter points out that the use of civil rights strategies by (or for) Indians has reinforced the assumption that Indians are Americans, which has had the effect of undermining Indian sovereignty. Rather than accepting a racial minority status and demanding rights that have been withheld on account of race, he says, Indians should be arguing that the United States has no authority over them at all.[19] Thus, northern states' incorporation of Indians as a matter of equal rights had an ambiguous motivation and has had a mixed legacy. In their focus on discourse of civil rights and equality in the Civil War and Reconstruction era, the states submerged the real issue of tribal autonomy, just as they had earlier used the concept of states' rights to bury the issue of tribal sovereignty.

THE FEDERAL GOVERNMENT TAKES UP
THE CITIZENSHIP PROJECT

Throughout the time period under study, each state government's ability to incorporate Indians was affected by the extent to which the federal government asserted authority over Indians in the state. Although some states tried to extract as many Indians as possible from exclusive federal control, most had to concede federal authority over sizeable tracts of land and large numbers of Indians within state borders. Compared with eastern regions, states in the trans-Mississippi west, where most reservation Indians lived, incorporated far fewer Indians on their own initiative. Those reservations were considered federally owned land, and the Indians living there were federal wards, which meant that state taxes and legislation were inapplicable. The states were unwilling to offer citizenship privileges to Indians who were not subject to state laws and taxation.

Around 1880 the federal government began a more active program to bring Indians into American citizenship, which was expected to make more of them subject to ordinary state legislation. In the 1850s, 1860s, and 1870s, rather than integrating Indians into American society, the federal government had forced "uncivilized" Indians onto reservations, organized by tribe and under the supervision of Indian agents. Beginning in the late 1870s, however, the government instituted a more concerted effort to govern Indians directly and shifted to a more aggressive policy of acculturation. Vast tracts of tribal lands were divided up and allotted to individual Indians in order to compel private property ownership and squelch collectivism; Indian agents were assigned the task of monitoring Indians' cultural progress more closely; regulations attempted to stamp out undesirable Indian rites and practices; and stepped-up education efforts endeavored to mold Indian youths into literate, disciplined, orderly, moral, civilized men and women.[20]

Federal case law buttressed Congress's assimilation efforts. In *The Cherokee Tobacco* case, the Supreme Court held that acts of Congress—including the taxation statute in question in the case—would apply to Indian tribes unless Congress explicitly excluded them, even when the acts conflicted with treaty guarantees. Effectively, the Court was deciding that congressional legislation could abrogate and supersede the provisions of treaties previously made with Indian tribes, thus asserting plenary federal authority over tribal Indians. In *United States v. Kagama*, the Court upheld the constitutionality of the Major Crimes Act, ruling that Congress had the power to legislate for Indians on reservations.[21]

The main goal of the federal government's aggressive assimilation policy of the late nineteenth century was to produce acculturated Indian citizens; ideally, they would be independent of their old tribes. Yet the federal government met limited success, despite the fact that it had power over larger numbers of Indians than the states did, and far more resources to devote to the assimilation effort. Many Indians did not want to give up tribal affiliation or abandon traditional cultural practices, and some were resistant to American citizenship.[22]

During the decades immediately following the period focused on in this book, Indian writers reacted to the federal government's shift to direct rule, and they especially responded to the newly intensified civilization effort by the federal government, taking complex (and sometimes different) positions on the issues of assimilation and citizenship. As Frederick Hoxie explains, during the Progressive Era a number of Indians who had been educated in white schools proposed that Indians would benefit from retention of Indian values and traditions even while they also took on many aspects of white American culture. These men and women honored indigenous heritage and wanted to shield Indian culture from the most totalizing American assimilation efforts but also lived much of their lives in white society. They criticized some aspects of white civilization, were particularly critical of the way in which the government administered Indians on reservations, and rejected full assimilation and acculturation; at the same time, many of them were strong advocates for Indian citizenship and rights in the United States. Prominent Native writers, activists, and anthropologists of that era included Charles Eastman (Santee Sioux, 1858–1939), Zitkala-Ša, also known as Gertrude Bonnin (Yankton Sioux, 1876–1938), Carlos Montezuma (Yavapai, 1866–1923), Black Elk (Oglala Lakota, 1863–1950), Francis La Fleche (Omaha, 1857–1932), Sarah Winnemucca (Northern Paiute, 1844–1891), Emmet Starr (Cherokee, 1870–1930), Luther Standing

Bear (Brule Sioux, 1868–1939), and Arthur C. Parker (Seneca, 1881–1955). Following them were prominent Indian voices of the 1930s and 1940s, such as John Joseph Mathews, D'Arcy McNickle, Ed Dozier, Vine Deloria Sr., and Francis Frazier. Many of these men and women acted through Pan-Indian political organizations, such as the Society of American Indians (founded in 1913), followed by the National Congress of American Indians (founded in 1944).[23]

Eventually, the federal government simply declared all Indians to be citizens but ruled that citizenship was not inconsistent with retention of tribal ties nor with guardianship status. Since such conditions restricted full state authority over Indians, many states found ways of excluding from the franchise Indians who were "under guardianship," "not taxed," or not "residents" of the state.[24] Such state actions contrast sharply with the role states had played between 1790 and 1880. During that earlier period, when the federal government acquiesced in state assertions of power to determine the political status of Indians, there was room for the states to act independently in incorporating Indians. During that period states had tried to extend their authority over Indians, had worked to entice Indians to join white society, and at times had even forced amalgamation of Indians into the state community. Once the states no longer had a say in determining the political status of Indians, however, they lost interest in admitting Indians to privileges under state law. After 1880, if Indians were to be incorporated into American society, the process would now be primarily in the hands of the federal government and the tribes, rather than the states.

APPENDIX

~

The bracketed info that follows each quotation refers to the state's session laws. Publishing info for the session laws is provided in the bibliography.

EXAMPLES OF LAWS PROHIBITING INDIANS FROM SELLING LAND

Connecticut, 1855: "All conveyances of any land, by any Indian or Indians, belonging to or which have belonged to the estate of such tribe, whether by deed or otherwise, shall be void." [12 June 1855, ch. 65, p. 79]

Maine, 1839: "it shall not be in the power of any Indian to sell or convey his lot or improvements on the same to any person other than some member of [the Penobscot] tribe." [16 February 1839, ch. 396, p. 567]

Maryland, 1790: "it shall not be lawful for the [Choptank] Indians to sell, grant, lease, or otherwise dispose of, the lands to be reserved to them by virtue of this act." [22 December 1790, ch. 43, no page number]

EXAMPLES OF LAWS PERMITTING INDIANS TO SELL LAND UNDER CERTAIN CONDITIONS

Indiana, 1861: "all *bona fide* sales, conveyances, purchases and devises heretofore made by any Indian ... are hereby legalized." [11 March 1861, ch. 79, p. 153]

Massachusetts, 1819: "all real estate acquired by the industry of the proprietors [of Mashpee] and members [of the Herring Pond tribe], and purchased by them, shall be the sole and separate property and estate of such proprietor or member, so acquiring and purchasing the same, and may be by him or her enjoyed, sold, alienated and disposed of, by deed, will or otherwise." [18 February 1819, ch. 105, p. 161]

North Carolina, 1802: "no lease, grant, demise, covenant or agreement made by [the Tuscarora] Indian Chiefs ... respecting [their] lands, or the rents thereof, shall be good or valid in law, unless the same shall be approved by [the] Commissioners ... in writing." [1802, ch. 4, p. 6]

Rhode Island, 1843: "Moses Stanton, Nancy Stanton, Daniel Moody and Eunice

Rogers, are hereby authorised to sell all their right, title and interest in and to any lands which they may hold individually, as members of the Narragansett tribe of Indians . . . *Provided*, the sale be made under the direction of the Commissioner of the Indian tribe and that said Commissioner be first satisfied of the intention of such persons to emigrate." [October 1843, p. 75]

Virginia, 1792: Whereas the Nottoway tribe of Indians have petitioned the assembly for permission to sell a tract of land, "It shall be lawful for the said tribe of Indians, under the direction and with the approbation of [their] trustees . . . to proceed to sell the said tract of land." [12 November 1792, ch. 41, p. 91]

Virginia, 1824: "all laws now in force forbidding contracts for the sale of real property between [Nottoway] Indians . . . and white persons citizens of this Commonwealth, shall cease in their operation and effect so far only as they concern . . . William G. Bozeman; and . . . after the allotment to him of his interest in the lands belonging to the said tribe, shall have been made as aforesaid, he, the said Bozeman, shall have the same power to sell, convey, or exchange the same, as free white persons of this Commonwealth possess and enjoy. And . . . whenever any descendant of a female of the Nottoway tribe of Indians, entitled to a share of property in common, in the county of Southampton, shall apply to the county court of the said county for privileges similar to those granted to William G. Bozeman, the said court . . . may, at their discretion [allow such applicant to] enjoy all the rights and privileges which, by the foregoing sections, are granted to the aforesaid William G. Bozeman: *Provided*, that it shall be the duty of the said court to grant such privileges only to such applicants, as in their opinion are of good moral character, and not likely to become chargeable to any part of the Commonwealth." [23 February 1824, ch. 99, p. 101]

EXAMPLES OF LAWS ALLOWING STATES
TO PURCHASE AND SELL INDIAN LANDS

Connecticut, 1873: "the overseer of said Pequot tribe of indians, and his successors in said office . . . are hereby authorized and empowered, to sell by public auction, all of the lands reserved by the state for said indians (except one hundred acres of the same)." [17 June 1873, p. 58]

Maryland, 1790: "the said commissioners . . . are authorized and empowered, with all convenient speed after the passage of this act, to repair to the Indian settlement, near Secretary's Creek, in Dorchester county, and to contract, covenant and agree, in behalf of this state, with the Choptank Indians inhabiting the said settlement, for the purchase of all and singular the lands, tenements and appertenances, belonging to the said Indians[. . .]; provided . . . that there shall be reserved to the said Indians, for their own cultivation and improvement, a quantity of the said land not exceeding three hundred acres[. . .]; And the [county] surveyor . . . shall proceed to lay off the remaining lands in lots, each lot to contain not less than one hundred, nor more than three hundred acres[. . .]; And the treasurer . . . shall proceed to expose the said lots to sale by the acre . . . to the highest bidder." [22 December 1790, ch. 43, no page number]

New Jersey, 1801: At the request of the Brotherton Indians, who plan to move to New Stockbridge, New York, the Indian commissioners are to "divide the lands held in trust for the use of the [Brotherton] Indians . . . into such convenient farms, or lots, not exceeding one hundred acres . . . and to sell the same, separately, at public sale." [3 December 1801, ch. 63, p. 131]

EXAMPLES OF LAWS VOIDING INDIAN CONTRACTS OR PROHIBITING INDIANS FROM SUING OR BEING SUED

Georgia, 1830: "no Cherokee Indian shall be bound by any contract hereafter to be entered into with a white person or persons, nor shall Indians be liable to be sued in any of the courts of law or equity in this State, on such contract." [23 December 1830, p. 118]

Indiana, 1841: "No white man or negro shall hereafter have the benefit of any of the legal remedies for the collection of debts hereafter contracted by an Indian within the limits of the state of Indiana, and all contracts hereafter made with Indians shall be null and void." [3 February 1841, ch. 51, p. 134]

EXAMPLES OF LAWS PERMITTING INDIANS TO MAKE ENFORCEABLE CONTRACTS AND TO SUE AND BE SUED UNDER CERTAIN CONDITIONS

Alabama, 1832: "contracts freely and voluntarily made, whereby any white man shall purchase an improvement or claim of any Indian, on any of the unceded territory in this State, and shall actually receive possession thereof, the same shall be obligatory on the parties to such contract: *Provided*, the same is made in the presence of one respectable free white person, and reduced to writing, in which shall be specified the terms of such contract; and provided a valuable consideration be paid for such claim." [16 January 1832, p. 7]

California, 1850: "Any person wishing to hire an Indian, shall go before a Justice of the Peace with the Indian, and make such contract as the Justice may approve . . . , and all contracts so made shall be binding between the parties; but no contract between a white man and an Indian, for labor, shall otherwise be obligatory on the part of an Indian." [22 April 1850, ch. 133, p. 408]

Connecticut, 1855: "No judgment shall be rendered against an Indian, for any debt or on any contract, except for the rent of land hired and occupied by such Indian." [12 June 1855, ch. 65, p. 79]

Massachusetts, 1810: "no promise made, or contract entered into by any of the [Chappaquiddick] Indians, or people of colour, shall be valid in law, unless the same be made or entered into with the written consent of two or more of their Guardians, and no action hereafter brought upon such promise or contract, made or entered into, without such written consent, shall be sustained in any Court of Law [and] no action shall be sustained in any Court of Law in this Commonwealth, wherein any of said Indians or people of colour shall be plaintiff, unless the original writ be endorsed by two or more of their Guardians." [27 February 1810, p. 109]

Michigan, 1841: "any Indian shall be capable of suing and being sued in any of the courts of justice of this state." [9 April 1841, no. 54, p. 137]

North Carolina, 1837: "all contracts and agreements of every description made . . . with any Cherokee Indian . . . for an amount equal to ten dollars or more, shall be null and void, unless some note or memorandum thereof be made in writing and signed by such Indian . . . in the presence of two creditable witnesses." [21 January 1837, ch. 8, p. 30]

South Carolina, 1808: "it shall and may be lawful for the Catawba Indians to grant and make to any person or persons, any lease or leases, for life or lives or term of years, of any of the lands vested in them by the laws of this state: *Provided*, That no lease shall exceed the term of ninety-nine years, or three lives in being." [15 December 1808, p. 72]

EXAMPLES OF LAWS PUNISHING THE SALE OF LIQUOR TO INDIANS

California, 1850: "If any person in this State shall sell, give, or furnish to any Indian, male or female, any intoxicating liquors (except when administered in sickness), for good cause shown, he, she, or they so offending shall, on conviction thereof, be fined not less than twenty dollars for each offence, or be imprisoned not less than five days, or fined and imprisoned, as the Court may determine." [22 April 1850, ch. 133, p. 408]

Florida, 1853: "it shall not be lawful for any person or persons to sell, barter, give, loan, or in any manner furnish to any of the Indians now remaining within the limits of this State . . . , any spirituous liquors, powder, lead, or any goods, wares, or merchandise of any description." [5 January 1853, ch. 538, p. 115]

Illinois, 1823: "no tavern keeper, grocer, or retailer of spirituous liquors, or other person or persons, shall sell, exchange, or otherwise deliver to any Indian or Indians, within the boundaries of this state, any spirituous liquors, under the penalty of twenty dollars for every such offence." [14 February 1823, p. 148]

Michigan, 1841: "if any person shall sell, exchange or give, barter, or dispose of any spirituous liquor, wine, mixed liquor, or other strong and intoxicating drink, to any Indian or Indians, male or female, such person shall forfeit and pay the sum of twenty dollars upon the first conviction thereof, and the sum of forty dollars for each subsequent offence." [9 April 1841, no. 54, p. 137]

Minnesota, 1862: "if any person shall sell, exchange, give, barter or dispose of any spirituous liquors or wines, to any Indians within this State, such person, on conviction thereof . . . shall be punished by imprisonment in the State prison for a period not exceeding two years, and shall be fined not more than three hundred dollars." [24 September 1862, ch. 11, p. 55]

Missouri, 1839: "It shall not be lawful for any person or persons to trade, traffic or barter with any Indian or Indians, either by selling, trading or exchanging them any spirituous liquors, horses, guns, blankets, or any other article or commodity whatever, within the limits of this State, unless such Indians shall be traveling through the State and have a written permit from their proper agent." [9 February 1839, p. 66]

Nevada, 1877: "Any person who shall, after the passage of this Act, sell, barter, give, or in any manner dispose of any spirituous or malt liquors of any kind or description whatever, to any Indian within this State, shall be deemed guilty of a misdemeanor, and upon due conviction thereof . . . shall be fined in any sum not exceeding five hundred dollars, or be imprisoned in the county jail for any time not exceeding six months." [2 March 1877, ch. 82, p. 133]

Ohio, 1809: "if any tavern-keeper, or other person or persons, shall sell or barter any spirituous or other liquids of intoxicating quality, to any Indian or Indians within this state, . . . unless authorised by the proper authority; such person or persons shall forfeit and pay a fine not exceeding one hundred dollars, nor less than five dollars, . . . and the person so offending shall, moreover, forfeit the article, of whatsoever nature or kind he, she or they may have received in exchange; which shall be restored to any Indian or Indians claiming the same, on giving satisfactory proof . . . that the articles so claimed, are actually the property of the Indian or Indians who make the claim." [11 February 1809, ch. 129, p. 584]

Texas, 1866: "If any person shall give, or barter, or cause to be sold, given or bartered, any ardent spirits, or any spirituous or intoxicating liquors, or fire arms, or ammunition to any Indian of the wild or unfriendly tribes, he shall be fined not less than ten nor more than one hundred dollars." [31 October 1866, ch. 73, p. 70]

Appendix

Massachusetts, 1840: "When any person shall unlawfully enter, intrude upon, or hold any land, the title to which is in the Commonwealth, for the use of any tribe or body of Indians in the Commonwealth, the same may be recovered upon an information filed and prosecuted by the attorney general or district attorney in the court of common pleas for the county where the land lies." [14 March 1840, ch. 34, p. 193]

New Jersey, 1796: The Indian commissioners "shall have full power . . . to commence, prosecute and carry on to effect any action or actions against any person or persons trespassing on [Indian] lands." [17 March 1796, ch. 594, p. 78]

Pennsylvania, 1822: "if any person . . . shall cut down or fell . . . any timber, tree, or trees, growing upon the lands of the [Seneca] Indians, without their consent, or that of their agent, he, she, or they so offending shall be liable to pay to them the said Indians, or their chief, double the value of such tree or trees." [2 April 1822, ch. 157, p. 217]

Rhode Island, 1798: "the Treasurer of the Narragansett Tribe of Indians . . . is hereby authorised and empowered, to sue and prosecute in Actions of Trespass, for any Trespasses upon the Lands of said Tribe, which may have been, or shall be made, contrary to the Regulations of the Committee, appointed by this General Assembly to regulate the Affairs of said Tribe." [January 1798, p. 9]

NOTES

PREFACE

1. This book primarily uses the term "Indians" to refer to the indigenous people of the Americas. Occasionally, the alternatives "Native people," "Natives," or, for a later period, "Native Americans" are used interchangeably with "Indians."

2. Donald Fixico, "Federal and State Policies and American Indians," in *A Companion to American Indian History*, ed. Philip J. Deloria and Neal Salisbury (Malden MA: Blackwell, 2004), 379–96. The quotation is on p. 390.

3. Vine Deloria Jr. and Clifford M. Lytle, *The Nations Within: The Past and Future of American Indian Sovereignty* (New York: Pantheon Books, 1984; reprint, Austin: University of Texas Press, 1998), 3.

4. David E. Wilkins, *American Indian Sovereignty and the U.S. Supreme Court: The Masking of Justice* (Austin: University of Texas Press, 1997) (quotation on p. 4); Robert A. Williams Jr., *The American Indian in Western Legal Thought: The Discourses of Conquest* (New York: Oxford University Press, 1990); Robert A. Williams Jr., "The Algebra of Federal Indian Law: The Hard Trail of Decolonizing and Americanizing the White Man's Indian Jurisprudence," *Wisconsin Law Review* 1986 (1986): 219–99; David Wilkins, "From Time Immemorial: The Origin and Import of the Reserved Rights Doctrine," in Richard A. Grounds et al, eds, *Native Voices: American Indian Identity and Resistance*, (Lawrence: University Press of Kansas, 2003), 81–96; and Vine Deloria Jr. and David E. Wilkins, *Tribes, Treaties, and Constitutional Tribulations* (Austin: University of Texas Press, 1999).

5. Vine Deloria Jr. and Clifford M. Lytle *American Indians, American Justice* (Austin: University of Texas Press, 1983), 50–57, 203–15, 222–46; and David Wilkins and Tsianina Lomawaima, *Uneven Ground: American Indian Sovereignty and Federal Law* (Norman: University of Oklahoma Press, 2001), 179 and 281 (note 4). See also the latter authors' description of the attitudes of the tribes, the federal government, and the states on the issue of federal-state-tribe relationships, on p. 198.

6. David J. Wishart, *An Unspeakable Sadness: The Dispossession of the Nebraska Indians* (Lincoln: University of Nebraska Press, 1994); H. Craig Miner and William E. Unrau, *The End of Indian Kansas: A Study of Cultural Revolution, 1854–1871* (Lawrence: University Press of Kansas, 1990); and Laurence M. Hauptman, *Conspiracy of Interests: Iroquois Dispossession and the Rise of New York State* (Syracuse: Syracuse University Press, 1999).

7. Jean M. O'Brien, *Dispossession by Degrees: Indian Land and Identity in Natick, Massachusetts, 1650–1790* (New York: Cambridge University Press, 1997). The quotation is on p. 214. O'Brien elaborates on ways in which colonial Massachusetts prefigured nineteenth- and twentieth-century American policies: "The ideological underpinnings of missionary programs, too, involved ideas about education, a sedentary agricultural economy supplemented by spinning and weaving by women, rigid organization of time and space, redefinitions of family structure, and the thoroughgoing alteration of gender roles that changed little into the twentieth century."

8. James H. Merrell, *The Indians' New World: Catawbas and Their Neighbors from European Contact through the Era of Removal* (Chapel Hill: University of North Carolina Press, 1989).

9. Jack Campisi, *The Mashpee Indians: Tribe on Trial* (Syracuse: Syracuse University Press, 1991); *Paul Brodeur, Restitution: The Land Claims of the Mashpee, Pasamaquoddy, and Penobscot Indians of New England* (Boston: Northeastern University Press, 1985); Robert N. Clinton and Margaret Tobey Hotopp, "Judicial Enforcement of the Federal Restraints on Alienation of Indian Land: The Origins of the Eastern Land Claims," *Maine Law Review* 31, no. 5 (1979): 17–90; and essays about the Mashpees by James Clifford ("Identity in Mashpee"), Francis G. Hutchins ("Mashpee: The Story of Cape Cod's Indian Town"), Campisi ("The Mashpee Indians: Tribe on Trial"), and Jo Carrillo ("Identity as Idiom: Mashpee Reconsidered") in *Readings in American Indian Law: Recalling the Rhythm of Survival*, ed. Jo Carrillo (Philadelphia: Temple University Press, 1998), 19–49; and Christopher Vecsey and William A. Starna, eds., *Iroquois Land Claims* (Syracuse: Syracuse University Press, 1988). On the background to land claims in New York, see also Gerald Gunther, "Governmental Power and New York Indian Lands—A Reassessment of a Persistent Problem of Federal-State Relations," *Buffalo Law Review* 8 (1958): 1–26; Theodore C. Max, "Conundrums along the Mohawk: Preconstitutional Land Claims of the Oneida Indian Nation," *New York University Review of Law and Social Change* 11 (1982–1983): 473–519; and Robert B. Porter, "Legalizing, Decolonizing, and Modernizing New York State's Indian Law," *Albany Law Review* 63 (1999): 125–200.

10. Tim Alan Garrison, *The Legal Ideology of Removal: The Southern Judiciary and the Sovereignty of Native American Nations* (Athens: University of Georgia Press, 2002).

11. Brad Asher, *Beyond the Reservation: Indians, Settlers and the Law in Washington Territory, 1853–1889* (Norman: University of Oklahoma Press, 1999).

12. Cynthia Cumfer, "Local Origins of National Indian Policy: Cherokee and Tennessean Ideas about Sovereignty and Nationhood, 1790–1811," *Journal of the*

Early Republic 23 (2003): 21–46; Ann Marie Plane and Gregory Button, "The Massachusetts Indian Enfranchisement Act: Ethnic Contest in Historical Context, 1849–1869," *Ethnohistory* 40 (1993): 587–618; and Sidney L. Harring, *Crow Dog's Case: American Indian Sovereignty, Tribal Law, and United States Law in the Nineteenth Century* (New York: Cambridge University Press, 1994), ch. 2.

THE COLONIAL FOUNDATIONS OF INDIAN LAW

1. On the history of the Spanish colonies in North America, see especially David J. Weber, *The Spanish Frontier in North America* (New Haven: Yale University Press, 1992); and Ramón A. Gutiérrez, *When Jesus Came, the Corn Mothers Went Away: Marriage, Sexuality, and Power in New Mexico, 1500–1846* (Stanford: Stanford University Press, 1991). For good descriptions of differences between Spanish and English colonial rule, see J. H. Elliott, "Afterword: Atlantic History: A Circumnavigation," in *The British Atlantic World, 1500–1800*, ed. David Armitage and Michael J. Braddick (New York: Palgrave Macmillan, 2002), 233–49; John H. Elliott, "Empire and State in British and Spanish America," in *Le Nouveau Monde, Mondes Nouveau: L'Expérience Américaine*, ed. Serge Gruzinski and Nathan Wachtel (Paris: Editions Recherche sur les civilizations; Editions de l'Ecole des hautes études en sciences sociales, 1996), 365–82; Anthony Pagden, *Lords of All the World: Ideologies of Empire in Spain, Britain, and France c. 1500–c. 1800* (New Haven: Yale University Press, 1995), ch. 5; and Richard J. Ross, "Legal Communications and Imperial Governance in Colonial British and Spanish America," in *Cambridge History of Law in America*, ed. Christopher Tomlins and Michael Grossberg (New York: Cambridge University Press, forthcoming 2006). I appreciate Professor Ross's providing me with an advance copy of his essay. For a more extensive description and comparison of the colonies settled by different European nations in the New World, see Alan Taylor, *American Colonies* (New York: Viking, 2001).

2. For an in-depth analysis of European concepts of the status of American Indians, see Robert A. Williams Jr., *The American Indian in Western Legal Thought: The Discourses of Conquest* (New York: Oxford University Press, 1990). On European justifications during the colonial period, see also Wilcomb E. Washburn, *Red Man's Land/White Man's Law: The Past and Present Status of the American Indian*, 2nd ed. (Norman: University of Oklahoma Press, 1995), part 2, ch. 1. More generally on European ideologies of empire in the sixteenth and seventeenth centuries, see Pagden, *Lords of All the World*.

3. On the early debates among Spaniards about how they should treat the Indians—i.e., how the Spanish could successfully colonize the New World, spread Christianity, and make the colonies economically profitable while still complying

with their Christian duty to be just and ethical and protecting the rights of the Native peoples they encountered—see Lewis Hanke, *The Spanish Struggle for Justice in the Conquest of America* (Philadelphia: University of Pennsylvania Press, 1949). On Spaniards' efforts to provide the Indians of New Spain with special protections against abuses, see C. H. Haring, *The Spanish Empire in America* (New York: Oxford University Press, 1947), ch. 3.

4. *Recopilación de Leyes de los Reinos de las Indias* (Madrid, 1680). The general provision requiring that the Indians be "protected, favored, and sustained" is in book 6, title 1, law 1 [6.1.1]. The other laws referred to in the text are, in order of reference, 6.10.1–23, 6.6.1–14, 4.12.18, 6.3.21 and 22, 4.12.12 and 4.17.10, 6.1.26, 2.1.4, 5.2.22, and 5.2.26.

5. Woodrow Borah, *Justice by Insurance: The General Indian Court of Colonial Mexico and the Legal Aides of the Half-Real* (Berkeley: University of California Press, 1983); Gretchen Koch Markov, "The Legal Status of Indians under Spanish Rule" (PhD diss., University of Rochester, 1983); P. E. B. Coy, "Justice for the Indian in Eighteenth Century Mexico," *American Journal of Legal History* 12 (1968): 41–49; Charles R. Cutter, *The Legal Culture of Northern New Spain, 1700–1810* (Albuquerque: University of New Mexico Press, 1995); and Edward H. Spicer, "Political Incorporation and Cultural Change in New Spain: A Study in Spanish-Indian Relations," in *Attitudes of Colonial Powers toward the American Indian*, ed. Howard Peckham and Charles Gibson (Salt Lake City: University of Utah Press, 1969), 107–35.

6. Report of Josef Mariano de la Peña, Alcalde Mayor of Albuquerque, 5 August 1819 (part of the proceedings concerning lands of the pueblo of San Felipe), contains an example of language that distinguished Pueblo Indians from "citizens" in New Mexico. For an English translation, see *Spanish Archives of New Mexico, 1621–1821, Series I, Translations*, 4 microfilm reels (Santa Fe: New Mexico State Records Center and Archives, 1981) [hereafter referred to as SANM], archive number 1234 (translated by M. Baca).

7. Proceedings in a dispute between the Indians of Santa Clara and San Ildefonso and certain Spanish citizens, 1786, SANM, archive number 1354; and Proceedings in a dispute between Santa Clara Pueblo and Canjuebe Indians, 11 November and 27 December 1815, SANM, archive numbers 1279 and 1280. See also the descriptions of these documents by Ralph Emerson Twitchell in *Spanish Archives of New Mexico*, 2 vols. (Cedar Rapids IA: Torch Press, 1914), 1:416–21, 371–72.

8. Law of 9 February 1811, reissued on 19 July 1820, and later proclaimed in New Spain, SANM, archive numbers 1082 (translated by I. L. Chaves) and 1334 (translated by Claribel Fischer Walker); and Laws of 9 November 1812 (reissued on 29 April 1820), and 4 January 1813 (revived in 1821). See SANM, archive number 1133.

9. King Ferdinand VII returned to the throne in 1814 and nullified the new laws and the Constitution of 1812. He did not accept the changes until 1820. When Governor Facundo Melgares received word that the liberal statutes were once again in effect, he proclaimed the end of the Indians' "minority" status. Henceforward, he said, they should be regarded "as Spaniards in all things, exercising their rights to vote and to stand as candidates for office." 18 April 1821, quoted in Marc Simmons, *Spanish Government in New Mexico* (Albuquerque: University of New Mexico Press, 1968), 213. Mexico declared independence on 28 September 1821.

10. Borah, *Justice by Insurance*, 412.

11. See the excellent description of this subject in G. Emlen Hall and David J. Weber, "Mexican Liberals and the Pueblo Indians, 1821–1829," *New Mexico Historical Review* 59 (1984): 5–32. Language of the Plan of Iguala is quoted at p. 8. The quotation of Pueblo Indians claiming the rights that every citizen enjoys is from a letter of 9 March 1829, by Rafael Aguilar and José Cota of Pecos Pueblo to Governor Antonio Narbona, quoted at 19. Hall and Weber point out that a decade after New Mexico became part of the United States, the Mexican government initiated a more vigorous effort to break up the communal lands of Indians in the remaining territory of the Republic.

12. Although there were up to 25 million Indians in pre-Columbian central Mexico and 9 million in Peru, there were only approximately 1 million Indians east of the Mississippi River in 1600. John Elliott, *Britain and Spain in America: Colonists and Colonized* (Reading, England: University of Reading, 1994), 14. Most notably, disease had significantly thinned the indigenous population along the coastline just before English colonization; Puritans assumed that God had thus cleared the land to make way for their holy endeavor. William Cronon, *Changes in the Land: Indians, Colonists, and the Ecology of New England* (New York: Hill and Wang, 1983).

13. Williams, *American Indian in Western Legal Thought*, chs. 4 and 5; and Pagden, *Lords of All the World*, ch. 3.

14. John Elliott analyzes the differences between Spanish and English approaches to Indians in *Britain and Spain in America*. His conclusion that the Spanish treated Indians as insiders while the English treated them as outsiders has also been noted in general historical scholarship, such as Francis Paul Prucha, *The Great Father: The United States Government and the American Indians* (Lincoln: University of Nebraska Press, 1984), 11–12; Weber, *Spanish Frontier*, 12; Alan Gallay, *The Indian Slave Trade: The Rise of the English Empire in the American South, 1670–1717* (New Haven: Yale University Press, 2002), 355–56; and Edward H. Spicer, *Cycles of Conquest: The Impact of Spain, Mexico, and the United States on the Indians of the Southwest, 1533–1960* (Tucson: University of Arizona Press, 1962), 281–82, 344. On English (and

other European) negotiation with Indian nations in North America, see Howard
R. Berman, "Perspectives on American Indian Sovereignty and International Law,
1600–1776," in Oren Lyons et al., *Exiled in the Land of the Free: Democracy, Indian
Nations, and the U.S. Constitution* (Santa Fe: Clear Light, 1992), 125–88; and Robert
A. Williams, *Linking Arms Together: American Indian Treaty Visions of Law and
Peace, 1600–1800* (New York: Oxford University Press, 1997). On Europeans' and
Indians' interactions in the colonies more generally, see Colin G. Calloway, *New
Worlds for All: Indians, Europeans, and the Remaking of Early America* (Baltimore:
Johns Hopkins University Press, 1997).

15. On the autonomy enjoyed by British colonists in North America, see Jack P.
Greene, *Peripheries and Center: Constitutional Development in the Extended Polities
of the British Empire and the United States, 1607–1788* (Athens: University of Georgia
Press, 1986); and Greene, "Transatlantic Colonization and the Redefinition of
Empire in the Early Modern Era: The British-American Experience," in *Negotiated
Empires: Centers and Peripheries in the Americas, 1500–1820*, ed. Christine Daniels
and Michael V. Kennedy (New York: Routledge, 2002), 267–82.

16. The eight named communities are those that are mentioned in documents
discussed in chapter 7. On the history of Massachusetts Indians and the English
colonial legal relationship with Indians in New England, see Jean M. O'Brien,
*Dispossession by Degrees: Indian Land and Identity in Natick, Massachusetts,
1650–1790* (New York: Cambridge University Press, 1997); Alden T. Vaughan, ed.,
New England Encounters: Indians and Euroamericans, ca. 1600–1850 (Boston:
Northeastern University Press, 1999); Alden T. Vaughan, *New England Frontier:
Puritans and Indians, 1620–1675*, 3rd ed. (Norman: University of Oklahoma Press,
1995); Neal Salisbury, *Manitou and Providence: Indians, Europeans, and the Making
of New England, 1500–1643* (New York: Oxford University Press, 1982); Francis
Jennings, *The Invasion of America: Indians, Colonialism, and the Cant of Conquest*
(Chapel Hill: University of North Carolina Press, 1975); Yasuhide Kawashima,
Puritan Justice and the Indian: White Man's Law in Massachusetts, 1630–1763
(Middletown CT: Wesleyan University Press, 1986); Yasu Kawashima, "Legal Origins
of the Indian Reservation in Colonial Massachusetts," *American Journal of Legal
History* 13 (1969): 45–56; Lyle Koehler, "Red-White Power Relations and Justice in
the Courts of Seventeenth-Century New England," *American Indian Culture and
Research Journal* 3, no. 4 (1979): 1–31; James Warren Springer, "American Indians
and the Law of Real Property in Colonial New England," *American Journal of Legal
History* 30 (1986): 25–58; and James P. Ronda, "Red and White at the Bench: Indians
and the Law in Plymouth Colony, 1620–1691," *Essex Institute Historical Collections*
110 (1974): 200–15. See also the scholarship relating to Indian land claims listed in
note 9 of the preface.

17. In this book, English colonial laws are cited to Alden T. Vaughan and Deborah A. Rosen, eds., *Early American Indian Documents: Treaties and Laws, 1607–1789*, 3 vols.: vol. 15, *Virginia and Maryland Laws* (Bethesda MD: University Publications of America, 1998); vol. 16, *Carolina and Georgia Laws* (Bethesda MD: University Publications of America, 1998); and vol. 17, *New England and Middle Atlantic Laws* (Bethesda MD: University Publications of America, 2004). Massachusetts Bay and Plymouth Colony statutes restricting Indians' freedom of movement and choice of dwelling places included laws moving Natives out of the way of new colonial settlements, allowing towns to exclude Indians, prohibiting Indians from coming into Boston, confining them to Deer Island during "King Philip's War," concentrating Indian settlements into four towns by the end of the seventeenth century. See Massachusetts laws of 1644, 1646, 1675, 1681, and 1694, and Plymouth laws of 1677, 1682, and 1689, in Vaughan and Rosen, *Indian Documents*, 17: Massachusetts Documents [hereafter abbreviated MD] 30, 39, 75, 82, 97, 118, and Plymouth Documents [hereafter abbreviated PD] 74, 79, 85. An example of a statute forbidding Indians from powwowing or worshiping false gods is a 1646 Massachusetts law (MD 40). See also statutes forbidding Indians from profaning the Sabbath (MD 18, 1637), blaspheming the name of God (MD 40, 1646), swearing (MD 149, 1747), and working on Sundays (PD 16, 1652; and PD 52, 1671). To see the development of Massachusetts Bay statutes regulating trade with Indians, see especially Massachusetts laws of 1632, 1636, 1637, 1641, 1644, 1650, 1657, 1666, 1668, 1675, 1676, 1694, 1695, 1699, 1713, 1721, 1726, and 1753 (MD 9, 14, 16, 22, 36, 48, 57, 66, 68, 81, 87, 116, 119, 123, 132, 136, 140, and 150). See also Plymouth Colony statutes relating to trade in 1640, 1671, and 1677 (PD 5, 6, 52, and 76). Examples of laws prohibiting the sale of liquor are Massachusetts laws of 1633, 1654, 1657, 1694, 1726, 1746, and 1777 (MD 11, 52, 56, 114, 140, 147, and 159), and Plymouth laws of 1639, 1667, and 1673 (PD 4, 44, and 58). Other laws prohibited the sale of guns in Massachusetts in 1637, 1642, and 1681 (MD 15, 26, and 96) and in Plymouth in 1667 and 1676 (PD 44 and 73); horses in Massachusetts in 1656 and Plymouth in 1656 and 1670 (MD 54 and PD 22 and 50); boats in both colonies in 1656 (MD 55 and PD20); and silver or gold money in Massachusetts in 1631 (MD 6).

18. MD 12 (1634), 98 (1685), and 125 (1701), and PD 8 (1643) and 47 (1668). See the exception made regarding lands purchased from Christiantown, MD 153 (1763).

19. Statutes forbidding suing Indians for debt include MD 130 (1709) and 155 (1773), and PD 81 (1682). Statutes allowing recovery of debts from Indians only under special circumstances include MD 134 (1718), 139 (1725), and 154 (1763).

20. MD 124 (1700), 134 (1718), 139 (1725), and 154 (1763).

21. MD 129 (1709) and 126 (1703).

22. MD 42 (1647), 43 (1647), 59 (1658), and 114 (1694), and PD 49 (1670) and 63 (1675). Note that sometimes Indians were allowed to bring business to regu-

lar courts on special dates set aside for Indians. A 1673 law of Plymouth Colony allowed Indians to initiate court proceedings, and a law of the following year allowed Indians to testify as witnesses in litigation between them and an English person. PD 59 (1673) and 60 (1674). A law of 1691 specifically provided that poor Indians claiming a share of war plunder could bring suits *in forma pauperis*. PD 89 (1691). It should also be noted that denying citizens' rights to Indians was normally accompanied by their exemption from citizens' duties, but this was not always the case. Indians were typically spared the obligation to pay taxes and were often excluded or exempted from the militia or military training. For an example of the former, see MD 138 (1723), which explicitly exempted Indian landowners in the town of Sutton from a land tax to support the minister, and for examples of the latter see MD 53 (1656) and 161 (1779). However, at times Indians served in the military. Specifically, a statute of 1652 ordered that all Indians who were servants to the English were to attend military training with the colonists; during King Philip's War, statutes included friendly Indians among those sent on expeditions against the enemy Indians; and during the Revolutionary War laws provided for hundreds of Massachusetts Indians to serve in the Continental Army. MD 49 (1652), 89 (1676), and 210 (1777).

23. MD 50 (1652) and PD 38 (1665). See also the laws of 1654 and 1657 that gave specific groups of Indians the liberty to establish towns. MD 51 (1654) and 58 (1657).

24. PD 79 (1682).

25. See Kawashima, "Legal Origins of the Indian."

26. MD 148 (1747).

27. MD 154 (1763). The statute required that the town clerk and treasurer of Mashpee had to be Englishmen, but significant power was still left in the hands of the Mashpees because they held a majority of the overseer positions. The overseers were authorized to (a) allot and apportion lands to the residents, (b) lease out the common lands and use the profits to support indigent people in the community; (c) bring actions against anyone who illegally gained possession of Mashpee lands or trespassed upon those lands; (d) regulate the fishery in Mashpee; and (e) call district meetings (just as selectmen in other towns did).

28. Vaughan and Rosen, *Indian Documents*, 16: Georgia Document 8 (1755). Similar language appeared in later Georgia legislation. E.g., see Georgia Document 28 (1770).

29. South Carolina laws that most extensively regulated Indian slaves include those enacted in 1696, 1712, 1722, and 1740 (Vaughan and Rosen, *Indian Documents*, 16: South Carolina Documents 11, 27, 55, and 77). Historian Alan Gallay estimates that in 1708 there were 1,400 Indian slaves in the Carolinas, constituting 15 percent of the population of the colony. Gallay, *Indian Slave Trade*, 200, 346. On Indians

and slavery in South Carolina, see also Peter H. Wood, *Black Majority: Negroes in Colonial South Carolina from 1670 to the Stono Rebellion* (New York: Knopf, 1974). For earlier studies of Indian slavery in the English colonies, see Almon Wheeler Lauber, *Indian Slavery in Colonial Times within the Present Limits of the United States* (New York: Columbia University Press, 1913); John Donald Duncan, "Servitude and Slavery in Colonial South Carolina, 1670–1776," PhD diss., Emory University, 1971; and Donald Grinde Jr., "Native American Slavery in the Southern Colonies," *Indian Historian* 10, no. 2 (1977): 38–42.

30. Examples of slave laws include Vaughan and Rosen, *Indian Documents*, 16: North Carolina Documents 7 (1715–1716) and 33 (1760); Vaughan and Rosen, *Indian Documents*, 15: Virginia Documents 103 (1677), 132 (1705), 162 (1748), and 173 (1755), Maryland Document 67 (1717); Vaughan and Rosen, *Indian Documents*, 17: New Jersey Documents 35 (1704) and 37 (1714), Pennsylvania Document 27 (1751), New York Documents 53 (1706) and 70 (1717), Connecticut Document 149 (1730), and Rhode Island Document 63 (1712). In addition, New Hampshire laws referred ambiguously to any "Indian, Negro or Mulatto servant or slave" in legislation enacted in 1714 (New Hampshire Document 20).

31. For examples of southern and middle colony regulations pertaining to Indian land, see Vaughan and Rosen, *Indian Documents*, 16: Georgia Document 14 (1758), and Vaughan and Rosen, *Indian Documents*, 17: New York Document 46 (1684); for laws pertaining to trade with Indians, see Georgia Document 2 (1735) and New York Document 67 (1714); and for laws pertaining to alcohol, see Georgia Document 3 (1735) and New York Document 61 (1709). On the history of English-Indian relations in the southern and middle colonies, see Gallay, *Indian Slave Trade*; J. Leitch Wright, Jr., *The Only Land They Knew: The Tragic Story of the American Indians in the Old South* (New York: Free Press, 1981); James H. Merrell, *The Indians' New World: Catawbas and Their Neighbors from European Contact through the Era of Removal* (Chapel Hill: University of North Carolina Press, 1989); Matthew Dennis, *Cultivating a Landscape of Peace: Iroquois-European Encounters in Seventeenth-Century America* (Ithaca NY: Cornell University Press, 1993); Daniel K Richter, *The Ordeal of the Longhouse: The Peoples of the Iroquois League in the Era of European Colonization* (Chapel Hill: University of North Carolina Press, 1992); and Eric Hinderaker, *Elusive Empires: Constructing Colonialism in the Ohio Valley, 1673–1800* (New York: Cambridge University Press, 1997). On relations between the English and Indians throughout all of the east coast colonies, see Karen Ordahl Kupperman, *Indians and English: Facing Off in Early America* (Ithaca NY: Cornell University Press, 2000).

32. Although the Spanish and the English were the dominant colonial powers in the territory that later became the United States, other European countries also

established settlements and followed either the English or the Spanish model of governance and Indian policy. Most notably, French rule over its sparsely populated colonies along the St. Lawrence River, by the Great Lakes, and in the Mississippi River Valley closely followed the Spanish model in two important respects. First, official French policy was to "Frenchify" and Christianize the Indians and then to assimilate them into French society and make them French citizens. Second, the absolutist French king exerted considerable centralized control over the colonial empire; most of the laws governing the colonies emanated from Paris, most conspicuously the codified customary law of Paris and the Île de France (known as the *Coutume de Paris*) and decrees of the king, such as the *Code Noir*. On the history of the French colonies in North America, see especially W. J. Eccles, *France in America*, rev. ed. (East Lansing: Michigan State University Press, 1990); Daniel H. Usner Jr., *Indians, Settlers, and Slaves in a Frontier Exchange Economy: The Lower Mississippi Valley before 1783* (Chapel Hill: University of North Carolina Press, 1992); Usner, "American Indians in Colonial New Orleans," in *Powhatan's Mantle: Indians in the Colonial Southeast*, ed. Peter H. Wood et al. (Lincoln: University of Nebraska Press, 1989), 104–27; Mathé Állain, *"Not Worth a Straw": French Colonial Policy and the Early Years of Louisiana* (Lafayette: Center for Louisiana Studies, University of Southwestern Louisiana, 1988); and Patricia Dillon Woods, *French-Indian Relations on the Southern Frontier, 1699–1762* (Ann Arbor MI: UMI Research Press, 1980). On efforts to incorporate Indians into the French colonial society and legal system, see Saliha Belmessous, "Assimilation and Racialism in Seventeenth and Eighteenth-Century French Colonial Policy," *American Historical Review* 110 (2005): 322–49; Mason Wade, "The French and the Indians," in Peckham and Gibson, *Attitudes of Colonial Powers*, 61–80; George F. G. Stanley, "The Policy of 'Francisation' as Applied to the Indians during the Ancien Regime," *Revue d'Histoire de l'Amérique Française* 3 (1949): 333–48; John A. Dickinson, "Native Sovereignty and French Justice in Early Canada," in *Essays in the History of Canadian Law*, ed. Jim Philips et al., vol. 5 (Toronto: University of Toronto Press, 1994), 17–40. See also the descriptions of Dutch, Swedish, and Russian colonies in Taylor, *American Colonies*.

33. For the most comprehensive history of American Indian policy, see Prucha, *Great Father*. On the British-Indian treaties, see Dorothy V. Jones, *License for Empire: Colonialism by Treaty in Early America* (Chicago: University of Chicago Press, 1982), chs. 3 and 4. On British Indian policy in the American revolutionary era, see Colin G. Calloway, *Crown and Calumet: British-Indian Relations, 1783–1815* (Norman: University of Oklahoma Press, 1987).

34. John Sevier to James Ore, 12 May 1798, quoted in Prucha, *Great Father*, 108. For an in-depth analysis of United States legal theory of colonization, see Williams, *American Indian in Western Legal Thought*, chs. 6 and 7.

35. Jones, *License for Empire*, 173.

36. For example, see the comments of Thomas Hart Benton (Missouri) and Alfred Cuthbert (Georgia) on the floor of the Senate in February 1835. Both senators denied that the "agreements" with Indian tribes were really "treaties" within the meaning of the word in the Constitution or in the law of nations. Senate, 23rd Cong., 2nd sess., 4 February 1835, *The Congressional Globe*, 2:196–97.

37. *Johnson v. McIntosh*, 21 U.S. 543 (1823); David E. Wilkins, *American Indian Sovereignty and the U.S. Supreme Court: The Masking of Justice* (Austin: University of Texas Press, 1997), 27–35; and David Wilkins, "Quit-Claiming the Doctrine of Discovery: A Treaty Based Reappraisal," *Oklahoma City University Law Review* 23 (1998): 277–315. (The first and third quotations are on p. 31 of *American Indian Sovereignty*; the second quotation is from "Quit-Claiming the Doctrine of Discovery," p. 310.) Wilkins comments that although "[a] solid argument can be made that *Johnson* was implicitly overruled by two later cases, *Worcester v. Georgia* (1832) and especially *Mitchel v. U.S.* (1835), [t]he fact remains . . . that this decision is still regularly cited by commentators and, more importantly, relied upon as 'good' precedent by the Supreme Court." *American Indian Sovereignty*, 35. See also Williams, *American Indian in Western Legal Thought*, 308–17.

38. *Johnson v. McIntosh*, 21 U.S. 543 (1823).

1. TRIBAL SOVEREIGNTY AND STATE JURISDICTION

1. "Murder," *Niagara Patriot*, 8 May 1821.

2. *Geneva Palladium*, 25 July 1821; and *Albany Argus*, 27 July 1821.

3. "State of Georgia vs. Tassels," *New-Hampshire Patriot and State Gazette* (Concord NH), 24 January 1831; and *Cherokee Phoenix*, 8 January 1831, printed in *Cherokee Editor: The Writings of Elias Boudinot*, ed. Theda Perdue (Knoxville: University of Tennessee Press, 1983; reprint, Athens: University of Georgia Press, 1996), 120–21. In the court case the Georgia Supreme Court referred to the defendant as "Tassels" rather than "Tassel."

4. Gary E. Moulton, *John Ross: Cherokee Chief* (Athens: University of Georgia Press, 1978).

5. Harry Robie, "Red Jacket's Reply: Problems in the Verification of a Native American Speech Text," *New York Folklore* 12 (1986): 99–117, at 100. In his article, Robie analyzes the authenticity of Red Jacket's famous Reply to Reverend Cram (1805); he concludes that the text of the reply appears to be an accurate reflection of the content and structure of Red Jacket's speech.

6. Vine Deloria Jr., "Self-Determination and the Concept of Sovereignty," in *Native American Sovereignty*, ed. John R. Wunder (New York: Garland, 1996),

118–124; Vine Deloria Jr., *Behind the Trail of Broken Treaties: An Indian Declaration of Independence* (New York: Delacorte Press, 1974); Vine Deloria Jr. and Clifford M. Lytle, *The Nations Within: The Past and Future of American Indian Sovereignty* (New York: Pantheon Books, 1984; reprint, Austin: University of Texas Press, 1998), chs. 1–2; David E. Wilkins, *American Indian Sovereignty and the U.S. Supreme Court: The Masking of Justice* (Austin: University of Texas Press, 1997), ch. 2; Glenn T. Morris, "Vine Deloria, Jr., and the Development of a Decolonizing Critique of Indigenous Peoples and International Relations," in *Native Voices: American Indian Identity and Resistance*, ed. Richard A. Grounds et al. (Lawrence: University Press of Kansas, 2003), 97–154; Robert A. Williams Jr., "The Algebra of Federal Indian Law: The Hard Trail of Decolonizing and Americanizing the White Man's Indian Jurisprudence," *Wisconsin Law Review* 1986 (1986): 219–99; and Taiaiake Alfred, "Sovereignty," in *A Companion to American Indian History*, ed. Philip J. Deloria and Neal Salisbury (Malden MA: Blackwell, 2004), 460–74. While modern white conceptions of sovereignty tend to focus on political elements, David Wilkins and Vine Deloria also explain that for Indians tribal sovereignty has both a political and a cultural or spiritual dimension. Wilkins, *American Indian Sovereignty*, 20–21; Deloria, "Self-Determination." For a recent comprehensive history of tribal sovereignty in a comparative context, see P. G. McHugh, *Aboriginal Societies and the Common Law: A History of Sovereignty, Status, and Self-Determination* (New York: Oxford University Press, 2004).

7. For a biography of Red Jacket, see Christopher Densmore, *Red Jacket: Iroquois Diplomat and Orator* (Syracuse: Syracuse University Press, 1999). For general background on the Senecas in the period prior to 1821, see Anthony F. C. Wallace, *The Death and Rebirth of the Seneca* (New York: Knopf, 1970).

8. Red Jacket's speeches of 1805, 1811, 1826, and an undated speech, in Alan R. Velie, ed., *American Indian Literature: An Anthology* (Norman: University of Oklahoma Press, 1979), 254–63 (quotations on pp. 257 and 260).

9. Report of proceedings in the Stiff-Armed George case by presiding judge Brockholst Livingston, 4 March 1803, printed in the *Morning Chronicle* (New York City), 15 March 1803.

10. *Chronicle Express* (New York City), 14 March 1803; Red Jacket's speech at the meeting of Seneca chiefs and white citizens, printed in full in William L. Stone, *The Life and Times of Red-Jacket or Sa-Go-Ye-Wat-ha* (New York: Wiley and Putnam, 1841), 173–78 (quotations on pp. 175 and 176); and *Journal of the Assembly of the State of New-York* (Albany: John Barber, 1803), 5, 7, 10, 11, and 12 March 1803. "An Act to pardon George, a Seneca Indian, otherwise called Stiff-Armed George, convicted of Murder" is in New York Session Laws, 12 March 1803, ch. 31 (p. 64). (In this book, post-Revolutionary statutes are cited to the state's official volumes of session

laws. In order to ensure that every law can be located, each citation provides a date, chapter number [if any], and starting page number of the statute. Alternative titles that are specific to each state's session laws, along with publication information, are included in the bibliography.)

11. *Albany Argus*, 27 July 1821; *Republican Chronicle* (Ithaca NY), 25 July 1821; and *New-York Evening Post* (New York City), 15 May 1821, reprint of an article originally published in the *Niagara (Buffalo) Journal*.

12. *Geneva Palladium*, 25 July 1821; "Imperium in Imperio, Or an independent State within an Independent civilized State," *American Journal* (Ithaca NY), 8 August 1821, reprint of an article originally published in the *New-York Journal* (New York City).

13. *Republican Chronicle* (Ithaca NY), 1 August 1821; "Indian Murder," *Essex Patriot* (Haverhill MA), 28 July 1821; *New-Hampshire Patriot & State Gazette* (Concord NH), 30 July 1821; and "Rights of Indians," *Columbian Centinel* (Boston), 8 August 1821.

14. "Law," *Albany Argus*, 17 August 1821; "Indian Jurisdiction," *Niles' Weekly Register*, 25 August 1821, reprint of an article originally published in the *Albany Daily Advertiser*, 4 August 1821; and *New-York Evening Post* (New York City), 18 August 1821, reprint of an article originally published in the *Albany Statesman*. The first and third quotations are from the *Albany Argus* article, while the second quotation is from the *Niles' Weekly Register* article.

15. "Law," *Albany Argus*, 17 August 1821; "Indian Jurisdiction," *Niles' Weekly Register*, 25 August 1821, reprint of an article originally published in the *Albany Daily Advertiser*, 4 August 1821. The quotations are from the *Albany Argus*. Although the state's attorneys pointedly did not distinguish between the state government and the federal government, the defendant's lawyer observed about the Senecas that "if jurisdiction was acquired over them by conquest, it was that of the United States and not of this state, and that the United States had never ceded it to this state." *Niles' Weekly Register* reprint of the *Albany Daily Advertiser* article. The federalism issue is discussed in depth in the next chapter.

16. "Law," *Albany Argus*, 17 August 1821; and "Indian Jurisdiction," *Niles' Weekly Register*, 25 August 1821, reprint of an article originally published in the *Albany Daily Advertiser*, 4 August 1821.

17. "Indian Jurisdiction," *Niles' Weekly Register*, 25 August 1821, reprint of an article originally published in the *Albany Daily Advertiser*, 4 August 1821.

18. New York Session Laws, "An Act declaring the Jurisdiction of the Courts of this State, and pardoning Soo-non-gize, otherwise called Tommy Jemmy," 12 April 1822, ch. 204.

19. In some newspaper accounts, Ketaukah's name is spelled "Hetaukah." A Menominee Indian, Kewabiskim, whom a court in Green Bay had found guilty of

murdering another white man, was executed in Detroit along with Ketaukah. For accounts of the two Michigan Territory cases, see the *New-York Evening Post*, 31 October 1821; "Supreme Court," *Boston Daily Advertiser*, 1 November 1821; "Crimes, &c," *Columbian Centinel* (Boston), 3 November 1821; *Essex Register* (Salem MA), 3 November 1821; "Indian Execution," *Essex Patriot* (Haverhill MA), 26 January 1822; and *Niles' Weekly Register* (Baltimore), 10 November 1821 and 26 January 1822. For a discussion of the general treatment of Indians in Michigan Territory during the period immediately following those cases, see Patrick J. Jung, "To Extend Fair and Impartial Justice to the Indian: Native Americans and the Additional Court of Michigan Territory, 1823–1836," *Michigan Historical Review* 23, no. 2 (1997): 25–48. Jung found that under the judgeship of James D. Doty, Indians generally were more fairly treated than has often been assumed; he also found that Indians effectively used the courts to further their own interests. However, Jung also concludes that the courts were less generous toward Indians after 1836. He attributes the change to the increased number of white settlers who were more interested in farming than in the fur trade. These newer settlers "had only limited and superficial contact with Native Americans and their culture" and were more racist than their predecessors (46–47). According to the newspaper accounts of Ketaukah's 1821 case, prior to ascending to the position of judge, Doty had served as one of Ketaukah's two defense lawyers.

20. See, for example, the Minnesota law asserting that the state had jurisdiction over certain Indian crimes committed outside of reservations: "if any Indian or Indians shall enter upon the limits of this State, or cross the boundary line of their reservation, and there take, steal, or destroy any property, real or personal, belonging to any citizen or inhabitant of this State, or shall commit any murder, violence, or outrage upon any such citizen or inhabitant, or shall commit any crime, offence or misdemeanor whatever, recognized by the laws of this State as a crime, offence or misdemeanor, he or they shall be subject to the existing laws of this State, and shall be punished accordingly; *Provided*, These laws shall not extend to crimes committed by one Indian against the person or property of another Indian, except in the case of murder." And see also the law of California enacted in its first year of statehood: "If any Indian shall commit an unlawful offence against a white person, such person shall not inflict punishment for such offence, but may, without process, take the Indian before a Justice of the Peace, and on conviction, the Indian shall be punished according to the provisions of this Act" and "An Indian convicted of stealing horses, mules, cattle, or any valuable thing, shall be subject to receive any number of lashes not exceeding twenty-five, or shall be subject to a fine not exceeding two hundred dollars, at the discretion of the Court or Jury." Minnesota Session Laws, 20 July 1858, ch. 44; California Session Laws, 22 April 1850, ch. 133.

21. New York Session Laws, "An Act declaring the Jurisdiction of the Courts of this State, and pardoning Soo-non-gize, otherwise called Tommy Jemmy," 12 April 1822, ch. 204. The legislature's reference to protecting the Indians most likely reflected the legislators' dim view of the nature of Seneca justice. The *Albany Argus* expressed the popular perception in one article that devoted half a column to the "dreadful" and "horridly revolting" punitive practices of the Senecas, who allegedly punished murderers by immolating their innocent relatives. *Albany Argus*, 27 July 1821. The same article was also printed in the *New-Hampshire Gazette*, 14 August 1821 (citing the *Albany Argus* as the original source of the text) and the *Essex Register* (Salem MA), 1 August 1821 (citing the *Erie Gazette* (Erie PA) as its source). Other newspaper articles omitted the details of the Senecas' punishments but conveyed a negative view nonetheless through the use of the headline "Aboriginal Severity." For example, that headline was used for identical articles published in the *Eastern Argus* (Portland ME), 21 August 1821, and in the *City Gazette and Daily Advertiser* (Charleston SC), 6 November 1821.

22. *Jackson ex dem. Smith v. Goodell*, 20 Johns. 188 (N.Y., 1822).

23. *Goodell v. Jackson ex dem. Smith*, 20 Johns. 693 (N.Y., 1823).

24. Chancellor Kent discussed the citizenship/sovereignty issue in the 1823 case at 709–18. It is interesting to note that two decades earlier, Kent had taken a somewhat different view of an Indian of the Brotherton (or Brothertown) tribe. In 1801, the Oneida County Court of Oyer and Terminer in Utica found Brotherton Indian George Peters guilty of murdering his wife (who was also an Indian) in the New York village of Rome. Judge Kent considered the question of whether the Brotherton Indians were subject to state laws for an offense against another Indian. He concluded that the Brothertons were "mere remnants" of tribes that had been conquered and destroyed, that they had never been an independent tribe in New York, and that they had never had a separate criminal justice system of their own. Therefore, he decided that they were subject to the state's criminal jurisdiction. This ruling was issued many years before the 1822 statute extended criminal jurisdiction over all Indians in the state. For a newspaper account of the proceedings presided over by Kent, see the *Albany Centinel*, 30 June 1801. The subsequent New York Supreme Court endorsement of Kent's position is *In re George Peters*, 2 Johns. Cas. 344 (N.Y., 1801). The court was careful to note in the *Peters* case that it was taking no position on whether Indians from other tribes in the state might be amenable to New York's civil and criminal laws.

Newspaper accounts evidence the fact that other Indians were tried in New York courts prior to 1822, but the articles do not always specify the defendants' tribal affiliation. Indians tried for murder include John Denny (convicted 1818) and Nicholas, an Oneida Indian (acquitted, 1797), and those tried for burglary include Peter Daniel (convicted, 1818) and David Bigbag (convicted, 1820). "Trials for Murder," *American Mercury* (Hartford CT) 6 January 1818; "Law Intelligence," *Boston Daily Advertiser*, 2 January 1818, reprint of article from the *Utica Patriot* (NY); *Otsego Herald; or, Western Advertiser* (Cooperstown NY), 13 July 1797; *New-York Evening Post*, 15 October 1818; *New-York Statesman* (Albany NY), 16 June 1820, reprint of article from the *Batavia Times* (NY). According to James H. Smith, *The History of Chenango and Madison Counties, New York* (Syracuse NY: D. Mason, 1880), other Indians who were executed for murder in early national New York include Mary Antoine (Oneida, executed 1814) and her father, Abram Antoine (Oneida, executed 1823).

25. In addition to the *Goodell v. Jackson* case, one can see another gesture toward tribal sovereignty by a New York court in *Hastings v. Farmer and Ellis*, 4 N.Y. 293 (1850). The court recognized that each Indian tribe was an independent sovereignty and that tribal laws governed its members but concluded that since the tribes needed protection against fraud by whites, New York was justified in forbidding whites to bring suit against Indians to enforce contracts with them.

26. *Strong and Gordon, Chiefs of the Seneca Nation of Indians v. Waterman*, 11 Paige 607 (1845).

27. *United States v. Elm*, 25 F. Cas. 1006 (D.C., N.D. N.Y., 1877).

28. Article 7, section 12, of the New York State Constitution of 1821.

29. New York Session Laws, "An Act relative to the lands appropriated by this State to the use of the Oneida Onondaga and Cayuga Indians," 11 March 1793, ch. 51; "An Act relative to the Indians resident within this State," 27 March 1794, ch. 59; "An Act for the better support of the Oneida Onondaga and Cayuga Indians, and for other purposes therein mentioned," 9 April 1795, ch. 70; "An Act authorizing the governor to appoint commissioners to treat with the Oneida Indians for the purchase of part of their lands," 26 February 1798, ch. 23; "An Act relative to the lands of the Cayuga Indians," 8 March 1799, ch. 25. Treaties between New York State and the Oneida, Onondaga, Cayuga, and St. Regis Indians were completed in 1795, 1796, and 1798. The Confederation era practice of having commissioners purchase Indian land is exemplified in New York Session Laws, "An Act for the payment of certain contingent expenses, and for other purposes therein mentioned," 29 November 1784.

30. New York Session Laws, "An Act to enable resident aliens to hold and convey real estate," 10 April 1843, ch. 87; "An Act for the benefit of Indians," 11 April 1849, ch. 420.

31. New York Session Laws, "An Act more effectually to protect certain tribes of Indians residing within this State from frauds," 22 March 1790, ch. 29; "An Act rela-

tive to Indians," 4 April 1801, ch. 147; "An Act to enable resident aliens to hold and convey real estate," 10 April 1843, ch. 87; "An Act to amend the act for the protection and improvement of the Seneca Indians residing on the Cattaraugus and Allegany reservations in this State," 15 November 1847, ch. 365. Prior to the 1847 statute, the legislature had permitted "The Seneca Nation of Indians" to bring suits in New York courts on behalf of the Nation. "An Act for the protection and improvement of the Seneca Indians, residing on the Cattaraugus and Allegany reservations in this state," 8 May 1845, ch. 150.

32. New York Session Laws, "An Act for the protection and improvement of the Seneca Indians, residing on the Cattaraugus and Allegany reservations in this state," 8 May 1845, ch. 150 (political organization); "An Act to fix the time of electing officers for the Seneca Indians," 12 April 1848, ch. 300 (elections); "An Act in reference to the new government of the Seneca Nation of Indians," 11 April 1849, ch. 378 (political organization); "An Act to enable resident aliens to hold and convey real estate," 10 April 1843, ch. 87 (taxation); "An Act in relation to the roads and bridges within the Allegany and Delaware Creek Reservations," 9 May 1840, ch. 254 (taxation); "An act authorizing the construction and repair of roads and bridges on the Indian lands in the Counties of Erie and Cattaraugus," 4 May 1841, ch. 166 (taxation); "An Act relative to Indians," 4 April 1801, ch. 147 (inheritance); and "An Act for the benefit of Indians," 11 April 1849, ch. 420 (marriage).

33. In addition to the categories of Indian laws described in the text, New York also enacted Indian-related laws on subjects that were already being regulated by the federal government. Specifically, New York also took it upon itself to punish whites who sold liquor to Indians, as well as to punish and remove white intruders or settlers on Indian land. For New York and the other twelve original states, such laws continued the practice of the pre-Revolutionary era, when all of the colonies passed numerous statutes punishing whites for such behavior that was thought to disrupt peaceful relations with neighboring Indians. When re-enacted after ratification of the U.S. Constitution, these laws either provided state remedies for white actions that were already prohibited by the federal government or strayed from federal law by allowing exceptions to such prohibitions. An example of an anti-liquor law that emulated the federal prohibition is New York's twenty-dollar fine imposed on any person who sold "ardent spirits" on lands owned by or reserved to Indians, as well as persons who sold ardent spirits within the counties of Oneida or Chenango to Indians belonging to the Oneida, Stockbridge, or Brotherton tribe. An example of an anti-trespass law that was similar to federal law except that it exempted trespassers from the fine under certain circumstances is New York's twenty-five-dollar fine for whites who entered on Stockbridge Indian property.

The law exempted from the fine any white person who first obtained permission from the tribal officers ("peace makers") elected pursuant to the statute. New York Session Laws, "An Act relative to Indians," 4 April 1801, ch. 147 (liquor); and "An Act supplementary to an act entitled 'An act for the relief of the Indians residing in New Stockbridge and Brothertown,'" 23 March 1797, ch. 44 (trespass). Naturally, the mere presence of these laws on the books did not necessarily mean that they were regularly enforced. Despite that fact, and despite the fact that these laws may not have been a direct challenge to tribal sovereignty, the statutes were perceived by some as challenges to exclusive federal authority over relations with Indian tribes because they presumed the state's right to govern Indians inside state boundaries. Accordingly, these statutes were relevant to the federalism issue, which is discussed in the next chapter.

34. Treaty of Buffalo Creek, signed 15 January 1838, proclaimed 4 April 1840 (Statutes at Large 7: 550), printed in Charles J. Kappler, ed., *Indian Affairs: Laws and Treaties*, 3 vols. (Washington: Government Printing Office, 1913), 2: 502–12. For an excellent and thorough examination of the dispossession of New York's Indians, see Laurence M. Hauptman, *Conspiracy of Interests: Iroquois Dispossession and the Rise of New York State* (Syracuse: Syracuse University Press, 1999). The description of treaty making of the 1830s and 1840s in the text is based on Hauptman's book. On the 1780s and 1790s, see Barbara Graymont, "New York State Indian Policy after the Revolution," *New York History* 57 (1976): 438–74; and J. David Lehman, "The End of the Iroquois Mystique: The Oneida Land Cession Treaties of the 1780s," *William and Mary Quarterly*, 3rd ser., 47 (1990): 523–47. On the connections between nineteenth-century New York statutes and court decisions and continuing state exercise of jurisdiction over Indians, see Robert B. Porter, "Legalizing, Decolonizing, and Modernizing New York State's Indian Law," *Albany Law Review* 63 (1999): 125–200.

35. Supplemental Treaty of Buffalo Creek, signed 20 May 1842, proclaimed 26 August 1842 (Statutes at Large 7: 586), printed in Kappler, *Indian Affairs*, 2: 537–42; New York State Assembly Resolution, 16 February 1847; concurrence by the state Senate, 19 February 1847 (printed with New York Session Laws of 1847).

36. Hauptman, *Conspiracy of Interests*, ch. 12. Later, the first Indian to serve as commissioner of Indian affairs, Ely S. Parker (commissioner from 1869 to 1871), came from the Tonawanda Seneca reservation. Having been educated in white schools throughout his childhood in the 1830s and 1840s, he provided support for the federal government's efforts to civilize Indians while he was commissioner. As a young man, however, he had also helped the tribe retain its reservation lands. For a biography of Ely Parker, see William H. Armstrong, *Warrior in Two Camps: Ely S. Parker, Union General and Seneca Chief* (Syracuse: Syracuse University Press, 1978).

37. New York State Senate, "Report of the committee on Indian affairs on the Assembly bill in relation to the Seneca Indians," 18 April 1845, included among the documents accompanying the "Declaration of the Seneca Nation of Indians in general council assembled" (Baltimore: Wm. Wooddy, printer, 1845), 16–27. The committee made the quoted statement in the context of a paragraph explaining why New York had always tolerated "a distinct, and to a certain extent, an independent [Indian] community, in the heart of our territorial dominions."

38. William G. McLoughlin, *Cherokee Renascence in the New Republic* (Princeton: Princeton University Press, 1986); Anthony F. C. Wallace, *The Long, Bitter Trail: Andrew Jackson and the Indians* (New York: Hill and Wang, 1993), and Robert J. Conley, *The Cherokee Nation: A History* (Albuquerque: University of New Mexico Press, 2005). In her examination of Indian-white relations in early Tennessee, Cynthia Cumfer explains how the view of frontier whites developed over time. Before 1790, she says, most settlers recognized the separate nationhood of the Cherokees. Their view shifted only during the 1790s, when they began to question the notion of Cherokee sovereignty. As she describes it, whites "reconstituted the Indian sovereign unit from a 'nation' with a country to a 'tribe' with territory, or, worse, to 'tenants' with mere claims." By the early nineteenth century, they had "denationalized" Indian communities, had devalued their land rights, and envisioned no place for Native people within the state. Cynthia Cumfer, "Local Origins of National Indian Policy: Cherokee and Tennessean Ideas about Sovereignty and Nationhood, 1790–1811," *Journal of the Early Republic* 23 (2003): 21–46. The quotation is on p. 44.

39. Report of the Joint Committee on the State of the Republic, 19 December 1827, and Resolutions of the Senate, 27 December 1827, printed with Georgia Session Laws for 1827 (p. 236).

40. Statutes relating to Cherokees and Cherokee lands are in Georgia Session Laws, 20 December 1828 (p. 88); 19 December 1829 (p. 98); 21, 22, and 23 December 1830 (pp. 127, 114, 115, and 118); 22 and 26 December 1831 (pp. 141, 143, and 144); 22 and 24 December 1832 (pp. 107, 102, and 106); 6 and 20 December 1833 (pp. 119 and 114); 20 December 1834 (pp. 152 and 156); and 21 December 1835 (p. 144). Even after the Treaty of New Echota provided for expulsion of the Cherokees within two years, Georgia could not leave the matter alone. In 1837 the legislature enacted a statute establishing eleven sixty-man companies of state soldiers to help federal troops remove Cherokees from Georgia. Georgia Session Laws, 26 December 1837 (p. 154). Historian Mary Young provides a fuller description of the succession of oppressive statutes enacted by the Georgia state legislature between 1827 and 1836 in "The Exercise of Sovereignty in Cherokee Georgia," *Journal of the Early Republic* 10 (1990): 43–63.

41. McLoughlin, *Cherokee Renascence.*

42. John Ross to David L. Child, 11 February 1831, printed in *The Papers of Chief John Ross*, ed. Gary E. Moulton, 2 vols. (Norman: University of Oklahoma Press, 1985), 1:214–15 [hereafter cited as "*Ross Papers*"]; and John Ross et al. to the Senate and House of Representatives, 27 February 1929, in *Ross Papers*, 1:154–57 (quotations on pp. 155 and 157). For a biography of Ross, see Moulton, *John Ross.*

43. John Ross and William Hicks, Annual Message, 13 October 1828, in *Ross Papers*, 1:140–44.

44. John Ross and Cherokee delegation, [11 February?] 1824, quoted in Conley, *Cherokee Nation*, 132.

45. McLoughlin, *Cherokee Renascence*, 307.

46. John Ross to Hugh Montgomery, 20 July 1830, in *Ross Papers*, 1:193–95 (quotation on p. 194). The italics and capitalization in the text are as modified by Ross for emphasis. For Robert A. Williams Jr.'s explanation of the meaning of treaties, see Williams, "'The People of the States Where They Are Found Are Often Their Deadliest Enemies': The Indian Side of the Story of Indian Rights and Federalism," *Arizona Law Review* 38 (1996): 981–97; and Williams, *Linking Arms Together: American Indian Treaty Visions of Law and Peace, 1600–1800* (New York: Oxford University Press, 1997).

47. Ross to Montgomery, 20 July 1830.

48. Andrew Denson, *Demanding the Cherokee Nation: Indian Autonomy and American Culture, 1830–1900* (Lincoln: University of Nebraska Press, 2004), 28–38.

49. Indian Removal Act, 28 May 1830, Statutes at Large 4: 411. The federal government's lead negotiator for the fraudulent Treaty of New Echota was John Schermerhorn, who, a few years later in New York, was also one of the chief negotiators of the fraudulent Treaty of Buffalo Creek. Sadly, by 1835 Ross and former ally Elias Boudinot had come to different conclusions about the path the Cherokees ought to take, and they ended up attacking each other bitterly. While Boudinot decided that the Cherokees had to leave Georgia in order to preserve their nation, Ross was determined to remain in the state, even if it meant submitting to the state's jurisdiction. In 1835, Boudinot was among those who signed the Treaty of New Echota, a document that Ross publicly derided as a subversion of the people's will.

50. *State of Georgia v. Tassels*, 1 Dud. 229 (1830). The trial and execution were also described in newspaper articles. See "State of Georgia vs. Tassels," *New-Hampshire Patriot and State Gazette* (Concord NH), 24 January 1831; "George Tassels," *Farmer's Cabinet* (Amherst NH), 22 January 1831; and "Execution of George Tassels," *Baltimore Patriot*, 10 January 1831. See also the discussion of *Tassels* in Tim Alan Garrison, *The Legal Ideology of Removal: The Southern Judiciary and the Sovereignty of Native American Nations* (Athens: University of Georgia Press, 2002), ch. 4.

51. Marshall's writ to the state of Georgia, the governor's letter to the legislature, and the legislature's authorization to the governor to ignore the writ are printed in "Georgia and the Supreme Court," *Baltimore Patriot*, 6 January 1831. John Ross's letter to the governor shortly before the execution, along with the Cherokee Nation's petition to the Supreme Court, was printed in the *Watch-Tower* (Cooperstown NY), 24 January 1831 (acknowledging the *Georgia Journal* as their source for the text). See also Garrison, *Legal Ideology of Removal*, ch. 4.

52. *Cherokee Nation v. State of Georgia*, 30 U.S. 1 (1831); Deloria and Lytle, *Nations Within*, 16–17.

53. *Worcester v. State of Georgia*, 31 U.S. 515 (1832).

54. For analysis of *Worcester*, see Jill Norgren, *The Cherokee Cases: The Confrontation of Law and Politics* (New York: McGraw Hill, 1996); Joseph C. Burke, "The Cherokee Cases: A Study in Law, Politics, and Morality," *Stanford Law Review* 21 (1969): 500–31; and Garrison, *Legal Ideology of Removal*, ch. 7.

55. Sidney L. Harring, *Crow Dog's Case: American Indian Sovereignty, Tribal Law, and United States Law in the Nineteenth Century* (New York: Cambridge University Press, 1994), 52.

56. Garrison, *Legal Ideology of Removal*, 238–39, 229.

57. Russell Thornton, "Cherokee Population Losses during the Trail of Tears: A New Perspective and a New Estimate," *Ethnohistory* 31 (1984): 289–300; and Ronald N. Satz, *American Indian Policy in the Jacksonian Era* (Lincoln: University of Nebraska Press, 1975), 97, 101, 112, 235. On Cherokee, Georgia, and U.S. policies on removal, see also Wallace, *Long, Bitter Trail*; McLoughlin, *Cherokee Renascence*; and Michael D. Green, *The Politics of Indian Removal: Creek Government and Society in Crisis* (Lincoln: University of Nebraska Press, 1982).

58. *State of Tennessee v. Forman*, 16 Tenn. 256 (1835); *Caldwell v. State of Alabama*, 1 Stew. & P. 327 (1832). For extensive discussion of these cases, see Garrison, *Legal Ideology of Removal*, chs. 6 and 8. For another southern case, see *State of North Carolina v. Ta-Cha-Na-Tah*, 64 N.C. 614 (1870), where the Supreme Court of North Carolina held that Cherokee Indians in the state were subject to its criminal laws.

59. *State of Wisconsin v. Doxtater*, 47 Wis. 278 (1879). The court in *Doxtater* focused mostly on states' rights issues rather than on tribal sovereignty. For more on this case, see chapter 2.

60. *Blue-Jacket v. Commissioners of Johnson County*, 3 Kan. 299 (1865); and *The Kansas Indians*, 72 U.S. 737 (1867).

61. E.g., Missouri, as shown in *Boyer v. Dively*, 58 Mo. 510 (1875); *Johnson v. Johnson's Administrator*, 30 Mo. 72 (1860); *Buchanan v. Harvey*, 35 Mo. 276 (1864); Alabama as shown in *Wall v. Williamson*, 8 Ala. 48 (1845); Arkansas, as shown in *Crabtree v. McDaniel*, 17 Ark. 222 (1856); and Tennessee, as shown in *Morgan v.*

McGhee, 24 Tenn. 13 (1844). New York recognized Indian marriages by statute enacted 11 April 1849 (ch. 420). See also *Dole v. Irish*, 2 Barb. 639 (N.Y., 1848), in which the court found that Seneca Indians have their own customs regarding inheritance and therefore the surrogate of Erie County had no authority over the estate of a deceased Seneca. But see *State of North Carolina v. Ta-Cha-Na-Tah*, in which North Carolina declined to recognize a marriage that followed Cherokee customs but did not conform to state law. State recognition of Indian customs is discussed further in chapter 3.

62. James Madison to James Monroe, 27 November 1784, quoted in Jack Campisi, "From Stanwix to Canandaigua: National Policy, States' Rights, and Indian Land," in *Iroquois Land Claims*, ed. Christopher Vecsey and William A. Starna (Syracuse: Syracuse University Press, 1988), 49–65, 56. After granting Congress authority to manage relations with Indians "not members of any of the States," the Articles of Confederation added the qualifying clause "provided that the legislative right of any State within its own limits be not infringed or violated." Madison concluded that the phrase "legislative right of any State" referred to the state right of pre-emption of lands from Indians, but others believed that the clause had broader meaning, allowing a state's regular laws to apply within Indian Territory. Francis G. Hutchins, *Tribes and the American Constitution* (Brookline MA: Amarta Press, 2000), 60–63.

2. THE STATE SOVEREIGNTY ARGUMENT

1. Regarding federal regulation of Indian land sales, executory contracts, and trading, see, for example, sections 7–12 of the trade and intercourse act of 1802 (Statutes at Large 2: 139), sections 2 and 12 of the 1834 act (Statutes at Large 4: 729), and section 3 of the 1847 act (Statutes at Large 9: 203). For assertions of exclusive federal control of treaty making with Indians, see, e.g., section 12 of the federal trade and intercourse acts of 1802 and 1834. For federal prohibitions on white intruders or settlers on Indian land and prohibitions on the sale of liquor to Indians, see sections 2, 3, and 5 of the 1802 trade and intercourse act and sections 10 and 11 of the 1834 act. Similar provisions appeared in other trade and intercourse acts. For a description of the trade and intercourse acts, see Francis Paul Prucha, *American Indian Policy in the Formative Years: The Indian Trade and Intercourse Acts, 1790–1834* (Cambridge MA: Harvard University Press, 1962), and for a particularly close analysis of the language in those acts relating to restraints on alienation, see Robert N. Clinton and Margaret Tobey Hotopp, "Judicial Enforcement of the Federal Restraints on Alienation of Indian Land: The Origins of the Eastern Land Claims," *Maine Law Review* 31 (5) (1979): 17–90.

2. For an in-depth study of how local laws were extended to cover Indians in the territory of Washington, see Brad Asher, *Beyond the Reservation: Indians, Settlers, and the Law in Washington Territory, 1853–1889* (Norman: University of Oklahoma Press, 1999).

3. Sidney L. Harring, *Crow Dog's Case: American Indian Sovereignty, Tribal Law, and United States Law in the Nineteenth Century* (New York: Cambridge University Press, 1994), 34, 49–50. The quotation is on p. 34. Richard W. Crawford's quantitative analysis of cases involving Indians in San Diego County in the late nineteenth century illustrates the consequences of the disadvantages encountered by Indians in state courts. Crawford, "The White Man's Justice. Native Americans and the Judicial System of San Diego County, 1870–1890," *Western Legal History* 5 (1992): 69–81.

4. Annual Report of Commissioner of Indian Affairs Charles E. Mix for 1858, in Wilcomb E. Washburn, *The American Indian and the United States: A Documentary History*, 4 vols. (New York: Random House, 1973), 1:69–73.

5. Population figures shown in the table are drawn from the *Report on Indians Taxed and Indians Not Taxed in the United States (except Alaska) at the Eleventh Census: 1890* (Washington DC: Government Printing Office, 1894), 17–18. Indians who may have been categorized as "free colored persons" are not included in these census figures. The census had routinely included Indians as "free colored persons" between 1790 and 1850, when there was no separate category for Indians.

6. That states other than New York also regulated Indian land sales by prohibiting them, permitting them broadly, permitting them conditionally, or permitting them to take place through state agents is evidenced in the first three tables in the appendix. The next two tables give examples of other state statutes regulating Indians' right to make enforceable contracts. Some states' laws, like federal laws, provided that Indians were not bound by contracts and not liable to be sued in court, and that whites could not obtain judgments against Indians to collect debts. In apparent contradiction to federal law, however, other states provided that Indians' contracts were valid and that Indians could sue and be sued in state courts. Additionally, some states ruled that Indian contracts were valid if approved by a state commissioner. Finally, almost every state and territory also enacted anti-liquor and anti-trespass legislation. A wide range of such laws is shown in the last two tables.

7. *State of Oregon v. Gilbert*, 55 Ore. 596 (1883). The "technicality" was that the judgment roll listed two separate indictments of the defendant for the two murders, but there was only one verdict, and nothing in the record indicated of which murder Gilbert had been convicted.

8. *Gibbons v. Ogden*, 22 U.S. 1 (1824); *Willson v. Black Bird Creek Marsh Co.*, 27 U.S. 245 (1829). For a masterful discussion of the implied limitation on state power

embodied in the Indian commerce clause, see Robert N. Clinton, "Sovereignty and the Native American Nation: The Dormant Indian Commerce Clause," *Connecticut Law Review* 27 (1995): 1055–1249.

9. Indian Agent Edmund Graves to Commissioner of Indian Affairs George W. Manypenny, 29 December 1853, in *Letters Received by the Office of Indian Affairs, 1824–1881: New Mexico Superintendency*, original manuscripts in National Archives, Washington DC, microfilm rolls 546–56, microcopy 234.

10. *Johnson v. McIntosh*, 21 U.S. 543 (1823); *Cherokee Nation v. State of Georgia*, 30 U.S. 1 (1831); *Worcester v. State of Georgia*, 31 U.S. 515 (1832); and *United States v. Kagama*, 118 U.S. 375 (1886).

11. Tim Alan Garrison, *The Legal Ideology of Removal: The Southern Judiciary and the Sovereignty of Native American Nations* (Athens: University of Georgia Press, 2002), 6. Garrison provides the fullest discussion of early nineteenth-century southern state appellate court decisions on Indian matters. Harring, *Crow Dog's Case*, ch. 2, also provides an overview of cases examining legislation extending state criminal jurisdiction over Indians.

12. It should be noted that although federal courts in the nineteenth century were more likely to address the conflict between federal and tribal authority, they nevertheless usually refused to take arguments about tribal sovereignty seriously, rarely allowed it to override Congress's presumed broad power over matters relating to Indians, and did not develop clear and consistent principles to govern the federal government's relationship with Indians. For scholarship describing the role of federal courts in the nineteenth century, see especially Nell Jessup Newton, "Federal Power over Indians: Its Source, Scope and Limitations," *University of Pennsylvania Law Review* 132 (1984): 195–288; David E. Wilkins, *American Indian Sovereignty and the U.S. Supreme Court: The Masking of Justice* (Austin: University of Texas Press, 1997); Harring, *Crow Dog's Case*; Vine Deloria Jr. and David E. Wilkins, *Tribes, Treaties, and Constitutional Tribulations* (Austin: University of Texas Press, 1999); and Petra T. Shattuck and Jill Norgren, *Partial Justice: Federal Indian Law in a Liberal Constitutional System* (Providence RI: Berg, 1991).

13. *Gibbons v. Ogden*, at 81–83.

14. *Mayor of New York v. Miln*, 36 U.S. 102 (1837).

15. *Murray v. Wooden*, 17 Wend. 531 (N.Y., 1837). It is understandable why the court focused on the commerce clause rather than on the trade and intercourse acts in this case. The 1802 act, which was in effect at the time of the deed in question, prohibited purchases from "any Indian" as well as from any Indian tribe. Other New York cases allowing certain Indians to convey land under state law were *Jackson ex dem. Tewahangarahkan v. Sharp*, 14 Johns. 472 (N.Y., 1817), and the related case *Jackson ex dem. Gillet v. Brown*, 15 Johns. 263 (N.Y., 1818). New York cases

that upheld state regulations prohibiting Indians from selling land include *Lee v. Glover*, 8 Cow. 189 (N.Y., 1828), and *Jackson ex dem. Gilbert v. Wood*, 7 Johns. 290 (1810).

16. In *Chandler v. Edson*, 9 Johns. 362 (N.Y., 1812), for example, an Indian's agreement to allow whites to cut timber was ruled invalid because of an 1801 state law; the white man cutting timber in accordance with the agreement was deemed a trespasser with no right to the wood.

17. See *Dana v. Dana*, 14 Johns. 181 (N.Y., 1817); *Jackson ex dem Van Dyke v. Reynolds*, 14 Johns. 335 (N.Y., 1817); *St. Regis Indians v. Drum*, 19 Johns. 127 (N.Y., 1821); and *Hastings v. Farmer and Ellis*, 4 N.Y. 293 (1850). However, another New York case allowed a Seneca Indian to maintain an action for trespass upon Tonawanda reservation land that he possessed individually. *Blacksmith v. Fellows and Kendle*, 7 N.Y. 401 (1852).

18. *People of New York ex rel. Cutler v. Dibble*, 18 Barb. 412 (N.Y., 1854); 16 N.Y. 203 (1857); 62 U.S. 366 (1859).

19. *Dibble* quotations are at 18 Barb., 414–15, 418; and at 16 N.Y., 212 and 216. U.S. Supreme Court Justice Robert Cooper Grier agreed with this analysis, calling the state statute a prudent and just police regulation to protect the weak Indians and keep peace in the state.

20. *Goodell v. Jackson ex dem. Smith*, 20 Johns. 693 (N.Y., 1823), quotations at 715, 722–23, 719.

21. In *Lee v. Glover* the court ruled that an Indian's disability to make contracts "is analogous to the disability of infants to contract, in not depending on the actual capacity to protect his own rights"; in *Jackson v. Wood* one of the attorneys analogized Indians to children, married women, and people who were categorized as *non compos mentis*, arguing that they were all under a legal disability and therefore unable to sell land even if they were freeholders; in *St. Regis Indians v. Drum* Justice Jonas Platt analogized Indians' contracts to those of children, married women, and persons *inops concilii* but argued that, unlike the latter, the contracts of Indians were not just voidable but were absolutely and automatically void and unenforceable on behalf of either party; and in *Wynehamer v. People*, 13 N.Y. 378 (1856), the court commented in dictum that laws prohibiting the sale of liquor to Indians were constitutional because Indians "are considered as persons *inops consilii* under the tutelage of government, and in the same category with minors, habitual drunkards, &c."

22. Ironically, as noted above, an Indian who demonstrated that he was fully competent risked being subjected to general municipal regulations on the ground that because he was so civilized he should be subject to the same laws as whites.

23. *Sunol v. Hepburn*, 1 Cal. 254 (1850), quotations at 279–80; *Doe ex dem. Lafontaine v. Avaline*, 8 Ind. 6 (1856). In the South, Mississippi, like California, com-

pared Indians' rights with those of women. The court pointed out that just because a married woman cannot convey land without the participation of her husband does not mean that that land is not liable for a debt that the woman might legally contract. *Saffarans v. Terry*, 20 Miss. 690 (1849). New York's argument that the state was entitled to protect its own citizens was echoed in the preamble to Florida's statute for the removal of the remaining Seminole Indians. The Seminoles had repeatedly left their reservation and had murdered whites and destroyed their property, "creating terror and insecurity," the legislature explained in the statute. Therefore, the law authorized the governor to raise troops and send them to remove the Indians. Florida Session Laws, 20 January 1851, ch. 418 (p. 149).

24. *Hicks v. Ewhartonah*, 21 Ark. 106 (1860); *Taylor v. Drew*, 21 Ark. 485 (1860); *Rubideaux v. Vallie*, 12 Kan. 28 (1873); and *Reed v. Brasher*, 9 Port. 438 (Ala., 1839).

25. For a survey of cases reviewing state criminal jurisdiction over Indians, see Harring, *Crow Dog's Case*, ch. 2.

26. *State of Tennessee v. Forman*, 16 Tenn. 256 (1835); *Caldwell v. State of Alabama*, 1 Stew. & P. 327 (1832), quotations at 71; *State of Wisconsin v. Doxtater*, 47 Wis. 278 (1879); and *Hicks v. Ewhartonah*, quotation at 107. [In the first case, the defendant's last name was more commonly spelled "Foreman," though it was recorded as "Forman" in the court decision. Garrison, *Legal Ideology of Removal*, 283.] See also *Taylor v. Drew*. A federal court in Tennessee agreed in 1834 that because federal government power under the commerce clause was limited to matters having "a direct relation to the object" of regulating trade, the provision of federal law that gave the United States jurisdiction over all crimes in Indian country was unconstitutional. *United States v. Bailey*, 24 F. Cas. 937 (C.C., D. Tenn., 1834). The state court argument that the Indian commerce clause did not authorize federal criminal jurisdiction over Indians or Indian territory was also later echoed in the U.S. Supreme Court decision in *United States v. Kagama*.

27. In *Forman*, the quotation is at 319; *State of Georgia v. Tassels*, 1 Dud. 229 (1830). Contrast the pre-removal case, *Holland v. Pack*, 7 Tenn. 151 (1823), where the Tennessee Supreme Court seemed comfortable with the concept of a Cherokee nation within state boundaries; in that case, the court held that an Indian in Cherokee country was governed by Cherokee laws and was not covered by state law except when she left the reservation and entered state lands.

28. The federalism issue in *Tassels* also extended to the conflict between the U.S. Supreme Court and Georgia state officials. While some people argued that the U.S. Supreme Court had no right to interfere with a state's criminal laws and proceedings and no right to summon a state to appear before the justices, others argued that the Constitution required state officials to submit to the rulings of the U.S. Supreme Court. Examples of arguments on each side are in "Georgia

vs. the United States," *Norwich (CT) Courier*, 12 January 1831 (pro-federal government); and "Georgia and the United States Court," *Ithaca (NY) Journal and General Advertiser*, 19 January 1831 (pro–states' rights).

29. *United States v. Ward*, 1 Kan. 601 (1863), 28 F. Cas. 397 (D.C., D. Kan., 1863). In *Forman*, the quotation is at 330; in *Caldwell*, the quotations are at 49, 138, 161. Similarly, in *United States v. Cisna*, 25 F. Cas. 422 (C.C., D. Ohio, 1835), the court mentioned actions by Georgia and New York in punishing their own citizens (and, in New York, Indians as well) for offenses on Indian reservations and acknowledged Ohio's power to do the same.

30. Andrew C. Lenner, *The Federal Principle in American Politics, 1790–1830* (Landham MD: Rowman & Littlefield, 2001), 130.

31. *In re George Peters*, 2 Johns. 344 (N.Y., 1801); *Danzell v. Webquish*, 108 Mass. 133 (1871). In 1866, the U.S. Supreme Court expressed agreement with the principle and listed criteria for assessing whether or not a tribe was federally recognized. *The Kansas Indians*, 72 U.S. 737 (1867).

32. *Clark v. Libbey*, 14 Kan. 435 (1875). See also the rulings of southeastern courts in the decades after the removal of Indians; they held that once the two-year removal period was completed, any Indian who remained in the state was a citizen subject to the state's civil and criminal jurisdiction. *State of North Carolina v. Ta-Cha-Na-Tah*, 64 N.C. 614 (1870); and *Morrow v. Blevins*, 23 Tenn. 223 (1843). A similar principle was applied in the territories. For example, the federal trade and intercourse acts were deemed to be inapplicable to New Mexico's Pueblo Indians or their lands, and the territorial legislature therefore was free to regulate them, once the territorial judiciary ruled that the Pueblo Indians were citizens. The basic concept was upheld by the U.S. Supreme Court, though without directly deciding the citizenship issue. *United States v. Lucero*, 1 N.M. 422 (1869); *United States v. Santistevan*, 1 N.M. 583 (1874); *United States v. Joseph*, 1 N.M. 593 (1874), 94 U.S. 614 (1877).

33. *Caldwell v. Alabama*. Three years later, in *Cisna*, a federal court in Ohio similarly ruled that it was impractical to try to enforce the trade and intercourse laws on the Wyandot reservation because the reservation was only twelve square miles, it was situated amid a dense white population, public roads ran through it, and whites regularly did business there. Since federal laws had effectively become "inoperative" with regard to the Wyandots, the state of Ohio, rather than the United States, held jurisdiction over crimes committed on Wyandot lands.

34. *Hicks v. Ewhartonah; Blue-Jacket v. Commissioners of Johnson County*, 3 Kan. 299 (1865), quotations at 355 and 358. The U.S. Supreme Court later rejected Kansas's arguments in *Blue-Jacket*, holding that the higher principle was the fact that the Shawnees were still a federally recognized and federally protected tribe. *The Kansas Indians*. See also the companion case, *The New York Indians*, 72 U.S. 761 (1867). In

Quinney v. Stockbridge, 33 Wis. 505 (1873), and in *Commissioners of Franklin Co. v. Pennock*, 18 Kan. 579 (1877), however, state courts upheld taxation of lands held by Indians in fee simple or "by purchase." Soon after the *Blue-Jacket* case, almost all Shawnees and other Indians were removed from Kansas to the Indian Territory. H. Craig Miner and William E. Unrau, *The End of Indian Kansas: A Study in Cultural Revolution, 1854–1871* (Lawrence: University Press of Kansas, 1990).

35. Another ambiguity arose in eastern cases after 1834: it was not clear whether or not the 1834 act repealed the "surrounded by settlements" exception as to states east of the Mississippi.

36. The Arkansas court's vagueness on the constitutional basis for this challenge to the federal government's protective, guardianship power over certain Indians is understandable, since federal courts, too, were unclear on exactly what the source of the U.S. guardianship role was. Courts readily accepted—but never really explained the basis of—the principle that Indians were wards or domestic subjects of the United States. Federal justices sometimes implied that the source of federal authority in this regard somehow came from the property clause, suggesting that the doctrine of discovery gave the United States ownership of Indian lands, and this in turn justified governance of the dependent Indians on those lands. Often, however, the guardianship power appeared to be entirely extra-constitutional, based simply on the perceived weakness and dependence of Indians. See the discussion of the guardianship power in Newton, "Federal Power over Indians"; and Vine Deloria Jr. and Clifford M. Lytle, *American Indians, American Justice* (Austin: University of Texas Press, 1983), ch. 2; and the description of wardship in Felix S. Cohen, *Handbook of Federal Indian Law* (Washington DC: U.S. Government Printing Office, 1942; reprint, Buffalo: William S. Hein, 1988), 169–73.

37. See also the decisions of New Mexico's territorial courts, holding that the trade and intercourse acts were only meant to apply to "wild, wandering savages." "Civilized" tribes like the Pueblo Indians were meant to be locally regulated, by territorial and state governments, and were exempt from the operation of the trade and intercourse laws. *United States v. Lucero;* and *United States v. Ortiz*, First Judicial District Court, Territory of New Mexico, 1867. (The *Ortiz* opinion is not contained in any printed reporter but is provided in full at the end of the *Lucero* decision.)

38. The Nevada, Alaska, and Oregon cases are *United States v. Leathers*, 26 F. Cas. 897 (D.C., D. Nev., 1879); *United States v. Seveloff*, 27 F. Cas. 1021 (D.C., D. Ore., 1872); and *United States v. Tom*, 1 Ore. 26 (1853). For a study of the unusual situation in Alaska, which describes how the territorial government (rather than federal Indian agents) established American Indian policy there in the nineteenth century, see Harring, *Crow Dog's Case*, ch. 7. The New Mexico decision, which apparently was never appealed to the territorial Supreme Court, is not included in any

printed reporter. It is referred to in reports and correspondence of the mid-1850s. See Governor David Meriwether's Annual Report to Commissioner of Indian Affairs George W. Manypenny, 4 September 1854; Meriwether to Manypenny, 30 October 1853, 1 October 1853, 31 August 1855, and September 1855; and Indian Agent Edmund A. Graves to Manypenny, 29 December 1853, all in *Letters Received by the Office of Indian Affairs, 1824–1881: New Mexico Superintendency*, original manuscripts in National Archives, Washington DC, microcopy 234, microfilm rolls 546–56. For an example of territorial courts explicitly considering the federal government's property interest in Indian lands, see the New Mexico cases *Lucero*, *Joseph*, and *Santistevan*, where the fact that the United States did not hold ultimate title to Pueblo Indian land was a crucial factor in the judicial ruling that the trade and intercourse acts did not apply to those Indians. The Pueblo Indians held full title to their own land by grants from Spain, as subsequently recognized by the Republic of Mexico and confirmed by the United States. The New Mexico courts focused on statutory interpretation rather than on constitutional principles, however. In these cases involving whites accused of intruding on Indian lands, the fact that the pertinent portion of the trade and intercourse act explicitly applied only to "lands belonging, secured, or granted by treaty with the United States to any Indian tribe" allowed the court to focus on the fact that the Pueblo Indian lands were not granted "by treaty," but rather by patent. See chapter 7 for further discussion of the status of Pueblo Indian lands.

39. *People of California v. Antonio*, 27 Cal. 404 (1865); *Hunt v. Kansas*, 4 Kan. 60 (1866); *Rubideaux v. Vallie*; *Taylor v. Drew*. Other courts have also analogized Indians to aliens, despite the ruling in *Cherokee Nation* that Indian tribes were not foreign nations. See, e.g., *Farrington v. Wilson*, 29 Wis. 383 (1872); *Gho v. Julles*, 1 Wash. Terr. 325 (1871); and *Goodell v. Jackson*.

40. *Caldwell* quotations at 57–58 and 79. Two years later, a federal court in Tennessee agreed with this principle. The court held that the state, rather than the United States, had jurisdiction over a case involving a white-on-white murder in Cherokee Territory. Although the federal government could exercise general criminal jurisdiction over offenses on Indian land in a territory, such general jurisdiction could not be assumed if the Indian land was located within a state. *United States v. Bailey*.

41. *Wisconsin v. Doxtater*.

42. *United States v. Ward*; *United States v. Sa-Coo-Da-Cot*, 27 F. Cas. 923 (C.C., D. Neb., 1870); and *Painter v. Ives*, 4 Neb. 122 (1875). For background information on the *Sa-Coo-Da-Cot* case, see David Wishart, *An Unspeakable Sadness: The Dispossession of the Nebraska Indians* (Lincoln: University of Nebraska Press, 1994), 182–85. Within a few years after the case was decided, the Pawnees were pushed

out of Nebraska; by 1875 they had moved to Indian Territory, and their reservation land was subsequently sold off to whites (187–202). On Indian dispossession from Kansas between 1854 and 1871, including the removal of the Shawnees (the *Ward* defendant's tribe), see Miner and Unrau, *End of Indian Kansas*. For similar legal arguments in other states, see also the "equal footing" language applied to Minnesota in *United States v. Forty-Three Gallons of Whisky*, 25 F. Cas. 1155 (D.C., D. Minn., 1874), and to Nevada in *Ex parte Sloan*, 22 F. Cas. 324 (D.C., D. Neb., 1877). Later, the U.S. Supreme Court used similar language in rejecting federal jurisdiction over whites accused of committing a crime on an Indian reservation in the new state of Colorado. *United States v. McBratney*, 104 U.S. 621 (1882).

43. See, e.g., María E. Montoya's description of incorporation and land dispossession in territorial New Mexico in *Translating Property: The Maxwell Land Grant and the Conflict over Land in the American West, 1840–1900* (Berkeley: University of California Press, 2002), 117–18.

44. For a general history of federal Indian policy, see especially Francis Paul Prucha, *The Great Father: The United States Government and the American Indians* (Lincoln: University of Nebraska Press, 1984).

45. For a comprehensive analysis of the purposes for which New Yorkers coveted Iroquois lands, as well as the process by which Indian lands were taken in New York State, see Laurence M. Hauptman, *Conspiracy of Interests: Iroquois Dispossession and the Rise of New York State* (Syracuse: Syracuse University Press, 1999).

3. SLAVERY AND RACIAL CLASSIFICATION

1. There is an extensive scholarly literature—and vigorous debate and disagreement—about the evolution of slavery and racism in early American history. For an excellent review and analysis of scholarship on this subject, see Alden T. Vaughan, "The Origins Debate: Slavery and Racism in Seventeenth-Century Virginia," in *Roots of American Racism: Essays on the Colonial Experience* (New York: Oxford University Press, 1995), 136–74.

2. Alden T. Vaughan, "From White Man to Redskin: Changing Anglo-American Perceptions of the American Indian," *American Historical Review* 86 (1982): 917–53; Kathleen Brown, "Native Americans and Early Modern Concepts of Race," in *Empire and Others: British Encounters with Indigenous Peoples, 1600–1850*, ed. Martin Daunton and Rick Halpern (Philadelphia: University of Pennsylvania Press, 1999), 79–100; and Karen Ordahl Kupperman, "Presentment of Civility: English Reading of American Self-Presentation in the Early Years of Colonization," *William and Mary Quarterly*, 3rd. ser., 54 (1997): 193–228.

3. Theda Perdue, *"Mixed Blood" Indians: Racial Construction in the Early South*

Notes to page 85

(Athens: University of Georgia Press, 2003); Reginald Horsman, *Race and Manifest Destiny: The Origins of American Racial Anglo-Saxonism* (Cambridge MA: Harvard University Press, 1981); and Robert F. Berkhofer Jr., *The White Man's Indian: Images of the American Indian from Columbus to the Present* (New York: Random House, 1978). On the French colonists' parallel shift from an optimistic view that focused on mutable cultural differences to a pessimistic attitude based on race, see Saliha Belmessous, "Assimilation and Racialism in Seventeenth and Eighteenth-Century French Colonial Policy," *American Historical Review* 110 (2005): 322–49.

4. The best-known Virginia case is *Hudgins v. Wrights*, 11 Va. 134 (1806). See also *Robin v. Hardaway*, Jeff. 109 (Va., 1772); *Pallas v. Hill*, 12 Va. 149 (1807), *Pegram v. Isabell*, 12 Va. 193 (1808); *Butt v. Rachel*, 18 Va. 209 (1814); and *Gregory v. Baugh*, 29 Va. 665 (1831). Courts in Kentucky, a state drawn from land once considered part of Virginia, cited and relied on the Virginia legal history, as did courts handling cases involving Indians whose ancestors had first been enslaved in Virginia. See *Gentry v. McMinnis*, 33 Ky. 382 (1835); *Gatliff's Administrator v. Rose*, 47 Ky. 629 (1848); and *Vaughn v. Phebe*, 8 Tenn. 5 (1827). On Indians and slavery in Virginia, see Peter Wallenstein, "Indian Foremothers: Race, Sex, Slavery, and Freedom in Early Virginia," in *The Devil's Lane: Sex and Race in the Early South*, ed. Catherine Clinton and Michele Gillespie (New York: Oxford University Press, 1997), 57-73; and Robert M. Cover, *Justice Accused: Antislavery and the Judicial Process* (New Haven: Yale University Press, 1975), 50-55. On Indians and slavery in South Carolina, see Peter H. Wood, *Black Majority: Negroes in Colonial South Carolina from 1670 to the Stono Rebellion* (New York: Knopf, 1974). Slaves who were descended from Europeans also brought actions in other southern courts. In her study of the process of racial determination in southern state courts, Ariela J. Gross found trial records in fourteen suits for freedom based on claims of European descent; in twelve of those cases the claim of whiteness was successful, resulting in freedom for the slave. Gross also found other contexts in which race was determined in the courtroom, such as suits for slander, paternity cases, and inheritances disputes in which the capacity to bequeath or inherit depended on whiteness. Gross, "Litigating Whiteness: Trials of Racial Determination in the Nineteenth-Century South," *Yale Law Journal* 108 (1998): 109–85. See also Gross's book, *Double Character: Slavery and Mastery in the Antebellum Southern Courtroom* (Princeton: Princeton University Press, 2000).

5. On Indian slavery in colonial Louisiana, see Stephen Webre, "The Problem of Indian Slavery in Spanish Louisiana, 1769-1803," *Louisiana History* 25 (1984): 117–35; Hans W. Baade, "The Law of Slavery in Spanish Luisiana, 1769-1803," in *Louisiana's Legal Heritage*, ed. Edward F. Haas Jr. (Pensacola FL: Louisiana State Museum, by Perdido Bay Press, 1983), 43–85; and Carl A. Brasseaux, "The Administration of Slave Regulations in French Louisiana, 1724-1766," *Louisiana History* 21 (1980): 139–58. In

255

a broader context, see also the references to Indian slaves in colonial Louisiana in Daniel H. Usner Jr., *American Indians in the Lower Mississippi Valley: Social and Economic Histories* (Lincoln: University of Nebraska Press, 1998).

6. *Séville v. Chrétien*, 5 Mart. (o.s.) 275 (La., 1817). See also the related court decision, *Agnès v. Judice*, 3 Mart. (o.s.) 171 (La., 1813). The full manuscript case file of the proceedings in all of the cases—*Agnès v. Judice, Séville v. Chrétien, Catherine v. Chrétien, Narcisse v. Chrétien, Pierre v. Chrétien, Thémier v. Chrétien,* and *Jeanne v. Chrétien*—in the court of the parish of St. Landry is in the Supreme Court of Louisiana Collection of the Earl K. Long Library, Special Collections, University of New Orleans, docket number 34.

7. Since children's status followed that of their mother, the plaintiffs did not make the argument that they were free because of their white male ancestor. See references to Agnès's father (Séville's grandfather) in the deposition of Madame Donatto Billo.

8. *Hart v. Burnett*, 15 Cal. 530, 559 (1860); *Ferris v. Coover*, 10 Cal. 589, 619 (1858); *United States v. Lucero*, 1 N.M. 422 (1869); *Charlotte v. Chouteau*, 25 Mo. 465, 478 (1857). Note that even antislavery northeastern state judges agreed that slavery and the slave trade did not violate the law of nations. See, e.g., *Commonwealth of Massachusetts v. Aves*, 35 Mass. 193, 211–15 (1836).

9. *Ulzère v. Poeyfarré*, 8 Mart. (o.s.) 155 (La., 1820) and 2 Mart. (n.s.) 504 (La., 1824).

10. *Marguerite v. Chouteau*, 2 Mo. 71 (1828) and 3 Mo. 540 (1834).

11. The quotation in the text is from *Marguerite v. Chouteau*, 3 Mo. 540 (1834). On suits for freedom in Missouri, see William E. Foley, "Slave Freedom Suits before Dred Scott: The Case of Marie Jean Scypion's Descendants," *Missouri Historical Review* 79 (1984): 1-23; and Helen Tunnicliff Catterall, "Some Antecedents of the Dred Scott Case," *American Historical Review* 30 (1924): 56–71.

12. *Scott v. Sandford*, 60 U.S. 393 (1857). The case is discussed further in chapter 6.

13. *Ulzère v. Poeyfarré*. The full manuscript case file of the trial in the court of the parish and city of New Orleans is at the Earl K. Long Library, Special Collections and Archives, University of New Orleans, docket numbers 468 and 989.

14. Specifically, the Louisiana Supreme Court said it was inappropriate for the parish court to have the jury make findings about the specific provisions of Spanish or French law pertaining to Indians as slaves, since the content of those legal provisions was, the Supreme Court said, a question of law to be decided by judges, not a question of fact to be submitted to a jury. The Supreme Court also found that the parish court should not have admitted oral evidence of decrees from colonial Louisiana pertaining to Indian slavery because parole evidence of the content of documents is admissible only when it has been shown that the written documents are unavailable.

15. As important as appearance was to determining someone's racial classification in antebellum suits for freedom, resort to such nonscientific evidence of race became even more established in the postbellum period, when judges were often explicit about the fact that racial classification in legal disputes would be determined by popular perception. See Ian F. Haney López's discussion of the prerequisite cases in *White by Law: The Legal Construction of Race* (New York: New York University Press, 1996), ch. 3.

16. *Boullemet v. Philips*, 2 Rob. 365 (La., 1842); *Spalding v. Taylor*, 1 La. Ann. 195 (1846). For an anthropological study of racial classification in Louisiana, see Virginia R. Domínguez, *White by Definition: Social Classification in Creole Louisiana* (New Brunswick NJ: Rutgers University Press, 1986).

17. The specific ways in which laws discriminated against Indians are discussed in chapter 4.

18. The most thorough study of this subject is Jack D. Forbes, *Africans and Native Americans: The Language of Race and the Evolution of Red-Black Peoples*, 2nd ed. (Urbana: University of Illinois Press, 1993). On the designation of Indians as "black" or "people of color" in revolutionary-era New England, see also Ruth Wallis Herndon and Ella Wilcox Sekatau, "The Right to a Name: The Narragansett People and Rhode Island Officials in the Revolutionary Era," *Ethnohistory* 44 (1997): 433–62.

19. The first law referred to is in Vaughan and Rosen, *Indian Documents*, 15: Virginia Document 124 (1705); the second law referred to is in Vaughan and Rosen, *Indian Documents*, 16: South Carolina Document 48 (1719). The colonial South Carolina law, which levied a lower tax on Indian slaves than on Negro slaves (because the former were "reputed of much less value" than the latter), provided that "for preventing all doubts and scruples that may arise what ought to be rated on mustees, mulattoes, &c. all such slaves as are not entirely Indian shall be accounted as negroe, and as such rated by the said assessors." The colonial Virginia law that included "the child of an Indian" in the term "mulatto" also included in that category "the child, grand child, or great grand child, of a negro." Thus, it seems that someone who had one Indian grandparent and three white grandparents was considered white, but a person who had one Negro grandparent, or even one Negro great-grandparent, was legally classified as a mulatto.

Although Virginia legislation of 1785 made no reference to Indians in its definition of the word "mulatto," later statutes made it clear that many Indians were in fact included in the category of "mulatto" or "colored person." For example, a Virginia law of 1866 explained that someone who had "one-fourth or more of Indian blood" was considered to be an "Indian" only if he or she "was not a colored person"; the statute decreed that every person who had "one-fourth or more of negro blood" would be considered a "colored person." Thus, an Indian who had one black grandparent would be classified as "colored" rather than "Indian," even if he or she had three Indian grandparents. Virginia Session Laws, October 1785, ch. 78 (p. 61); and 27 February 1866, ch. 17 (p. 84).

20. Forbes, *Africans and Native Americans*, 199–207. Prior to 1860, the U.S. census included no "Indian" category; Forbes has found that Indians were routinely listed among the "free colored persons."

21. There were a few post-Revolution laws that did mention Indian slaves. A 1798 New Jersey slave law provided that "every negro, indian, mulatto or mestee, within this State, who, at the time of passing this act, is a slave for his or her life, shall continue such during his or her life, unless he or she shall be manumitted and set free." New Jersey Session Laws, 14 March 1798, ch. 727 (p. 364). In addition, an 1847 Maryland law defining who could serve as witnesses in court applied both to free Indians and Indian slaves. Maryland Session Laws, 26 January 1847, ch. 27 (no page number).

22. Ira Berlin, *Many Thousands Gone: The First Two Centuries of Slavery in North America* (Cambridge MA: Harvard University Press, 1998), 145. For discussion of people of mixed African and Indian descent and analysis of blacks' and Indians' shared histories, see James F. Brooks, ed., *Confounding the Color Line: The Indian-Black Experience in North America* (Lincoln: University of Nebraska Press, 2002); and Forbes, *Africans and Native Americans*.

23. In 1797 the New Jersey Supreme Court swiftly disposed of an Indian slave's suit for freedom initiated in the form of a habeas corpus action. Because state laws clearly recognized that Indians, like Africans, could be slaves in New Jersey, the court did not see any need to examine the slave's racial background nor the manner in which her ancestors had originally lost their freedom. As Chief Justice James Kinsey noted in his opinion, freeing the slave on the ground that she was an Indian would violate long-established property rights. *State of New Jersey v. Van Waggoner*, 1 N.J.L. 374 (1797).

24. *State of North Carolina v. Jacobs*, 51 N.C. 284 (1859). For discussions of American "racial science" in the nineteenth century, see Bruce Dain, *A Hideous Monster of the Mind: American Race Theory in the Early Republic* (Cambridge MA: Harvard University Press, 2002); and Robert E. Bieder, *Science Encounters the Indian, 1820–1880: The Early Years of American Ethnology* (Norman: University of Oklahoma Press, 1986).

25. For a more detailed analysis of the importance of reputation and behavior, including a more in-depth discussion of *Bryan v. Walton*, see Gross, "Litigating Whiteness." Gross, the leading expert on racial identity trials in American history, argues that "law made the 'performance' of whiteness increasingly important to the determination of racial status" (112).

26. *Bryan v. Walton*, 20 Ga. 480 (1856). Other aspects of the case were explained at 14 Ga. 185 (1853), 30 Ga. 834 (1860), and 33 Ga. Supp. 11 (1864).

27. Virginia Session Laws, 27 February 1866, ch. 17 (p. 84); California Session Laws, 22 April 1850, ch. 142 (p. 428). It should be noted that in 1854 California found it convenient to classify Chinese people as "Indians" in order to include them in the prohibition against testifying in cases involving white parties. *People of California v. Hall*, 4 Cal. 399 (1854). Nevada's witness statute also provided that a person with "one-half or more of Indian blood" would be deemed an Indian. The fraction of Indian ancestry varied, however, depending on the state and the legal context. Indiana applied its protective law for Indians to tribal members "down to those having one-eighth Indian blood." Nevada Session Laws, 14 March 1865, ch. 136 (p. 403). Indiana Session Laws, 3 February 1841, ch. 51 (p. 134). Later in the nineteenth century, states started to adopt the "one-drop" rule for racial classification.

28. *People of Michigan ex rel. Dean v. Board of Registration of Nankin*, 15 Mich. 156 (1866); *People of Michigan ex rel. Wood v. Board of Registration of Fourth Ward, City of Detroit*, 17 Mich. 427 (1868). For more analysis of the racial classification issue in the *Dean* case, see the earlier decision, *People of Michigan v. Dean*, 14 Mich. 406 (1866). That opinion focused on the Board of Registration's allegation that Dean was a Negro; the court decided that a person who had "less than one-fourth of African blood" was "white" under the constitutional provision that only "white male citizens" could vote.

29. *Doe ex dem. Lafontaine v. Avaline*, 8 Ind. 6 (1856).

30. *Jeffries v. Ankeny*, 11 Ohio 372 (1842); *Gray v. State of Ohio*, 4 Ohio 353 (1831); *Lane v. Baker*, 12 Ohio 237 (1843).

31. *Harris v. Doe ex dem. Barnett and another*, 4 Blackf. 369 (Ind., 1837).

32. *Morgan v. Fowler*, 10 Tenn. 450 (1830); *Tuten's Lessee v. Martin*, 11 Tenn. 452 (1832).

33. For a broad discussion of similarities and differences in the historical experiences of Native Americans and African Americans in the United States, see David E. Wilkins, "African Americans and Aboriginal Peoples: Similarities and Differences in Historical Experiences," *Cornell Law Review* 90 (2005): 515–30.

34. *Morgan v. McGhee*, 24 Tenn 13 (1844). But see later cases to the contrary, such as *State of North Carolina v. Ta-Cha-Na-Tah*, 64 N.C. 614 (1870). (Since cohabitation between a Cherokee man and woman according to tribal customs, which allowed both parties to be free to dissolve the relationship at any time, did not create a legal marriage, the woman may be compelled to testify against the man in a murder trial.)

35. *Wall v. Williamson*, 8 Ala. 48 (1845) and 11 Ala. 826 (1847).

36. New York Session Laws, 11 April 1849, ch. 420 (p. 576).

37. *Johnson v. Johnson's Administrator,* 30 Mo. 72 (1860).

38. *Boyer and Charley v. Dively, Donnelly, and Black,* 58 Mo. 510 (1875). The marriage in question predated Missouri's law against interracial marriage, which was enacted in 1835. Such laws were usually directed particularly at black-white marriages but were sometimes also applied to Indian-white marriages as well. Statutory prohibitions on intermarriage are discussed in chapter 4.

39. *Fisher v. Allen,* 3 Miss. 611 (1837).

40. *Holland v. Pack,* 7 Tenn. 151 (1823). This decision was issued well before Tennessee's extension statute, the removal of Indians from the state, and the *Forman* case. Had the decision been issued in the 1830s, the Tennessee Supreme Court clearly would not have treated the Cherokees as an "independent nation."

41. *Jones v. Laney,* 2 Tex. 342 (1847).

42. *Duval v. Marshall,* 30 Ark. 230 (1875). Since the Creek Nation was not another state in the Union, if resolution of the case depended on whether George W. Marshall had the general power to assign property, the court could not presume the applicability of general principles of Anglo-American common law. Instead, Creek usages and customs would govern the question, because Ben Marshall had been a Creek Indian, officials of the Creek Nation had appointed George W. Marshall as administrator of the intestate's estate, and the assignment of property that was in dispute took place in the Creek Nation. The justice noted, however, that even if George W. Marshall had the authority to assign property, he could not have the power to assign property situated outside the Creek Nation. Justice Walker concluded that the assigned property in this case—a judgment obtained in an Arkansas court—was located not in the Creek Nation but in a "foreign country," and with regard to that property George W. Marshall was a "foreign" administrator. Thus, Marshall's assignment of the judgment (which he alleged was induced by fraud) was void. In addition to respecting Indian customs, states also signaled acknowledgement of some degree of Indian separateness and self-governance when they (reluctantly) refrained from taxing reservation lands.

43. *Herbert v. Moore,* Dallam 592 (Tex., 1844).

44. Ira Berlin, *Slaves without Masters: The Free Negro in the Antebellum South* (New York: Vintage Books, 1974), 71–78, 286–315; and Leon F. Litwack, *North of Slavery: The Negro in the Free States, 1790–1860* (Chicago: University of Chicago Press, 1961), 187–213.

4. INDIANS AND RACIAL DISCRIMINATION

1. *Ex parte Smith and Ex parte Keating,* 38 Cal. 702 (1869).

2. *Ex parte Smith and Ex parte Keating; Wynehamer v. People of New York,* 13 N.Y. 378 (1856); and *Murphy and Glover Test Oath Cases,* 41 Mo. 339 (1867).

3. On the role of racialized ideology to build an American national identity during the early national period, see especially the essays in Michael A. Morrison and James Brewer Stewart, eds., *Race and the Early Republic: Racial Consciousness and Nation-Building in the Early Republic* (New York: Rowman & Littlefield, 2002). Other examples of scholarship dealing with the broad subject of nineteenth-century national expansion, national identity, and racial constructions include Alexander Saxton, *The Rise and Fall of the White Republic: Class Politics and Mass Culture in Nineteenth-Century America* (New York: Verso, 1990); David R. Roediger, *The Wages of Whiteness: Race and the Making of the American Working Class*, rev. ed. (New York: Verso, 1999); and Ronald Takaki, *Iron Cages: Race and Culture in 19th-Century America* (New York: Oxford University Press, 1990).

4. Reginald Horsman, *Race and Manifest Destiny: The Origins of American Racial Anglo-Saxonism* (Cambridge MA: Harvard University Press, 1981), ch. 6; and Elise Marienstras, "The Common Man's Indian: The Image of the Indian as a Promoter of National Identity in the Early National Era," in *Native Americans and the Early Republic*, ed. Frederick E. Hoxie et al. (Charlottesville: University Press of Virginia, 1999), 261–96. See also Bernard W. Sheehan, *Seeds of Extinction: Jeffersonian Philanthropy and the American Indian* (Chapel Hill: University of North Carolina Press, 1973), ch. 9. Mixed in with an imagined vision of Indians as too savage for civilization was a sense that they were too independent to become citizens (in contrast to Africans, who were seen as too dependent to become citizens). See John Wood Sweet's discussion of Indian-white relations in the colonial and early national periods in *Bodies Politic: Negotiating Race in the American North, 1730–1830* (Baltimore: Johns Hopkins University Press, 2003), 301–303.

5. Theda Perdue, *"Mixed Blood" Indians: Racial Construction in the Early South* (Athens: University of Georgia Press, 2003), ch. 3; Horsman, *Race and Manifest Destiny*; Robert F. Berkhofer Jr., *The White Man's Indian: Images of the American Indian from Columbus to the Present* (New York: Random House, 1978); Robert E. Bieder, *Science Encounters the Indian, 1820–1880: The Early Years of American Ethnology* (Norman: University of Oklahoma Press, 1986), chs 1–3; Bruce Dain, *A Hideous Monster of the Mind: American Race Theory in the Early Republic* (Cambridge MA: Harvard University Press, 2002); and Audrey Smedley, *Race in North America: Origin and Evolution of a Worldview* (Boulder: Westview Press, 1993).

6. Daniel K. Richter, "'Believing That Many of the Red People Suffer Much for the Want of Food': Hunting, Agriculture, and a Quaker Construction of Indianness in the Early Republic," in Morrison and Stewart, *Race and the Early Republic*, 27–53; Perdue, *"Mixed Blood" Indians*, ch. 3 (quotation is on p. 97); and James P. Ronda, "'We Have a Country': Race, Geography, and the Invention of Indian Territory," in Morrison and Stewart, *Race and the Early Republic*, 159–75.

7. Mary Young, "Racism in Red and Black: Indians and Other Free People of Color in Georgia Law, Politics, and Removal Policy, *Georgia Historical Quarterly* 73 (1989): 492–518, at 515; and Young, "The Cherokee Nation: Mirror of the Republic," *American Quarterly* 33 (1981): 502–24, at 521–22.

8. "Memorial of a Council Held at Running Waters," 28 November 1834, H.R. Doc 91, 23rd Cong., 2d sess., quoted in Young, "Cherokee Nation," 522.

9. Circe Sturm, *Blood Politics: Race, Culture, and Identity in the Cherokee Nation of Oklahoma* (Berkeley: University of California Press, 2002), 43–57. As to present-day Cherokees, Sturm concludes that they tend to "conflate blood, color, race, and culture to demarcate their sociopolitical community" (169–70). Historian Theda Perdue notes that in the nineteenth century, culture and kinship, rather than race, remained the more important determinant of membership in the Cherokee community. Thus, although some Cherokees, like whites, objected to Ridge's and Boudinot's marriages to white women, Perdue argues, the Cherokees' discomfort with those pairings was not based on race. They were uneasy about Ridge's and Boudinot's wives not because the women were white, but because they did not seek to join a clan; since clan membership was determined by the maternal line, the children of such marriages would lack clan identity, leaving them without formal kinship ties to the Cherokees. Consistent with the fact that inclusion in the community was not determined primarily by race, Perdue also points out, generally the Cherokees, like other Indians, tended not to recognize any racial distinction between "full-blood" and "mixed-blood" (Cherokee-white) tribal members. Perdue, *"Mixed Blood" Indians*, 93–95; and Perdue, *Slavery and the Evolution of Cherokee Society, 1540–1866* (Knoxville: University of Tennessee Press, 1979), ch. 4. On Cherokees' view of race as reflected in their miscegenation laws, see Karen M. Woods, "Lawmaking: A 'Wicked and Mischievous Connection': The Origins of Indian-White Miscegenation Law," *Legal Studies Forum* 23 (1999): 37–70, at 61–70.

On Indians' role in situating themselves in relation to Europeans, see also Nancy Shoemaker's argument that the Cherokees and other Indians of the Southeast were the first to identify themselves as "red." Shoemaker, "How Indians Got to Be Red," *American Historical Review* 102 (1997): 625–44. On racial attitudes of New England's Indians, see Daniel R. Mandell, "Shifting Boundaries of Race and Ethnicity: Indian-Black Intermarriage in Southern New England, 1760–1880," *Journal of American History* 85 (1998): 466–501, 474–79. Mandell concludes that "with few exceptions, Indians did not seem concerned about drawing racial lines or creating a racial hierarchy that paralleled the surrounding society." When they did express hostility toward blacks and "foreigners," it came out of the tribes' history of outsider men marrying Indian women, triggering "community conflicts [that were] rooted in issues of gender and power rather than race or skin color" (477–78).

10. For a comparison of whites' treatment of Indians and blacks in Georgia, see Young, "Racism in Red and Black." On the colonial-era use of the race-based institution of slavery to enhance freedom and democracy among whites, see Edmund S. Morgan, *American Slavery, American Freedom: The Ordeal of Colonial Virginia* (New York: Norton, 1975).

11. Horsman, *Race and Manifest Destiny*, ch. 10.

12. On the status and rights of "free colored persons" in the antebellum period, see Ira Berlin, *Slaves without Masters: The Free Negro in the Antebellum South* (New York: Vintage Books, 1974); and Leon F. Litwack, *North of Slavery: The Negro in the Free States, 1790–1860* (Chicago: University of Chicago Press, 1961).

13. For a thorough history of state slave laws, see Thomas D. Morris, *Southern Slavery and the Law, 1619–1860* (Chapel Hill: University of North Carolina Press, 1996).

14. Recent publications on the history of miscegenation regulation include Peggy Pascoe, "Miscegenation Law, Court Cases, and Ideologies of 'Race' in Twentieth-Century America," *Journal of American History* 83 (1996): 44–69; Woods, "A 'Wicked and Mischievous Connection'"; Peter Wallenstein, *Tell the Court I Love My Wife: Race, Marriage, and Law—An American History* (New York: Palgrave Macmillan, 2002); Werner Sollors, ed., *Interracialism: Black-White Intermarriage in American History, Literature, and Law* (New York: Oxford University Press, 2000); and Joshua D. Rothman, *Notorious in the Neighborhood: Sex and Families across the Color Line in Virginia, 1787–1861* (Chapel Hill: University of North Carolina Press, 2003).

15. The colonial North Carolina laws of 1715–1716 and 1741 are in Vaughan and Rosen, *Indian Documents*, 16: North Carolina Documents 7 (sec. 16–17) and 18 (sec. 13–14). For the nineteenth century, see North Carolina Session Laws, 8 January 1839, ch. 24 (p. 33); and *State of North Carolina v. Melton and Byrd*, 44 N.C. 49 (1852). North Carolina courts did not always assess Indian racial identity by determining blood quantum. See, e.g., the decision in *State of North Carolina v. Jacobs*, 51 N.C. 284 (1859), discussed in chapter 3.

16. Massachusetts Session Laws, 22 June 1786, ch. 3 (p. 437).

17. David H. Fowler provides a list of state miscegenation laws in *Northern Attitudes towards Interracial Marriage: Legislation and Public Opinion in the Middle Atlantic and the States of the Old Northwest, 1780–1930* (New York: Garland, 1987), 339–439. Eventually, twelve states enacted miscegenation laws that specifically mentioned Indians. The pre-1880 states that never enacted a miscegenation law are Connecticut, Kansas, Minnesota, New Hampshire, New Jersey, New York, Vermont, and Wisconsin. (The Territory of Kansas prohibited miscegenation in 1855 but repealed the prohibition in 1859, before being admitted as a state.) See 336.

18. Marc Simmons, *Kit Carson and His Three Wives: A Family History* (Albuquerque: University of New Mexico Press, 2003).

19. Randall Kennedy, *Race, Crime, and the Law* (New York: Vintage Books, 1997), chs. 2 and 3. (The quoted language is from pages 29 and 88). On the early history of race and criminal law, see also Paul Finkelman, "The Crime of Color," *Tulane Law Review* 67 (1993): 2063–112.

20. The Kentucky law on striking whites is in Kentucky Session Laws, 8 February 1798, ch. 54 (p. 105); the colonial Virginia law on striking whites is in Vaughan and Rosen, *Indian Documents*, 15: Virginia Document 162 (1748); and the Kentucky laws on rape are in Kentucky Session Laws, 22 December 1802, ch. 53 (p. 107), and 25 January 1811, ch. 235 (p. 59). The criminal laws also imposed harsher penalties on rapists (and other criminals) who were slaves than on those who were free men, a distinction that was obviously likely to have a disparate racial impact.

21. Mississippi Session Laws, 14 October 1852, ch. 6 (p. 27), and 2 December 1858, ch. 98 (p. 180).

22. For a description of how law and custom made a point of excluding black women from the category of "ladies" in a different context, see Barbara Young Welke's discussion of black female train passengers in the nineteenth century in *Recasting American Liberty: Gender, Race, Law, and the Railroad Revolution, 1865–1920* (New York: Cambridge University Press, 2001).

23. Territorial Indiana Laws, 22 September 1803 (p. 26), and 17 September 1807, ch. 48 (p. 340). Kentucky had a similar law, which provided that "[n]o negro, mulatto or indian shall at any time purchase any servant, other than of their own complexion." Kentucky Session Laws, 16 January 1798, ch. 3 (p. 8).

24. Virginia Session Laws, 10 January 1818, ch. 50 (p. 66) (witnesses); 28 February 1866, ch. 24 (p. 89) (witnesses); and 27 February 1866, ch. 17 (p. 84) (racial classification). These laws had their precedent in the colonial period. For colonial Virginia statutes limiting Indians' capacity to testify in court proceedings, see Vaughan and Rosen, *Indian Documents*, 15: Virginia Documents 131 (1705), 150 (1732), 159 (1748), and 162 (1748). Kentucky continued the prohibition on Negro, mulatto, and Indian witnesses—along with the provisions of many other Virginia laws—after it became a separate state. Kentucky Session Laws, 6 February 1798, ch. 47 (p. 90).

25. Georgia Session Laws, 19 December 1829 (p. 98); Maryland Session Laws, 26 January 1847, ch. 27 (no page number); North Carolina Session Laws, November–December 1821, ch. 46 (p. 41), and 23 January 1837, no. 90 (p. 82); and Laws of the Republic of Texas, 22 December 1836, continued by the state after joining the United States.

26. On Mississippi, see Mississippi Session Laws, 19 January 1830, ch. 1 (p. 7); *Doe ex dem. Harris v. Newman*, 11 Miss. 565 (1844); and *Coleman v. Doe ex dem. Tish-ho-mah*, 12 Miss. 40 (1844). On Georgia, see Georgia Session Laws, 19 December 1829 (p. 98); and 24 December 1832 (p. 102).

27. California Session Laws, 22 April 1850, ch. 142 (p. 428); 22 April 1850, ch. 133 (p. 408); California Session Laws, 15 May 1854, ch. 54 (p. 59); 28 April 1855, ch. 144 (p. 179); *People of California v. Hall*, 4 Cal. 399 (1854); California Session Laws, 16 March 1863, ch. 68 (p. 60). Five years after the *Hall* case, the court ruled that a Turkish man did not fall within the racial prohibition and could testify against a white person. The justices explained that although the Turkish man had a dark complexion, "the indicium of color cannot be relied upon as an infallible test of competency under the statute." Since the Caucasian race predominated in Turkey, Justice Warner W. Cope wrote, this witness would be presumed racially eligible to testify. *People of California v. Elyea*, 14 Cal. 144 (1859).

28. Oregon Session Laws, 7 January 1854 (p. 130); Nevada Session Laws, 14 March 1865, ch. 136 (p. 403).

29. Territorial Indiana Laws, 17 September 1807, ch. 46 (p. 311); Indiana Session Laws, 28 January 1818, ch. 3 (p. 22), 29 January 1831, ch. 78 (p. 399), and 14 February 1853, ch. 42 (p. 60); Illinois Session Laws, 22 March 1819 (p. 139); and Nebraska Session Laws, 16 March 1855 (p. 134) and 13 February 1857 (p. 107). The language of the 1857 Nebraska law was repeated the next year. Nebraska Session Laws, 1 November 1858 (p. 109).

30. Cynthia Cumfer explains that Return Meigs, Indian agent to the Cherokee in Tennessee from 1801 to 1823, allowed Indians to testify in hearings that he conducted, and he argued that Indian testimony should also be allowed in trials in state courts. Cumfer, "Local Origins of National Indian Policy: Cherokee and Tennessean Ideas about Sovereignty and Nationhood, 1790–1811," *Journal of the Early Republic* 23 (2003): 21–46, at 33.

31. *Booth v. Commonwealth of Virginia*, 57 Va. 519 (1861). Parallel to Indians' exclusion from juries was their exclusion from the militia in some states. While most states simply restricted militia service to white males, several states—including Illinois (1818 and 1848), Indiana (1816), and Kentucky (1799 and 1850)—provided in their state constitutions that Indians were excluded from the militia.

32. This argument parallels one of the responses to assertions that the federal government's exclusive powers under the commerce clause served as a barrier to states' regulating Indians' right to make contracts or sell land (as discussed in chapter 2). That commerce clause counterargument was based on the ground that the states were not regulating commerce when they regulated Indians' contract and property rights. Similarly, the counterargument on the issue of suffrage was based on the ground that the states were not making decisions about citizenship or naturalization at all when they determined who could vote, even if they included Indians and other noncitizens in the franchise.

The other counterargument on the commerce clause was based on the assertion that the states enjoyed a concurrent power over commerce. The parallel argument on the suffrage issue was based on the assertion that the states retained a concurrent power over citizenship—that the states had the power to decide who would be citizens of the state. This argument is spelled out in connection with the discussion of citizenship in chapter 6.

33. *Tennessee v. Claiborne,* 19 Tenn. 331 (1838). In this case the court also held that free blacks were not citizens entitled to the protections of the privileges and immunities clause of the U.S. Constitution.

34. *Wall v. Williams,* 11 Ala. 826 (1847). Other state courts, however, did not question the "citizenship" language in the treaty and accepted the Indian land grantees as citizens. See, e.g., *Newman v. Doe ex dem. Harris and Plummer,* 5 Miss. 522 (1840).

35. *Amy v. Smith,* 11 Ky. 326 (1822). Well before the *Dred Scott* case, the Kentucky Supreme Court declared in this case that free blacks could not be citizens of the United States. The dissenting judge in the case described what he thought citizenship meant: "A citizen . . . is one who owes to government allegiance, service, and money by way of taxation, and to whom the government, in turn, grants and guarantees liberty of person and of conscience, the right of acquiring and possessing property, of marriage and the social relations, of suit and defence, and security in person, estate and reputation." Both the majority and the dissent agreed that since federal law allowed only whites to become citizens, no nonwhite person could have become a citizen since the Constitution went into effect in 1789.

36. *Laurent v. Kansas,* 1 Kan. 313 (1863). Although various draft constitutions written in the mid- to late 1850s allowed all men who were U.S. citizens to vote, the final ratified state constitution inserted a racial qualification for the suffrage.

37. Population figures for "civilized" and "unenumerated" (tribe-affiliated) Indians are available in the *Report on Indians Taxed and Indians Not Taxed in the United States (except Alaska) at the Eleventh Census: 1890* (Washington DC, Government Printing Office, 1894), 17–18. Article II, section 1 of Maine's first constitution phrased the elective franchise qualifications as follows: "Every male citizen of the United States of the age of twenty-one years and upwards, excepting paupers, persons under guardianship, and Indians not taxed, having his residence established in this State for the term of three months next preceding any election, shall be an elector for Governor, Senators and Representatives." Maine did not grant reservation Indians the right to vote until the twentieth century.

38. All of the antebellum state constitutions are available in William F. Swindler, ed., *Sources and Documents of United States Constitutions,* 12 vols. (Dobbs Ferry NY: Oceana, 1973–1979).

39. On the framing of the Fourteenth Amendment, see William E. Nelson, *The*

Fourteenth Amendment: From Political Principle to Judicial Doctrine (Cambridge MA: Harvard University Press, 1988); and (specifically with regard to Indians) Earl M. Maltz, "The Fourteenth Amendment and Native American Citizenship," *Constitutional Commentary* 17 (2000): 555–73. On judicial interpretation of the Fourteenth Amendment in race discrimination cases arising in various contexts, see Robert J. Kaczorowski, *The Politics of Judicial Interpretation: The Federal Courts, Department of Justice and Civil Rights, 1866–1876* (Dobbs Ferry NY: Oceana, 1985); A. Leon Higginbotham Jr., *Shades of Freedom: Racial Politics and Presumptions of the American Legal Process* (New York: Oxford University Press, 1996); Kennedy, *Race, Crime, and the Law*; Charles A. Lofgren, *The Plessy Case: A Legal-Historical Interpretation* (New York: Oxford University Press, 1987). See also Angelo N. Ancheta, *Race, Rights, and the Asian American Experience* (New Brunswick NJ: Rutgers University Press, 1998) for a scholarly examination of racial discrimination against Asian Americans after ratification of the Fourteenth Amendment.

40. *Senate Report No. 268*, 41st Cong., 3rd sess., 1870.

41. *United States v. Elm*, 25 F. Cas. 1006 (D.C., N.D. N.Y., 1877). The *Elm* case involved an Oneida Indian who had been charged with illegally voting in the election of 1876. The district court held that New York could not prohibit the defendant from voting, because, as a male citizen who satisfied the age and residence requirements, he met the state constitution's qualifications for the franchise.

42. *United States ex rel. Standing Bear v. Crook*, 25 F. Cas. 695 (C.C., D. Neb., 1879). For a book-length discussion of the case, see Valerie Sherer Mathes and Richard Lowitt, *The Standing Bear Controversy: Prelude to Indian Reform* (Urbana: University of Illinois Press, 2003).

43. *Elk v. Wilkins*, 112 U.S. 94 (1884). For discussion of the exclusion of Indians from protective guarantees of the Bill of Rights and subsequent constitutional amendments, see John R. Wunder, *"Retained by the People": A History of American Indians and the Bill of Rights* (New York: Oxford University Press, 1994); and Vine Deloria Jr. and David E. Wilkins, *Tribes, Treaties, and Constitutional Tribulations* (Austin: University of Texas Press, 1999).

44. *California v. Brady*, 40 Cal. 198 (1870). The court in Brady disagreed with the reasoning in *California v. Washington*, 36 Cal. 658 (1869), which ruled that the 1866 Civil Rights Act invalidated the state's prohibition on testimony by Chinese witnesses against a mulatto defendant. For scholarly discussions of the *Brady* case in the context of Chinese-American legal history, see Charles J. McClain, *In Search of Equality: The Chinese Struggle against Discrimination in Nineteenth-Century America* (Berkeley: University of California Press, 1994); and Tom I. Romero II, "Exploring the History, Evolution, and Future of the Fourteenth Amendment:

The 'Tri-Ethnic' Dilemma: Race, Equality, and the Fourteenth Amendment in the American West," *Temple Political and Civil Rights Review* 13 (2004): 817–56.

45. Kentucky Session Laws, 14 February 1866, ch. 563 (p. 38); *Bowlin v. Commonwealth of Kentucky*, 65 Ky. 5 (1867). Contrast *Kelley v. State of Arkansas*, 25 Ark. 392 (1869), in which the Arkansas Supreme Court held that the provisional courts of Arkansas (in trials prior to the state's re-admission to the Union in 1868) were bound to follow the Civil Rights Act, which clearly prohibited a ban on blacks testifying against whites. Thus the court upheld the decision of an 1866 trial court to allow a black victim of robbery to testify against the white man charged with the crime. Because the trial occurred prior to ratification of the Fourteenth Amendment, the Arkansas Supreme Court did not address the question of how the amendment would apply.

46. Nevada Session Laws, 2 March 1877, ch. 82 (p. 403); Nebraska Session Laws, 1866 Code of Civil Procedure, in force as of 1 July 1866 (p. 449).

47. *Priest and Walker v. Nebraska*, 10 Neb. 393 (1880); *Smith v. Brown*, 8 Kan. 608 (1871).

48. Indiana Session Laws, 20 December 1865, ch. 56 (p. 162), and 11 March 1867, ch. 120 (p. 225); Texas Session Laws, 10 November 1866, ch. 126 (p. 129); and 19 May 1871, ch. 104 (p. 108); North Carolina Session Laws, 13 September 1861, ch. 14 (p. 16); Tennessee Session Laws, 25 May 1866, ch. 56 (p. 80); and Minnesota Session Laws, 6 March 1868, ch. 70 (p. 110).

49. Fowler, *Northern Attitudes towards Interracial Marriage*. For a list of late nineteenth-century decisions upholding miscegenation statutes (as well as the few that voided such laws), see Pascoe, "Miscegenation Laws," 50 (note 16).

50. California Session Laws, 4 April 1870 (begins on p. 824, section 56 at p. 839); *Ward v. Flood*, 48 Cal. 36 (1874).

51. Nevada Session Laws, 8 March 1867, ch. 52 (begins on p. 89, relevant provision appears on p. 95); *State ex rel. Stoutmeyer v. Duffy*, 7 Nev. 342 (1872).

52. For example, as early as 1829 Ohio had excluded blacks and mulattos from common schools set up for whites, and later statutes provided for separate schools for white and "colored" children; case decisions show that Native Americans, like African Americans, were considered "colored." See laws enacted 10 February 1829 (p. 72); and 10 February 1849 (p. 17). Even after passage of the federal Civil Rights Act and ratification of the Fourteenth Amendment, Ohio laws of the postbellum period provided that school districts "may organize separate schools for colored children." Ohio Session Laws, 11 May 1878 (p. 513). Despite the federal amendment and federal laws, the Ohio Supreme Court continued to uphold racial classifications in the state's school districts. *Ohio ex rel. Garnes v. McCann*, 21 Ohio 198 (1871). Indiana, too, had excluded Negroes and mulattoes from common schools established for

whites before the Civil War and continued to permit school districts to segregate children on the basis of race long after the war. Indiana Session Laws, 5 March 1855, ch. 86 (p. 161); 13 May 1869, ch. 16 (p. 41); and 5 March 1877, ch. 81 (p. 124).

53. See, e.g. *United States v. Elm*, in which Judge Wallace proclaimed that "by the fourteenth amendment . . . , the whole subject of citizenship was transferred to the jurisdiction of congress."

54. Swindler, ed., *Sources and Documents of United States Constitutions*. The quotation is from the South Dakota Constitution of 1889, Article VII, section 8.

55. *Van Valkenburg v. Brown*, 43 Cal. 43 (1872).

56. *People of California ex rel. Kimberly v. De La Guerra*, 40 Cal. 311 (1870).

57. State constitution convention delegates expressing concern about suffrage limitations conflicting with the treaty were Edward Gilbert, L. W. Hastings, J. D. Hoppe, and H. W. Halleck. Delegates asserting the state's right to set voter qualifications were Charles T. Botts (lawyer), Kimball H. Dimmick (lawyer), W. M. Gwin (farmer), Lewis Dent (lawyer), J. M. Jones (lawyer), and Winfield S. Sherwood (lawyer). Members of the latter group were more likely to have been born in a slave state (two-thirds of the latter group compared to one-quarter of the former and three-tenths of all delegates), which might have affected their eagerness to assert states' rights positions. J. Ross Browne, comp., *Report of the Debates in the Convention of California on the Formation of the State Constitution* (Washington DC: John T. Towers, 1850), 63–71, 305, 478–79.

58. Population figures are based on the *Report on Indians Taxed and Indians Not Taxed in the United States (except Alaska) at the Eleventh Census: 1890* (Washington DC, Government Printing Office, 1894), 17–18.

59. On the disfranchisement of African Americans in the late nineteenth century, see Robert M. Goldman, *Reconstruction and Black Suffrage: Losing the Vote in Reese and Cruikshank* (Lawrence: University Press of Kansas, 2001).

60. Jeanette Wolfley, "Jim Crow, Indian Style: The Disfranchisement of Native Americans," *American Indian Law Review* 16 (1991): 167–202; and Orlan J. Svingen, "Jim Crow, Indian Style," *American Indian Quarterly* 11 (1987): 275–86, reprinted in *The American Indian Past and Present*, ed. Roger L. Nichols (New York: McGraw Hill, 1992), 268–77.

5. RACE, CULTURE, AND POLITICAL STATUS

1. The names "Sioux" and "Chippewa" (rather than the proper terms used today, "Dakota" and "Ojibwe") are used in this chapter because those were the terms used in nineteenth-century debates on Indian policy in Michigan and Minnesota.

2. On the history of Indians in Michigan and Minnesota, see Charles E. Cleland,

Rites of Conquest: The History and Culture of Michigan's Native Americans (Ann Arbor: University of Michigan Press, 1992); Susan E. Gray, "Limits and Possibilities: Indian-White Relations in Western Michigan in the Era of Removal," *Michigan Historical Review* 20 (1994): 71–91; James A. Clifton, "Michigan's Indians: Tribe, Nation, Estate, Racial, Ethnic, or Special Interest Group?" *Michigan Historical Review* 20 (1994): 93–152; Roy W. Meyer, *History of the Santee Sioux: United States Indian Policy on Trial* (Lincoln: University of Nebraska Press, 1967); Gary Clayton Anderson, *Kinsmen of Another Kind: Dakota-White Relations in the Upper Mississippi Valley, 1650–1862* (Lincoln: University of Nebraska Press, 1984); William E. Lass, "The Removal from Minnesota of the Sioux and Winnebago Indians," *Minnesota History* 38 (1963): 353–64; and Richard White, *The Middle Ground: Indians, Empires, and Republics in the Great Lakes Region, 1650–1815* (New York: Cambridge University Press, 1991).

3. Among the states in 1860, only California reported a larger number of Indians (17,798 civilized plus 13,540 others) than there were in Michigan or Minnesota. Also listing a high population of Indians was the Territory of New Mexico (6,467 civilized plus 55,100 others). *Report on Indians Taxed and Indians Not Taxed in the United States (except Alaska) at the Eleventh Census: 1890* (Washington DC: Government Printing Office, 1894), 17–18. For historical census data from the states (but not the territories), see also University of Virginia Geospatial and Statistical Data Center, *United States Historical Census Data Browser* (1998), http://fisher.lib. virginia.edu/collections/stats/census/.

4. Treaty with the Sioux (Sisseton and Wahpaton), signed 19 June 1858, proclaimed 31 March 1859 (Statutes at Large 12: 1037), printed in Charles J. Kappler, ed., *Indian Affairs: Laws and Treaties, 1778–1883*, 3 vols. (Washington DC: Government Printing Office, 1913; reprint ed., New York: Interland, 1972), 2:785–89.

5. For leading studies of the history of early Michigan and Minnesota and of Indians in those states, see the sources cited in note 2 and also, more generally, Bruce A. Rubenstein and Lawrence E. Ziewacz, *Michigan: A History of the Great Lakes State*, 3rd ed. (Wheeling IL: Harlan Davidson, 2002); William E. Lass, *Minnesota: A Bicentennial History* (New York: W. W. Norton, 1977); Theodore C. Blegen, *Minnesota, A History of the State* (Minneapolis: University of Minnesota Press, 1963); and William Watts Folwell, *A History of Minnesota*, rev. ed., 4 vols. (St. Paul: Minnesota Historical Society, 1956–69).

6. On the evolution of political parties and their positions on alien and black suffrage in antebellum Michigan, see Ronald P. Formisano, *The Birth of Mass Political Parties: Michigan, 1827–1861* (Princeton: Princeton University Press, 1971).

7. Peggy Pascoe, "Miscegenation Law, Court Cases, and Ideologies of 'Race' in Twentieth-Century America," *Journal of American History* 83 (1996): 44–69, 48.

Pascoe argues in her article that in the early twentieth century, racialism gave way to new ideologies that viewed race and culture as separate and distinct.

8. *The Michigan Constitutional Conventions of 1835–36: Debates and Proceedings* (Ann Arbor: University of Michigan Press, 1940), 171–243.

9. *Michigan Constitutional Conventions 1835–36*, 246–48 (Wilkins, McDonnell, and Norvell [on tax-based qualification]). On the history of property and taxpaying qualifications for suffrage, see Alexander Keyssar, *The Right to Vote: The Contested History of Democracy in the United States* (New York: Basic Books, 2000), ch. 2.

10. *Michigan Constitutional Conventions of 1835–36*, 246–48 (Biddle, McDonnell, Norvell). For Michigan Supreme Court justices' views on how "whiteness" should be assessed and measured for purposes of determining who could vote, see *People of Michigan v. Dean*, 14 Mich. 406 (1866).

11. *Michigan Constitutional Conventions of 1835–36*, 246–49, 384 (Williams and McDonnell).

12. Rubenstein and Ziewacz, *Michigan*, 74, 88; Formisano, *Birth of Mass Political Parties*, 83.

13. Michigan Session Laws, 9 April 1841, no. 54 (p. 137); Joint Resolutions in relation to Indian claims, 19 February 1851, no. 1 (printed with Michigan Session Laws, 1851, p. 258).

14. "Joint Resolution relative to certain Ottawa Indians residing at L'Arbre Croche, on Lake Michigan," 11 March 1844, Resolution No. 27 (printed with Michigan Session Laws, 1844, p. 176).

15. *Report of the Proceedings and Debates in the Convention to Revise the Constitution of the State of Michigan, 1850* (Lansing: R. W. Ingals, 1850), discussion at 485–86 and 495–96; quotations at 486 (Raynale) and 495 (Williams).

16. *Report of Proceedings . . . Michigan, 1850*, 93 (petitions), 420 (McLeod amendment); *Constitution of Michigan*, 1850, Article 7, section 1 (qualification of electors). Article 4, section 5 of the 1850 constitution also explicitly made satisfaction of the qualifications for electors a condition for eligibility to hold legislative office.

17. *Report of Proceedings . . . Michigan, 1850*, 241 (militia, including Leach motion), 62–63 (right to bear arms; Bagg, Cornell, and McLeod quotations); Constitution of Michigan, 1850, Article 18, section 7 (right to bear arms); Article 17, section 1 (militia). Article 1, section 13 of the constitution of 1835 had guaranteed the same broad right to bear arms as the final constitution of 1850; there was no racial qualification.

18. Cleland, *Rites of Conquest*, 248–56.

19. *Debates and Proceedings of the [Republican] Constitutional Convention for the Territory of Minnesota* (St. Paul: George W. Moore, 1858) [hereafter *Minnesota Republican Convention*], 337.

20. *The Debates and Proceedings of the Minnesota [Democratic] Constitutional Convention* (St. Paul: Earle S. Goodrich, 1857) [hereafter *Minnesota Democratic Convention*], 422–23.

21. *Minnesota Republican Convention*, 338 (Mantor), 393–97 (Mantor, Hudson, Colburn, Robbins, Billings); *Minnesota Democratic Convention*, 422–28.

22. Sibley subsequently withdrew the proposed amendment. *Minnesota Democratic Convention*, 435 (Brown); 178, 180 (Sibley).

23. George Bonga (1802–1880) is an example of a man of African and Indian descent who might have been seen as meeting the cultural criteria for "whiteness." He was a prominent fur trader who spoke English, French, and Ojibwe, was fully literate, and had served as an interpreter during Indian treaty negotiations. See his name listed among those present at the signing of the Treaty of the Chippewa, 19 May 1867 (Statutes at Large 16: 719), printed in Kappler, *Indian Affairs*, 2: 974–76. On George Bongo and on blacks in early Minnesota, see Earl Spangler, "The Negro in Minnesota, 1800–1865, *Transactions of the Historical and Scientific Society of Manitoba* 3 (20) (1965): 13–26; and Max L. Grivno, "'Black Frenchmen' and 'White Settlers': Race, Slavery, and the Creation of African-American Identities along the Northwest Frontier, 1790–1840," *Slavery and Abolition* 21 (3) (2000): 75–93. On Indian-black intermarriage more generally, see James F. Brooks, ed., *Confounding the Color Line: The Indian-Black Experience in North America* (Lincoln: University of Nebraska Press, 2002); and Daniel R. Mandell, "Shifting Boundaries of Race and Ethnicity: Indian-Black Intermarriage in Southern New England, 1760–1880," *Journal of American History* 85 (1998): 466–501. On fur traders and their families, see Jennifer S. H. Brown, *Strangers in Blood: Fur Trade Company Families in Indian Country* (Vancouver: University of British Columbia Press, 1980; reprint ed., Norman: University of Oklahoma Press, 1996).

24. *Minnesota Republican Convention*, 346 (Balcombe), 392 (Foster), 394 (Messer); *Minnesota Democratic Convention*, 431 (Flandrau).

25. *Minnesota Republican Convention*, 347 (Wilson).

26. Anderson, *Kinsmen of a Different Kind*, 232, 237–40.

27. *Minnesota Republican Convention*, 348 (McKune), 380 (Coggswell).

28. *Minnesota Democratic Convention*, 434 (Flandrau), 435 (Brown).

29. In addition, during the last few years of Minnesota's territorial period, the mixed-blood Indians, or Métis, living in settled communities along the territory's Red River Valley had supported the Democratic Party, playing a role in electing those fur traders to the territorial legislature and the constitutional convention. The Democrats may also have hoped that offering the suffrage to civilized Indians might attract more (Democratic-voting) Métis to move south from the Canadian portion of the river valley into the U.S.-controlled territory. As it turned out, how-

ever, Congress did not include the Red River Valley within the boundaries of the new state of Minnesota, even though it had been a part of the Minnesota Territory since it was established in 1849. As a consequence, few Métis actually ended up obtaining the right to vote through the provisions of the Minnesota state constitution. Jeremy Mumford, "Métis and the Vote in 19th-Century America," *Journal of the West*, 39 (3) (2000): 38–45.

30. Henry Sibley, a prominent fur trader, had played a major role in negotiating treaties with the Sioux in the 1850s; a significant amount of the money that was supposed to go to the Sioux in exchange for land cessions in that decade went instead to Sibley, in payment of debts owed to him in connection with the fur trade. Sibley later became governor of the state. Historian Robert M. Utley refers to the situation in 1850s Minnesota as "a classic example of the corruption of the federal Indian system" and uses Sibley as an example of a Minnesotan who profited from his role in Indian affairs. Utley, *The Indian Frontier of the American West, 1846–1890* (Albuquerque: University of New Mexico Press, 1984), 78.

31. *Minnesota Democratic Convention*, 435–36 (Emmett).

32. *Minnesota Democratic Convention*, 430 (Becker).

33. *Minnesota Democratic Convention*, 432 (Flandrau); *Minnesota Republican Convention*, 341 (Foster).

34. *Minnesota Republican Convention*, 394 (Messer). In 1860 there were approximately six thousand eastern Sioux Indians in Minnesota. Approximately 15 percent of those living on reservations were of mixed Indian and European heritage. Gary Clayton Anderson and Alan R. Woolworth, introduction to *Through Dakota Eyes: Narrative Accounts of the Minnesota Indian War of 1862*, ed. Anderson and Woolworth (St Paul: Minnesota Historical Society Press, 1988), 1–17, at 5, 8.

35. *Minnesota Democratic Convention*, 435–36 (Emmett).

36. *Minnesota Democratic Convention*, 432 (Sibley).

37. Anderson, *Kinsmen of a Different Kind*.

38. Jennifer Brown and Theresa Schenck point out a general tendency on the part of white Americans "to separate the mixed-bloods from the rest of the Native people" and, specifically, "to try to entice mixed-bloods to leave the reservations and become citizens." Jennifer Brown and Theresa Schenck, "Métis, Mestizo, and Mixed-Blood," in *A Companion to American Indian History*, ed. Philip J. Deloria and Neal Salisbury (Malden MA: Blackwell, 2002), 321–38, quotations on 331.

39. Theda Perdue, *"Mixed Blood" Indians: Racial Construction in the Early South* (Athens: University of Georgia Press, 2003), 86–98.

40. As in Michigan, Minnesota's 1857 constitution mandated that state legislators had to be qualified electors in the state, though this issue attracted little attention during the convention debates. *Constitution of the State of Minnesota* (1857),

Article 7, section 1 (voter qualifications); and Article 4, section 25 (qualifications for legislative office). A few years later, the legislature spelled out the cultural conditions under which adult male Indians would be deemed "civilized" enough to obtain district court certification of their suitability to exercise state citizenship rights. The criteria focused particularly on ensuring that voting Indians had a "civilized" form of housing, attire, occupation, and moral standards. Through evidence presented by at least two witnesses, including one white man, an Indian seeking citizenship had to establish that he (1) understood "the nature of an oath," (2) had a "fixed residence in a house, as distinguished from a teepee or wigwam," (3) was "engaged in the cultivation of the soil, or in the trades or in any other strictly civilized pursuit," (4) had "assumed the habits and worn the dress of civilization," and (5) was "a man of correct general demeanor, and possessed of good moral character." Minnesota Session Laws, 11 March 1861, ch. 48 (p. 171).

41. *Minnesota Democratic Convention*, 149–55, 177–81 (quotations at 149 [Ames] and 253 [Flandreau and Ames]); *Constitution of the State of Minnesota* (1857), Article 12, section 1.

42. Kenneth Carley, *The Sioux Uprising of 1862* (St. Paul: Minnesota Historical Society Press, 1976); Waziyatawin Angela Wilson, "Decolonizing the 1862 Death Marches," *American Indian Quarterly* 28 (2004): 185–215; Meyer, *History of the Santee Sioux*; Anderson, *Kinsmen of Another Kind*; Blegen, *Minnesota*; Folwell, *History of Minnesota*; and Lass, "Removal from Minnesota. All prior treaties with the Sisseton, Wahpaton, Mdeawakanton, and Wahpakoota bands of Sioux were nullified by Congress in 1863, laying the foundation for the Indians' expulsion from the state. Statutes at Large 12: 652.

43. A Minnesota law of 1861 went beyond offering suffrage rights; it formally extended the opportunity for civilized Indians to become citizens if they satisfied a detailed list of cultural criteria. Minnesota Session Laws, 11 March 1861, ch. 48 (p. 171). That this statute received little attention in nineteenth- or twentieth-century histories of the state suggests that it may not have had much impact. If few Indians were able to take advantage of the law, it could have been because so many were expelled from the state after the 1862 conflict. Furthermore, once Congress's 1863 law nullifying treaties with Minnesota Indians apparently retracted the federal government's offer of U.S. citizenship to certain members of the Sisseton and Wahpaton bands, the state might have become less interested in following through with their own offer of state citizenship rights to Indians. Statutes at Large 12: 652.

44. William Blair Lord and David Wolfe Brown, comp., *The Debates and Proceedings of the Constitutional Convention of the State of Michigan*, 2 vols. (Lansing: John A. Kerr, 1867), 2:270–271 (Shearer's comments on equal justice); 262 and 780, 785, 273, and 780 (Van Valkenburgh, Farmer, T. Smith, and Warner, respectively, on

distinctions based on race); 259 and 780, and 781 (Leach and Conger, respectively, on Indians as longtime voters); 266, 780, 270, and 273 (Conger, Van Valkenburgh, Shearer, and Smith, respectively, on Indians as the original owners of the soil); and 266 and 263 (Conger and McKernan, respectively, on past Indian military service). Knowledgeable experts reported that Indian suffrage would do no harm since only a few hundred of Michigan's eight thousand Indians had shown any interest in voting. *Constitutional Convention of . . . Michigan* (1867), 260 (Leach); and 784 (Richard M. Smith, in a letter presented at the convention).

45. *Constitutional Convention of . . . Michigan* (1867), 272 (Norris); 782–83 (Coolidge).

46. *Constitutional Convention of . . . Michigan* (1867), 260, 268, and 783 (Leach), 265–66 and 781–82 (Conger) and 780–81 (Van Valkenburgh); 262–63 (McKernan).

47. *Constitutional Convention of . . . Michigan* (1867), 784–85 (quotation from letter from Indian agent Richard M. Smith); 266 (Conger); 273–74 (T. Smith); 268 (Leach).

48. *Constitutional Convention of . . . Michigan* (1867), 263–64, 269–70, and 782 (Henry R. Lovell); 261 and 271–73 (Lyman D. Norris); 262 (Henry H. Coolidge); 779 (Solomon L. Withey); and 263 (William S. Utley).

49. For pre-statehood treaties, see, most notably, treaties of 1807, 1819, 1821, and 1836 (Statutes at Large 7:105, 203, 218, 491, and 503), printed in Kappler, *Indian Affairs*, 2:92–95, 185–87, 198–201, 450–56, and 461–62. The 1855 treaty (Statutes at Large 11:621) is in Kappler, *Indian Affairs*, 2:725–35. Treaties signed before Michigan attained statehood had provided that the Chippewa, Ottawa, and Potawatomi Indians ceded most of their land in Michigan; the first two tribes continued to retain reserved land in the state after the 1836 treaties. A treaty with the Chippewa and Ottawa Indians signed in 1855 and ratified the next year nullified any liability under the earlier agreements and established a new arrangement. The United States pledged to grant individual lots of land to heads of families and single people, but patents on the land would be withheld for ten years, during which time the land would be held in trust by the U.S. government and would be inalienable by the Indian occupants unless the president gave special permission. At the end of the decade-long trust period, the patents would issue except in cases where the president deemed the occupant incapable of managing his own affairs, in which cases the patents would be withheld as long as the president deemed "necessary and proper." Indians could also purchase unallocated lands from the tracts covered by the treaty. The treaties further provided that the United States would pay off debts owed by the Chippewas and Ottawas and would pay annuities to the Indians over a period of ten years. The treaties do not specify any action that could only be carried out by an organized tribe; tribal leaders are given no role in identifying those

eligible for land allotments or in distributing annuities, and any further issues were to be worked out by the particular individuals involved rather than by the tribes as a whole.

50. *Constitutional Convention of . . . Michigan* (1867), 263–64, 269–70 (Lovell); 779–80 (Bills); 263 (Utley); 258–61 (Estee).

51. *Constitutional Convention of . . . Michigan* (1867), 260–61 and 264 (Leach); 780 (Van Valkenburgh); 266 (Conger).

52. *Constitutional Convention of . . . Michigan* (1867), 785 (Farmer); 271 (Birney); 259 and 274 (Warner); 779 and 785 (Stockwell); and 274–75, 280–81, and 784–85 (votes). Before they decided to eliminate the constitutional provision allowing male Indians to vote, the delegates had already agreed to insert the word "civilized," thus proposing to enfranchise only "civilized male Indians, natives of the United States." The final draft of the constitution omitted the qualification that voters be white but retained the requirement that they be male. The proposed constitution also continued the practice of allowing declarant aliens to vote.

53. *United States v. Nice*, 241 U. S. 591 (1916).

54. At the same time the racial requirement for militia service was also elimi-nated. A statute enacted the following year provided that no school district could keep separate schools on account of race or color, in 1883 the legislature validated intermarriages between whites and blacks, and in 1885 a state civil rights law pro-hibited denial of access to public places on account of race or color. 1870 amend-ments to Article 7, section 1, and Article 17, section 1, quoted in William F. Swindler, ed. *Sources and Documents of United States Constitutions*, 12 vols. (Dobbs Ferry NY: Oceana Publications, 1973–1979). Michigan Session Laws, 17 April 1871, no. 170 (p. 271); 11 April 1883, no. 23 (p. 16); and 28 May 1885, no. 130 (p. 131).

55. Though the Minnesota electorate agreed to eliminate the whiteness require-ment qualifying the first two categories of legal voters (citizens and declarant aliens), the state's constitution's third and fourth categories of electors, which applied to civilized mixed-blood and full-blood Indians, remained unchanged. "Declarant aliens" were foreigners who had declared their intention to become citizens. The proposed amendment to delete the word "white" from the first two categories of legal voters ("White citizens of the United States" and "White persons of foreign birth, who shall have declared their intentions to become citizens") was finally approved by Minnesota voters on the third try, in 1868. Minnesota Laws, 24 February 1865, ch. 57; 27 February 1867, ch. 25; 6 March 1868, ch. 106.

56. Considerations of race and culture did not, of course, entirely disappear from Indian identity issues. In the twentieth century the federal Bureau of Indian Affairs came to use "blood quantum" measures for determining who was an Indian eligible for social services that depend on Indian identity. Yet, to Indians them-

selves, culture was and is also very important for marking who is a member of the tribe. For an excellent discussion of the ways in which race, blood, color, and culture are used by people of the Cherokee Nation to define Cherokee community, see Circe Sturm, *Blood Politics: Race, Culture, and Identity in the Cherokee Nation of Oklahoma* (Berkeley: University of California Press, 2002). For analysis of the ways in which race, culture, political structure, anthropology, and history were used by a twentieth-century trial court to determine whether the Mashpee Indians of Massachusetts were a tribe, see James Clifford, "Identity in Mashpee"; Francis G. Hutchins, "Mashpee: The Story of Cape Cod's Indian Town"; and Jack Campisi, "The Mashpee Indians: Tribe on Trial"; all in *Readings in American Indian Law: Recalling the Rhythm of Survival*, ed. Jo Carrillo (Philadelphia: Temple University Press, 1998), 19–42.

57. *Opsahl v. Johnson*, 138 Minn. 42 (1917).

58. *Elk v. Wilkins*, 112 U.S. 94 (1884).

59. *United States v. Kagama*, 118 U.S. 375 (1886). In *State of Minnesota v. Campbell*, 53 Minn. 354 (1893), the Minnesota Supreme Court signaled its acceptance of federal authority over reservation Indians, acknowledging that Indians in tribal relations were not subject to state criminal laws for acts committed on their reservation.

6. STATE CITIZENSHIP BY LEGISLATIVE ACTION

1. On the early history of American citizenship, see Rogers M. Smith, *Civic Ideals: Conflicting Visions of Citizenship in U.S. History* (New Haven: Yale University Press, 1997); and James H. Kettner, *The Development of American Citizenship, 1608–1870* (Chapel Hill: University of North Carolina Press, 1978). The Supreme Court cases referred to are *Chirac v. Lessee of Chirac*, 15 U.S. 259 (1817); and *American Insurance Company v. Canter*, 26 U.S. 511 (1828).

2. The case referred to is *Worcester v. State of Georgia*, 31 U.S. 515 (1832). An example of a New England protest against Cherokee removal is a memorial from William B. Calhoun and other prominent Massachusetts men to Congress on the subject of the "Rights of Indians," 22 February 1830.

3. For examples of treaty provisions allowing some Indians to remain in Southeastern states as citizens, see Article 14 of the Treaty of Dancing Rabbit Creek (Choctaws) and Article 12 of the Treaty of New Echota (Cherokees). The former treaty was signed 27 September 1830 and was proclaimed on 24 February 1831 (Statutes at Large 7:333) and is printed in Charles J. Kappler, ed., *Indian Affairs: Laws and Treaties, 1778–1883*, 3 vols. (Washington DC: Government Printing Office, 1913; reprint ed., New York: Interland, 1972), 2:310–19. The latter treaty was signed on 29 December 1835 and proclaimed 23 May 1836 (Statutes at Large 7:478) and is

printed in Kappler, *Indian Affairs*, 2: 439–48. Preemption rights accorded by the 1835 treaty to Cherokees who chose to remain were revoked by a supplemental treaty the next year. The supplement was signed 1 March 1836 and proclaimed 23 May 1836 (Statutes at Large 7:488) and is printed in Kappler, *Indian Affairs*, 2:448–49.

4. Mary E. Young, "Indian Removal and Land Allotment: The Civilized Tribes and Jacksonian Justice," *American Historical Review* 64 (1958): 31–45; Reginald Horsman, *Race and Manifest Destiny: The Origins of American Racial Anglo-Saxonism* (Cambridge MA: Harvard University Press, 1981), 201; and Ronald Takaki, *Iron Cages: Race and Culture in 19th-Century America* (New York: Oxford University Press, 1990), 98–99.

5. Examples of the Georgia laws granting citizenship status to individual male and female Cherokee Indians and their children include those passed on 21 December 1839 (for the wife and children of Daniel Davis, for Mrs. Burnhill and her children, for Benjamin R. Dougherty and his children, and for the wife of Isaac Morris and her children), 22 December 1840 (for David Keel and John Tucker and their children, for Mary R. Post, Tattnall H. Post, J. M. Post, and William A. Coleman and family), 27 December 1842 (for the wife and children of Lewis Ralston, and for George Ward, Andrew J. Senard, and Jane Senard), 26 December 1845 (for George Michael Lavender and Matthew Thompson), and 27 December 1845 (for Isabella Hicks and her children, and for Neely Justice). For examples in other southern states, see private laws approved in Tennessee on 8 November 1833 (ch. 16); in Alabama on 30 January 1852 (no. 442) and 5 February 1852 (no. 414); and in Mississippi in its constitution of 1832, Article 3, section 18.

6. For Kansas, see the treaty with the Wyandots signed 31 January 1855 and proclaimed 1 March 1855 (Statutes at Large 10:1159), printed in Kappler, *Indian Affairs*, 2: 677–81; Laws of the Territory of Kansas, 23 February 1860, ch. 74 (listed as ch. 115 of the laws in force in 1862); and Constitution of Kansas, 1859 (in effect with statehood in 1861). For Minnesota, see the treaty with the Sioux, signed 19 June 1858, proclaimed 31 March 1859 (Statutes at Large 12:1037), printed in Kappler, *Indian Affairs*, 2:785–89; and Minnesota Session Laws, 11 March 1861, ch. 48 (p. 171). For a broad description of northern and southern Indian removal, see Francis Paul Prucha, *The Great Father: The United States Government and the American Indians* (Lincoln: University of Nebraska Press, 1984), chs. 7–9. Rogers Smith estimates that before the 1887 General Allotment Act, 3,072 Native Americans had gained citizenship rights through treaties connected to removal efforts. Smith, *Civic Ideals*, 236.

7. *Scott v. Sandford*, 60 U.S. 393 (1857). Elsewhere, Taney had declined to recognize Indian tribes as "foreign" or "independent" governments. See *United States v. Rogers*, 45 U.S. 567 (1846). Rogers Smith analyzes this point in *Civic Ideals*, 266–67.

8. Massachusetts Session Laws, 27 March 1858, ch. 44 (p. 170), and 26 May 1857,

ch. 224 (p. 558); Maine Session Laws, 15 April 1857, ch. 112 (p. 60) and ch. 53 (p. 38); Resolution of New Hampshire Senate and House of Representatives, 26 June 1857, ch. 1999, printed with the New Hampshire Session Laws of 1857 (p. 1925); New Hampshire House of Representatives inquiry to the Supreme Judicial Court, 20 June 1861, printed at the beginning of the *Opinion of the Justices of the Supreme Judicial Court*, 41 N.H. 553 (1857); Vermont Session Laws, 25 November 1858, no. 37 (p. 42); Connecticut Laws, 25 June 1857, ch. 13 (p. 11). Moreover, Massachusetts declared that slavery would not be tolerated in the commonwealth, while the other four legislatures explicitly accorded free status to any slaves who were voluntarily brought into the state by their masters, or with their masters' knowledge or consent. In addition, in 1857 New York's legislature passed resolutions critical of the *Dred Scott* decision, and in 1857 Ohio enacted laws to protect the liberty of slaves entering Ohio (repealed soon after). Resolution of the New York State Assembly and Senate, 16 April 1857, printed with the New York Session Laws of 1857 (p. 797); Ohio Session Laws, 16 April 1857 (p. 170), 17 April 1857 (p. 186), 23 February 1858 (p. 10), and 27 March 1858 (p. 19).

9. *Opinion of the Justices of the Supreme Court, on Question Propounded by the Senate*, 44 Me. 505 (1857). Judge Appleton's ninety-three-page opinion also laid out historical facts supporting his argument that African Americans had been recognized as U.S. citizens since the founding of the country following the Revolution. Judge Davis focused much of his opinion on the principle that "birth makes a person a citizen by natural right," which could not be denied by government and on the argument that racial requirements for citizenship necessarily injected uncertainty and lack of uniformity into the citizenship determination. New Hampshire's Supreme Court also spoke to the issues, upholding the constitutionality of its state statute. *Opinion of the Justices of the Supreme Judicial Court*, 41 N.H. 553 (1857). State courts in both New York and Ohio freed slaves who were brought or sent temporarily into the state by their owners. *Lemmon v. People of New York*, 20 N.Y. 562 (1860); *Anderson v. Poindexter*, 6 Ohio St. 622 (1856).

10. On federal government debates and policy regarding Indian citizenship in the nineteenth century, see Smith, *Civic Ideals*; Kettner, *Development of American Citizenship*; Jill E. Martin, "'Neither Fish, Flesh, Fowl nor Good Red Herring': The Citizenship Status of American Indians, 1830–1924," *Journal of the West* 29 (1990): 75–87; Alexandra Witkin, "To Silence a Drum: The Imposition of United States Citizenship on Native Peoples," *Historical Reflections/Réflections historiques* 21 (1995): 353–83; R. Alton Lee, "Indian Citizenship and the Fourteenth Amendment," *South Dakota History* 4 (1974): 198–221; Earl M. Maltz, "The Fourteenth Amendment and Native American Citizenship," *Constitutional Commentary* 17 (2000): 555–73;

and Michael T. Smith, "The History of Indian Citizenship," *Great Plains Journal* 10 (1970): 25–35.

11. Massachusetts Session Laws, 6 April 1859, ch. 266 (p. 419); 30 April 1862, ch. 184 (p. 149); and 23 June 1869, ch. 463 (p. 780).

12. Connecticut Laws, 31 July 1872, ch. 67 (p. 36); and 14 June 1876, ch. 19 (p. 93).

13. Rhode Island laws, 31 March 1880, ch. 800 (p. 101). In addition, freeholder Indians in New York were declared citizens by a Reconstruction-era federal district court decision; the court ruled that the 1843 law pertaining to Indian freeholders had effectively made such Indians citizens and that the disintegration of Oneida tribal organization placed all Oneida Indians in the citizenship category. *United States v. Elm*, 25 F. Cas. 1006 (1877).

14. See the introduction for the colonial background to the legal history of Indians in Massachusetts.

15. For an example of a Massachusetts naturalization statute, see the legislation declaring George William Erving to be a free citizen of the commonwealth entitled to all the privileges and immunities of a citizen. Massachusetts Session Laws, 9 March 1793, ch. 19 (p. 242).

16. "Report of the Commissioners Relating to the Condition of the Indians in Massachusetts," 21 February 1849 [hereafter cited as 1849 Report], 49.

17. Benjamin Franklin Hallett, "Rights of the Marshpee Indians: Argument of Benjamin F. Hallett, Counsel for the Memorialists of the Marshpee Tribe, Before a Joint Committee of the Legislature of Massachusetts," 7 March 1834, 11; and William Apess, "Indian Nullification of the Unconstitutional Laws of Massachusetts Relative to the Marshpee Tribe; or, The Pretended Riot Explained," in *On Our Own Ground: The Complete Writings of William Apess, a Pequot*, ed. Barry O'Connell (Amherst: University of Massachusetts Press, 1992), 166–274, quotation at 240. Note that Apess's name is also sometimes spelled "Apes" and that the tribe currently known as the "Mashpees" was referred to as the "Marshpees" in the nineteenth century.

18. Vaughan and Rosen, *Indian Documents*, 17: Massachusetts Documents 50 (1652) and 139 (1725). The 1719 provision is printed in *Acts and Laws Passed by the Great and General Court or Assembly of His Majesty's Province of Massachusetts Bay in New England* (Boston: B. Green, 1719), 320. See Benjamin Hallett's observation that the language of colonial laws seemed to recognize that Indians did in fact "own" the land they occupied. Hallett, "Rights of the Marshpee Indians."

19. Massachusetts Session Laws, 14 March 1840, ch. 34 (p. 193); and 9 March 1855, ch. 245 (p. 665).

20. Massachusetts Session Laws, 27 February 1810, ch. 69 (p. 109); and 10 March 1828, ch. 114 (p. 803). See also the short-term allotment of parcels of Gay Head land by a statute of 25 June 1811 (p. 254), contrasted with the permanent allotment of land in Deep Bottom by a statute of 28 May 1856, ch. 206 (p. 120).

21. See, for example, the 1842 law pertaining to partition of the Mashpee lands. Massachusetts Session Laws, 3 March 1842, ch. 72 (p. 522).

22. Massachusetts Session Laws, 13 June 1788, ch. 2 (p. 695). The statute further iterated that no Mashpee proprietor could sell or lease out any of his or her lands, bind out his or her children to others as servants or apprentices, or be sued on a contract unless approved by the guardians.

23. In some ways the political arrangement for the Mashpees continued to be somewhat different from that of other tribes, however. Most notably, the proprietors were allowed to elect certain public officials who would play a role in governing the tribe and its land, though they were not entrusted with the management of their own funds. For laws pertaining to the Mashpees enacted during the early national period and the antebellum period, see especially Massachusetts Session Laws, 9 March 1808 (p. 31); 18 February 1819, ch. 105 (p. 161); 31 March 1834, ch. 166 (p. 231); 21 March 1840, ch. 65 (p. 210); 17 March 1841, ch. 102 (p. 380); 3 March 1842, ch. 72 (p. 522); and 23 April 1853, ch. 186 (p. 466). To some extent these laws also applied to the Herring Pond Indians. For discussions of recent legal claims of the Mashpee Indians based in large part on the history of their relations with the commonwealth, see Jack Campisi, *The Mashpee Indians: Tribe on Trial* (Syracuse: Syracuse University Press, 1991); Paul Brodeur, *Restitution: The Land Claims of the Mashpee, Pasamaquoddy, and Penobscot Indians of New England* (Boston: Northeastern University Press, 1985); and essays about the Mashpees by James Clifford ("Identity in Mashpee"), Francis G. Hutchins ("Mashpee: The Story of Cape Cod's Indian Town"), Campisi ("The Mashpee Indians: Tribe on Trial"), and Jo Carrillo ("Identity as Idiom: *Mashpee* Reconsidered") in *Readings in American Indian Law: Recalling the Rhythm of Survival*, ed. Jo Carrillo (Philadelphia: Temple University Press, 1998), 19–49.

24. For an example of a law expanding the powers of the guardians, see the 1828 statute pertaining to the guardians of Chappaquiddick, Christiantown, and Gay Head. Massachusetts Session Laws, 10 March 1828, ch. 114 (p. 803).

25. *Inhabitants of Andover v. Inhabitants of Canton*, 13 Mass. 547 (1816); *City of Lynn v. Inhabitants of Nahant*, 113 Mass. 433 (1873); *Mayhew v. District of Gay Head*, 95 Mass. 129 (1866); and *Danzell v. Webquish*, 108 Mass. 133 (1871).

26. *Clark v. Williams*, 36 Mass. 499 (1837). In explaining the court's opinion, Chief Justice Lemuel Shaw rejected the defendants' argument that Jane Barker should be able to claim her uncle's property because colonial laws of 1633 and 1701 had prohibited Indians from selling their land. The justice noted that since there was no evidence that this piece of land had been reserved to the use of Indians, the presumption was that aboriginal title to this piece of land in an "old settled town" had been extinguished by the government and therefore the colonial laws against alienation did not apply.

27. *Thaxter v. Grinnell*, 43 Mass. 13 (1840). In this case, the court said, the guardian's approval of Goodridge's employment as a seaman satisfied the provisions of the statute of 1827, which empowered the guardian to grant licenses to worthy Indians to make contracts. The court also took note of the fact that the defendants did not know that Goodridge was an Indian when they made the arrangement with him.

28. Massachusetts Senate and House of Representatives, "Resolve concerning the relations of the United States with the Indian tribes," 25 April 1838, ch. 100, printed with the Massachusetts Session Laws for 1838 (p. 763); 1849 Report.

29. "Massachusetts Indians," *Pittsfield (MA) Sun*, 5 April 1849, reprinted from an article published in the *Boston Courier*.

30. Massachusetts Session Laws, 6 April 1859, ch. 266 (p. 419).

31. John Milton Earle, "Report to the governor and Council, concerning the Indians of the Commonwealth, under the act of April 6, 1859" (Boston: William White, printer, 1861) [hereafter cited as Earle Report].

32. Earle Report, 120–37.

33. Massachusetts Session Laws, 30 April 1862, ch. 184 (p. 149); 27 April 1863, ch. 183 (p. 494); and 23 June 1869, ch. 463 (p. 780).

34. Ann Marie Plane and Gregory Button, "The Massachusetts Indian Enfranchisement Act: Ethnic Contest in Historical Context, 1849–1869," *Ethnohistory* 40 (1993): 587–618. Plane and Button fruitfully supplement the printed documents that are widely available on microfilm—such as the state laws, the legislative reports, and the transcript of the hearing at Mashpee—with archival materials, such as correspondence to and from leading figures in the Indian citizenship discussion. They also report that the printed version of the transcript of the hearing is an accurate rendition of the original manuscript, which is kept in the Massachusetts State Archives. See 616 (note 92).

35. Hallett, "Rights of the Marshpee Indians; and Apess, "Indian Nullification." See Barry O'Connell's analysis of Apess's ideas and language in his superb introduction to the collection of Apess's writings in O'Connell, *On Our Own Ground*, xiii–lxxvii.

36. 1849 Report, 49, 59.

37. Earle Report, 121 and 128.

38. Massachusetts Session Laws, 8 February 1864, ch. 15 (p. 12); and 16 May 1865, ch. 277 (p. 650). The Massachusetts Senate ratified the Fifteenth Amendment on 9 March and the House of Representatives ratified on 12 March 1869. *Journal of the House of Representatives of the Commonwealth of Massachusetts* 1869 (Boston: Wright & Potter, printers, 1869).

39. Governor William Claflin's Address to the legislature of Massachusetts in

January 1869, quoted in "Report of the Committee to Whom was Referred so much of the Governor's Address as Relates to the Indians of the Commonwealth," 3 June 1869 (Boston, 1869) [hereafter cited as 1869 Report].

40. *Journal of the House*, 11 January 1869, 15–16.

41. *Journal of the House*, 3 June 1869, 542; 1869 Report. Francis W. Bird, who was a member of the Committee on Indians in 1869, had been one of the three authors of the 1849 Report. In addition, Plane and Button point out that Bird was "a close advisor to the state's Radical Republican Senator, Charles Sumner." They also note that John Milton Earle, author of the 1861 Report, was a Quaker who had been the editor of an abolitionist newspaper. Thus, the two authors observe, there were close connections between abolitionists, Radical Republicans, and the supporters of Indian citizenship in Massachusetts before and after the Civil War. Plane and Button, "Massachusetts Indian Enfranchisement Act," 611 (notes 38 and 42).

42. The quotations are from the 1869 Report, 8, 13, and 16–17.

43. Another economic factor for the legislature was the prospect of saving the expenditures that had previously been made for personal aid and relief to Indians. The Committee on Indians said such aid had totaled $15,000 within the preceding five years. From 1869 Report, 9.

44. 1849 Report, 51.

45. Earle Report, 17 (Chappaquiddick), 48–50 and quotation at 41 (Mashpee), 71–72 (Natick), 111–12 (Dartmouth), 117 (Middleborough), 73–77 (Punkapog), 100–101 (Hassanamisco), and 101–103 (Dudley).

46. Earle Report. Quotations at 128 and 24, respectively. See also 129.

47. Most commonly in Anglo-American law, land that was entailed could be inherited by only the owner's heirs, or certain classes of the owner's heirs. When the term "entailment" was used to refer to Indians' land, it referred to the statutory limitation that such land could be inherited by or conveyed to only other members of the owner's tribe.

48. 1869 Report, 8; S. C. Howland, "Report of the Treasurer of the District of Mashpee to the Governor and Executive Council of Massachusetts," Public Document no. 32, 30 September 1866, 7; and 1849 Report, 7.

49. Plane and Button, "Massachusetts Indians Enfranchisement Act," 600–601. Plane and Button also found that there were more intermarried people among supporters of change. A similar pattern emerged at the legislative hearing in Mashpee in February 1869, where three of the five Mashpee supporters of citizenship and the end of entailment were non-Indians.

50. Massachusetts House of Representatives, Committee on Indians, "Hearing Before the Committee on Indians, at Marshpee," 9 February 1869 (Boston: Wright & Potter, State Printers, 1869) [hereafter cited as Hearing at Mashpee].

51. Earle Report, Appendix, xx–xxi.

52. Massachusetts Session Laws, 19 February 1867, ch. 41 (p. 491).

53. The Amos quotation was reported in the Hearing at Marshpee, 11; Amos's comment about other men buying Mashpee land, 12–13; Attaquin's statement, 33; and Sewell's assertions, 6–7 and 17. No first name was provided for Mr. Sewell.

54. These statements are from the Hearing at Marshpee, as follows: Pocknett, 22 and 23; Simons, 15; J. Amos, 18; Brown, 25–28. According to Earle's 1861 Report, these four opponents of change owned property worth only a quarter to half the value of the property held by supporters of change. At the end of the meeting in 1869, 26 Mashpee Indians who were present voted to oppose the proposal to end the entailment, while 14 supported it. Hearing at Mashpee, 34.

55. Hearing at Mashpee, 6.

56. See, for example, Jack Campisi's description of the Mashpees after citizenship in his book *The Mashpee Indians*, 116 and 120.

57. See Linda K. Kerber, *Women of the Republic: Intellect and Ideology in Revolutionary America* (Chapel Hill: University of North Carolina Press, 1980), especially p. 31.

58. Plane and Button, "Massachusetts Indians Enfranchisement Act," 604; Daniel R. Mandell, "Shifting Boundaries of Race and Ethnicity: Indian-Black Intermarriage in Southern New England, 1760–1880," *Journal of American History* 85 (1998): 466–501, 497; and Earle Report, 136. Mandell points out that at the Mashpee hearing, African American men who had married Mashpee women made clear that they "had made Anglo-American concepts of property, virtuous labor, and gender roles their keys to freedom and dignity." Mandell, "Shifting Boundaries," 498.

59. The quotations are reported in the Hearing at Mashpee, as follows: Attaquin, 33; Amos, 11; and Sewall, 4, 6, 7, 7, 5, and 6, respectively.

60. The quotations are reported in Hearing at Mashpee, as follows: Godfrey, 20; Holden, 20; Hinckley, 28 and 29, respectively; and Gouch, 25.

61. 1849 Report, 16.

62. Massachusetts Session Laws, 31 March 1834, ch. 166 (p. 231). The earlier statute quoted in the text was enacted in 1819. Massachusetts Session Laws, 18 February 1819, ch. 105 (p. 161).

63. Most of the 146 petitions in favor of woman suffrage came from more than one person. The *Journal of the House* for the 1869 term also mentions one petition opposed to woman suffrage. The vote rejecting "An Act to secure the Elective Franchise to Women in this Commonwealth" took place on 16 June 1869, *Journal of the House*, 615–17. Petitions in support of women's suffrage continued to pour into the house in subsequent years, to no avail.

64. *Journal of the House*, 4 June, 7 June, 8 June, 14 June, 15 June, 16 June, and 23

June 1869, pp. 550, 558, 602, 608, 610, 614, 651, and 654. While the Committee on Indians was studying the issue, there were several related petitions to the house: on 4 February, Representative Rodney French presented a petition from a group of Gay Head Indians who asked that they might remain in their present condition and not be made to assume the burdens of citizenship; on 2 March, Representative French presented a petition from a group of Deep Bottom Indians asking for the right of citizenship; and on 11 May French presented another petition from Gay Head Indians asking to be enfranchised. *Journal of the House*, 4 February, 2 March, and 11 May 1869, pp. 87, 177, 469.

65. *Pells v. Webquish*, 129 Mass. 469 (1880).

66. *Drew v. Carroll*, 154 Mass. 181 (1891). This case involved property that had belonged to the Herring Pond Indians. On 20 January 1870, a member of the tribe had mortgaged "all the real estate I own" in several towns, including Plymouth, where the Herring Pond plantation was located. The court held that even though the common lands of Herring Pond were not yet formally partitioned by the commissioners appointed by the probate judges, the 1870 mortgage did include the mortgagor's individual interest in the common lands of the Herring Pond tribe, which vested in him immediately when the 1869 statute went into effect.

67. Massachusetts Session Laws, 30 April 1870, ch. 213 (p. 140) (Gay Head); and 28 May 1870, ch. 293 (p. 213) (Mashpee).

68. *In re Coombs*, 127 Mass. 278 (1879).

69. General Allotment Act, Statutes at Large 24 (1887): 388. It was not until 1924 that the federal Indian Citizenship Act made all Indians born in the United States citizens. Statutes at Large 43 (1924): 253.

7. THE POLITICS OF INDIAN CITIZENSHIP

1. On the history of New Mexico, see Marc Simmons, *New Mexico: A Bicentennial History* (New York: Norton, 1977); Ramón A. Gutiérrez, *When Jesus Came, the Corn Mothers Went Away: Marriage, Sexuality, and Power in New Mexico, 1500–1846* (Stanford: Stanford University Press, 1991); David J. Weber, *The Spanish Frontier in North America* (New Haven: Yale University Press, 1992); and Howard R. Lamar, *The Far Southwest, 1846–1912: A Territorial History* (New Haven: Yale University Press, 1966). On the history of the Pueblo Indians, see Joe S. Sando, *Pueblo Nations: Eight Centuries of Pueblo Indian History* (Santa Fe: Clear Light, 1992); Herbert O. Brayer, *Pueblo Indian Land Grants of the "Rio Abajo," New Mexico* (Albuquerque: University of New Mexico Press, 1938); and Marc Simmons, "History of the Pueblos since 1821," in *Southwest*, ed. Afonso Ortiz, vol. 9 of *Handbook of North American Indians*, William C. Sturtevant, gen. ed. (Washington DC: Smithsonian Institution,

1979), 206–23. For a discussion of the (often inaccurate) common presumption that tribe-affiliated Indians were nomadic and hunting oriented (though in an earlier time period), see Daniel K. Richter, "'Believing That Many of the Red People Suffer Much for the Want of Food': Hunting, Agriculture, and a Quaker Construction of Indianness in the Early Republic," in *Race and the Early Republic: Racial Consciousness and Nation-Building in the Early Republic*, ed. Michael A. Morrison and James Brewer Stewart (New York: Rowman & Littlefield, 2002), 27–53. The issue of Pueblo Indian status in the nineteenth century has arisen in other scholarship, particularly in scholarly works discussing rights to Pueblo Indian land grants. See especially G. Emlen Hall, *Four Leagues of Pecos: A Legal History of the Pecos Grant, 1800–1933* (Albuquerque: University of New Mexico Press, 1984); and Myra Ellen Jenkins, "The Baltasar Baca 'Grant': History of an Encroachment," *El Palacio* 68 (1961): 47–64 and 87–105.

2. Population figures for "civilized" and "unenumerated" (tribe-affiliated) Indians are available in United States Bureau of the Census, *Report on Indians Taxed and Indians Not Taxed in the United States (except Alaska) at the Eleventh Census: 1890* (Washington DC: Government Printing Office, 1894), 17–18.

3. For example, see Governor David Meriwether to Commissioner of Indian Affairs George W. Manypenny, 31 August 1853, and Meriwether to Manypenny, Annual Report, 4 September 1854; Edmund A. Graves to Meriwether, 31 August 1853; David V. Whiting to Commissioner of Indian Affairs Luke Lea, 4 August 1852; and William F. M. Arny to the Legislative Assembly of New Mexico, 16 December 1865, in *Letters Received by the Office of Indian Affairs, 1824–1881: New Mexico Superintendency*, original manuscripts in National Archives, Washington DC, microcopy 234, microfilm rolls 546–56 [hereafter *Letters*]. See also Edward H. Wingfield to Lea, 6 February 1752, in Annie Heloise Abel, ed., *The Official Correspondence of James S. Calhoun while Indian Agent at Santa Fé and Superintendent of Indian Affairs in New Mexico* (Washington DC: Government Printing Office, 1915) [hereafter *Correspondence of Calhoun*], 469–71.

4. "An Act to enable Pueblo Indians to bring and defend actions," Territorial New Mexico Laws, December 1847 (p. 418).

5. For the different provisions of other incorporation statutes, see "An act incorporating the City of Santa Fe," Territorial New Mexico Laws, 4 July 1851 (p. 112); "An Act incorporating the New Mexico Mining Company," Territorial New Mexico Laws, 2 February 1854 (p. 38); and "An Act to incorporate the fraternity of the Independent Order of Odd Fellows of the Territory of New Mexico," Territorial New Mexico Laws, 12 July 1851 (p. 160).

6. Acting Governor W. W. H. Davis to Manypenny, 29 March 1856; Meriwether to Manypenny, September 1855; and Pueblo Agent Abraham G. Mayers to Manypenny, 3 January 1857, all in *Letters*.

7. "An Act to regulate trade and intercourse with the Indian tribes, and to preserve peace on the frontiers," Statutes at Large 4 (1834): 729.

8. Calhoun to Commissioner of Indian Affairs Orlando Brown, 8 November 1849, 16 July 1850, 12 August 1850, and 30 August 1850, and "Treaty Between the United States of America and Certain Indian Pueblos or Towns," in *Correspondence of Calhoun*, 75, 227, 237–46, 249–50, 255.

9. Calhoun to Commissioner of Indian Affairs William Medill, 1 October 1849, and 4 October 1849; Calhoun to Brown, 3 February 1850, 18 February 1850, and 30 March 1850; Brown to Smith, 27 February 1850; Smith to Brown, 9 March 1850; and Brown to Calhoun, 24 April 1850, in *Correspondence of Calhoun*, 36, 40, 139, 152–53, 176, 190–94, 223–26. The appointment of John Ward is described in Governor William Carr Lane to Lea, 30 October 1852, *Letters*.

10. Statutes at Large 10 (1851): 574 (at p. 587, section 7).

11. Meriwether to Manypenny, Annual Report, 4 September 1854; Meriwether to Manypenny, 30 October 1853, 1 October 1853, 31 August 1855, and September 1855; and Graves to Manypenny, 29 December 1853, in *Letters*.

12. Meriwether to Manypenny, 24 November 1853 and 1 October 1 1853, in *Letters*.

13. "An Act to prevent the sale of Spirituous Liquor to Indians in the Territory of New Mexico," Territorial New Mexico Laws, 10 January 1853 (p. 29).

14. Graves to Manypenny, 29 December 1853, *Letters*.

15. Davis to Manypenny, 14 November 1855, *Letters*; Meriwether to Manypenny, 18 January 1856, *Letters*. The first statute referred to in the text is cited in note 13 above. The second statute is "An Act to facilitate the punishment and suppression of crime against the laws of the United States, regulating trade and intercourse with the Savage Indian tribes, and to preserve peace on the frontiers," Territorial New Mexico Laws, 12 July 1851 (p. 157). This enforcement law provided that it was the duty of the prefects and justices of the peace to apprehend and bind over to the courts any person who violated U.S. laws governing trade and intercourse with Indian tribes.

16. Superintendent of Indian Affairs James L. Collins to Commissioner of Indian Affairs James W. Denver, 26 March 1859, Collins to Commissioner of Indian Affairs Alfred B. Greenwood, 23 December 1859; Superintendent of Indian Affairs Felipe Delgado to Commissioner of Indian Affairs Dennis N. Cooley, 11 June 1866; and Pueblo Agent John D. Henderson to Cooley, 7 October 1866, all in *Letters*.

17. Calhoun to Brown, 16 November 1849; Calhoun to Medill, 15 October 1849; and Calhoun to Brown, 3 February 1850, in *Correspondence of Calhoun*, 79, 54, and 140.

18. The federal law that created the Territory of New Mexico is Statutes at Large 9 (1850): 446. An example of a racial restriction on voting is section 19 of "Election Laws," Territorial New Mexico Laws, 20 July 1851. On the U.S. citizenship require-

ment for justices of the peace, see section 1 of "An Act establishing Justices' Courts . . . ," Territorial New Mexico Laws, 9 January 1852 (p. 303).

19. Calhoun to Brown, 2 February 1850, and Calhoun to the Indians of the Pueblo of Taos, 2 February 1850, in *Correspondence of Calhoun*, 132–35 and 136–38. It is difficult to determine the actual views of Pueblo Indians on these matters from written records, since documents purporting to describe their opinions were most often actually written by American agents.

20. Meriwether to Manypenny, Annual Report, 4 September 1854, *Letters*; Collins to Denver, 26 March 1859, *Letters*; and Message of W. W. H. Davis, Acting Governor of the Territory of New Mexico, Delivered to the Legislative Assembly, 3 December 1855, printed in the *Santa Fe Weekly Gazette*, 15 December 1855; and William Watts Hart Davis, *El Gringo; or, New Mexico and her People* (1857; reprint, New York: Arno Press, 1973), 148–52. Davis's observation before he became acting governor can be found in the newspaper he published, *Santa Fe Weekly Gazette*, 22 April 1854.

21. Mayers to Manypenny, 3 January 1857, *Letters*; Wingfield to Lea, 6 February 1752, in *Correspondence of Calhoun*, 469–71; Graves to Manypenny, 29 December 1853, *Letters*; Manypenny to Graves, 17 February 1854, p. 424, *Records of the Office of Indian Affairs, Letters Sent*, original manuscript in National Archives, Washington DC, microcopy 21, microfilm roll 48; and Indian Agent Samuel M. Yost to Acting Commissioner of Indian Affairs Charles E. Mix, 14 April 1858, *Letters*.

22. *Santa Fe Weekly Gazette*, 21 January 1854; Section 3 of "An Act amending the election law," Territorial New Mexico Laws, 16 February 1854 (p. 142); and "An Act providing and establishing means for the education of the youth in the Territory of New Mexico," Territorial New Mexico Laws, 4 February 1856, ch. 34 (p. 74). Emlen Hall explains that Pueblo agent John Ward, hoping to protect the land and resources of the Pueblos, initially arranged the tax exemption. If the territory would not tax the Pueblo Indians, they would not vote in territorial elections. Hall, *Four Leagues of Pecos*, 84–95.

23. *United States v. Benigno Ortiz* (an 1867 case heard in the U.S. District Court of the First Judicial District of New Mexico, which was printed in the *New Mexican* (Santa Fe), 3 August 1867); *United States v. José Juan Lucero*, 1 N.M. 422 (1869); *United States v. Anthony Joseph*, 1 N.M. 593 (1874), 94 U.S. 614 (1877); *United States v. Juan Santistevan*, 1 N.M. 583 (1874); *United States v. Manuel Varela*, 1 N.M. 593 (1874); and *United States v. Martin Koslowski*, 1 N.M. 593 (1874).

24. Secretary of the Territory of New Mexico Herman H. Heath to Commissioner of Indian Affairs Nathaniel G. Taylor, 8 August 1867, *Letters*.

25. Norton to Taylor, 3 August 1867, and Norton to the Governors of the Pueblos of New Mexico, 6 August 1867; Pueblo Agent John D. Henderson to Taylor, 6 March 1868; Ward to Taylor, 10 April 1868; and Indian Agent William F. M. Arny to

Mix, 11 August 1867, Arny to Senator John B. Henderson, Chairman of the Senate Committee on Indian Affairs, 8 August 1867, Arny to Representative William Windom, Chairman of the House Committee on Indian Affairs, 11 August 1867, and Arny to Secretary of the Interior Orville H. Browning, 10 August 1867, in *Letters*. New Mexico's delegate to Congress, José Francisco Chavez, also expressed disagreement with the courts' decisions. See Chavez to President Ulysses S. Grant, 11 December 1869, *Letters*. The agents' concerns about Pueblo lands apparently turned out to be warranted. Marc Simmons has estimated that the cost of the courts' removal of federal protection was that "some thirty percent or more of the Pueblos' best acreage shortly passed into non-Indian hands." Simmons, *New Mexico*, 170.

26. On the salary of Indian agents, see Statutes at Large 9 (1851): 574 (at 587); and 19 (1876): 176. For the superintendent's salary after the position was separated from that of the governor, see 11 (1857): 169 (at 185).

27. According to James Calhoun, in addition to daily rations, blacksmiths earned $40 a month, whereas servants earned a monthly salary of $10 to $15. Calhoun to Brown, 17 November 1849, in *Correspondence of Calhoun*, 82–83.

28. Federal statutes allocated the following sums for the Indian service in New Mexico (excluding treaty making and tentative allocations): $25,000 in 1854, $47,500 in 1856, $47,500 in 1857, $75,000 in 1858, $25,000 in 1863, $50,000 in 1871, $73,153.85 in 1874, $40,000 in 1875, $15,000 in 1876, and $20,000 in 1877. These allocation figures are contained within long statutes appropriating funds for various purposes. Citations are to the page numbers on which the relevant Indian-related allocation is specified. Statutes at Large 10 (1854): 330; 11 (1856): 79; 11 (1857): 184; 11 (1858): 330; 12 (1863): 789–90; 16 (1871): 566; 18 (1874): 141; 18 (1874): 171; 18 (1875): 445; 19 (1876): 198; and 19 (1877): 293.

29. Report of Julius K. Graves, Special Commissioner for New Mexico, Part 9, "Indian Appropriations," 1866, *Letters*.

30. John S. Watts to Secretary of the Interior Jacob D. Cox, 10 May 1869, *Letters*.

31. Charles P. Clever to Mix, 2 October 1868, *Letters*.

32. Simmons, *New Mexico*, 155.

33. Based on their study of primary sources such as the Report of the Indian Peace Commission (1868), observations in contemporary newspapers, and commentary in other writings from that period, historians have amply described the criticisms of the Indian service as well as the efforts to cleanse the service of corruption. On the alleged corruption of Indian agents, see especially H. Craig Miner and William E. Unrau, *The End of Indian Kansas: A Study of Cultural Revolution, 1854–1871* (Lawrence: University Press of Kansas, 1978), ch. 3; Francis Paul Prucha, *The Great Father: The United States Government and the American Indians* (Lincoln: University of Nebraska Press, 1984), chs. 18 and 23; Francis Paul Prucha, *American*

Indian Policy in Crisis: Christian Reformers and the Indian, 1865–1900 (Norman: University of Oklahoma Press, 1975); Robert M. Utley, *The Indian Frontier of the American West, 1846–1890* (Albuquerque: University of New Mexico Press, 1984), 41–46, 78; Hana Samek, "No 'Bed of Roses': The Careers of Four Mescalero Indian Agents, 1871–1878," *New Mexico Historical Review* 57 (1982): 138–57; Langdon Sully, "The Indian Agent: A Study in Corruption and Avarice," *American West* 70, no. 2 (1973): 4–9; and William E. Unrau, "The Civilian as Indian Agent: Villain or Victim?" *Western Historical Quarterly* 3 (1972): 405–20.

34. Often traveling the judicial circuit together, lawyers and judges had the opportunity to become well acquainted. Furthermore, many judges had been practicing lawyers before they were appointed to the bench and returned to legal practice when their judicial terms expired. Three of the seven New Mexico attorneys who represented defendants in the cases under study had previously served on the New Mexico Supreme Court (Kirby Benedict, Joab Houghton, and Henry Waldo). Justices of the district courts and the Supreme Court of New Mexico received an annual salary of $2,500 in 1854 and $3,000 by 1876. Statutes at Large 10 (1854): 311 and 19 (1876): 159.

35. Document no. 12, 5 December 1854, Arther Bibo Collection of Acoma and Laguna Documents, New Mexico State Records Center and Archives, Santa Fe.

36. Attorneys in other states and territories found ways to profit from Indian tribes that were under the jurisdiction of the federal government. For example, lawyers represented the tribes in their efforts to collect annuities. Likewise, other occupational groups that had official dealings with Indians often had personal financial interests in Native affairs. For instance, soldiers serving in the western territories often took advantage of opportunities to purchase Indian lands. See Miner and Unrau, *End of Kansas Indians*, chs. 3 and 5.

37. Mayers to Manypenny, 3 January 1857; Henderson to Cooley, 7 October 1866; and Meriwether to Manypenny, September 1855, *Letters*.

38. Victor Westphall, "The Public Domain in New Mexico, 1854–1891," *New Mexico Historical Review* 33 (1958): 24–52 and 128–43.

39. Willard H. Rollings, "Indian Land and Water: The Pueblos of New Mexico (1848–1924)," *American Indian Culture and Research Journal* 6, no. 4 (1982): 1–21, 9; and Kenneth Philp, "Albert B. Fall and the Protest from the Pueblos, 1921–23," *Arizona and the West* 12 (1970): 237–54, at 239–40.

40. On lawyers' challenges to community grants, see Malcolm Ebright, *The Tierra Amarilla Grant: A History of Chicanery* (Santa Fe: Center for Land Grant Studies, 1980), 4–6; and William deBuys, "Fractions of Justice: A Legal and Social History of the Las Trampas Land Grant, New Mexico," *New Mexico Historical Review* 56 (1981): 71–97. For a discussion of the conflicting views on the owner-

ship of communal lands, see also Malcolm Ebright, *Land Grants and Lawsuits in Northern New Mexico* (Albuquerque: University of New Mexico Press, 1994), ch. 9, especially p. 209. It should be noted that lawyers also viewed decision making by federal courts as contributing to the marketability of land. As a general rule in the American West, lawyers and others who had a stake in the marketability of land favored the transfer of decision-making power from local authorities to national courts. As historian María E. Montoya has observed, "[l]ocal interests and customs only interfered with investors' interest in creating titles that were marketable anywhere and to anyone." Land speculators were confident that transferring authority to more remote locations would be more likely to result in their property interests being interpreted in such a way that they would be recognizable in a world market. María E. Montoya, *Translating Property: The Maxwell Land Grant and the Conflict over Land in the American West, 1840–1900* (Berkeley: University of California Press, 2002), 117–18.

41. Herbert O. Brayer, *William Blackmore: The Spanish-Mexican Land Grants of New Mexico and Colorado, 1863–1878*, vol. 1 of *A Case Study in the Economic Development of the West* (Denver: Bradford-Robinson, 1949), 17–18; Victor Westphall, *Thomas Benton Catron and His Era* (Tucson: University of Arizona Press, 1973), 35–36, 72; Robert W. Larson, *New Mexico's Quest for Statehood, 1846–1912* (Albuquerque: University of New Mexico Press, 1968), 141–42; Ebright, *Land Grants*, 42–43; and David Benavides, *Lawyer-Induced Partitioning of New Mexican Land Grants: An Ethical Travesty* (Guadalupita NM: Center for Land Grant Studies, 1994).

42. Ralph Emerson Twitchell, *The Leading Facts of New Mexican History*, 5 vols. (Cedar Rapids IA: Torch Press, 1911–1917), 2:401–402, 483–85; 5:261–62; Westphall, *Catron*, 34, 39–46, 100–104, 109, 113–14, 125, 132, 201; Ebright, *Land Grants*, 43, 205; Larson, *Quest for Statehood*, 142–43, 328; Robert W. Larson, "Territorial Politics and Cultural Impact," *New Mexico Historical Review* 60 (1985): 249–69, at 256–57; Brayer, *Blackmore*, 56, 78, 134, 166–67, 210, 241, 278, 309; Ebright, *Tierra Amarilla Grant*, 3; Philip J. Rasch, "The People of the Territory of New Mexico vs. the Santa Fe Ring," *New Mexico Historical Review* 47 (1972): 185–202; Lamar, *Far Southwest*, 140, 147; and William A. Keleher, *Maxwell Land Grant: A New Mexico Item*, rev. ed. (New York: Argosy-Antiquarian, 1964), 18. Evarts's brief is part of the Transcript of Record in the *Joseph* case.

Some historians have even asserted that lawyers so dominated the Santa Fe Ring that it was essentially the equivalent of the New Mexico bar association. Larson, "Territorial Politics," 256; and Westphall, *Catron*, 201. It was thought that the lawsuit against Antonio Joseph, along with hundreds of other similar cases, was filed by the U.S. attorney in order to pressure the defendants into voting for Elkins as congressional delegate. Note also that the defendant in the primary Supreme Court case, Antonio Joseph, was also among the members of the Santa Fe Ring. Joseph was a major land speculator who owned substantial interests in the Maxwell Grant, Cieneguilla Grant, and Chama Grant. In addition, he helped other land grantees obtain confirmation of their titles. Brayer, *Blackmore*, 1:148, 149, 197–98, 253–61, 298; Ebright, *Land Grants*, 43; and Larson, *Quest for Statehood*, 144.

43. Hall, *Four Leagues of Pecos*, 119–20; Lamar, *Far Southwest*, 140–43, 160; Brayer, *Blackmore*, 131–34, 212, 255; and Jim Berry Pearson, *The Maxwell Land Grant* (Norman: University of Oklahoma Press, 1961), 24–25.

44. Statutes at Large 16 (1871): 566, and 24 (1887): 388.

45. Examples include the removal of Indians from Georgia and other southeastern states in order to permit the extension of cotton plantations, and Indian removal from New York to make way for transportation lines, as discussed in chapter 1.

It should be noted, however, that the lawyers' interests did not always coincide with the broader American point of view. Most notably, Americans of the mid- to late nineteenth century tended to believe in the principle of equal access to land as a means to reinforce the ideal of a democratic nation of independent, enterprising republican citizens. Such a principle required that large tracts of unimproved lands be treated as public domain and made available to individual settlers. In contrast, lawyers in New Mexico most often supported the confirmation of large, private land grants from which individual settlers would be ejected. See references to the two different conceptions of western land ownership in Twitchell, *Leading Facts*, 2:467–68; Lamar, *Far Southwest*, 155; and Montoya, *Translating Property*, ch. 5.

46. Although the *Joseph* case provided a firm resolution of the debate of the early territorial period, it was destined to be an impermanent settlement. Over time new jurisdictional conflicts emerged, especially once New Mexico became a state in 1912. In 1910 the New Mexico Enabling Act provided that "the terms 'Indian' and 'Indian country' shall include the pueblo Indians of New Mexico and the lands now owned and occupied by them." That definition meant the Pueblo Indians would be covered by federal Indian laws. See Statutes at Large 36 (1910): 557. The U.S. Supreme Court upheld the constitutionality of this statute in *United States v. Sandoval*, 231 U.S. 28 (1913). Later, a battle would emerge as Congress tried to resolve the ambiguities of claims to Pueblo Indian lands. The Bursum Bill was brought to Congress in the early 1920s to settle the land titles in favor of the non-Indian claimants, but the proposal met strong resistance and failed to pass. Finally, in 1924 the Pueblo Lands Act established a Pueblo Lands Board to determine Pueblo Indians' title to lands using a more equitable approach. Over two decades later, the Pueblo Indians were finally acknowledged (once again) to be citizens of the United States.

47. Lucy Maddox, "American Indians, Civilized Performance and the Question of Rights," *Comparative American Studies* 1 (2003): 317–26. The quotation is on p. 325.

STATE LAW AND DIRECT RULE OVER INDIANS

1. Lauren Benton, *Law and Colonial Cultures: Legal Regimes in World History, 1400–1900* (New York: Cambridge University Press, 2002). See especially chapter 4, where Benton discusses nineteenth-century expansion of colonizing states' jurisdictional authority in Bengal and West Africa.

2. Mahmood Mamdani, *Citizen and Subject: Contemporary Africa and the Legacy of Late Colonialism* (Princeton NJ: Princeton University Press, 1996), definitions on 16–18.

3. Robert A. Williams Jr., "The Algebra of Federal Indian Law: The Hard Trail of Decolonizing and Americanizing the White Man's Indian Jurisprudence," *Wisconsin Law Review* 1986 (1986): 219–99; Robert B. Porter, "The Demise of the Ongwehoweh and the Rise of the Native Americans: Redressing the Genocidal Act of Forcing American Citizenship upon Indigenous Peoples," *Harvard BlackLetter Law Journal* 15 (1999): 107–83; Devon A. Mihesuah, "Choosing America's Heroes and Villains: Lessons Learned from the Execution of Silon Lewis," *American Indian Quarterly* 20 no. 1/2 (2005): 239–62; Devon Abbott Mihesuah, *Indigenous American Women: Decolonization, Empowerment, Activism* (Lincoln: University of Nebraska Press, 2003); Carol Chiago Lujan and Gordon Adams, "U.S. Colonization of Indian Justice Systems: A Brief History," *Wicazo Sa Review* 19, no. 2 (2004): 9–23; Waziyatawin Angela Wilson, "Decolonizing the 1862 Death Marches," *American Indian Quarterly* 28 (2004): 185–215; Susan A. Miller, "Seminoles and Africans under Seminole Law: Sources and Discourses of Tribal Sovereignty and 'Black Indian' Entitlement," *Wacazo Sa Review* 20 (2005): 23–47; Bonita Lawrence, "Gender, Race, and the Regulation of Native Identity in Canada and the United States: An Overview," *Hypatia* 18, no. 2 (2003): 3–31; and Elizabeth Cook-Lynn and James Riding In, "Editors' Commentary," *Wicazo Sa Review* 19, no. 1 (2004): 5–10 (quotation on p. 6). These authors are only a small sampling of the many Native scholars who have categorized U.S.-Indian relations as colonial.

4. On federal government efforts to assimilate Indians both culturally and politically in the 1880s and 1890s, see especially Frederick E. Hoxie, *A Final Promise: The Campaign to Assimilate the Indians, 1880–1920* (Lincoln: University of Nebraska Press, 1984); and Francis Paul Prucha, *American Indian Policy in Crisis: Christian Reformers and the Indian, 1865–1900* (Norman: University of Oklahoma Press, 1975). Although U.S. treatment of Indians has been identified as a form of colonization, there has been little scholarly analysis of the particular style of American colonial administration. The few existing publications on that subject focus not on the nineteenth-century shift from indirect to direct rule but, rather, on the later shift back to indirect rule in the twentieth century. For example, Laurence Hauptman has described the ways in which John Collier, commissioner of Indian affairs from 1933

to 1945, consciously and explicitly patterned American Indian policy on Britain's new approaches to administering its African colonies. Collier shared the view of British reformers who saw the established model of direct rule in Africa as unduly intrusive, destructive, and oppressive and who were trying to engineer a shift to a gentler and more decentralized indirect rule. In U.S. Indian policy the new model of indirect rule was manifested in the Indian Reorganization Act of 1934, which, among other things, provided for establishment of tribal political organizations to manage internal tribal governance (under the supervision of federal government officials). Collier regarded the new approach as far more enlightened than the form of direct rule that, by the beginning of his term, dominated federal policy. Prior to institution of direct rule in the nineteenth century, federal administration of Indians had been by indirect rule, and Collier advocated a return to that more enlightened approach. Since the publication of Hauptman's article on Collier, other historians have described how the 1930s shift from direct to indirect colonial rule affected specific tribes, as exemplified by Akim D. Reinhardt's recent case study of the Indian New Deal and the Pine Ridge Reservation of South Dakota. Laurence M. Hauptman, "Africa View: John Collier, the British Colonial Service and American Indian Policy, 1933–1945," *Historian* 48 (1986): 359–74; and Akim D. Reinhardt, "A Crude Replacement: The Indian New Deal, Indirect Colonialism, and Pine Ridge Reservation," *Journal of Colonialism and Colonial History* 6, no. 1 (2005).

5. Brad Asher, *Beyond the Reservation: Indians, Settlers, and the Law in Washington Territory, 1853–1889* (Norman: University of Oklahoma Press, 1999).

6. Globally, Lauren Benton observes, colonial officials sometimes extended legal jurisdiction over an outsider group for the purpose of facilitating the outsiders' progress toward civilization. Focusing specifically on U.S. relations with Indians, Sidney Harring also stresses the crucial importance of law in the process of acculturation. To emphasize the coercive and violent nature of the process of imposing law on Indians, he writes that the law "overshadowed the army as the method of choice to force assimilation," and he describes the law "replacing the gun as the agent of civilization." Benton, *Law and Colonial Cultures*, 65; Sidney L. Harring, *Crow Dog's Case: American Indian Sovereignty, Tribal Law, and United States Law in the Nineteenth Century* (New York: Cambridge University Press, 1994), 13.

7. Benton, *Law and Colonial Cultures*, ch. 1 and 154–56; Mamdani, *Citizen and Subject*, 16–17.

8. *United States v. Monte*, 3 N.M. 173 (1884). In support of its decision, the New Mexico Supreme Court cited the 1883 opinion of the U.S. Supreme Court relating to courts in the Territory of Dakota, *Ex parte Crow Dog (Kan-gi-Shun-ca)*, 109 U.S. 556 (1883).

9. John Ross, Annual Message to the Cherokee Nation, 24 October 1831, printed

in Gary E. Moulton, ed., *The Papers of Chief John Ross*, 2 vols. (Norman: University of Oklahoma Press, 1985), 1:224–31. The quotations are on p. 226.

10. For the colonial antecedent to the nineteenth-century use of racial hierarchies to mitigate class conflicts among whites, see Edmund S. Morgan, *American Slavery, American Freedom: The Ordeal of Colonial Virginia* (New York: Norton, 1975).

11. Asher, *Beyond the Reservation*. The quoted sentence is on p. 111.

12. Benton, *Law and Colonial Cultures*, ch. 5. The quotation is on p. 209.

13. In this regard, too, parallels can be seen to nineteenth-century African colonies. As Mamdani explains, white-dominated civil society in Africa was racialized; the colonial laws frequently discriminated on the basis of race. Mamdani, *Citizen and Subject*, 18–21. For an analysis of the meaning of "inclusion" and "exclusion" as applied to blacks in the United States, see Devon W. Carbado, "Racial Naturalization," *American Quarterly* 57 (2005): 633–58. Carbado observes that, for blacks, "inclusion in the category of formal citizenship has not meant exclusion from racial inequality"; in fact, blacks' treatment as subordinate people in U.S. history illustrates that "inclusion can be a social vehicle for exclusion." (Quotations on pp. 645 and 638.)

14. David Waldstreicher, *In the Midst of Perpetual Fetes: The Making of American Nationalism, 1776–1820* (Chapel Hill: University of North Carolina Press, 1997), ch. 5; and Susan-Mary Grant, *North over South: Northern Nationalism and American Identity in the Antebellum Era* (Lawrence: University Press of Kansas, 2000).

15. Joanne Pope Melish, *Disowning Slavery: Gradual Emancipation and "Race" in New England, 1780–1860* (Ithaca NY: Cornell University Press, 1998), especially ch. 6.

16. Joshua David Bellin, "Apostle of Removal: John Eliot in the Nineteenth Century," *New England Quarterly* 69 (1996): 3–32. The Everett quotation is on p. 12. Indians might have been perceived as "vanishing" for another reason as well. Daniel Mandell argues that as the rate of intermarriage between Indians and blacks increased, "the difficulty that whites had defining 'Indians' and 'Negroes' and distinguishing between them similarly increased." Mandell explains that many whites came to see local Indians as "part of the undifferentiated 'people of color.'" To whites, the children of mixed-race marriages may not have appeared to be true Indians. Daniel R. Mandell, "Shifting Boundaries of Race and Ethnicity: Indian-Black Intermarriage in Southern New England, 1760–1880," *Journal of American History* 85 (1998): 466–501, 471, 497.

17. Jean M. O'Brien, *Dispossession by Degrees: Indian Land and Identity in Natick, Massachusetts, 1650–1790* (New York: Cambridge University Press, 1997). Quotation at p. 213.

18. Bruce A. Rubenstein, "Justice Denied: An Analysis of American Indian-White Relations in Michigan, 1855–1889," PhD diss., Michigan State University, 1974, ch. 5; John Wood Sweet, *Bodies Politic: Negotiating Race in the American North, 1730–1830* (Baltimore: Johns Hopkins University Press, 2003); and Philip J. Deloria, *Indians in Unexpected Places* (Lawrence: University Press of Kansas, 2004).

19. Vine Deloria Jr. and David E. Wilkins, *Tribes, Treaties, and Constitutional Tribulations* (Austin: University of Texas Press, 1999), 147; and Porter, "Demise of the Ongwehoweh and the Rise of the Native Americans," part 3. Likewise, with regard to New Zealand's indigenous people, Moana Jackson, a member of the Ngati Kahungunu and Ngati Iwi (tribal nations), argues that it "is actually inappropriate to see the Maori as simply another economic minority or under-class in their own country. Rather, they need to be accepted as sovereign parties to the Treaty of Waitangi," and the "truth of Maori self-determination" needs to be acknowledged. Jackson, "Justice and Political Power: Reasserting Maori Legal Processes," in *Legal Pluralism and the Colonial Legacy: Indigenous Experiences of Justice in Canada, Australia, and New Zealand*, ed. Kayleen M. Hazlehurst (Brookfield vt: Ashgate, 1995), 243–63, 259.

20. For a comparative study of efforts to assimilate Aboriginal people in Canada through a similar combination of disciplinary training and regulation of behavior, see John Pratt, "Aboriginal Justice and the 'Good Citizen': An Essay on Population Management," in Hazlehurst, *Legal Pluralism and the Colonial Legacy*, 39–71. Scholarship on late nineteenth-century federal Indian policy in the United States includes Hoxie, *Final Promise*; and Prucha, *American Indian Policy in Crisis*.

21. *The Cherokee Tobacco*, 78 U.S. 616 (1871); and *United States v. Kagama*, 118 U.S. 375 (1886). *Kagama* was the case in which Justice Samuel F. Miller commented that, historically, the states had been the Indians' "deadliest enemies." For discussion of these important federal cases, see David E. Wilkins, *American Indian Sovereignty and the U.S. Supreme Court: The Masking of Justic*e (Austin: University of Texas Press, 1997), 54–63 and 67–81.

22. Indeed, U.S. citizenship was unilaterally imposed even on tribes that rejected it. An article that emphasizes Indian citizenship as forced incorporation is Alexandra Witkin, "To Silence a Drum: The Imposition of United States Citizenship on Native Peoples," *Historical Reflections/Réflexions Historiques*, 21 (1995): 353–83.

23. For discussions of the views of American Indian intellectuals writing after 1880, see Frederick E. Hoxie, ed., *Talking Back to Civilization: Indian Voices from the Progressive Era* (Boston: Bedford/St. Martin's, 2001); Margot Liberty, ed., *American Indian Intellectuals of the Nineteenth and Early Twentieth Centuries* (1978; reprint ed., Norman: University of Oklahoma Press, 2002); R. David Edmunds, *The New Warriors: Native American Leaders since 1900* (Lincoln: University of Nebraska

Press, 2001); Peter Iverson, *Carlos Montezuma and the Changing World of American Indians* (Albuquerque: University of New Mexico Press, 1982); and Thomas W. Cowger, *The National Congress of American Indians: The Founding Years* (Lincoln: University of Nebraska Press, 1999).

24. States excluding Indians from the franchise on these grounds included Arizona, Idaho, Nevada, New Mexico, North Dakota, Utah, and Washington. Even today, some states remain reluctant to extend social services to Indians and seek ways to dilute the votes of tribal Indians. For a description of a twentieth-century dispute over Indian voting rights in Arizona, see Glenn A. Phelps, "Representation without Taxation: Citizenship and Suffrage in Indian Country," *American Indian Quarterly* 9 (1985): 135–48.

BIBLIOGRAPHY

REPORTED COURT CASES

In case names, specific state names have been used in place of "the State," "the Commonwealth," and "the People."

Agnès v. Judice, 3 Mart. (o s.) 171 (La., 1813)

American Insurance Company v. Canter, 26 U.S. 511 (1828)

Amy v. Smith, 11 Ky. 326 (1822)

Anderson v. Poindexter, 6 Ohio St. 622 (1856)

Blacksmith v. Fellows, 7 N.Y. 401 (1852)

Blue-Jacket v. Commissioners of Johnson County, 3 Kan. 299 (1865)

Booth v. Virginia, 57 Va. 519 (1861)

Boullemet v. Philips, 2 Rob. 365 (La., 1842)

Bowlin v. Kentucky, 65 Ky. 5 (1867)

Boyer v. Dively, 58 Mo. 510 (1875)

Bryan v. Walton, 14 Ga. 185 (1853), 20 Ga. 480 (1856), 30 Ga. 834 (1860), and 33 Ga. Supp. 11 (1864)

Buchanan v. Harvey, 35 Mo. 276 (1864)

Butt v. Rachel, 18 Va. 209 (1814)

Caldwell v. Alabama, 1 Stew. & P. 327 (1832)

California v. Antonio, 27 Cal. 404 (1865)

California v. Brady, 40 Cal. 198 (1870)

California v. Elyea, 14 Cal. 144 (1859)

California v. Hall, 4 Cal. 399 (1854)

California ex rel. Kimberly v. De La Guerra, 40 Cal. 311 (1870)

California v. Washington, 36 Cal. 658 (1869)

Chandler v. Edson, 9 Johns. 362 (N.Y., 1812)

Charlotte v. Chouteau, 25 Mo. 465 (1857)

Cherokee Nation v. Georgia, 30 U.S. 1 (1831)

Cherokee Tobacco, 78 U.S. 616 (1871)

Chirac v. Lessee of Chirac, 15 U.S. 259 (1817)

City of Lynn v. Inhabitants of Nahant, 113 Mass. 433 (1873)

Clark v. Libbey, 14 Kan. 435 (1875)

Clark v. Williams, 36 Mass. 499 (1837)

Bibliography

Coleman v. Doe ex dem. Tish-ho-mah, 12 Miss. 40 (1844)

Commissioners of Franklin Co. v. Pennock, 18 Kan. 579 (1877)

In re Coombs, 127 Mass. 278 (1879)

Crabtree v. McDaniel, 17 Ark. 222 (1856)

Ex parte Crow Dog, 109 U.S. 556 (1883)

Dana v. Dana, 14 Johns. 181 (N.Y., 1817)

Danzell v. Webquish, 108 Mass. 133 (1871)

Doe ex dem. Harris v. Newman, 11 Miss. 565 (1844)

Doe ex dem. Lafontaine v. Avaline, 8 Ind. 6 (1856)

Dole v. Irish, 2 Barb. 639 (N.Y., 1848)

Drew v. Carroll, 154 Mass. 181 (1891)

Duval v. Marshall, 30 Ark. 230 (1875)

Elk v. Wilkins, 112 U.S. 94 (1884)

Farrington v. Wilson, 29 Wis. 383 (1872)

Ferris v. Coover, 10 Cal. 589 (1858)

Fisher v. Allen, 3 Miss. 611 (1837)

Gatliff's Administrator v. Rose, 47 Ky. 629 (1848)

Gentry v. McMinnis, 33 Ky. 382 (1835)

Georgia v. Tassels, 1 Dud. 229 (1830)

Gho v. Julles, 1 Wash. Terr. 325 (1871)

Gibbons v. Ogden, 22 U.S. 1 (1824)

Goodell v. Jackson ex dem. Smith, 20 Johns. 693 (N.Y., 1823)

Gray v. Ohio, 4 Ohio 353 (1831)

Gregory v. Baugh, 29 Va. 665 (1831)

Harris v. Doe ex dem. Barnett, 4 Blackf. 369 (Ind., 1837)

Hart v. Burnett, 15 Cal. 530 (1860)

Hastings v. Farmer, 4 N.Y. 293 (1850)

Herbert v. Moore, Dallam 592 (Tex., 1844)

Hicks v. Ewhartonah, 21 Ark. 106 (1860)

Holland v. Pack, 7 Tenn. 151 (1823)

Hudgins v. Wrights, 11 Va. 134 (1806)

Hunt v. Kansas, 4 Kan. 60 (1866)

Inhabitants of Andover v. Inhabitants of Canton, 13 Mass. 547 (1816)

Jackson ex dem. Gilbert v. Wood, 7 Johns. 290 (N.Y., 1810)

Jackson ex dem. Gillet v. Brown, 15 Johns. 263 (N.Y., 1818)

Jackson ex dem. Smith v. Goodell, 20 Johns. 188 (N.Y., 1822)

Jackson ex dem. Tewahangarahkan v. Sharp, 14 Johns. 472 (N.Y., 1817)

Jackson ex dem. Van Dyke v. Reynolds, 14 Johns. 335 (N.Y., 1817)

Jeffries v. Ankeny, 11 Ohio 372 (1842)

Johnson v. Johnson's Administrator, 30 Mo. 72 (1860)

Johnson v. McIntosh, 21 U.S. 543 (1823)

Jones v. Laney, 2 Tex. 342 (1847)

Kansas Indians, 72 U.S. 737 (1867)

Kelley v. Arkansas, 25 Ark. 392 (1869)

Lane v. Baker, 12 Ohio 237 (1843)

Laurent v. Kansas, 1 Kan. 313 (1863)

Lee v. Glover, 8 Cow. 189 (N.Y., 1828)

Lemmon v. New York, 20 N.Y. 562 (1860)

Marguerite v. Chouteau, 2 Mo. 71 (1828) and 3 Mo. 540 (1834)

Massachusetts v. Aves, 35 Mass. 193 (1836)

Mayhew v. District of Gay Head, 95 Mass. 129 (1866)

Mayor of New York v. Miln, 36 U.S. 102 (1837)

Michigan v. Dean, 14 Mich. 406 (1866)

Michigan ex rel. Dean v. Board of Registration of Nankin, 15 Mich. 156 (1866)

Michigan ex rel. Wood v. Board of Registration of Fourth Ward, City of Detroit, 17
    Mich. 427 (1868)

Minnesota v. Campbell, 53 Minn. 354 (1893)

Morgan v. Fowler, 10 Tenn. 450 (1830)

Morgan v. McGhee, 24 Tenn. 13 (1844)

Morrow v. Blevins, 23 Tenn. 223 (1843)

Murphy and Glover Test Oath Cases, 41 Mo. 339 (1867)

Murray v. Wooden, 17 Wend. 531 (N.Y., 1837)

Nevada ex rel. Stoutmeyer v. Duffy, 7 Nev. 342 (1872)

New Jersey v. Van Waggoner, 6 N.J.L. 374 (1797)

New York ex rel. Cutler v. Dibble, 18 Barb. 412 (N.Y., 1854); 16 N.Y. 203 (1857); 62 U.S.
    366 (1859)

New York Indians, 72 U.S. 761 (1867)

Newman v. Doe ex dem. Harris, 5 Miss. 522 (1840)

North Carolina v. Jacobs, 51 N.C. 284 (1859)

North Carolina v. Melton, 44 N.C. 49 (1852)

North Carolina v. Ta-Cha-Na-Tah, 64 N.C. 614 (1870)

Ohio ex rel. Garnes v. McCann, 21 Ohio 198 (1871)

Opinion of the Justices of the Supreme Court, on Question Propounded by the Senate,
    44 Me. 505 (1857)

Opinion of the Justices of the Supreme Judicial Court, 41 N.H. 553 (1857)

Opsahl v. Johnson, 138 Minn. 42 (1917)

Oregon v. Gilbert, 55 Ore. 596 (1883)

Painter v. Ives, 4 Neb. 122 (1875)

Pallas v. Hill, 12 Va. 149 (1807)

Pegram v. Isabell, 12 Va. 193 (1808)

Pells v. Webquish, 129 Mass. 469 (1880)

In re Peters, 2 Johns. Cas. 344 (N.Y., 1801)

Priest v. Nebraska, 10 Neb. 393 (1880)

Quinney v. Stockbridge, 33 Wis. 505 (1873)

Reed v. Brasher, 9 Port. 438 (Ala., 1839)

Robin v. Hardaway, Jeff. 109 (Va., 1772)

Rubideaux v. Vallie, 12 Kan. 28 (1873)

Saffarans v. Terry, 20 Miss. 690 (1849)

Scott v. Sandford, 60 U.S. 393 (1857)

Séville v. Chrétien, 5 Mart. (o.s.) 275 (La., 1817)

Ex parte Sloan, 22 F. Cas. 324 (D.C., D. Neb., 1877)

Ex parte Smith and Ex parte Keating, 38 Cal. 702 (1869)

Smith v. Brown, 8 Kan. 608 (1871)

Spalding v. Taylor, 1 La. Ann. 195 (1846)

St. Regis Indians v. Drum, 19 Johns. 127 (N.Y., 1821)

Strong and Gordon v. Waterman, 11 Paige 607 (N.Y., 1845)

Sunol v. Hepburn, 1 Cal. 254 (1850)

Taylor v. Drew, 21 Ark. 485 (1860)

Tennessee v. Claiborne, 19 Tenn. 331 (1838)

Tennessee v. Forman, 16 Tenn. 256 (1835)

Thaxter v. Grinnell, 43 Mass. 13 (1840)

Tuten's Lessee v. Martin, 11 Tenn. 452 (1832)

Ulzère v. Poeyfarré, 8 Mart. (o.s.) 155 (La., 1820) and 2 Mart. (n.s.) 504 (La. 1824)

United States v. Bailey, 24 F. Cas. 937 (C.C., D. Tenn., 1834)

United States v. Cisna, 25 F. Cas. 422 (C.C., D. Ohio, 1835)

United States v. Elm, 25 F. Cas. 1006 (D.C., N.D., N.Y., 1877)

United States v. Forty-Three Gallons of Whisky, 25 F. Cas. 1155 (D.C., D. Minn., 1874)

United States v. Joseph, 1 N.M. 593 (1874), 94 U.S. 614 (1877)

United States v. Kagama, 118 U.S. 375 (1886)

United States v. Koslowski, 1 N.M. 593 (1874).

United States v. Leathers, 26 F. Cas. 897 (D.C., D. Nev., 1879)

United States v. Lucero, 1 N.M. 422 (1869)

United States v. McBratney, 104 U.S. 621 (1882)

United States v. Monte, 3 N.M. 173 (1884)

United States v. Nice, 241 U.S. 591 (1916)

United States v. Rogers, 45 U.S. 567 (1846)

United States v. Sa-Coo-Da-Cot, 27 F. Cas. 923 (C.C., D. Neb., 1870)

United States v. Sandoval, 231 U.S. 28 (1913)

United States v. Santistevan, 1 N.M. 583 (1874)

United States v. Seveloff, 27 F. Cas. 1021 (D.C., D. Ore., 1872)

United States v. Tom, 1 Ore. 26 (1853)

United States v. Varela, 1 N.M. 593 (1874)

United States v. Ward, 1 Kan. 601 (1863), 28 F. Cas. 397 (D.C., D. Kan., 1863)

United States ex rel. Standing Bear v. Crook, 25 F. Cas. 695 (C.C., D. Neb., 1879)

Van Valkenburg v. Brown, 43 Cal. 43 (1872)

Vaughn v. Phebe, 8 Tenn. 5 (1827)

Wall v. Williamson, 8 Ala. 48 (1845)

Wall v. Williams, 11 Ala. 826 (1847)

Ward v. Flood, 48 Cal. 36 (1874)

Willson v. Black Bird Creek Marsh Co., 27 U.S. 245 (1829)

Wisconsin v. Doxtater, 47 Wis. 278 (1879)

Worcester v. Georgia, 31 U.S. 515 (1832)

Wynehamer v. New York, 13 N.Y. 378 (1856)

LAWS

The titles of official state session laws varied slightly, as they were published serially from 1790 to 1880. In such situations the alternative title listed in italics after the state's general "Session Laws" title is the one predominantly used during the years covered. Since the Hein microfiches do not identify the date of their production, the approximate dates provided here are based on catalog entries.

Alabama Session Laws. *Laws (and Joint Resolutions) of the Legislature of Alabama.* Montgomery: State of Alabama, 1819–. Microfiche. Buffalo NY: William S. Hein, 1979.

Arkansas Session Laws. *Acts of the General Assembly.* Little Rock: General Publishing, 1836– . Microfiche. Buffalo NY: William S. Hein, 1979.

California Session Laws. *Statutes of California and Digest of Measures.* Sacramento, s.n., 1850–. Microfiche. Buffalo NY: William S. Hein, 1979.

Colorado Session Laws. *Laws Passed at the . . . Session of the General Assembly of the State of Colorado.* Denver: Bradford Printing, 1879–. Microfiche. Buffalo NY: William S. Hein, 1979.

Connecticut Session Laws. *Public and Special Acts.* Hartford: s.n., 1776–. Microfiche. Buffalo NY: William S. Hein, n.d.

Delaware Session Laws. *Laws of the State of Delaware.* Wilmington: Secretary of State, 1734–. Microfiche. Buffalo NY: William S. Hein, 1975–76.

Florida Session Laws. *Acts and Resolutions Adopted by the Legislature of Florida.* Tallahassee: State Printer, 1845–. Microfiche. Buffalo NY: William S. Hein, 1986.

Georgia Session Laws. *Acts and Resolutions of the General Assembly of the State of Georgia.* Milledgeville and Atlanta: Clark & Hines, State Printers, 1700s–. Microfiche. Buffalo NY: William S. Hein, 1979.

Illinois Session Laws. *Laws of the State of Illinois.* Springfield: State Printers, 1830s–. Microfiche. Buffalo NY: William S. Hein, n.d.

Indiana Session Laws. *Laws of the State of Indiana.* Indianapolis: Indiana Legislative Council, 1816–. Microfiche. Buffalo NY: William S. Hein, 1978.

Iowa Session Laws. *Acts and Joint Resolutions Passed at the . . . General Assembly of the State of Iowa.* Des Moines: State of Iowa, 1846–. Microfiche. Buffalo NY: William S. Hein, n.d.

Kansas Session Laws. *Session Laws of Kansas.* Topeka: Secretary of State, 1861–. Microfiche. Buffalo NY: William S. Hein, 1979.

Kentucky Session Laws. *Acts of the General Assembly of the Commonwealth of Kentucky.* Frankfort: Legislative Research Commission, 1792–. Microfiche. Buffalo NY: William S. Hein, 1978.

Laws Adopted by the Governor and Judges of the Indiana Territory. Frankfort: William Hunter, 1801– Microfiche. Buffalo NY: William S. Hein, 1986.

Laws of the Territory of New Mexico Passed by the . . . Legislative Assembly. Santa Fe: J. L. Collins, 1851–. Microfiche. Buffalo NY: William S. Hein, n.d.

Louisiana Session Laws. *Acts Passed at the . . . Session of the General Assembly of the State of Louisiana.* New Orleans: Thierry, State Printer, 1812–. Microfiche. Buffalo NY: William S. Hein, 1986.

Maine Session Laws. *Laws of the State of Maine.* Portland: F. Douglas, State Printer, 1820–. Microfiche. Buffalo NY: William S. Hein, n.d.

Maryland Session Laws. *Laws of the State of Maryland.* Annapolis: State Department of Legislative Reference, 1777–. Microfiche. Buffalo NY: William S. Hein, 1979.

Massachusetts Session Laws. *Acts and Resolves Passed by the General Court of Massachusetts.* Boston: Secretary of the Commonwealth, 1780–. Microfiche. Buffalo NY: William S. Hein, 1978.

Michigan Session Laws. *Acts of the Legislature of the State of Michigan.* Lansing: W. S. George, 1836–. Microfiche. Buffalo NY: William S. Hein, n.d.

Minnesota Session Laws. *Session Laws of the State of Minnesota.* St. Paul: State of Minnesota, 1849–. Microfiche. Buffalo NY: William S. Hein, n.d.

Mississippi Session Laws. *Laws of the State of Mississippi.* Jackson: Secretary of State, 1817–. Microfiche. Buffalo NY: William S. Hein, 1979.

Missouri Session Laws. *Laws of Missouri.* Jefferson City: Secretary of State, 1800s–. Microfiche. Buffalo NY: William S. Hein, 1978.

Bibliography

Nebraska Session Laws. *Laws, Joint Resolutions, and Memorials Passed at the . . . Session of the Legislative Assembly of the State of Nebraska.* Omaha: St. A. D. Balcombe, State Printer, 1867–. Microfiche. Buffalo NY: William S. Hein, n.d.

Nevada Session Laws. *Statutes of the State of Nevada Passed at the . . . Session of the Legislature.* Carson City: J. Church, State Printer, 1864– Microfiche. Buffalo NY: William S. Hein, 1979.

New Hampshire Session Laws. *Laws of the State of New Hampshire.* Concord: Secretary of State, 1700s–. Microfiche. Buffalo NY: William S. Hein, 1978.

New Jersey Session Laws. *Acts of the Legislature of the State of New Jersey.* Trenton: Secretary of State, 1776– Microfiche. Buffalo NY: William S. Hein, 1977.

New York Session Laws. *Laws of the State of New York Passed at the . . . Session of the Legislature.* Albany: State of New York, 1777– Microfiche. Buffalo NY: William S. Hein, 1978.

North Carolina Session Laws. *Session Laws and Resolutions Passed by the General Assembly, State of North Carolina.* Raleigh: Secretary of State, 1777– Microfiche. Buffalo NY: William S. Hein, n.d.

Ohio Session Laws. *Acts of the State of Ohio.* Chillicothe: N. Willis, State Printer, 1803– Microfiche. Buffalo NY: William S. Hein, 1986.

Oregon Session Laws. *Laws of the State of Oregon Enacted During the . . . Session of the Legislative Assembly.* Salem: A. Bush, 1859–. Microfiche. Buffalo NY: William S. Hein, n.d.

Pennsylvania Session Laws. *Acts of the General Assembly of the Commonwealth of Pennsylvania.* Philadelphia: s.n., 1776–. Microfiche. Buffalo NY: William S. Hein, 1986.

Public Statutes at Large of the United States of America. Boston: Charles C. Little and James Brown, 1789–1845.

Recopilación de Leyes de los Reynos de las Indias. Madrid, 1681. Reprint, Madrid: Boix, 1841.

Rhode Island Session Laws. *Acts and Resolves Passed by the General Assembly of the State of Rhode Island and Providence Plantations.* Providence: Oxford Press, 1700s– Microfiche. Buffalo NY: William S. Hein, n.d.

South Carolina Session Laws. *Acts and Joint Resolutions of the General Assembly of the State of South Carolina.* Columbia: Printed under direction of Code Commissioner, 1776–. Microfiche. Buffalo NY: William S. Hein, 1979.

Statutes at Large of the United States of America. Washington DC: Government Printing Office, 1846–1937.

Tennessee Session Laws. *Acts Passed at the . . . Session of the General Assembly of the State of Tennessee.* Knoxville: G. Roulstone, State Printer, 1796–. Microfiche. Buffalo NY: William S. Hein, n.d.

Bibliography

Texas Session Laws. *General and Special Laws of the State of Texas.* Austin: Ford & Cronican, 1846– Microfiche. Buffalo NY: William S. Hein, 1997.

United States Statutes at Large. Washington DC: Government Printing Office, 1937–.

Vermont Session Laws. *Acts and Resolves Passed by the General Assembly of the State of Vermont.* Montpelier: Secretary of State, 1778–. Microfiche. Buffalo NY: William S. Hein, n.d.

Virginia Session Laws. *Acts of the General Assembly of the State of Virginia.* Richmond: s.n., 1776–. Microfiche. Buffalo NY: William S. Hein, 1986.

West Virginia Session Laws. *Acts of the Legislature of West Virginia.* Charleston: s.n., 1861–. Microfiche. Buffalo NY: William S. Hein, 1984.

Wisconsin Session Laws. *Wisconsin Session Laws . . . Including All the Acts and Certain Joint Resolutions.* Madison: s.n., 1836–. Microfiche. Buffalo NY: William S. Hein, n.d.

ARCHIVAL COLLECTIONS

Supreme Court of Louisiana Collection, Earl K. Long Library, Special Collections, University of New Orleans

Manuscript case file of the proceedings in *Séville v. Chrétien, Agnès v. Judice, Catherine v. Chrétien, Narcisse v. Chrétien, Pierre v. Chrétien, Thémier v. Chrétien,* and *Jeanne v. Chrétien,* in the court of the parish of St. Landry, docket number 34.

Manuscript case file of the trial of *Ulzère v. Poeyfarré* in the court of the parish and city of New Orleans, docket number 468 and docket number 989.

National Archives, Washington DC

Letters Received by the Office of Indian Affairs, 1824–1881: New Mexico Superintendency, microcopy 234, microfilm rolls 546–556.

Records of the Office of Indian Affairs, Letters Sent, microcopy 21, microfilm roll 48

New Mexico State Archives and Records Center, Santa Fe

Arthur Bibo Collection of Acoma and Laguna Documents

PUBLISHED SOURCES

Abel, Annie Heloise, ed. *The Official Correspondence of James S. Calhoun While Indian Agent at Santa Fé and Superintendent of Indian Affairs in New Mexico.* Washington DC: Government Printing Office, 1915.

Bibliography

Alfred, Taiaiake. "Sovereignty." In *A Companion to American Indian History*, ed. Philip J. Deloria and Neal Salisbury, 460–74. Malden MA: Blackwell, 2004.

Állain, Mathé. *"Not Worth a Straw": French Colonial Policy and the Early Years of Louisiana*. Lafayette: Center for Louisiana Studies, University of Southwestern Louisiana, 1988.

Ancheta, Angelo N. *Race, Rights, and the Asian American Experience*. New Brunswick NJ: Rutgers University Press, 1998.

Anderson, Gary Clayton. *Kinsmen of Another Kind: Dakota-White Relations in the Upper Mississippi Valley, 1650–1862*. Lincoln: University of Nebraska Press, 1984.

Anderson, Gary Clayton, and Alan R. Woolworth. Introduction to *Through Dakota Eyes: Narrative Accounts of the Minnesota Indian War of 1862*, ed. Anderson and Woolworth, 1–17. St. Paul: Minnesota Historical Society Press, 1988.

Apess, William. "Indian Nullification of the Unconstitutional Laws of Massachusetts Relative to the Marshpee Tribe; or, The Pretended Riot Explained." In *On Our Own Ground: The Complete Writings of William Apess, a Pequot*, ed. Barry O'Connell, 166–274. Amherst: University of Massachusetts Press, 1992.

Armstrong, William H. *Warrior in Two Camps: Ely S. Parker, Union General and Seneca Chief*. Syracuse: Syracuse University Press, 1978.

Asher, Brad. *Beyond the Reservation: Indians, Settlers and the Law in Washington Territory, 1853–1889*. Norman: University of Oklahoma Press, 1999.

Baade, Hans W. "The Law of Slavery in Spanish Luisiana, 1769-1803." In *Louisiana's Legal Heritage*, ed. Edward F. Haas, 43–85. Pensacola: Louisiana State Museum, by Perdido Bay Press, 1983.

Bellin, Joshua David. "Apostle of Removal: John Eliot in the Nineteenth Century." *New England Quarterly* 69 (1996): 3–32.

Belmessous, Saliha. "Assimilation and Racialism in Seventeenth and Eighteenth-Century French Colonial Policy." *American Historical Review* 110 (2005): 322–349.

Benavides, David. *Lawyer-Induced Partitioning of New Mexican Land Grants: An Ethical Travesty*. Guadalupita NM: Center for Land Grant Studies, 1994.

Benton, Lauren. *Law and Colonial Cultures: Legal Regimes in World History, 1400–1900*. New York: Cambridge University Press, 2002.

Berkhofer, Robert F., Jr. *The White Man's Indian: Images of the American Indian from Columbus to the Present*. New York: Random House, 1978.

Berlin, Ira. *Many Thousands Gone: The First Two Centuries of Slavery in North America*. Cambridge MA: Harvard University Press, 1998.

———. *Slaves without Masters: The Free Negro in the Antebellum South*. New York: Vintage Books, 1974.

Berman, Howard R. "Perspectives on American Indian Sovereignty and International Law, 1600 to 1776." In *Exiled in the Land of the Free: Democracy, Indian Nations, and the U.S. Constitution*, by Oren Lyons et al., 125–188. Santa Fe: Clear Light, 1992.

Bieder, Robert E. *Science Encounters the Indian, 1820–1880: The Early Years of American Ethnology*. Norman: University of Oklahoma Press, 1986.

Blegen, Theodore C. *Minnesota, A History of the State*. Minneapolis: University of Minnesota Press, 1963.

Borah, Woodrow. *Justice by Insurance: The General Indian Court of Colonial Mexico and the Legal Aides of the Half-Real*. Berkeley: University of California Press, 1983.

Brasseaux, Carl A. "The Administration of Slave Regulations in French Louisiana, 1724-1766." *Louisiana History* 21 (1980): 139-158.

Brayer, Herbert O. *Pueblo Indian Land Grants of the "Rio Abajo," New Mexico*. Albuquerque: University of New Mexico Press, 1938.

———. *William Blackmore: The Spanish-Mexican Land Grants of New Mexico and Colorado, 1863–1878*. Vol. 1 of *A Case Study in the Economic Development of the West*. Denver: Bradford-Robinson, 1949.

Brodeur, Paul. *Restitution: The Land Claims of the Mashpee, Pasamaquoddy, and Penobscot Indians of New England*. Boston: Northeastern University Press, 1985.

Brooks, James F., ed. *Confounding the Color Line: The Indian-Black Experience in North America*. Lincoln: University of Nebraska Press, 2002.

Brown, Jennifer S. H. *Strangers in Blood: Fur Trade Company Families in Indian Country*. Vancouver: University of British Columbia Press, 1980; reprint, Norman: University of Oklahoma Press, 1996.

Brown, Jennifer, and Theresa Schenck. "Métis, Mestizo, and Mixed-Blood." In *A Companion to American Indian History*, ed. Philip J. Deloria and Neal Salisbury, 321–338. Malden MA: Blackwell, 2002.

Brown, Kathleen. "Native Americans and Early Modern Concepts of Race." In *Empire and Others: British Encounters with Indigenous Peoples, 1600–1850*, ed. Martin Daunton and Rick Halpern, 79–100. Philadelphia: University of Pennsylvania Press, 1999.

Burke, Joseph C. "The Cherokee Cases: A Study in Law, Politics, and Morality." *Stanford Law Review* 21 (1969): 500–531.

Calhoun, William B., et al. Memorial from William B. Calhoun and other prominent Massachusetts men to Congress on the subject of the "Rights of Indians," 22 February 1830.

California Constitutional Convention. *Report of the Debates in the Convention of California on the Formation of the State Constitution*. Comp. J. Ross Browne. Washington DC: John T. Towers, 1850.

Bibliography

Calloway, Colin G. *Crown and Calumet: British-Indian Relations, 1783–1815.* Norman: University of Oklahoma Press, 1987.

———. *New Worlds for All: Indians, Europeans, and the Remaking of Early America.* Baltimore: Johns Hopkins University Press, 1997.

Campisi, Jack. "From Stanwix to Canandaigua: National Policy, States' Rights, and Indian Land." In *Iroquois Land Claims,* ed. Christopher Vecsey and William A. Starna, 49–65. Syracuse: Syracuse University Press, 1988.

———. *The Mashpee Indians: Tribe on Trial.* Syracuse: Syracuse University Press, 1991.

———. "The Mashpee Indians: Tribe on Trial." In *Readings in American Indian Law: Recalling the Rhythm of Survival,* ed. Jo Carrillo, 32–42. Philadelphia: Temple University Press, 1998.

Carbado, Devon W. "Racial Naturalization." *American Quarterly* 57 (2005): 633–658.

Carley, Kenneth. *The Sioux Uprising of 1862.* St. Paul: Minnesota Historical Society Press, 1976.

Carrillo, Jo. "Identity as Idiom: *Mashpee* Reconsidered." In *Readings in American Indian Law: Recalling the Rhythm of Survival,* ed. Jo Carrillo, 43–49. Philadelphia: Temple University Press, 1998.

Catterall, Helen Tunnicliff. "Some Antecedents of the Dred Scott Case." *American Historical Review* 30 (1924): 56–71.

Cleland, Charles E. *Rites of Conquest: The History and Culture of Michigan's Native Americans.* Ann Arbor: University of Michigan Press, 1992.

Clifford, James. "Identity in Mashpee." In *Readings in American Indian Law: Recalling the Rhythm of Survival,* ed. Jo Carrillo, 19–26. Philadelphia: Temple University Press, 1998.

Clifton, James A. "Michigan's Indians: Tribe, Nation, Estate, Racial, Ethnic, or Special Interest Group?" *Michigan Historical Review* 20 (1994): 93–152.

Clinton, Robert N. "Sovereignty and the Native American Nation: The Dormant Indian Commerce Clause." *Connecticut Law Review* 27 (1995): 1055–1249.

Clinton, Robert N., and Margaret Tobey Hotopp. "Judicial Enforcement of the Federal Restraints on Alienation of Indian Land: The Origins of the Eastern Land Claims." *Maine Law Review* 31, no. 5 (1979): 17–90.

Cohen, Felix S. *Handbook of Federal Indian Law.* Washington DC: U.S. Government Printing Office, 1942; reprint, Buffalo NY: William S. Hein, 1988.

Conley, Robert J. *The Cherokee Nation: A History.* Albuquerque: University of New Mexico Press, 2005.

Cook-Lynn, Elizabeth, and James Riding In. "Editors' Commentary." *Wicazo Sa Review* 19 (1) (2004): 5–10.

Cover, Robert M. *Justice Accused: Antislavery and the Judicial Process.* New Haven: Yale University Press, 1975.

Cowger, Thomas W. *The National Congress of American Indians: The Founding Years.* Lincoln: University of Nebraska Press, 1999.

Coy, P. E. B. "Justice for the Indian in Eighteenth Century Mexico." *American Journal of Legal History* 12 (1968): 41–49.

Crawford, Richard W. "The White Man's Justice: Native Americans and the Judicial System of San Diego County, 1870–1890." *Western Legal History* 5 (1992): 69–81.

Cronon, William. *Changes in the Land: Indians, Colonists, and the Ecology of New England.* New York: Hill and Wang, 1983.

Cumfer, Cynthia. "Local Origins of National Indian Policy: Cherokee and Tennessean Ideas about Sovereignty and Nationhood, 1790–1811." *Journal of the Early Republic* 23 (2003): 21–46.

Cutter, Charles R. *The Legal Culture of Northern New Spain, 1700–1810.* Albuquerque: University of New Mexico Press, 1995.

Dain, Bruce. *A Hideous Monster of the Mind: American Race Theory in the Early Republic.* Cambridge MA: Harvard University Press, 2002.

Daniels, Christine, and Michael V. Kennedy, eds. *Negotiated Empires: Centers and Peripheries in the Americas, 1500–1820.* New York: Routledge, 2002.

Davis, William Watts Hart. *El Gringo; or, New Mexico and Her People.* 1857; reprint, New York: Arno Press, 1973.

DeBuys, William. "Fractions of Justice: A Legal and Social History of the Las Trampas Land Grant, New Mexico." *New Mexico Historical Review* 56 (1981): 71–97.

Deloria, Philip J. *Indians in Unexpected Places.* Lawrence: University Press of Kansas, 2004).

Deloria, Vine, Jr. *Behind the Trail of Broken Treaties: An Indian Declaration of Independence.* New York: Delacorte Press, 1974.

———. "Self-Determination and the Concept of Sovereignty." In *Native American Sovereignty*, ed. John R. Wunder, 118–124. New York: Garland, 1996.

Deloria, Vine, Jr., and Clifford M. Lytle. *American Indians, American Justice.* Austin: University of Texas Press, 1983.

———. *The Nations Within: The Past and Future of American Indian Sovereignty.* New York: Pantheon Books, 1984; reprint, Austin: University of Texas Press, 1998.

Deloria, Vine, Jr., and David E. Wilkins. *Tribes, Treaties, and Constitutional Tribulations.* Austin: University of Texas Press, 1999.

Dennis, Matthew. *Cultivating a Landscape of Peace: Iroquois-European Encounters in Seventeenth-Century America.* Ithaca NY: Cornell University Press, 1993.

Densmore, Christopher. *Red Jacket: Iroquois Diplomat and Orator*. Syracuse: Syracuse University Press, 1999.

Denson, Andrew. *Demanding the Cherokee Nation: Indian Autonomy and American Culture, 1830–1900*. Lincoln: University of Nebraska Press, 2004.

Dickinson, John A. "Native Sovereignty and French Justice in Early Canada." In *Essays in the History of Canadian Law*, vol. 5, ed. Jim Philips et al., 17–40. Toronto: University of Toronto Press, 1994.

Domínguez, Virginia R. *White by Definition: Social Classification in Creole Louisiana*. New Brunswick NJ: Rutgers University Press, 1986.

Duncan, John Donald. "Servitude and Slavery in Colonial South Carolina, 1670–1776." PhD diss., Emory University, 1971.

Earle, John Milton. "Report to the governor and Council, concerning the Indians of the Commonwealth, under the act of April 6, 1859." Boston: William White, 1861.

Ebright, Malcolm. *Land Grants and Lawsuits in Northern New Mexico*. Albuquerque: University of New Mexico Press, 1994.

———. *The Tierra Amarilla Grant: A History of Chicanery*. Santa Fe: Center for Land Grant Studies, 1980.

Eccles, W. J. *France in America*. Rev. ed., East Lansing: Michigan State University Press, 1990.

Edmunds, R. David. *The New Warriors: Native American Leaders since 1900*. Lincoln: University of Nebraska Press, 2001.

Elliott, J. H. "Afterword: Atlantic History: A Circumnavigation." In *The British Atlantic World, 1500–1800,* ed. David Armitage and Michael J. Braddick, 233–249. New York: Palgrave Macmillan, 2002.

Elliott, John. *Britain and Spain in America: Colonists and Colonized*. Reading, England: University of Reading, 1994.

Elliott, John H. "Empire and State in British and Spanish America." In *Le Nouveau Monde, Mondes Nouveau: L'Expérience Américaine*, ed. Serge Gruzinski and Nathan Wachtel, 365–382. Paris: Editions Recherche sur les civilizations; Editions de l'Ecole des hautes études en sciences sociales, 1996.

Finkelman, Paul. "The Crime of Color." *Tulane Law Review* 67 (1993): 2063–2112.

Fixico, Donald. "Federal and State Policies and American Indians." In *A Companion to American Indian History*, ed. Philip J. Deloria and Neal Salisbury, 379–396. Malden MA: Blackwell, 2004.

Foley, William E. "Slave Freedom Suits before Dred Scott: The Case of Marie Jean Scypion's Descendants." *Missouri Historical Review* 79 (1984): 1–23.

Folwell, William Watts. *A History of Minnesota*. Rev. ed. 4 vols. St. Paul: Minnesota Historical Society, 1956–1969.

Forbes, Jack D. *Africans and Native Americans: The Language of Race and the Evolution of Red-Black Peoples*. 2nd ed. Urbana: University of Illinois Press, 1993.

Formisano, Ronald P. *The Birth of Mass Political Parties: Michigan, 1827–1861*. Princeton NJ: Princeton University Press, 1971.

Fowler, David H. *Northern Attitudes towards Interracial Marriage: Legislation and Public Opinion in the Middle Atlantic and the States of the Old Northwest, 1780–1930*. New York: Garland, 1987.

Gallay, Alan. *The Indian Slave Trade: The Rise of the English Empire in the American South, 1670–1717*. New Haven: Yale University Press, 2002.

Garrison, Tim Alan. *The Legal Ideology of Removal: The Southern Judiciary and the Sovereignty of Native American Nations*. Athens: University of Georgia Press, 2002.

Goldman, Robert M. *Reconstruction and Black Suffrage: Losing the Vote in* Reese *and* Cruikshank. Lawrence: University Press of Kansas, 2001.

Grant, Susan-Mary. *North over South: Northern Nationalism and American Identity in the Antebellum Era*. Lawrence: University Press of Kansas, 2000.

Gray, Susan E. "Limits and Possibilities: Indian-White Relations in Western Michigan in the Era of Removal." *Michigan Historical Review* 20 (1994): 71–91.

Graymont, Barbara. "New York State Indian Policy after the Revolution." *New York History* 57 (1976): 438–474.

Green, Michael D. *The Politics of Indian Removal: Creek Government and Society in Crisis*. Lincoln: University of Nebraska Press, 1982.

Greene, Jack P. *Peripheries and Center: Constitutional Development in the Extended Polities of the British Empire and the United States, 1607–1788*. Athens: University of Georgia Press, 1986.

———. "Transatlantic Colonization and the Redefinition of Empire in the Early Modern Era: The British-American Experience." In *Negotiated Empires: Centers and Peripheries in the Americas, 1500–1820*, ed. Christine Daniels and Michael V. Kennedy, 267–282. New York: Routledge, 2002.

Grinde, Donald, Jr. "Native American Slavery in the Southern Colonies." *Indian Historian* 10, no. 2 (1977): 38–42.

Grivno, Max L. "'Black Frenchmen' and 'White Settlers': Race, Slavery, and the Creation of African-American Identities along the Northwest Frontier, 1790–1840." *Slavery and Abolition* 21, no. 3 (2000): 75–93.

Gross, Ariela J. *Double Character: Slavery and Mastery in the Antebellum Southern Courtroom*. Princeton: Princeton University Press, 2000.

———. "Litigating Whiteness: Trials of Racial Determination in the Nineteenth-Century South." *Yale Law Journal* 108 (1998): 109–185.

Bibliography

Gunther, Gerald. "Governmental Power and New York Indian Lands—A Reassessment of a Persistent Problem of Federal-State Relations." *Buffalo Law Review* 8 (1958): 1–26.

Gutiérrez, Ramón A. *When Jesus Came, the Corn Mothers Went Away: Marriage, Sexuality, and Power in New Mexico, 1500–1846.* Stanford: Stanford University Press, 1991.

Hall, G. Emlen. *Four Leagues of Pecos: A Legal History of the Pecos Grant, 1800–1933.* Albuquerque: University of New Mexico Press, 1984.

Hall, G. Emlen, and David J. Weber. "Mexican Liberals and the Pueblo Indians, 1821–1829." *New Mexico Historical Review* 59 (1984): 5–32.

Hallett, Benjamin Franklin. "Rights of the Marshpee Indians: Argument of Benjamin F. Hallett, Counsel for the Memorialists of the Marshpee Tribe, Before a Joint Committee of the Legislature of Massachusetts." 7 March 1834.

Haney López, Ian F. *White by Law: The Legal Construction of Race.* New York: New York University Press, 1996.

Hanke, Lewis. *The Spanish Struggle for Justice in the Conquest of America.* Philadelphia: University of Pennsylvania Press, 1949.

Haring, C. H. *The Spanish Empire in America.* New York: Oxford University Press, 1947.

Harring, Sidney L. *Crow Dog's Case: American Indian Sovereignty, Tribal Law, and United States Law in the Nineteenth Century.* New York: Cambridge University Press, 1994.

Hauptman, Laurence M. "Africa View: John Collier, the British Colonial Service and American Indian Policy, 1933–1945." *Historian* 48 (1986): 359–374.

———. *Conspiracy of Interests: Iroquois Dispossession and the Rise of New York State.* Syracuse: Syracuse University Press, 1999.

Herndon, Ruth Wallis, and Ella Wilcox Sekatau. "The Right to a Name: The Narragansett People and Rhode Island Officials in the Revolutionary Era." *Ethnohistory* 44 (1997): 433–462.

Higginbotham, A. Leon, Jr. *Shades of Freedom: Racial Politics and Presumptions of the American Legal Process.* New York: Oxford University Press, 1996.

Hinderaker, Eric. *Elusive Empires: Constructing Colonialism in the Ohio Valley, 1673–1800.* New York: Cambridge University Press, 1997.

Horsman, Reginald. *Race and Manifest Destiny: The Origins of American Racial Anglo-Saxonism.* Cambridge MA: Harvard University Press, 1981.

Howland, S. C. "Report of the Treasurer of the District of Mashpee to the Governor and Executive Council of Massachusetts." Public Document No. 32, 30 September 1866.

Hoxie, Frederick E. *A Final Promise: The Campaign to Assimilate the Indians, 1880–1920.* Lincoln: University of Nebraska Press, 1984.

————, ed. *Talking Back to Civilization: Indian Voices from the Progressive Era.* Boston: Bedford/St. Martin's, 2001.

Hoxie, Frederick E., et al., eds. *Native Americans and the Early Republic.* Charlottesville: University Press of Virginia, 1999.

Hutchins, Francis G. "Mashpee: The Story of Cape Cod's Indian Town." In *Readings in American Indian Law: Recalling the Rhythm of Survival*, ed. Jo Carrillo, 27–31. Philadelphia: Temple University Press, 1998.

————. *Tribes and the American Constitution.* Brookline MA: Amarta Press, 2000.

Iverson, Peter. *Carlos Montezuma and the Changing World of American Indians.* Albuquerque: University of New Mexico Press, 1982.

Jackson, Moana. "Justice and Political Power: Reasserting Maori Legal Processes." In *Legal Pluralism and the Colonial Legacy: Indigenous Experiences of Justice in Canada, Australia, and New Zealand*, ed. Kayleen M. Hazlehurst, 243–263. Brookfield VT: Ashgate, 1995.

Jenkins, Myra Ellen. "The Baltasar Baca 'Grant': History of an Encroachment." *El Palacio* 68 (1961): 47–64 and 87–105.

Jennings, Francis. *The Invasion of America: Indians, Colonialism, and the Cant of Conquest.* Chapel Hill: University of North Carolina Press, 1975.

Jones, Dorothy V. *License for Empire: Colonialism by Treaty in Early America.* Chicago: University of Chicago Press, 1982.

Jung, Patrick J. "To Extend Fair and Impartial Justice to the Indian: Native Americans and the Additional Court of Michigan Territory, 1823–1836." *Michigan Historical Review* 23, no. 2 (1997): 25–48.

Kaczorowski, Robert J. *The Politics of Judicial Interpretation: The Federal Courts, Department of Justice and Civil Rights, 1866–1876.* Dobbs Ferry NY: Oceana, 1985.

Kappler, Charles J., ed. *Indian Affairs: Laws and Treaties, 1778–1883.* 3 vols. Washington DC: Government Printing Office, 1913; reprint, New York: Interland, 1972.

Kawashima, Yasu. "Legal Origins of the Indian Reservation in Colonial Massachusetts." *American Journal of Legal History* 13 (1969): 42–56.

Kawashima, Yasuhide. *Puritan Justice and the Indian: White Man's Law in Massachusetts, 1630–1763.* Middletown CT: Wesleyan University Press, 1986.

Keleher, William A. *Maxwell Land Grant: A New Mexico Item.* Rev. ed. New York: Argosy-Antiquarian, 1964.

Kennedy, Randall. *Race, Crime, and the Law.* New York: Vintage Books, 1997.

Kerber, Linda K. *Women of the Republic: Intellect and Ideology in Revolutionary America.* Chapel Hill: University of North Carolina Press, 1980.

Kettner, James H. *The Development of American Citizenship, 1608–1870.* Chapel Hill: University of North Carolina Press, 1978.

Keyssar, Alexander. *The Right to Vote: The Contested History of Democracy in the United States.* New York: Basic Books, 2000.

Bibliography

Koehler, Lyle. "Red-White Power Relations and Justice in the Courts of Seventeenth-Century New England." *American Indian Culture and Research Journal* 3, no. 4 (1979): 1–31.

Kupperman, Karen Ordahl. *Indians and English: Facing Off in Early America.* Ithaca NY: Cornell University Press, 2000.

———. "Presentment of Civility: English Reading of American Self-Presentation in the Early Years of Colonization." *William and Mary Quarterly*, 3rd. ser., 54 (1997): 193–228.

Lamar, Howard R. *The Far Southwest, 1846–1912: A Territorial History.* New Haven: Yale University Press, 1966.

Larson, Robert W. *New Mexico's Quest for Statehood, 1846–1912.* Albuquerque: University of New Mexico Press, 1968.

———. "Territorial Politics and Cultural Impact." *New Mexico Historical Review* 60 (1985): 249–269.

Lass, William E. *Minnesota: A Bicentennial History.* New York: W.W. Norton, 1977.

———. "The Removal from Minnesota of the Sioux and Winnebago Indians." *Minnesota History* 38 (1963): 353–364.

Lauber, Almon Wheeler. *Indian Slavery in Colonial Times within the Present Limits of the United States.* New York: Columbia University Press, 1913.

Lawrence, Bonita. "Gender, Race, and the Regulation of Native Identity in Canada and the United States: An Overview." *Hypatia* 18, no. 2 (2003): 3–31.

Lee, R. Alton. "Indian Citizenship and the Fourteenth Amendment." *South Dakota History* 4 (1974): 198–221.

Lehman, J. David. "The End of the Iroquois Mystique: The Oneida Land Cession Treaties of the 1780s." *William and Mary Quarterly*, 3rd. ser., 47 (1990): 523–547.

Lenner, Andrew C. *The Federal Principle in American Politics, 1790–1833.* Landham MD: Rowman & Littlefield, 2001.

Liberty, Margot, ed. *American Indian Intellectuals of the Nineteenth and Early Twentieth Centuries.* 1978; reprint, Norman: University of Oklahoma Press, 2002.

Litwack, Leon F. *North of Slavery: The Negro in the Free States, 1790–1860.* Chicago: University of Chicago Press, 1961.

Lofgren, Charles A. *The Plessy Case: A Legal-Historical Interpretation.* New York: Oxford University Press, 1987.

Lujan, Carol Chiago, and Gordon Adams. "U.S. Colonization of Indian Justice Systems: A Brief History." *Wicazo Sa Review* 19, no. 2 (2004): 9–23.

Maddox, Lucy. "American Indians, Civilized Performance and the Question of Rights." *Comparative American Studies* 1 (2003): 317–326.

Maltz, Earl M. "The Fourteenth Amendment and Native American Citizenship." *Constitutional Commentary* 17 (2000): 555–573.

Bibliography

Mamdani, Mahmood. *Citizen and Subject: Contemporary Africa and the Legacy of Late Colonialism*. Princeton: Princeton University Press, 1996.

Mandell, Daniel R. "Shifting Boundaries of Race and Ethnicity: Indian-Black Intermarriage in Southern New England, 1760–1880." *Journal of American History* 85 (1998): 466–501.

Marienstras, Elise. "The Common Man's Indian: The Image of the Indian as a Promoter of National Identity in the Early National Era." In *Native Americans and the Early Republic*, ed. Frederick E. Hoxie et al., 261–296. Charlottesville: University Press of Virginia, 1999.

Markov, Gretchen Koch. "The Legal Status of Indians under Spanish Rule." PhD diss., University of Rochester, 1983.

Martin, Jill E. "'Neither Fish, Flesh, Fowl nor Good Red Herring': The Citizenship Status of American Indians, 1830–1924." *Journal of the West* 29 (1990): 75–87.

Massachusetts. Commissioners to Examine into the Condition of the Indians in the Commonwealth. "Report of the Commissioners Relating to the Condition of the Indians in Massachusetts." 21 February 1849.

Massachusetts House of Representatives. Committee on Indians. "Hearing Before the Committee on Indians, at Marshpee." 9 February 1869. Boston: Wright & Potter, State Printers, 1869.

————. *Journal of the House of Representatives of the Commonwealth of Massachusetts*, 1869. Boston: Wright & Potter, State Printers, 1869.

————. "Report of the Committee to Whom was Referred so much of the Governor's Address as Relates to the Indians of the Commonwealth." 3 June 1869. Boston: 1869.

Mathes, Valerie Sherer, and Richard Lowitt. *The Standing Bear Controversy: Prelude to Indian Reform*. Urbana: University of Illinois Press, 2003.

Max, Theodore C. "Conundrums along the Mohawk: Preconstitutional Land Claims of the Oneida Indian Nation." *New York University Review of Law and Social Change* 11 (1982–1983): 473–519.

McClain, Charles J. *In Search of Equality: The Chinese Struggle against Discrimination in Nineteenth-Century America*. Berkeley: University of California Press, 1994.

McHugh, P. G. *Aboriginal Societies and the Common Law: A History of Sovereignty, Status, and Self-Determination*. New York: Oxford University Press, 2004.

McLoughlin, William G. *Cherokee Renascence in the New Republic*. Princeton: Princeton University Press, 1986.

Melish, Joanne Pope. *Disowning Slavery: Gradual Emancipation and "Race" in New England, 1780–1860*. Ithaca NY: Cornell University Press, 1998.

Merrell, James H. *The Indians' New World: Catawbas and Their Neighbors from European Contact through the Era of Removal*. Chapel Hill: University of North Carolina Press, 1989.

Bibliography

Meyer, Roy W. *History of the Santee Sioux: United States Indian Policy on Trial.* Lincoln: University of Nebraska Press, 1967.

Michigan Constitutional Convention. *The Debates and Proceedings of the Constitutional Convention of the State of Michigan.* 2 vols. Comp. William Blair Lord and David Wolfe Brown. Lansing: John A. Kerr, 1867.

———. *The Michigan Constitutional Conventions of 1835–36: Debates and Proceedings.* Ann Arbor: University of Michigan Press, 1940.

———. *Report of the Proceedings and Debates in the Convention to Revise the Constitution of the State of Michigan, 1850.* Lansing: R. W. Ingals, 1850.

Mihesuah, Devon A. "Choosing America's Heroes and Villains. Lessons Learned from the Execution of Silon Lewis." *American Indian Quarterly* 20 (1 and 2) (2005): 239–262.

Mihesuah, Devon Abbott. *Indigenous American Women: Decolonization, Empowerment, Activism.* Lincoln: University of Nebraska Press, 2003.

Miller, Susan A. "Seminoles and Africans under Seminole Law: Sources and Discourses of Tribal Sovereignty and 'Black Indian' Entitlement." *Wacazo Sa Review* 20 (2005): 23–47.

Miner, H. Craig, and William E. Unrau. *The End of Indian Kansas: A Study of Cultural Revolution, 1854–1871.* Lawrence: University Press of Kansas, 1978.

Minnesota Constitutional Convention. *The Debates and Proceedings of the Minnesota [Democratic] Constitutional Convention.* St. Paul: Earle S. Goodrich, 1857.

———. *Debates and Proceedings of the [Republican] Constitutional Convention for the Territory of Minnesota.* St. Paul: George W. Moore, 1858.

Montoya, María E. *Translating Property: The Maxwell Land Grant and the Conflict over Land in the American West, 1840–1900.* Berkeley: University of California Press, 2002.

Morgan, Edmund S. *American Slavery, American Freedom: The Ordeal of Colonial Virginia.* New York: Norton, 1975.

Morris, Glenn T. "Vine Deloria, Jr., and the Development of a Decolonizing Critique of Indigenous Peoples and International Relations." In *Native Voices: American Indian Identity and Resistance,* ed. Richard A. Grounds et al., 97–154. Lawrence: University Press of Kansas, 2003.

Morris, Thomas D. *Southern Slavery and the Law, 1619–1860.* Chapel Hill: University of North Carolina Press, 1996.

Morrison, Michael A., and James Brewer Stewart, eds. *Race and the Early Republic: Racial Consciousness and Nation-Building in the Early Republic.* New York: Rowman & Littlefield, 2002.

Moulton, Gary E. *John Ross: Cherokee Chief.* Athens: University of Georgia Press, 1978.

————, ed. *The Papers of Chief John Ross.* 2 vols. Norman: University of Oklahoma Press, 1985.

Mumford, Jeremy. "Métis and the Vote in 19th-Century America." *Journal of the West* 39, no. 3 (2000): 38–45.

Nelson, William E. *The Fourteenth Amendment: From Political Principle to Judicial Doctrine.* Cambridge MA: Harvard University Press, 1988.

New Mexico. *Spanish Archives of New Mexico, 1621–1821, Series I, Translations.* 4 microfilm reels. Santa Fe: New Mexico State Records Center and Archives, 1981.

New York State Assembly. *Journal of the Assembly of the State of New-York.* Albany NY: John Barber, 1803.

New York State Senate. Committee on Indian Affairs. "Report of the committee on Indian affairs on the Assembly bill in relation to the Seneca Indians." 18 April 1845.

Newton, Nell Jessup. "Federal Power over Indians: Its Source, Scope and Limitations." *University of Pennsylvania Law Review* 132 (1984): 195–288.

Norgren, Jill. *The Cherokee Cases: The Confrontation of Law and Politics.* New York: McGraw Hill, 1996.

O'Brien, Jean M. *Dispossession by Degrees: Indian Land and Identity in Natick, Massachusetts, 1650–1790.* New York: Cambridge University Press, 1997.

Pagden, Anthony. *Lords of All the World: Ideologies of Empire in Spain, Britain, and France c. 1500–c. 1800.* New Haven: Yale University Press, 1995.

Pascoe, Peggy. "Miscegenation Law, Court Cases, and Ideologies of 'Race' in Twentieth-Century America." *Journal of American History* 83 (1996): 44–69.

Pearson, Jim Berry. *The Maxwell Land Grant.* Norman: University of Oklahoma Press, 1961.

Perdue, Theda, ed. *Cherokee Editor: The Writings of Elias Boudinot.* Knoxville: University of Tennessee Press, 1983; reprint, Athens: University of Georgia Press, 1996.

————. *"Mixed Blood" Indians: Racial Construction in the Early South.* Athens: University of Georgia Press, 2003.

————. *Slavery and the Evolution of Cherokee Society, 1540–1866.* Knoxville: University of Tennessee Press, 1979.

Phelps, Glenn A. "Representation without Taxation: Citizenship and Suffrage in Indian Country." *American Indian Quarterly* 9 (1985): 135–148.

Philp, Kenneth. "Albert B. Fall and the Protest from the Pueblos, 1921–23." *Arizona and the West* 12 (1970): 237–254.

Plane, Ann Marie, and Gregory Button. "The Massachusetts Indian Enfranchisement Act: Ethnic Contest in Historical Context, 1849–1869." *Ethnohistory* 40 (1993): 587–618.

Porter, Robert B. "The Demise of the Ongwehoweh and the Rise of the Native Americans: Redressing the Genocidal Act of Forcing American Citizenship upon Indigenous Peoples." *Harvard BlackLetter Law Journal* 15 (1999): 107–183.

———. "Legalizing, Decolonizing, and Modernizing New York State's Indian Law." *Albany Law Review* 63 (1999): 125–200.

Pratt, John. "Aboriginal Justice and the 'Good Citizen': An Essay on Population Management." In *Legal Pluralism and the Colonial Legacy: Indigenous Experiences of Justice in Canada, Australia, and New Zealand,* ed. Kayleen M. Hazlehurst, 39–71. Brookfield VT: Ashgate, 1995.

Prucha, Francis Paul. *American Indian Policy in Crisis: Christian Reformers and the Indian, 1865–1900.* Norman: University of Oklahoma Press, 1975.

———. *American Indian Policy in the Formative Years: The Indian Trade and Intercourse Acts, 1790–1834.* Cambridge MA: Harvard University Press, 1962.

———. *The Great Father: The United States Government and the American Indians.* Lincoln: University of Nebraska Press, 1984.

Rasch, Philip J. "The People of the Territory of New Mexico vs. the Santa Fe Ring." *New Mexico Historical Review* 47 (1972): 185–202.

Reinhardt, Akim D. "A Crude Replacement: The Indian New Deal, Indirect Colonialism, and Pine Ridge Reservation." *Journal of Colonialism and Colonial History* 6, no. 1 (2005).

Richter, Daniel K. "'Believing That Many of the Red People Suffer Much for the Want of Food': Hunting, Agriculture, and a Quaker Construction of Indianness in the Early Republic." In *Race and the Early Republic: Racial Consciousness and Nation-Building in the Early Republic,* ed. Michael A. Morrison and James Brewer Stewart, 27–53. New York: Rowman & Littlefield, 2002.

———. *The Ordeal of the Longhouse: The Peoples of the Iroquois League in the Era of European Colonization.* Chapel Hill: University of North Carolina Press, 1992.

Robie, Harry. "Red Jacket's Reply: Problems in the Verification of a Native American Speech Text." *New York Folklore* 12 (1986): 99–117.

Roediger, David R. *The Wages of Whiteness: Race and the Making of the American Working Class.* Rev. ed. New York: Verso, 1999.

Rollings, Willard H. "Indian Land and Water: The Pueblos of New Mexico (1848–1924)." *American Indian Culture and Research Journal* 6, no. 4 (1982): 1–21.

Romero, Tom I., II. "The 'Tri-Ethnic' Dilemma: Race, Equality, and the Fourteenth Amendment in the American West." *Temple Political and Civil Rights Review* 13 (2004): 817–856. Paper presented at symposium titled "Exploring the History, Evolution, and Future of the Fourteenth Amendment," November 14–15, 2003, Temple University, Philadelphia.

Ronda, James P. "Red and White at the Bench: Indians and the Law in Plymouth Colony, 1620–1691." *Essex Institute Historical Collections* 110 (1974): 200–215.

———. "'We Have a Country': Race, Geography, and the Invention of Indian Territory." In *Race and the Early Republic: Racial Consciousness and Nation-Building in the Early Republic,* ed. Michael A. Morrison and James Brewer Stewart, 159–175. New York: Rowman & Littlefield, 2002.

Ross, Richard J. "Legal Communications and Imperial Governance in Colonial British and Spanish America." In *Cambridge History of Law in America,* ed. Christopher Tomlins and Michael Grossberg. New York: Cambridge University Press, forthcoming.

Rothman, Joshua D. *Notorious in the Neighborhood: Sex and Families across the Color Line in Virginia, 1787–1861.* Chapel Hill: University of North Carolina Press, 2003.

Rubenstein, Bruce A. "Justice Denied: An Analysis of American Indian-White Relations in Michigan, 1855–1889." PhD diss., Michigan State University, 1974.

Rubenstein, Bruce A., and Lawrence E. Ziewacz. *Michigan: A History of the Great Lakes State.* 3rd ed. Wheeling IL: Harlan Davidson, 2002.

Salisbury, Neal. *Manitou and Providence: Indians, Europeans, and the Making of New England, 1500–1643.* New York: Oxford University Press, 1982.

Samek, Hana. "No 'Bed of Roses': The Careers of Four Mescalero Indian Agents, 1871–1878." *New Mexico Historical Review* 57 (1982): 138–157.

Sando, Joe S. *Pueblo Nations: Eight Centuries of Pueblo Indian History.* Santa Fe: Clear Light, 1992.

Satz, Ronald N. *American Indian Policy in the Jacksonian Era.* Lincoln: University of Nebraska Press, 1975.

Saxton, Alexander. *The Rise and Fall of the White Republic: Class Politics and Mass Culture in Nineteenth-Century America.* New York: Verso, 1990.

Shattuck, Petra T., and Jill Norgren. *Partial Justice: Federal Indian Law in a Liberal Constitutional System.* Providence RI: Berg, 1991.

Sheehan, Bernard W. *Seeds of Extinction: Jeffersonian Philanthropy and the American Indian.* Chapel Hill: University of North Carolina Press, 1973.

Shoemaker, Nancy. "How Indians Got to Be Red." *American Historical Review* 102 (1997): 625–644.

Simmons, Marc. "History of the Pueblos since 1821." In *Southwest,* ed. Afonso Ortiz, 206–223. Vol. 9 of *Handbook of North American Indians,* William C. Sturtevant, gen. ed., Washington DC: Smithsonian Institution, 1979.

———. *Kit Carson and His Three Wives: A Family History.* Albuquerque: University of New Mexico Press, 2003.

———. *New Mexico: A Bicentennial History.* New York: Norton, 1977.

Bibliography

Smedley, Audrey. *Race in North America: Origin and Evolution of a Worldview.* Boulder: Westview Press, 1993.

Smith, James H. *The History of Chenango and Madison Counties, New York.* Syracuse NY: D. Mason, 1880.

Smith, Michael T. "The History of Indian Citizenship." *Great Plains Journal* 10 (1970): 25–35.

Smith, Rogers M. *Civic Ideals: Conflicting Visions of Citizenship in U.S. History.* New Haven: Yale University Press, 1997.

Sollors, Werner, ed. *Interracialism: Black-White Intermarriage in American History, Literature, and Law.* New York: Oxford University Press, 2000.

Spangler, Earl. "The Negro in Minnesota, 1800–1865." *Transactions of the Historical and Scientific Society of Manitoba* 3, no. 20 (1965): 13–26.

Spicer, Edward H. *Cycles of Conquest: The Impact of Spain, Mexico, and the United States on the Indians of the Southwest, 1533–1960.* Tucson: University of Arizona Press, 1962.

———. "Political Incorporation and Cultural Change in New Spain: A Study in Spanish-Indian Relations." In *Attitudes of Colonial Powers toward the American Indian,* ed. Howard Peckham and Charles Gibson, 107–135. Salt Lake City: University of Utah Press, 1969.

Springer, James Warren. "American Indians and the Law of Real Property in Colonial New England." *American Journal of Legal History* 30 (1986): 25–58.

Stanley, George F. G. "The Policy of 'Francisation' as Applied to the Indians during the Ancien Régime." *Revue d'Histoire de l'Amérique Française* 3 (1949): 333–348.

Stone, William L. *The Life and Times of Red-Jacket or Sa-Go-Ye-Wat-ha.* New York: Wiley and Putnam, 1841.

Sturm, Circe. *Blood Politics: Race, Culture, and Identity in the Cherokee Nation of Oklahoma.* Berkeley: University of California Press, 2002.

Sully, Langdon. "The Indian Agent: A Study in Corruption and Avarice." *American West* 10, no. 2 (1973): 4–9.

Svingen, Orlan J. "Jim Crow, Indian Style." *American Indian Quarterly* 11 (1987): 275–286. Reprinted in *The American Indian Past and Present,* ed. Roger L. Nichols, 268–277. New York: McGraw Hill, 1992.

Sweet, John Wood. *Bodies Politic: Negotiating Race in the American North, 1730–1830.* Baltimore: Johns Hopkins University Press, 2003.

Swindler, William F., ed. *Sources and Documents of United States Constitutions.* 12 vols. Dobbs Ferry, NY: Oceana, 1973–1979.

Takaki, Ronald. *Iron Cages: Race and Culture in 19th-Century America.* New York: Oxford University Press, 1990.

Taylor, Alan. *American Colonies.* New York: Viking, 2001.

Thornton, Russell. "Cherokee Population Losses during the Trail of Tears: A New Perspective and a New Estimate." *Ethnohistory* 31 (1984): 289–300.

Twitchell, Ralph Emerson. *The Leading Facts of New Mexican History.* 5 vols. Cedar Rapids IA: Torch Press, 1911–1917.

———. *Spanish Archives of New Mexico,* 2 vols. Cedar Rapids IA: Torch Press, 1914.

University of Virginia Geospatial and Statistical Data Center. *United States Historical Census Data Browser* (1998). http://fisher.lib.virginia.edu/collections/stats/census/.

Unrau, William E. "The Civilian as Indian Agent: Villain or Victim?" *Western Historical Quarterly* 3 (1972): 405–420.

U.S. Bureau of the Census. *Report on Indians Taxed and Indians Not Taxed in the United States (except Alaska) at the Eleventh Census: 1890.* Washington, DC: Government Printing Office, 1894.

U.S. Congress. Senate. *Senate Report No. 268,* 41st Cong., 3d sess., 1870.

Usner, Daniel H., Jr. "American Indians in Colonial New Orleans." In *Powhatan's Mantle: Indians in the Colonial Southeast,* ed. Peter H. Wood et al., 104–127. Lincoln: University of Nebraska Press, 1989.

———. *American Indians in the Lower Mississippi Valley: Social and Economic Histories.* Lincoln: University of Nebraska Press, 1998.

———. *Indians, Settlers, and Slaves in a Frontier Exchange Economy: The Lower Mississippi Valley before 1783.* Chapel Hill: University of North Carolina Press, 1992.

Utley, Robert M. *The Indian Frontier of the American West, 1846–1890.* Albuquerque: University of New Mexico Press, 1984.

Vaughan, Alden T. "From White Man to Redskin: Changing Anglo-American Perceptions of the American Indian." *American Historical Review* 87 (1982): 917–53.

———, ed. *New England Encounters: Indians and Euroamericans ca. 1600–1850.* Boston: Northeastern University Press, 1999.

———. *New England Frontier: Puritans and Indians, 1620–1675.* 3rd ed. Norman: University of Oklahoma Press, 1995.

———. "The Origins Debate: Slavery and Racism in Seventeenth-Century Virginia." In *Roots of American Racism: Essays on the Colonial Experience,* 136–174. New York: Oxford University Press, 1995.

Vaughan, Alden T., and Deborah A. Rosen, eds. *Early American Indian Documents: Treaties and Laws, 1607–1789.* 3 vols. Vol. 15, *Virginia and Maryland Laws* (Bethesda MD: University Publications of America, 1998). Vol. 16, *Carolina and Georgia Laws* (Bethesda MD: University Publications of America, 1998). Vol. 17, *New England and Middle Atlantic Laws* (Bethesda MD: University Publications of America, 2004).

Vecsey, Christopher, and William A. Starna, eds. *Iroquois Land Claims*. Syracuse: Syracuse University Press, 1988.

Velie, Alan R., ed. *American Indian Literature: An Anthology*. Norman: University of Oklahoma Press, 1979.

Wade, Mason. "The French and the Indians." In *Attitudes of Colonial Powers Toward the American Indian*, ed. Howard Peckham and Charles Gibson, 61–80. Salt Lake City: University of Utah Press, 1969.

Waldstreicher, David. *In the Midst of Perpetual Fetes: The Making of American Nationalism, 1776–1820*. Chapel Hill: University of North Carolina Press, 1997.

Wallace, Anthony F. C. *The Death and Rebirth of the Seneca*. New York: Knopf, 1969.

———. *The Long, Bitter Trail: Andrew Jackson and the Indians*. New York: Hill and Wang, 1993.

Wallenstein, Peter. "Indian Foremothers: Race, Sex, Slavery, and Freedom in Early Virginia." In *The Devil's Lane: Sex and Race in the Early South*, ed. Catherine Clinton and Michele Gillespie, 57–73. New York: Oxford University Press, 1997.

———. *Tell the Court I Love My Wife: Race, Marriage, and Law—An American History*. New York: Palgrave Macmillan, 2002.

Washburn, Wilcomb E., ed. *The American Indian and the United States: A Documentary History*, 4 vols. New York: Random House, 1973.

———. *Red Man's Land/White Man's Law: The Past and Present Status of the American Indian*. 2nd ed. Norman: University of Oklahoma Press, 1995.

Weber, David J. *The Spanish Frontier in North America*. New Haven: Yale University Press, 1992.

Webre, Stephen. "The Problem of Indian Slavery in Spanish Louisiana, 1769-1803." *Louisiana History* 25 (1984): 117–135.

Welke, Barbara Young. *Recasting American Liberty: Gender, Race, Law, and the Railroad Revolution, 1865–1920*. New York: Cambridge University Press, 2001.

Westphall, Victor. "The Public Domain in New Mexico, 1854 1891." *New Mexico Historical Review* 33 (1958): 24–52 and 128–143.

———. *Thomas Benton Catron and His Era*. Tucson: University of Arizona Press, 1973.

White, Richard. *The Middle Ground: Indians, Empires, and Republics in the Great Lakes Region, 1650–1815*. New York: Cambridge University Press, 1991.

Wilkins, David E. "African Americans and Aboriginal Peoples: Similarities and Differences in Historical Experiences." *Cornell Law Review* 90 (2005): 515–530.

———. *American Indian Sovereignty and the U.S. Supreme Court: The Masking of Justice*. Austin: University of Texas Press, 1997.

———. "From Time Immemorial: The Origin and Import of the Reserved Rights

Doctrine." In *Native Voices: American Indian Identity and Resistance*, ed. Richard A. Grounds et al., 81–96. Lawrence: University Press of Kansas, 2003.

———. "Quit-Claiming the Doctrine of Discovery: A Treaty Based Reappraisal." *Oklahoma City University Law Review* 23 (1998): 277–315.

Wilkins, David, and Tsianina Lomawaima. *Uneven Ground: American Indian Sovereignty and Federal Law*. Norman: University of Oklahoma Press, 2001.

Williams, Robert A., Jr. "The Algebra of Federal Indian Law: The Hard Trail of Decolonizing and Americanizing the White Man's Indian Jurisprudence." *Wisconsin Law Review* 1986 (1986): 219–299.

———. *The American Indian in Western Legal Thought: The Discourses of Conquest*. New York: Oxford University Press, 1990.

———. *Linking Arms Together: American Indian Treaty Visions of Law and Peace, 1600–1800*. New York: Oxford University Press, 1997.

———. "'The People of the States Where They Are Found Are Often Their Deadliest Enemies': The Indian Side of the Story of Indian Rights and Federalism." *Arizona Law Review* 38 (1996): 981–997.

Wilson, Waziyatawin Angela. "Decolonizing the 1862 Death Marches." *American Indian Quarterly* 28 (2004): 185–215.

Wishart, David J. *An Unspeakable Sadness: The Dispossession of the Nebraska Indians*. Lincoln: University of Nebraska Press, 1994.

Witkin, Alexandra. "To Silence a Drum: The Imposition of United States Citizenship on Native Peoples." *Historical Reflections/Réflexions historiques* 21 (1995): 353–383.

Wolfley, Jeanette. "Jim Crow, Indian Style: The Disfranchisement of Native Americans." *American Indian Law Review* 16 (1991): 167–202.

Wood, Peter H. *Black Majority: Negroes in Colonial South Carolina from 1670 to the Stono Rebellion*. New York: Knopf, 1974.

Woods, Karen M. "Lawmaking: A 'Wicked and Mischievous Connection': The Origins of Indian-White Miscegenation Law." *Legal Studies Forum* 23 (1999): 37–70.

Woods, Patricia Dillon. *French-Indian Relations on the Southern Frontier, 1699–1762*. Ann Arbor MI: UMI Research Press, 1980.

Wright, J. Leitch, Jr. *The Only Land They Knew: The Tragic Story of the American Indians in the Old South*. New York: Free Press, 1981.

Wunder, John R. *"Retained by the People": A History of American Indians and the Bill of Rights*. New York: Oxford University Press, 1994.

Young, Mary. "The Cherokee Nation: Mirror of the Republic." *American Quarterly* 33 (1981): 502–524.

Bibliography

————. "The Exercise of Sovereignty in Cherokee Georgia." *Journal of the Republic* 10 (1990): 43–63.

————. "Racism in Red and Black: Indians and Other Free People of Col(Georgia Law, Politics, and Removal Policy." *Georgia Historical Quarterl* (1989): 492–518.

Young, Mary E. "Indian Removal and Land Allotment: The Civilized Tribes ; Jacksonian Justice." *American Historical Review* 64 (1958): 31–45.

INDEX